The Colonels' Coup
AND THE AMERICAN EMBASSY

ADST-DACOR
Diplomats and Diplomacy Series
Series Editor: Margery Boichel Thompson

Since 1776, extraordinary men and women have represented the United States abroad under all sorts of circumstances. What they did and how and why they did it remain little known to their compatriots. In 1995 the Association for Diplomatic Studies and Training (ADST) and DACOR, an organization of foreign affairs professionals, created the Diplomats and Diplomacy book series to increase public knowledge and appreciation of the role of American diplomats in world history. The series seeks to demystify diplomacy through the stories of those who have conducted U.S. foreign relations, as they lived, influenced, and reported them. Robert Keeley's account of Embassy Athens and the events surrounding the 1967 Colonels' coup fulfills these aims in depth.

OTHER TITLES IN THE SERIES

Gordon S. Brown, *Toussaint's Clause: The Founding Fathers and the Haitian Revolution*
Herman J. Cohen, *Intervening in Africa: Superpower Peacemaking in a Troubled Continent*
Charles T. Cross, *Born a Foreigner: A Memoir of the American Presence in Asia*
Brandon Grove, *Behind Embassy Walls: The Life and Times of an American Diplomat*
Paul Hacker, *Slovakia on the Road to Independence: An American Diplomat's Eyewitness Account*
Parker T. Hart, *Saudi Arabia and the United States: Birth of a Security Partnership*
Cameron R. Hume, *Mission to Algiers: Diplomacy by Engagement*
Dennis Kux, *The United States and Pakistan, 1947–2000: Disenchanted Allies*
Bo Lidegaard, *Defiant Diplomacy: Henrik Kauffmann, Denmark, and the United States in World War II and the Cold War, 1939–1958*
Jane C. Loeffler, *The Architecture of Diplomacy: Building America's Embassies*
William B. Milam, *Bangladesh and Pakistan: Flirting with Failure in South Asia*
Robert Hopkins Miller, *Vietnam and Beyond: A Diplomat's Cold War Education*
Richard B. Parker, *Uncle Sam in Barbary: A Diplomatic History*
Ralph Pezzullo, *Plunging into Haiti: Clinton, Aristide, and the Defeat of Diplomacy*
Yale Richmond, *Practicing Public Diplomacy: A Cold War Odyssey*
Howard B. Schaffer, *Ellsworth Bunker: Global Troubleshooter, Vietnam Hawk*
James Stephenson, *Losing the Golden Hour: An Insider's View of Iraq's Reconstruction*
Ulrich Straus, *The Anguish of Surrender: Japanese POWs of World War II*

Robert V. Keeley
with a Prologue by John O. Iatrides

The Colonels' Coup
AND THE AMERICAN EMBASSY

A Diplomat's View of the Breakdown of Democracy in
Cold War Greece

The Pennsylvania State University Press
University Park, Pennsylvania

An ADST-DACOR Diplomats and Diplomacy Book

The opinions and characterizations in this book are those of the author and do not necessarily represent official positions of the United States Government, the Association for Diplomatic Studies and Training, or DACOR.

Library of Congress Cataloging-in-Publication Data

Keeley, Robert V.
The colonels' coup and the American embassy : a diplomat's view of the breakdown of democracy in cold war Greece / Robert V. Keeley.
    p. cm.
(ADST-DACOR diplomats and diplomacy series)
Includes bibliographical references and index.
Summary: "A first-hand account, by a U.S. diplomat, of the 1967 military coup in Greece, and of how U.S. policy was formulated, debated, and implemented during this period. Explores Greek-U.S. relations within the larger historical framework of the Cold War"—Provided by publisher.
ISBN 978-0-271-03758-5 (cloth : alk. paper)
ISBN 978-0-271-05011-9 (pbk. : alk. paper)
1. United States—Foreign relations—Greece.
2. Greece—Foreign relations—United States.
3. Greece—History—Coup d'État, 1967 (April 21).
4. Greece—Politics and government—1967–1974.
5. Democracy—Greece—History—20th century.
6. Diplomatic and consular service, American—Greece—History—20th century.
7. Cold War—Diplomatic history.
8. Keeley, Robert V.
I. Title.

E183.8.G8K44 2010
327.730495—dc22
2010029013

Text copyright © 2010 Robert V. Keeley

Prologue copyright © 2010 Penn State University Press
All rights reserved
Printed in the United States of America
Published by The Pennsylvania State University Press,
University Park, PA 16802–1003

It is the policy of The Pennsylvania State University Press to use acid-free paper. Publications on uncoated stock satisfy the minimum requirements of American National Standard for Information Sciences—Permanence of Paper for Printed Library Material, ANSI Z39.48–1992.

*To all those
who maintained their faith
in democratic ideals,
and particularly to
the political prisoners, exiles,
and other victims
of the regime of April 21,
this book is dedicated.
Of the virtues for which
their classical ancestors
were renowned, they displayed
especially these:
bravery, sacrifice, pride, endurance.*

*. . . and to the memory of
GEORGE SEFERIS, 1900–1971,
Greek, poet, diplomat, linguist,
critic, democrat, gentleman,
teacher, interlocutor, friend.*

Wherever I travel Greece wounds me.

—George Seferis, "In the Manner of G. S." (1936)

It is almost two years since a regime was imposed upon us utterly contrary to the ideals for which our world—and so magnificently our people—fought in the last World War. It is a state of enforced torpor in which all the intellectual values that we have succeeded, with toil and effort, in keeping alive are being submerged in a swamp, in stagnant waters. I can well imagine that for some people these losses do not matter. Unfortunately this is not the only danger that threatens.

We have all learnt, we all know, that in dictatorial regimes the beginning may seem easy, yet tragedy waits at the end, inescapably. It is this tragic ending that consciously or unconsciously torments us, as in the ancient choruses of Aeschylus.

The longer the abnormal situation lasts, the greater the evil.

—George Seferis, public statement of March 28, 1969

Contents

Preface		ix
Prologue by John O. Iatrides		xiii
1	INTRODUCTION WITH DRAMATIS PERSONAE	1
2	SETTING THE SCENE	
	First Impressions	18
	The Political Situation	23
	The Phenomenon of Andreas Papandreou	26
	The Monarchy	34
	Trials and Negotiations	36
	An Alternative: U.S. Intervention?	40
3	THE AUTHOR GETS INVOLVED	
	Andreas's March 1 Speech	44
	A Policy Assessment	51
	Preparing for Elections	58
4	THE DAYS BEFORE THE COUP	
	Presentiments and Alarums	66
	Washington Weighs In	79
5	THE COUP	
	The Coup of April 21, 1967	81
	Assessing the Coup	83
	Coup Vignettes	93
6	REACTING TO THE COUP	
	"Our Present Dilemma"	99
	Other Reactions	103
	Mac Thompson's Attempt	108
	A Draft Telegram	112
	Mac and I Try Again	114

7	DEALING WITH THE NEW GOVERNMENT	
	A Call on Kollias	118
	A Postmortem	123
	A Visit by Nixon	127
	Shift of Focus	130

8	ANDREAS PAPANDREOU AND PROSPECTS FOR DEMOCRACY	
	Andreas in Danger	132
	Bits and Pieces	136
	Meeting Margaret	140
	Speculations	144

9	THE COUNTERCOUP	
	Planning the King's Coup	146
	Crisis in Cyprus	150
	Checkmate of Constantine	152
	Aftermath of Failure	157

10	ASSESSING THE COLONELS' REGIME	
	The *FDR* Fiasco	161
	Andreas Released	162
	"Dear Charley"	170
	Harassment Continues	170
	The Meaning of Fascism	172

11	FRICTION AT THE EMBASSY	
	Kay Leaves, I Continue	174
	Go Along to Get Along	177
	Parallels with Pakistan	180

12	LOOKING TO THE FUTURE OF GREECE	
	Assessment of Andreas	183
	The Papandreou Funeral	185
	Was Greece Ever a Democracy?	190
	Don't Make Waves	193

13	FINAL THOUGHTS	
	Postscript	197
	All's Well That Ends Well?	200

Appendix A: Seferis and the Clinton Speech		203
Appendix B: Internal Embassy Memoranda, March–June 1968		206
Notes		257
Index		265

Preface

HISTORY IS USUALLY, THOUGH NOT ALWAYS,
WRITTEN BY THE WINNING SIDE.

This book was originally written in 1971 and 1972 in Princeton, New Jersey, and Kampala, Uganda. Its genesis might be of some interest to the prospective reader.

For thirty-four years, from 1956 through 1989, I was an officer in the Foreign Service of the United States, the career diplomatic corps. After initial postings in Washington in the executive secretariat of the International Cooperation Administration, the foreign aid agency, and overseas as a junior political officer at our embassies in Jordan and Mali, I was transferred back to the State Department to serve as the junior desk officer for the Congo (called Zaire from 1971 to 1997) in the Bureau of African Affairs. In 1965, after two frenetic years on that desk, I won a competitive fellowship from the National Institute of Public Affairs that enabled me to enjoy an academic year as a non-degree-seeking graduate student at one of eight universities around the country. I chose Stanford, where I studied mostly economics, an important subject for diplomacy that I had neglected as an undergraduate and graduate student at Princeton.

Every year on April 1 in those days, Foreign Service officers (FSOs) around the world would fill out and submit a brief form listing onward postings that interested them should vacancies become available. This became known as "the April fool's card," as it rarely produced an assignment to a post of one's preference. (Many years later, a new system replaced this form, with people bidding against the competition for posts that were actually becoming available.) For some seven years I had listed three posts—Athens, Thessaloniki, and Nicosia—where Greek was the local language.

Sometime early in 1966 I placed a call to Robert Houghton, director of State's Mid-career Personnel Division. It was clear that he had noted my pack of April fool's cards, and he had also found my name on a list of Greek-speaking officers. "How is your Greek?" Houghton asked.

"Somewhat rusty," I said, "as I've visited there only once since I lived there twenty years ago [as the son of a diplomat]. But my accent is first rate, since I learned the language as a kid. I think I could regain my fluency with some work."

He said he had an opening coming up that summer in Athens for a Greek-speaking political officer to replace John Owens, a Greek-language specialist who was being transferred to Washington after six years in Greece. Houghton said,

> This is a language-designated position, so I have to fill it with a Greek-speaking officer, but not just any Greek-speaking officer. There are lots of Greek speakers in the Athens mission, mostly Greek-Americans in various capacities, but I think they could use a non-Greek who speaks Greek, if you know what I mean. You have the right rank and a good background for that assignment. There's a new ambassador out there since last fall, a first-class guy, Phil Talbot. He was the assistant secretary of the NEA Bureau in the early Kennedy administration, and he needs a lot of help, because the domestic political situation is very turbulent, I'm told.

The upshot was that Houghton got my assignment approved by the personnel system, and I promised him that I would hire a tutor (at my expense) to help me regain my fluency in Greek during the remainder of the academic year at Stanford.

In 1970, after my four-year tour in Greece, I was lucky enough to be given another year of academic training, this time at the Woodrow Wilson School at Princeton. The two FSO Fellows were required to take at least three Wilson School seminars each term for credit, plus any other courses we wished to audit at the school or anywhere else in the university. The three seminars I took in the spring term were International Economics, the History and Dynamics of Modern Revolutionary Movements, and Studies in American Foreign Policy. The latter was the prize offering of the entire program.

Which brings me to where this book originated. My faculty adviser was Richard Ullman, and his course covering U.S. foreign policy since 1943 was a requirement for the FSOs. Ullman used as a primary text an influential (in academia and elsewhere) 1969 article by Graham Allison and Morton Halperin titled "Bureaucratic Politics: Theory and Policy Implications." It proposed a bureaucratic-organizational model for analyzing how American foreign policy gets crafted, namely through the interactions of various departments, agencies, and other power centers in Washington. Ullman also counted on the FSO Fellows to participate intensively in the seminar and to provide concrete examples based on our personal experiences in diplomatic practice, what we like to call our "war stories."

After some discussion, I suggested to Ullman that I would like my seminar session to address the performance of the American Embassy in Athens in reaction to the April 21, 1967, military coup d'état that brought "the Colonels" to power there. I said the policy struggles within the American mission and between the Embassy and Washington well illustrated the Allison-Halperin analytic approach. He heartily concurred, and I set to work writing what became the first draft of this memoir. The original was a paper of only thirty or so pages.

My seminar was a success—largely attributed, I believe, to the fact that the seminar leader, the author, was speaking from personal experience, not from research. Afterward, Ullman urged me to expand my "term paper" into a full-length book, as it seemed to be a somewhat unique account of events that had not been well covered in the media in recent years. Since at that stage it was mostly based on memory, he did not think classification or secrecy would be a problem. With that encouragement I embarked on the project that eventually turned into this book.

In June 1971 I departed Princeton for my next posting, in Kampala, Uganda, where I was to be the deputy chief of mission. I took with me the first draft of the Embassy Athens 1966–69 memoir, which I completed during the next year as time permitted. The text that appears here is largely that second draft. At that point I put the book on a shelf at home for very good reasons, namely, that I had not been promoted for six years (since 1967), largely because of unfavorable performance ratings owing to my vocal dissents in Athens, and if those six years became eight, my career would be terminated. Publication back then would have had that unwelcome result even more prematurely. Why I suppressed it for eighteen years after retirement from the Service I cannot readily explain.

The text that follows remains essentially as I wrote it in 1971–72, with only minor editorial changes. The few additions made in 2010 are enclosed between two text ornaments.

It may also be of interest to prospective readers that I served as the American ambassador to Greece from 1985 to 1989. This no doubt surprised some people with knowledge of my earlier tour there in the 1960s. But even those who doubted the wisdom of this assignment could not argue that I was unqualified.

I WISH TO FORMALLY EXPRESS MY PROFOUND GRATITUDE for the essential—in fact, crucial—assistance and support of several individuals who have helped bring this project to fruition some forty-plus years after the events recounted: first of all, Professor Evanthis Hatzivassiliou of the University of Athens, who worked assiduously with Patakis S. A. Publishers to transform it into a book in the Greek language; also in Athens, Elisabet Papadopoulou, for her masterful translation into contemporary Greek; on this side of the world, Professor John O. Iatrides, for providing a much-needed prologue and for vetting the translation; the Association for Diplomatic Studies and Training in Washington, D.C., and specifically its publishing director, Margery Thompson, who gave the book a much-needed boost by accepting it for the Diplomats and Diplomacy book series that it sponsors with DACOR, Inc.; my brother, Professor Edmund L. Keeley, and my daughter and copyeditor, Michal M. Keeley, for their encouragement and contributions; and most of all, my wife, Louise, who not only wrote part of the book but participated in a major way in the events that are here narrated, playing the role of the foreign service spouse who is seldom recognized much less fully appreciated.

—Robert V. Keeley

JOHN O. IATRIDES

In the fall of 1944, as the war in Europe entered its final phase, the liberation of Greece from Nazi occupation appeared imminent. Lincoln MacVeagh, the American ambassador to Greece (1933–41, 1943–47), prepared to fly from Cairo to Athens and to the post he had occupied since 1933. While eager to return, he was worried that the country he had once called "his life's passion" was heading toward powerful social and political upheaval, whose impact was likely to cause more pain and suffering to a war-devastated nation and poison relations among the Allies. He had urged his friend, President Franklin D. Roosevelt, and State Department officials to take a closer look at the dangerous situation he had been following with increasing concern and defuse it before it was too late. In Greece, as elsewhere in the Balkans, the war and brutal foreign occupation had unleashed radical new forces that were determined to block the restoration of the prewar order and carry out sweeping revolutionary changes. Britain's high-handed handling of Greek affairs, ostensibly in the name of the Allies, and particularly its rigid support of the monarchy and the government in exile, had exacerbated the situation, making civil violence increasingly likely. Equally important, British-Russian rivalry in the Balkans was moving toward a dangerous confrontation, with broader international implications. In one of his "Dear Franklin" letters, MacVeagh reiterated his warning that "eventually what goes on in the Balkans and the Near East generally will have to be recognized as of prime importance to us despite the fact that the countries involved are small and remote."[1] To prevent the collapse of social order in the region and open conflict between the Allies, he urged the president to assume in southeastern Europe the role of the universally respected honest broker. Aware of the pressing priorities dictated by the war, he suggested that the naming of an American general to oversee postliberation developments in the region would go a long way toward ameliorating the situation.

In Washington, MacVeagh's Cassandra-like warnings fell on deaf ears. The global war effort, the myriad of plans and preparations for the postwar international order, and America's traditional official indifference toward Eastern Europe's politics allowed no room for Balkan issues. The ambassador's hope that the United States might avert a clash between Britain and Russia in the region was dashed at the very top. For the president, the prospect of Anglo-Russian friction over postwar Eastern Europe was the main reason he was determined to avoid any American involvement in that faraway area: "It isn't so bad now," Roosevelt told MacVeagh in August 1944, "but may become worse, and I don't want our men to be involved."[2]

MacVeagh's failure to draw Washington's attention to his concerns is best illustrated by his inability to have his embassy staffed properly. As he prepared to be flown to Athens by the U.S. military (he refused to sail with the Greek government in exile and its British diplomatic and troop escort), the three Foreign Service officers and two of the four auxiliary staff who had been attached to him in Cairo were given new assignments. Feeling ignored and abandoned by his superiors, he poured out his frustration in a letter of resignation, which, in the end, he did not mail:

> I cannot but feel that the post I now occupy is of small importance to the Department, and since, in addition, when I saw the President for ten minutes in Washington recently and asked him what instructions he wished to give me for my future guidance here, he replied none, except that I should bear in mind that the United States is not going to be involved in Balkan affairs, I see no other course open to me than to offer my resignation. . . . I am sure that it will not be difficult to find someone else willing to accept the rank and emoluments of an Ambassador in return for the discharge of the unimportant and diminishing duties now devolving on this Mission.[3]

In the end, during the first months in postliberation Athens, several diplomats and a number of military and OSS men, including William H. McNeill, the future distinguished historian, and Thomas Karamessines, the future top CIA official, were attached temporarily to the Embassy, and a small

Greek staff performed important support services. Virtually all communications to Washington were reports on the deteriorating local situation, often repeating what had been learned from British officials in the capital. MacVeagh's frequent and lengthy dispatches, which he wrote with the greatest of care, were widely circulated in the Department, where they were much admired for their eloquence and wit. But he received no instructions or comments of any consequence.

In December 1944, when fighting broke out in Athens between the British-backed government and the Communists, who had refused to demobilize their resistance army, MacVeagh wrote to the president that "at bottom, the handling of this fanatically freedom-loving country . . . as if it were composed of natives under the British Raj, is what is the trouble." His recommendation that an international commission with American, British, and Russian participation be created to bring political stability and reconstruction to Greece received little attention and no support in Washington.[4]

As had been decided at the Yalta conference, an allied mission, which included a large contingent of Americans (the Russians refused to participate), was sent to observe the Greek elections of March 1946, the first in ten years. Among them, James Hugh Keeley, a Foreign Service officer with previous experience in Greece and the Near East, served as special assistant to the chief of the observers' mission and then stayed on as counselor of embassy under MacVeagh. In April the U.S. battleship *Missouri* paid a purely ceremonial visit to the port of Piraeus, giving Greek officialdom cause to celebrate and raising hopes for more substantial American interest. In December 1946, following discussions in the UN Security Council of the escalating political violence in Greece, the Council sent a commission to investigate charges of Soviet Bloc involvement in the emerging Greek civil war. The commission brought to the region a number of American representatives, led by Mark Ethridge, a respected newspaper publisher. Although the Embassy's workload increased, its basic function as a remote diplomatic outpost did not appear to change, and its regular personnel remained small. Until the end of 1946, as the fighting intensified, Washington policy makers gave no indication that they were paying any special attention to events in Greece. But appearances were deceptive.

In February 1947 MacVeagh, increasingly preoccupied with the threat of Communism in Greece, joined Ethridge in advising Washington that the economic situation in the country was so bad that it "must soon cause revolution on a nationwide scale."[5] A few days later, Paul Porter, the head of a small economic mission investigating conditions in Greece, reported from Athens that, to the Soviets, Greece was a "ripe plum ready to fall into their hands."⁶ Echoing Porter's warning, MacVeagh concluded, "If Greece falls to communism the whole Near East and part of North Africa as well are certain to pass under Soviet influence."⁷ In Washington, Under Secretary of State Dean Acheson used MacVeagh's reasoning to emphasize the Soviet factor in the Greek crisis. He advised Secretary of State George Marshall on February 21 that "the capitulation of Greece to Soviet domination through lack of adequate support from the U.S. and Great Britain might eventually result in the loss of the whole Near and Middle East and northern Africa."⁸ On the same day, the British Embassy in Washington informed the State Department that, for economic reasons, the British government had decided to terminate its assistance to Greece and Turkey as of March 31. In a matter of weeks, as the transformation of American foreign policy got under way, MacVeagh's small and remote diplomatic outpost became a beehive of activity and the Athens embassy would never be the same again.

Having decided to "contain" further Soviet expansionism in Europe and the Middle East, the Truman administration adopted the arguments of its representatives in Athens and perceived the Greek civil war as Moscow's way of testing the resolve of the West to defend its perimeter. In the hyperbolic words of a senior American diplomat, Greece had become "the test tube which the peoples of the world are watching in order to ascertain whether the determination of the Western powers to resist aggression equals that of international Communism to acquire new territory and new bases for further expansion."⁹ East-Central Europe was already under Soviet control, and strong pressures on Turkey were interpreted as another indication of Stalin's aggressive schemes. As a result, the Truman Doctrine, announced on March 12, 1947, elevated Greece and Turkey to the status of America's front-line allies in the emerging Cold War and paved the way for their eventual membership in the Atlantic alliance.

American officials of every kind were now suddenly needed in Athens and Ankara, and in virtually every corner of the two countries. The inclusion of Greece in the European Recovery Program (the Marshall Plan) also necessitated the rapid buildup of the American presence in that country. By the end of 1947, scores of Foreign Service officers, civilian administrators, and military attachés and an assortment of experts and advisers had joined the cadre at the unpretentious embassy on Queen Sophia Avenue, around the corner from the royal residence. In addition, large economic, military, and cultural missions, initially housed in and around the large Metohikon Tameion building on University Avenue, just off Constitution Square, sprang into existence. Their operations expanded rapidly as the United States intensified its commitment to help the Greek government crush the Communist insurgency and put the country on the road to recovery. A large CIA station, nominally part of the Embassy, soon followed, destined to become a major intelligence-gathering outpost directed at the Soviet Bloc. In 1961 the Embassy and its principal agencies were moved to an imposing and more secure complex of buildings in a less congested part of the capital.

Under the bilateral agreements covering the various assistance programs, American officials were given authority to supervise virtually every function of the Greek state, especially if it involved the use of American funds. Because of the country's enormous needs, the weak and ineffective coalition governments, the glaring inadequacies of the state bureaucracy, and the determination of the Americans to achieve results quickly, foreign advice and oversight amounted to direct and often high-handed intervention. Although institutionalized American interference in Greece's domestic matters effectively ended in the early 1950s, its poisonous legacy persisted for decades. To be sure, the vast majority of Greeks appreciated the magnitude and importance of American assistance. One Greek diplomat called it the "life preserver and the only hope that Greece would not only survive as a country according to our liberal traditions, but would be assured of its economic well-being."[10]

However, over time, the corrosive effects of the "asymmetrical relationship" between a superpower and a small and weak state intensified. They were aggravated by frustrations over the Cyprus controversy, in which the Greeks demanded self-determination for the island (confident that it would eventually lead to union with the "motherland"), a development opposed by Britain and Turkey and, tacitly, by the United States. Thanks in part to the inflammatory rhetoric of an irresponsible Greek press, the Greek-Turkish rivalry generated in Greece a virulent brand of anti-Americanism that lingers to this day. In time, American officials were no longer welcomed or even safe. On the opposite side of the relationship, Washington's barely concealed impatience and irritation with the troubling situation in Greece were bluntly and undiplomatically expressed by President Truman, who, in July 1947, scribbled on a memo: "Greeks and Jews suffer from an inferiority complex as well as a persecution complex. I've tried to help both and so far they've only given me a pain in the neck."[11]

Although in theory the ambassador remained the top American official in Greece, in practice the military mission and the CIA station quickly evolved into autonomous agencies whose heads, with Washington's tacit consent, could operate virtually on their own. MacVeagh, a classical scholar and a patrician gentleman of the old school, was temperamentally unsuited for bureaucratic infighting. His only political asset, direct access to the president, was lost with Roosevelt's death. Despite his efforts, he could not maintain his embassy's authority over other American agencies in the country. He was also upset that the openly interventionist practices of American officials were damaging the image of Greece as a sovereign state. His principal nemesis, Dwight Griswold, a Republican ex-governor of Nebraska and head of the U.S. economic mission with the rank of ambassador, missed no opportunity to undermine MacVeagh's standing and took pleasure in being labeled in the press "the Most Powerful Man in Greece."[12] The Department's halfhearted and inept attempts to delineate authority between its two ambassadors in Athens merely prolonged an unsatisfactory situation. In the new era of "shirtsleeve diplomacy" openly assertive tactics were the order of the day. In the end, an ailing and recently widowed MacVeagh was recalled and given another ambassadorial assignment. One of his last important tasks in Athens (in August 1947) was to ask Prime Minister Constantine Tsaldaris to step down in favor of the opposition leader, Themistocles Sofoulis, in a coalition government that Griswold, with Washington's backing, had demanded. A confused and tearful Tsaldaris (who stayed on as deputy prime minister and foreign minister) muttered to MacVeagh: "Does this mean you declare war on us?"[13]

Dignified and reserved to the bitter end, MacVeagh summed up his personal feelings in a letter to his brother:

> The facts are that I tried to carry out the Department's policy in Greece, which was to try and unite the political factions without siding with any, and so far as our aid to Greece was concerned, to make it effective through the cooperation of the Greeks, and not have to wave the big stick and thus both endanger that cooperation and give support to the Communist charge that our "imperialism" is making slaves of the local inhabitants. . . . It isn't every smart operator in this country who is able to handle foreign affairs successfully. . . . If we subordinate our experts all around Europe to the interruption and interference and dictation of politically ambitious amateurs, we certainly are heading for disaster.[14]

While sacrificing MacVeagh to Washington's partisan politics, the Department successfully resisted Republican efforts to have Griswold named ambassador to Greece. To clarify and strengthen the chain of command in Athens, the new ambassador, Henry Grady (1948–50), originally head of the American mission to observe the Greek elections and, more recently, ambassador to India, was named also chief of the military mission and special representative of the Economic Cooperation Administration (ECA) in Greece. Although the ECA's Greek program continued under its own mandate, it functioned under the overall supervision of the Department and, in the field, of the ambassador. Similarly, the large military mission carried out its normal responsibilities under the direct authority of the Department of Defense, while its senior officials, as well as the military attachés and the head of the CIA station, were ex officio members of the Embassy's "country team," the ambassador's inner circle of advisers. This arrangement, which allowed the military and particularly the CIA virtual autonomy, did not openly challenge the ambassador's role as the top American official in Greece. After 1952, the curtailment of economic assistance programs and the channeling of infrastructure and military aid through NATO's command structure also helped restore the political authority and prestige of the Embassy and its head.

Grady, a good administrator with a genial personality, sought to smooth over the impact of the American presence in Greece and to observe more strictly diplomatic niceties. On the other hand, without fanfare, he did not hesitate to make it clear that despite the obvious failings of the coalition government and the dangers of the continuing civil war, he opposed a "strongman solution" that the palace and certain Greek and American circles were promoting. His successor, John Peurifoy (1950–53), a senior Department administrator without previous diplomatic experience, was more openly blunt in his dealings with the powerful in the world of Greek politics, and especially the palace and its supporters. In January 1952 he let it be known that the country's problems called for a stronger government, which could be achieved if the upcoming national elections were held under a simple majority system. Such elections, it was generally believed, would result in a sweeping victory by the conservative Greek Rally Party, which the recently retired Marshall Alexandros Papagos had formed. Dismissing Peurifoy's advice, King Paul reportedly retorted that if the Americans wanted to have a new government in Athens, "they could kick the present one out themselves."[15] Undaunted, Peurifoy announced that unless the elections were conducted under a simple majority system, American assistance might be drastically reduced.

The elections of November 1952, conducted in fact under a simple majority system, produced a clear victory for Papagos's Rally Party and ushered in a new era of stability and economic development under a staunchly pro-West government. It continued under the leadership of Papagos's successor, Constantine Karamanlis, a strong-willed and dynamic politician, staunchly anticommunist and an admirer of Western culture and of America's political institutions. Washington's powerful influence in Greece could now be exerted through more traditional diplomacy and fewer intrusive tactics. Moreover, with NATO emerging as an effective mechanism of coordination, planning, and support among its members, and given American officials' growing preoccupation with Cold War issues outside Europe, they became increasingly passive regarding internal developments in Greece. The ambassador remained the most powerful foreign official in Athens, whose counsel and support were sought by most politicians of the Right and Center, and his relations with the leaders of the ruling party and with the royal family were often quite cordial. On occasion the ambassador's political bias was hardly a secret: in his 1961 Christmas letter to the American community, Ambassador Ellis O. Briggs (1959–62) cheerfully exclaimed: "Aren't we all glad that Karamanlis won the elections!"[16] Briggs refused to communicate directly with leaders of the opposition, assigning that function to his staff, and would rarely invite them to embassy functions. His successors, Henry Labouisse (1962–65) and Phillips Talbot (1965–69), were also clearly pleased to see Karamanlis and the conservatives remain in power but avoided making their preferences public and were accessible to the leaders of all parties except the Left.

As long as Karamanlis remained in office, relations between Washington and Athens appeared to be close and harmonious. In May 1957 the Greek government endorsed the Eisenhower Doctrine. Two years later President Eisenhower visited Athens and praised Greece as an important ally and called its prime minister a valued friend of America. In April 1960 Secretary of State Christian Herter traveled to the Greek capital to reiterate Washington's commitment to protect Greece against Soviet aggression. The following year Karamanlis was honored by President John F. Kennedy in the White House and addressed the House of Representatives, where he received a standing ovation. But beneath the facade of cordiality and harmonious cooperation the two allies were drifting apart. Already in November 1957 the Embassy was warning Washington's decision makers: "We can no longer be as certain as we have been in the past that we shall have Greece's support in foreign policy matters that are crucial to us."[17]

Despite the Embassy's persistent efforts to alert its superiors to changes in the political climate in Greece, policy makers in the Department, the National Security Council, and the White House had failed to appreciate the extent to which domestic developments and frustrations, including growing anti-American sentiment across the political spectrum, had undermined Karamanlis's standing. Although the Communist Party remained outlawed, a strong leftist movement, spearheaded by the Communist-controlled Union of the Democratic Left (EDA), had briefly emerged as the main opposition party and continued to attack the government on every issue. The refusal of the Eisenhower administration to support the Greek demand for self-determination in Cyprus and to satisfy demands for additional military and economic assistance had damaged Karamanlis's prestige in the country and even within his own party. Washington officials handling Greek affairs remained confident that the prime minister's ability to govern was intact. In their view, any increased support was not only unnecessary but might tie the United States too strongly to one particular politician and add fuel to perennial complaints in Greece that Washington was playing favorites and using its influence to keep Karamanlis in power. In August 1961, in anticipation of new elections, Ambassador Briggs warned that the Karamanlis government "would suffer in forthcoming electoral contest . . . if it did not produce additional American aid" for psychological reasons.[18] The following month, in the wake of a new Cold War crisis over Berlin, Briggs reported that the prime minister wanted "a simple US statement to effect we are on Greece's side and have no intention letting Greece go down Soviet drainpipe."[19] The Department remained unmoved.

During the 1961 electoral campaign both Karamanlis's ERE and George Papandreou's Center Union parties received contributions from the CIA's secret funds. Afterward, Briggs expressed satisfaction over ERE's victory and commented favorably on Karamanlis's new government. He labeled "irresponsible" George Papandreou's charge that ERE's victory was an "electoral coup" to be undone through a "relentless struggle" against the government. In February 1963 the CIA station chief, Jack Maury, a frequent guest of the royal family, reported that Queen Frederika found Karamanlis "increasingly hard to get along with" and that "the time may be approaching when elections and a new government are in order." Maury concluded that "all her political judgments are based on the assumption that what is good for the Monarchy is good for Greece."[20]

In addition to reporting on the troubling views of the royal couple, the Embassy also kept the Department informed about the suspected machinations of another major player on the Greek political scene: the military. Since the 1950s there had been rumors about army officers' cliques threatening to take action to prevent politicians with any "leftist tinge" from coming to power. Increasingly the Greek military establishment, a favorite client of Washington's Pentagon, viewed Papandreou's Center Union with suspicion and hostility. In early April 1963 Ambassador Labouisse warned Secretary of State Dean Rusk of a possible "overthrow in Greece sometime in the coming months." A recently retired army chief, General Vassilis Kardamakis, had told the Embassy's military attaché that a coup was "no longer a question of whether, but when." One of the conspirators named was a certain Lieutenant Colonel Georgios Papadopoulos, whom the Embassy professed not to know (despite his CIA contacts). On his own authority, but along the lines of established policy, the ambassador had sent word to Kardamakis "in emphatic terms" warning that a coup would damage Greece's international standing as well as its economy.[21]

In its prompt response, the Department applauded Labouisse's action and, uncharacteristically, reiterated in fairly explicit terms its basic policy on Greece for the foreseeable future: "In view of our long involvement and large investment in Greece, we could not stand by and witness the creation of a Latin American type of totalitarian government in Greece, nor do we want a return to the Metaxas kind of tyranny. We are therefore unalterably opposed to such a 'solution.' . . . Greece with a totalitarian government in the Balkans would be a staggering blow to the cause of democracy in the area." The ambassador was instructed to warn Kardamakis, and through him the Greek military, that "the use of United States equipment to achieve such a 'solution' would be regarded with grave misgiving and disappointment by the United States" and might lead to the reduction of military assistance to Greece. The Kennedy administration was prepared to work with another Greek government, "should it come to power through constitutional means" and not include Communists. However, "in the meantime we would not wish to do anything to compromise the effectiveness of Karamanlis' Government as it still has considerable time to serve in office."[22]

Washington's professed confidence in Karamanlis was expressed again, on June 6, 1963, by Secretary Rusk, who told a visiting member of the Greek cabinet that the prime minister "is less sure and confident about his relationship with the United States than he should be. . . . The United States realizes that the Prime Minister has problems, like all political leaders, but [Rusk] hopes he realizes that Greece is regarded as a special, more mature friend which, unlike others, does not require periodic indications of reassurance."[23]

Rusk's vacuous comments obscured either his ignorance or his indifference to the real situation in Athens. In May 1963 the murder of a leftist deputy in Salonika by right-wing thugs with ties to senior police officials embarrassed the Karamanlis government and emboldened its critics. A few days later Karamanlis became embroiled in a feud with the palace, ostensibly over the royal couple's determination to go on a state visit to Britain against the advice of the prime minister, who feared violent demonstrations by Communist sympathizers. A man of authoritarian temperament and highly sensitive to personal attacks, Karamanlis resigned (on June 11, 1963) and left for Zurich. He returned briefly to take part in the fall elections, which he lost to Papandreou, and left again, eventually settling in Paris. He remained abroad until July 24, 1974, when, following the collapse of the military dictatorship (1967–74), he returned to lead a government of national unity that prepared the country for elections and the restoration of democracy.

Unfazed by the fall of its most dependable ally in Greece, the Department remained sanguine about the situation in Athens. When President Kennedy asked whether there was anything Washington "could or should do about . . . possible renewed instability in Greek politics," the Department predicted that Karamanlis would return to power and added reassuringly: "Since any United States actions which could be construed as interference in Greek domestic politics would almost certainly reduce rather than enhance this probability [of Karamanlis's return] and would be welcomed by both the palace and the opposition elements as grounds for attack against Karamanlis, the U.S. should refrain from such steps." The Department advised the president that "we must constantly bear in mind that Greeks are in general suspicious and resentful of real or imagined foreign intervention in their domestic political affairs. Greek public opinion is particularly alert to the operation of the so-called 'American Factor.'" Besides, if, contrary to expectations, Karamanlis did not make a comeback, "there is no reason to fear that a Center Union government or a coalition government excluding EDA would, at least in the foreseeable future, represent a threat to Greece's pro-Western foreign policy."[24]

As the Department had predicted, the fall of Karamanlis and the emergence of Papandreou's Center Union as the ruling party did not at first affect U.S.-Greek relations. In November 1963, when Foreign Minister Sophocles Venizelos sought to assure Secretary Rusk that the new Greek cabinet consisted of "great friends of the United States," the secretary responded that he foresaw "no difficulty in continuing our cooperation with Greece through one party or another."[25] At the same time, Rusk made it very clear to his visitor that the Johnson administration had no intention of becoming involved in efforts to find a solution to the Cyprus problem. This position proved easier to declare than to uphold. In the spring of 1964, as intercommunal violence in Cyprus escalated and Turkey appeared ready to send troops to the island, President Johnson, in a statement characterized by an American official as "the diplomatic equivalent of an atomic bomb," bluntly cautioned Ankara not to invade Cyprus.[26] While the warning had the desired effect, it paved the way for Washington's direct involvement in the Greek-Turkish feud, in which it provided hands-on mediation in the hope of averting war between two NATO allies. Johnson and his top advisers suggested several formulas that, they believed, met the basic objective of the Greek side: union of most of the island with Greece, while also satisfying Turkish demands for partition by ceding to the Turkish Cypriots a small part of its territory. However, neither Athens nor Ankara would accept the "Acheson plan" (actually three different plans were presented), and several American clandestine schemes to precipitate a solution also had to be abandoned. Washington officials blamed the setback on George Papandreou's failure to rein in Makarios, the unpredictable and independent-minded Greek Cypriot leader and president of the Cyprus Republic, and concluded that both men were pursuing unrealistic and dangerous policies.

During 1964–65 the Cyprus problem was a major factor in the political turmoil that engulfed the Greek capital and led to the collapse of the Papandreou government in July 1965. As a result of Washington's direct efforts to mediate in the Cyprus crisis, the Athens embassy became a key conduit of messages and analysis concerning the ongoing negotiations. At the same time, the Embassy continued to perform its basic function of monitoring the unfolding Greek political drama. Following Ambassador Labouisse's transfer in May 1965, and until the arrival in October of his successor, Phillips Talbot, (1965–69), the Embassy was headed by Deputy Chief of Mission (DCM) Norbert Anschuetz. Although a career diplomat with many years of service in Greece, Anschuetz did not, at least in the eyes of Greeks, carry the weight of a fully accredited ambassador. By the same token, the six-month delay in the arrival of the new ambassador, and the Department's failure to provide the Embassy with clear guidance on current Greek issues, suggested that, having given up hope that it could mediate between Greece and Turkey to solve the Cyprus problem, the Johnson administration was too preoccupied elsewhere to pay sufficient attention to the unraveling situation in Athens.

In June 1965 Anschuetz reported that the government was afflicted by a "new phase of malaise." Papandreou had come under attack from factions of his own party, and there was widespread speculation that prominent members of the cabinet planned to defect. The army leadership was upset by the government's ongoing investigation of the so-called Pericles Plan, made public by Papandreou in February 1965 as the plot to secure Karamanlis's reelection in 1961 through electoral fraud carried out by the armed forces. To add to the prime minister's troubles, in May 1965 George Grivas, the right-wing veteran of the Cypriots' armed struggle and political maverick whom Papandreou had appointed commander of the Greek troops in Cyprus, charged that a conspiracy of junior Greek officers stationed in

Cyprus, code-named ASPIDA, plotted to bring the army under the influence of the Left. Their leader was alleged to be the prime minister's son, Andreas. The young Papandreou had left Greece in 1939, at the age of twenty, and, following a distinguished academic career in the United States, returned in 1959 at the invitation of Prime Minister Karamanlis to establish a center of economic research.

An expert on economic development with influential friends in America, Andreas had entered politics and, following his election to parliament, emerged as a senior cabinet member and his father's principal adviser and confidant. Brilliant, arrogant, and combative, by 1965 Andreas had become the lightning rod attracting the hostility of the conservatives, the military and the palace, as well as of key members of the Center Union party. In Anschuetz's words, Andreas was his father's "most vulnerable point."[27]

The growing suspicion and animosity with which Andreas was regarded in Athens gradually spread to official Washington. An April 1966 internal memorandum written by the head of the Department's Greek Desk characterized the younger Papandreou as "politically naïve, unscrupulous, unstable (with paranoiac tendencies), venal, and above all [with] such an overweening ambition that he would resort to almost any means to achieve his goals." He was suspected of conspiring with Communists, and it was said that, given the opportunity, he "would try to move Greece toward a non-aligned, neutralist stance."[28] Washington's alarmist views on Andreas were becoming a major factor in American attitudes toward internal developments in Greece.

Despite the brewing "perfect storm" in Greek politics, the Embassy continued to believe that Papandreou was likely to survive at least through the summer of 1965. However, when Papandreou forced Defense Minister Petros Garoufalias to resign over the investigation of ASPIDA and the filling of top army posts, Anschuetz advised the Department that a showdown between Papandreou and King Constantine was a "distinct possibility." The DCM observed that such a clash would harm Greece as well as American interests but refrained from passing judgment on the merits of the dispute.[29] On the other hand, embassy reports to the Department became increasingly critical of Andreas for his anti-American rhetoric but primarily for his efforts to bring the armed forces and the Greek CIA (KYP) under the effective control of his father's government.

On June 30, without prodding from the Department, Anschuetz visited George Papandreou to discuss the impasse over the appointment of a new army chief and its political ramifications. He stressed that his only motive in raising the issue was his desire to assist in preserving political stability in Athens and ensure the continuation of American military assistance. While conceding that the army should be kept out of politics, he reminded the prime minister that the Greek king had "over [a] period of time acquired a generally recognized interest in [the] armed forces," and appealed to Papandreou to adopt a more conciliatory stand toward the palace. Not surprisingly, the old man of Greek politics did not appreciate the American diplomat's advice. As Anschuetz reported, Papandreou "was in a very serious mood and showed a degree of stubbornness to my prodding."[30] Undeterred, in additional talks with ERE leaders and palace officials, the DCM offered the opinion that the deadlock over the naming of a new minister of defense and army chief was undermining the monarchy and was "a tragedy for Greece from which only the Communists would profit." Once again, however, he was forced to concede to his superiors that "this position has naturally been received with lack of enthusiasm by those elements on both sides who hoped to win the unqualified support of the U.S."[31]

Anschuetz knew that he was offering platitudes and innocuous advice to Greeks who wanted to hear instead that, in the brewing crisis, the Embassy would side with them against their rivals. He was obviously anxious to assure the Department that he was careful not to exceed his authority or depart from established policy. On July 23 he reported, "Situation has not developed to point where US attitude might be decisive. Consequently we are endeavoring to maintain greatest possible discretion. . . . Given incredibly sensitive political acoustics in Athens and virtuosity of Greek talent for misrepresentation and distortion, Embassy position is constant subject for local exploitation. . . . This spectrum of commentary suggests that although our attempt not to become involved may not prove to be completely successful, the effort is at least a valiant one." In its prompt and peremptory response, the Department agreed that "discretion needed to avoid untimely involvement of American factor," at least while there was no U.S. ambassador in Athens.[32]

The Embassy's "valiant effort" to avoid becoming involved in the escalating political crisis was less than "completely successful." While various Greek factions intensified their efforts to secure Washington's endorsement of their particular position, Anschuetz became increasingly concerned that, in challenging the palace and arousing the fears of the military and the opposition, Papandreou was pushing the country toward political collapse and chaos. Yet there is no evidence that the resignation of prominent Center Union deputies and cabinet members, which forced Papandreou to resign on July 15, was encouraged by the Embassy's diplomatic personnel. On the other hand, on August 10 Anschuetz informed the Department that King Constantine had sent word that he would appreciate the Embassy's support for a new cabinet under Stephanos Stephanopoulos, a respected conservative politician and former foreign minister. The same message was received from several among the leading "defectors" from the Center Union party, including Constantine Mitsotakis, Elias Tsirimokos, and John Tsouderos, the last saying that "a word of encouragement from Embassy at this point could be extremely important." Reporting these developments to the Department the DCM expressed the opinion that if the proposed Stephanopoulos "solution" failed, "other possible solutions are certainly not very attractive." He concluded: "Under these circumstances . . . Embassy should not withhold word of encouragement which might just possibly provoke necessary impetus to break current impasse and provide interim political solution. Situation had developed to point where issue apparently hung in balance and where cautious effort on our part justified." Therefore, "within limitations of resources available, Embassy has provided maximum support" to Stephanopoulos "consistent with discretion which we have been endeavoring maintain." He hoped that the Department would endorse the action already taken and approve a plan for further clandestine activity in support of the anti-Papandreou forces.[33]

The Department's prompt reaction was to rebuke Anschuetz for his decision to lend support to a particular solution in the political stalemate: "Appreciate intense nature of pressure employed to force American involvement in crisis. However, believe response to any further approaches . . . should be reiteration that ultimate solution will be healthier politically and more permanent if Greeks work it out without interference."[34] As for further clandestine efforts to prevent the Papandreous' return to office, the DCM's proposal was referred to the president's national security adviser, McGeorge Bundy, who promptly rejected it.[35] When in mid-September the king again solicited the Embassy's support for the Stephanopoulos "solution," Anschuetz remained carefully noncommittal.

The proposed Stephanopoulos "solution" prompted Papandreou to launch once again his "relentless struggle" against his opponents and to agitate for new elections, which it was generally believed he would win. Requests from various political quarters that the Embassy play a catalytic role also continued. Through the spring and early summer of 1966, Ambassador Talbot and his embassy divided their time between the intensified diplomatic activity regarding the Cyprus problem and the unfolding Greek political drama.

In August 1966, twenty years after James H. Keeley assumed his duties as counselor of embassy in Athens, his son, Robert V. Keeley, also a career

Foreign Service officer with a fair knowledge of Greek and pleasant memories of his childhood days in that small corner of the Balkans, arrived to take up his post as a political analyst. He was to return in 1985 as the U.S. ambassador to Greece (1985–89). His baptism in the ways of American diplomacy and of Greek politics is recounted in this remarkably candid and historically valuable memoir. Keeley takes the reader inside the Embassy and paints a revealing picture of the complex, fractious, and often frustrating process through which the ambassador and his senior staff were involved in the formulation and execution of American policy during a particularly delicate period in U.S.-Greek relations. Among the many important facets of this process are the inner workings of the Embassy, in which senior staff members are shown to be anything but receptive to the differing views of their junior colleagues toward the relationship between the Embassy and the main protagonists of the Greek political crisis of 1966–67 and toward the exchanges between the Embassy and the Department before and after the Colonels' coup of April 21, 1967. Students of that period will be especially interested in Keeley's portrayal of Andreas Papandreou, which is far more nuanced and less alarmist than that of his superiors, who played a decisive role in establishing Washington's policy on Greece. Equally valuable is his account of the reaction of American officials to the coup, and to the dictatorship that followed. As the reader will discover, Washington's passive acquiescence to the new regime caused the young diplomat much frustration and disappointment, and may be presumed to be a primary motive behind his decision, many years later, to publish this memoir. The fact that his own interpretation of the Greek crisis in 1966–67, and subsequent recommendations for a more assertive American response, were largely ignored does not in the least diminish their importance for historians. On the contrary, they give us a much clearer understanding of American decision making and of both sides in the troubled relationship between the United States and Greece, whose reverberations were destined to prove lasting.

The Colonels' Coup
AND THE AMERICAN EMBASSY

INTRODUCTION WITH DRAMATIS PERSONAE

In setting out to write an account that is admittedly personal, and labeled as such, one should not have to apologize for presenting the story strictly from one's own perspective. Yet so much historical writing by public servants purports to be the inside-story-as-it-actually-happened rather than only one man's version of the story that it seems proper to admit at the beginning that what follows necessarily emphasizes my own role (or what I thought it to be) in the events described, that it suffers from the human tendency to remember occasions when one was right and to forget instances when one was wrong, that the views and actions of others with whose policies I was in disagreement are obviously presented less sympathetically than they would be by those other persons, and that a history of the same place and period by any other participant/observer would read vastly differently. If it is a truism that all history is memoir, it nevertheless bears repeating.[1]

It may strike the reader as curious that a number of the policy disagreements mentioned in the account to follow were recorded in memoranda and are thus available for quotation. Anyone with experience of an American Embassy knows that most discussions of and disagreements about policy matters occur orally—in face-to-face meetings of officers, in staff meetings, and in ad hoc "country team" meetings—and are therefore hardly ever recorded on paper. The final result, that is, the policy arrived at, is recorded, but not the often contradictory inputs.

One explanation for the existence of a written record in this case is that during the period covered I was not working on Greek "internal" (i.e., domestic) political affairs and was therefore not a member of the inner circle of officers regularly consulted by the ambassador about policy matters other than the Cyprus problem. Thus, I had to try to inject my views from "outside," and that required in most cases an unsolicited memorandum to my boss, the political counselor.

But why did I not simply tell her what I thought and save the trouble of preparing a formal memorandum? One reason is that most bureaucrats can more easily ignore an oral demarche than they can a piece of paper. ("Demarche" is diplomatic jargon for a presentation of an argument for, or an explanation of, a policy position, usually made by a diplomat to a foreign government interlocutor.) Secondly, during a crisis period it is extremely difficult to get a senior officer's undivided attention long enough to present a coherent case for a different policy approach. Thirdly, one can go over the head of one's superior—acceptably if not too subtly—by passing a copy of one's memo up the line to the deputy chief of mission or the ambassador or both without violating the hierarchical niceties too profoundly.[2] If one's boss won't pass one's ideas along, one can do it oneself by using this technique.

It was furthermore known that one could more readily obtain access to Ambassador Phillips Talbot's mind through a written document than orally. He liked to mull over ideas at his leisure. His successor, Ambassador Henry Tasca, was just as likely to ignore anything in writing; the way to reach him was through the ear. Finally, writing a memorandum is an exercise in self-discipline: if one cannot organize and present one's ideas coherently on paper, they are probably not worth bothering anyone else with.

My assignment to Athens came about principally because an acquaintance of mine, Robert Houghton, happened to be in charge of the Personnel section dealing with political officers of my rank, and he knew that I would welcome an assignment to Athens. For some seven years I had regularly listed Greece as my first choice on my annual "Post Preference Report," a bureaucratic form notorious for the lack of use made of it by personnel officers and usually referred to as the "April fool's card," in reference to the date of its annual submission to Washington. But the IBM computer used by Personnel had included my name on a list of Greek-speaking officers (probably because some other form showed that I had once spoken the language fluently), which brought my name to the attention of Houghton, who was looking for a "warm body" to fill an upcoming vacancy in the Political Section of Embassy Athens.

Another officer, who had to approve my assignment in his capacity as personnel officer of the Near East/South Asia Bureau, had formerly served in Athens. I understood from him that he thought it would be a good thing for me to replace John Owens as "internal political affairs officer" in the Athens Political Section, because the section needed some new blood, a new point of view, someone not a member of the clique of Greek-language specialists trained by the Foreign Service Institute.

Owens had served in Greece for six straight years, four in Athens after two in Thessaloniki. His Greek was good, he had a wide range of contacts, and he was a key officer on the political side who did a large portion of the Embassy's political reporting. After my arrival in Athens, I read the back files and found the quality of his reporting quite superior, although too focused on the superficialities—the daily tactical maneuvers of the most active players in the Athenian political game—and too little on analysis of the fundamental forces shaping the political life of the country. A protégé of Deputy Chief of Mission Norbert Anschuetz, Owens went along with the Embassy's policies, or nonpolicies, of the precoup period (according to what I heard about him), and he shared in the general anti–Andreas Papandreou animus of the official American community. He had some good contacts in Center Union party circles, notably the playboy-politician with a famous name, Nikitas Venizelos, but most of these contacts were not the most reputable types. Some people, unfairly no doubt, did not take Owens seriously, because he had developed a reputation as a womanizer. Frankly, this trait was not uncommon among the Greek political establishment that was Owens's terrain of responsibility, and certainly no handicap therein.

Unfortunately for me, I had no overlap with Owens. When I arrived in Athens, I discovered that I was to work on "external political affairs" (primarily the Cyprus problem); John Day, an officer slightly junior to me who had been handling the Cyprus portfolio for three years, had been moved into Owens's slot on internal political affairs just prior to my arrival. This arrangement did not seem entirely pleasing to Political Counselor Kay Bracken, who explained to me that she could do nothing about it, as it had been worked out by DCM Minister-Counselor Anschuetz prior to her own arrival in Athens a couple of months earlier. Day, like Owens, was an Anschuetz protégé. It became clear to me that Mrs. Bracken merely wished to avoid any disputes with Anschuetz because she hoped shortly to succeed him as DCM.

This switch of assignments with Day did not bother me a great deal at the time, because I thought it would be just as well for me to work on Cyprus for a year while learning about the internal political situation. I could then replace Day when he left on transfer a year later. In fact, he was already quietly planning to extend his tour a year, so it was two years before I replaced him. I hasten to add that what Anschuetz had done was in no way improper or unusual, for the senior embassy managers—including in this case the ambassador, the DCM, and the political counselor—have the right, even the obligation, to deploy their staffs in the manner they deem most appropriate, efficient, and effective.

I dwell on this matter here only because it helps explain why I was an "outsider" in trying to influence policy outcomes during the period recounted. Had I been allowed to fill the slot to which Personnel had assigned me, I would have automatically been a member of the inner circle dealing with the internal political crisis of 1966–67. I will not claim that the policy outcomes would have been different than they were, for an insider could have been ignored just as readily as an outsider. But since I feel strongly that we committed grievous errors in Athens during that period, I continue to regret that I was unable to bring to bear even the limited influence that would have been mine as the low man on the internal affairs policy totem pole.

DRAMATIS PERSONAE

Since this is essentially a story about the human (or bureaucratic) elements in foreign policy making, some background on the principal actors is necessary to an understanding of what follows.

Phillips Talbot became ambassador to Greece in the fall of 1965. He had been named early in the summer, but his departure from Washington had been postponed (I have been told on good authority) so that he could participate in a seminar at Aspen and because Secretary of State Dean Rusk asked him to stay on board as assistant secretary for the Near East and South Asia to deal with the gathering India/Pakistan crisis of that summer. I heard from Greeks in Athens their view that he had deliberately delayed his arrival in Athens until the Greek political crisis that began on July 15 with the ouster of George Papandreou had been resolved by the installation of the bare-majority Stephanopoulos government, but this may have been an unfair anti-Talbot canard. In any case, he traveled to Greece by ship, so apparently was in no hurry to get there that fall.

Talbot's expertise was notably South Asia, where he had served during World War II in the navy and both before and after the war as a newspaper correspondent for the *Chicago Daily News*. For ten years he had been an academic administrator, as executive director of the American Universities Field Service Staff. President Kennedy had appointed him assistant secretary for the Near East and South Asia at the beginning of his administration after being impressed with a preinaugural foreign policy task force report on that geographic region, for the drafting of which Talbot had been largely responsible. Talbot had good connections with a number of leading personalities in the liberal wing of the Democratic Party, including Hubert Humphrey, and was himself considered to be a liberal. (However, a longtime member of his personal staff once remarked to me, "He's a lot more conservative than you think.")

Visibly unemotional, even-tempered to a fault, he was not a difficult man to work for, nor an easy man. It was extremely difficult to tell what was going on in his mind because he never gave the slightest reaction to anything one said, not even a nod. One wondered if he ever had strong feelings, and if so, about what. Talbot was articulate, liked to draft his own telegrams, which he did very capably, and had never entirely thrown off the mantle of newspaper reporter. He was reputedly on extremely good terms with Dean Rusk, apparently because he never brought him any major problems and would report daily at the secretary's morning staff meeting that all was well in his area, all quiet on the Near Eastern–South Asian front. Rusk, with a full plate of crises indeed, appreciated anyone who didn't bring him problems.

Obviously all was not well, for the conditions that led to such untoward events as the 1965 Indo-Pak War and the 1967 Arab-Israeli "Six Day War" were brewing all during Talbot's tenure as assistant secretary. But the former situation did not reach the point of a major crisis until the last weeks of his service in Washington, and the latter crisis erupted into a major conflagration nearly two years after Talbot had moved to Athens. From my observation of the ambassador's attitude in Athens, I doubt he realized from the perspective of his post in Washington that the crisis that landed in his lap in Athens in April 1967 really had its beginnings in the Greek elections of 1961, some time after the start of his own State Department career.

In personality Talbot curiously resembled Arthur Schlesinger's description of Rusk, who "would sit quietly by, with his Buddha-like face and half-smile," keeping his views to himself so that his position on all major issues remained a mystery. Perhaps that is why they had got along so well together; they were so much alike. Although one was from the Middle West and the other from the South, they shared similar experience in the China-Burma-India theater in World War II and were each "nurtured in the successive bosoms of the university, the Army, the government department, the foundation." They both preferred banal language, conventional policies, and regularity of procedures, and they "rejoiced in the 'tedium' of diplomacy."

In describing Talbot one cannot improve on what Schlesinger wrote of Rusk:

The stereotypes of diplomacy were his native tongue. At times one wondered whether the harshness of life—the seething planet of revolutionary violence, ferocity and hate, shadowed by nuclear holocaust—ever penetrated the screen of clichés, ever shook that imperturbable blandness. . . . The inscrutability which made him a good aide and a gifted negotiator made him also a baffling leader. When Assistant Secretaries brought him problems, he listened courteously, thanked them and let them go; they would often depart little wiser than they came. Since his subordinates did not know what he thought, they could not do what he wanted. In consequence, he failed to imbue the Department with positive direction and purpose. He had authority but not command.[3]

Talbot ran his embassy in much the same manner—except that for people from the other agencies it was not a question of their not knowing what he wanted and therefore failing to perform adequately. Since he did not know what he wanted—or chose not to communicate it—they did as they pleased. In fairness, my own impression was that the senior staff of the mission did not serve the ambassador well, because they avoided the obligation to make forceful presentations of their own views when and if they disagreed with policies we were pursuing, which was of course rare enough. This left the ambassador unaware of any serious dissension in the ranks, or of possible policy alternatives to what we were doing. Talbot resigned his ambassadorship effective the day that Richard Nixon was inaugurated as president of the United States. He then became president of the Asia Society in New York.

Norbert Anschuetz, out of Kansas via Harvard Law School, was in appearance and personality—good looks, graying wavy hair, English-tailored but slightly fraying suits, urbane manner, smooth talk—the epitome of the American diplomat as typecast by Hollywood. He knew everyone worth knowing in town, traveled in the best circles, got invited to Onassis's island, was clever and witty (although the longer one knew him the smaller became his repertoire of wisecracks, usually tinged with sarcasm). Behind his back he was called "the Snake" by some establishment circles in Athens, because he played the diplomatic game to the hilt by dealing with all political factions without playing favorites (except his own).

Anschuetz had started his diplomatic career in Greece, on the staff of UNSCOB (UN Special Committee on the Balkans), which investigated Greek government charges against its northern neighbors in the years immediately after World War II. He was officer in charge of Greek affairs in the State

Department in 1950-51 and then entered the Foreign Service as first secretary–political officer in Athens. There he became the protégé of Jack Peurifoy, the very activist ambassador who literally ran Greece under the Truman Doctrine in the early fifties, later arranged the overthrow of President Jacobo Arbenz in Guatemala, and was killed in an auto accident in Thailand.

Anschuetz served as Peurifoy's political counselor in Bangkok, and was later deputy chief of mission in Cairo, political counselor in Paris, and then minister-counselor DCM in Athens from 1964 to 1967. He was in charge of the Embassy (between Henry Labouisse's and Talbot's tenures as ambassador) during the crisis of the summer of 1965. He was by that time overdue for appointment as an ambassador, but for some reason Talbot kept him on as his DCM when tradition called for his transfer after an extended period as chargé. During the period in question Anschuetz gave the impression of being most unhappy to stay on under Talbot. He apparently thought it was an insult to remain in Athens as DCM under a former assistant secretary of state and was heard to remark that he would have been happy to stay on with a "dress manufacturer from Brooklyn," or some such type, who would, of course, have needed the real skills and expertise the DCM could have provided to a needy diplomatic amateur, with no diminution of Anschuetz's position in Athens.

Originally considered sympathetic to the Center Union when it came to power in 1964, Anschuetz had been a good friend of the Andreas Papandreous and kept in touch with them from time to time in the period leading up to the coup. During the time I knew him, Anschuetz seemed to have no real work, would spend much of the day out of the office visiting with friends, was full of details about the political intrigues of the town. He rarely recorded any of his juicy conversations but would occasionally pass along a tidbit to John Day for him to use in one of his daily "spot" political reports.

Anschuetz's ambassadorial assignment never came through; he was assigned to the Senior Seminar in Washington in the summer of 1967, apparently decided he would never make it to the top, and quit to go to work for the First National City Bank as head of its Beirut office.

Mrs. **Katherine (Kay) Bracken** was one of the most senior female officers in the Foreign Service, winner of the Federal Women's Award and many other honors. Who or what Mr. Bracken had been no one knew, and no one had the audacity to ask, but he had not been around for a very long time. A southern girl born in Georgia, Kay had started her diplomatic career as a clerk in Latin America during World War II, had become an officer at the end of the war, and had had more service in her area of specialization (Greece-Turkey-Iran) than probably any other contemporary FSO: tours in

Thessaloniki, Athens, Izmir, Ankara, Istanbul, Teheran, and Isfahan. She had had Turkish and Persian language and area training (she also spoke fairly good Greek) and had also had experience in India and Latin America. By luck or design she had acquired signal expertise in all three of the countries that were covered by the Office of Greek, Turkish, and Iranian Affairs (known in the Department as "GTI"), part of the Bureau of Near Eastern and South Asian Affairs.

Although by this time a class 1 officer, she had apparently decided that she would not be made an ambassador and as a final "retirement" post had settled for the number two job (she thought) in Athens under Talbot, who had been her boss in the Department during the four years she had headed GTI, which also covered Cyprus. She came out to Athens with Talbot's approval as political counselor, reportedly with the intention of replacing Anschuetz as DCM when he departed. When Anschuetz left a year later, Talbot changed his mind, apparently in response to the prompting of Mrs. Talbot, who wanted a married DCM so that the latter's wife could share the load of official entertaining and the other chores of an ambassadorial wife. Talbot brought in a new DCM from Washington, and in the aftermath Mrs. Bracken became bitter about her treatment and retired from the Service in the spring of 1968.

A tall and large woman, and therefore somewhat imposing, Mrs. Bracken was highly intelligent, very knowledgeable about the area going back twenty years, somewhat inarticulate in speech and in writing, brusque with her subordinates, and obviously close to Talbot from the days they had worked together on the Cyprus crisis of 1963–64 in Washington. She had Talbot's ear, and he relied on her greatly for her presumed knowledge of Greece and the Greeks. She did not rely on any supposed femininity to gain a hearing or win an argument but rather on toughness and force of mind and determination, doubtless all necessary qualities for a woman to succeed in what was still very much a male profession. Kay seemed to go out of her way to avoid appearing in any way sentimental or even emotional, perhaps to prevent people from saying, or thinking, "There goes Kay, acting just like a woman!" She undoubtedly discounted most other people's views because she believed them (in most cases rightly) to be based on a less thorough knowledge of the country and area than her own. What she lacked was not knowledge but rather understanding.

Roswell D. McClelland, a career Foreign Service officer of class 1 with twenty-two years of experience, replaced Anschuetz as deputy chief of mission in August of 1967. An ambassador in Athens such as Talbot would ordinarily have had his pick of the senior officers in the Service in choosing his DCM, but Talbot apparently knew very few people despite his recent years in the Department. All through the winter of 1966 and the spring of 1967 he kept asking the Department for suggestions for a new DCM but evidently made none of his own, as was his right by tradition. In June he went to the United States on leave and to receive an honorary degree from his university (Illinois). McClelland flew to Illinois to be interviewed. He passed muster and was assigned to Athens. It was said that Talbot wanted someone who would concentrate on the management and administrative area—on running the Mission—a DCM's task that Anschuetz had allegedly neglected while he played at Greek politics. McClelland had no background for a Greek assignment and was happy to take on the assigned chore.

During the Second World War McClelland had served with the Quakers in Switzerland working with refugee relief and had entered government service with the War Refugee Board in Bern toward the end of the war. In the Foreign Service he had had a variety of assignments, in Bern, Madrid, and the Department. I had first met him in Dakar, Senegal, where he was DCM in 1960–64, while I was serving as a political officer in neighboring Bamako, Mali. He later served as consul general in Salisbury, and was withdrawn when the Rhodesian government declared unilateral independence from Great Britain in 1965.

"Ross" McClelland was a competent officer, cautious, outwardly calm but apparently inwardly nervous and tense, prone to ulcers. He drafted easily and well, ran a fairly smooth operation. His personal political convictions were exceedingly conservative. Finding himself in an embassy divided on the issue of policy toward Greece (though the division was lopsided in numbers), McClelland liked to think of his role as that of a mediator among the divergent schools of thought attempting to prevail in the Embassy. He asserted that his job and his goal were to achieve a necessary compromise between disagreeing advocates. But his judgments almost invariably came down on the side of a conservative approach, of not rocking the boat, avoiding anything that might antagonize the Greek Colonels, although their gaffes and ineptitudes would sometimes exasperate him to the point that he would exclaim aloud about their stupidity.

In the early months Ross did not have an easy time of it, for his mere presence in Athens irritated Kay Bracken. He was occupying the job that she had envisioned for herself, although it was obviously no fault of his that he was doing so. I was the only person in the Embassy whom McClelland knew from before, so he sought me out in the first days and pumped me for whatever information I could provide that would help ease his relations with irascible types like Mrs. Bracken. This didn't help much, for he found he had to keep his head down until she departed the post some months later. I recall one memorable occasion when McClelland felt inspired to prepare a memorandum on possible motivations for French government policy toward the Colonels—a subject in which he had some expertise, surely more than any other officer in the Embassy. When she saw the document Mrs. Bracken flew into a rage, marched into the ambassador's office, and announced that the DCM had no business preparing political reports as that was in the province of the political counselor, herself, and she would not countenance any interference in the work of her section, etc. McClelland decided the better part of wisdom would be to concentrate on running the Embassy until she departed the scene.

McClelland was chargé d'affaires for the period of nearly a year between the departure of Ambassador Talbot in January 1969 and the arrival of Ambassador Tasca in January 1970. There were no highly visible disasters in the performance of the Embassy during this time—as we continued to drift along without a policy to speak of—and he received his reward (some people would consider it so) when he was named ambassador to the Niger Republic in the summer of 1970, to cap his Foreign Service career. As the subsequent narrative will show, my personal relations with McClelland became thoroughly entangled with our policy differences as time progressed.

Small World Department item: Following McClelland's retirement and the death of his wife, he traveled to Kansas City, Missouri, and for reasons now lost in my defective memory, he there met the widow of my Keeley cousin who had lived in that city, and whom I had met only once. Ross and this cousin's widow were subsequently married, moved to Arkansas, and Ross died there. He and I were never reconciled after we said good-bye in Athens, which I regret, even more so because of this—I must say peculiar—development.

The second-ranking officer in the Political Section was **Malcolm Thompson**, a New Englander, product of Harvard and the Fletcher School of Law and Diplomacy at Tufts, and of the U.S. Navy. A Turkish specialist, he had been schooled in politico-military affairs in Washington, and following a tour on detail to the Defense Department had been assigned to Athens as political/military officer. He had had experience in Germany and two tours in Turkey (Ankara and Iskenderun) and spoke French, German, and Turkish. He had not had a happy tour in Athens, because the Greek specialist clique (including Kay Bracken) thought he was an anomaly: a Turk serving in Greece made no sense, they felt; it went against the grain. He was therefore ignored on most subjects, even on Greece's relations with Turkey and the Cyprus problem, on which he presumably could have provided some expertise. His first boss as political counselor (Bracken's predecessor) had formerly been the political/military officer, who never really turned that job over to him, except for its drearier aspect of holding the hands of the senior officers in the American military mission in Athens. Mrs. Bracken also tended to do this job herself, at least when anything important was involved, such as military assistance policy.

When his tour in Athens was over, Thompson went to Istanbul on transfer. His difficulties in Athens had done nothing good for his performance file, and he was not promoted. When he reached the maximum of ten years in grade without a promotion, he was involuntarily retired from the Service, which thus lost another very fine officer, whose problem was that he maintained his individuality and declined to succumb to the imperative demands of bureaucratic advancement.

John Day, another New Englander (Bowdoin, Fletcher, Freiburg), became a Greek language specialist after tours in Naples and The Hague. He served in the Athens embassy from 1963 to 1968, the first three years on the Cyprus problem and the last two as the internal affairs political officer. A competent political reporting officer, he worked in the shadow of John Owens, even after the latter had long since left the post. Though Day took the precaution of appropriating Owens's title, office, phone number, and secretary prior to my arrival—to ensure that no one in town made the mistake of thinking that I rather than he had replaced Owens as *the* embassy political officer—Day was never able to completely fill Owens's shoes. Primarily he lacked Owens's charm and resourcefulness, though they were clearly both among the abler political officers in the Foreign Service of that era, especially among those specializing in Greek affairs.

Day never developed Owens's wide range of contacts and was not nearly his equal as a drafting officer, nor as a linguist, but he was highly intelligent, worked hard at his job, had no limiting idiosyncrasies, and performed most capably for his superiors. He was normally ambitious, without exaggerated expectations of his future Foreign Service career. For two years he was a key officer in the Embassy because of his knowledge of Greece and background in its immediate past history.

He was not fairly appreciated by Mrs. Bracken. It may have been that their competitive instincts clashed, or she may have simply resented his status as a protégé of Anschuetz. His performance ratings written by her were not of the best and did not do his performance justice—most likely because of this "personality conflict" with Mrs. Bracken—and his next promotion came only after six years, three years after leaving Athens. (The reader may have noticed that this phenomenon was endemic at the Embassy in Athens at that time, which tells us something.) Day's attitude toward Greece and the Greeks was one of tolerant disdain, a trait especially prevalent among the Greek specialists in the Service, although he may have been overly influenced by the venality he attributed to the Greek politicians who were the flowers of the garden he cultivated. It was always difficult to discover what Day stood for, other than the U.S. of A. in the largest sense. He was a capable professional diplomat, in the good as well as the more limiting meanings of that term.

Jack Maury, the Central Intelligence Agency (CIA) station chief, was a Virginia gentleman of the old school. Pipe smoking, wearing a sportcoat in the office, smooth talking, he did not seem to have a sinister bone in his body. Of superb politeness, he exuded cooperativeness and absence of conflict. He was a professional intelligence officer, but one had the impression that if fox hunting and running after beagles had not gone out of style he would never have left Virginia for the supposedly exciting life of clandestine intelligence. During the war he had been a colonel in the marines. His career after that he did not talk about. He had been in Greece for about four years prior to the period under study. He ran a large organization apparently smoothly and with himself fully in control. Although he liked to startle people with his secretly obtained stories of nefarious activities, one had the feeling that he held back the best items for more private ears (perhaps the ambassador's alone).

Everyone liked Jack; he seemed to enjoy life. There were rumors that he had a mistress: no one cared; if he didn't have one, he should have. It went with his role. Maury's tour in Athens was supposed to end in the summer of 1967, but after the coup it was apparently decided that he should stay on, for he was close to the king, and Constantine was a key element in the post-coup political situation (even more than he had been earlier). Following the disastrously abortive countercoup undertaken by the king in December of 1967, Maury was recalled, presumably because his palace connection no longer counted for much. Doubtless the Athens job is one of the top overseas posts in CIA and is much sought after. In any case, Maury was replaced by the man who ran the Greek desk at headquarters. My identification of Jack Maury as the top CIA man in Greece is not "blowing his cover"; everyone in

Athens knew what Maury was, and the name of his successor was no secret either.

Major General **Samuel Knox Eaton** was a West Pointer, a fairly typical career army officer with enough of the social graces (his wife had even more) to become a sort of specialist in semidiplomatic assignments in NATO and as head of the military mission (JUSMAGG) in Greece. (The acronym stood for "Joint United States Military Assistance Group Greece.") He engaged in a running battle with all three of the service attachés in the Embassy—a losing battle for the latter, who despite being criminally overstaffed could not bring to bear the heavy artillery that Eaton could as the senior officer present, disposing of an even larger staff and around a hundred million dollars of military aid per annum. The attachés had fancy uniforms, but General Eaton had the dough.

Eaton was reasonably intelligent (within the rigidities characteristic of military minds), and a fairly articulate, somewhat personable senior officer. But Athens was his final post before retirement, a fact that perhaps affected his emotional equilibrium. He was peculiarly susceptible to social slights from the Greek military (which became common and apparently significant after the coup and the resultant partial embargo on U.S. military assistance). He would worry that certain officers whom he had invited to a reception at his very representational home had not shown up. Why? What did it mean? His personal relations with the senior officers of the Embassy were mostly quite good, although he naturally felt that not enough attention was paid to military considerations in the policy decisions reached. He also fretted about where he was ranked in the overall American mission hierarchy, especially vis-à-vis Kay Bracken; he had to rank below Anschuetz, for the DCM is always number two. He sometimes had difficulty understanding why anyone was concerned that Greece was ruled by a junta. "What's wrong with them?" he would ask. "Are you against them just because they're military officers?" It was difficult to convince him that one's objection was not to the fact that they wore uniforms but rather that they sat in the chairs of the prime minister and the other cabinet members.

Colonel **Oliver K. Marshall** was the army attaché and the defense attaché, the last army man to occupy the latter post, for during Marshall's tenure Athens was designated as one of the posts where the navy would hold the top spot. "OK," as he was called, was a career army man but not a West Pointer (he graduated from the Citadel). He was competent at the dual functions his job demanded: wearing the starched white uniforms covered with braid in a conspicuous manner at diplomatic receptions and other ceremonials, and picking up a bit of intelligence on the Greek military's extracurricular concerns and activities when such could be obtained without too much trouble in the generally friendly atmosphere that prevailed. It wasn't a tough job: we knew the order of battle, since we drew it up, and to find out what equipment the Greek forces disposed of all we had to do was examine our own vouchers, for we supplied them with everything bigger than a popgun.

OK had some excellent contacts among the senior Greek officers, some good friends in fact. He had been in Greece since 1963 and loved the country to such an extent that after his retirement in 1969 he tried his damnedest to find a civilian job that would send him back to Greece. As for so many of the other key figures in this story, Athens was OK's penultimate post, and he retired within less than a year after his departure. He was supposed to leave in the summer of 1967, but, as in the case of Maury, his very close relations with key royalist figures were considered such a valuable asset after the April 21 coup that his tour of duty was extended so that we could keep tabs on what the king's men in the army were up to.

OK did not approve of the April coup, because it violated the hierarchical values upon which all military organizations are founded. But more than that, he had been anxiously awaiting the "Generals' coup" that never came off; they would have been "his" generals. Through the summer and fall of 1967 Marshall kept in close touch with royalist officers, and he gave us more than enough warning of the king's countercoup attempt in December, although his prediction that it would be carried out smoothly and would succeed was of course 100 percent wrong. He made a tour through northern Greece in late November, visiting all of the major unit commanders, and reported that all was set, all they were waiting for was the signal from the king.

Although somewhat ambivalent, O. K. Marshall's attitude toward the April coup was that he basically didn't like it, mainly because the "little junta" purged a lot of his friends from the army. He liked them even less after they put down the king's coup, on which Marshall had staked so much, and which saw the further purge of the remainder of Marshall's Greek Army buddies. He left the post soon afterward, and the true depth of his feelings was not apparent until July 1971, when he testified before the House Foreign Affairs Subcommittee on Europe that the 1967 Greek coup "had not been an action of military leaders to head off Communism, as so frequently represented, but 'an open mutiny within the armed forces and a rebellion by those mutineers against their King and the constitutional government of Greece.'" According to the *New York Times* editorial (July 19) reporting this event, the then retired Colonel Marshall saw "the greatest danger to future Greek-American and Greek-NATO relationships" in the widely held belief that "the United States supported this military mutiny and continues to do so." In other words, by sustaining the junta this country would jeopardize its own and NATO's security rather than protect it.

Colonel Marshall advocated an all-out effort to convince Greeks that the United States did not back the junta and to persuade the junta to keep its promise to restore democratic government. Contradicting the State-Pentagon line, he said this effort should take priority over "our immediate military needs on Greek soil."[4]

It would be an understatement to say that O. K. Marshall was not your ordinary, garden-variety U.S. Army colonel.

The two officials at the State Department end of the line most responsible for U.S. policy toward Greece during the period under examination were **Stuart Rockwell** and **Daniel Brewster**. The former was the NEA Bureau deputy assistant secretary responsible for Greece, Turkey, Iran, and Cyprus, and the latter was the head of the Greek desk, the "country director" for Greek affairs.

Tall, handsome, with wavy, graying hair and cold blue eyes, Rockwell vied with Norbert Anschuetz for the prize of looking most like the Hollywood version of an American diplomat. But they differed widely in personality. Rockwell was more the traditional stuffed-shirt type, humorless, sober, tough, with no small talk and less wit. He had the reputation of having ruined the careers of a number of Foreign Service subordinates with his slashing performance ratings. It was also said that he was aware of how many people disliked him and had been trying in recent years to unbend a little, be more human, relax a bit. He had a fine mind and wrote exceedingly well. His tastes and attitudes were conservative.

A graduate of Harvard, Rockwell had had a rapid rise in the Foreign Service. Although lacking prior experience with Greece, he had served in both Turkey and Iran (recently as DCM in Teheran for six years), as well as in Panama and Spain, and had headed the Office of Near Eastern Affairs in an earlier manifestation. Like Anschuetz he was considered to be overdue for an ambassadorship. His stiff personality and total inability to suffer fools gladly were considered accountable for his delay in reaching the top. In 1969 he finally made it, as ambassador to Morocco.

Dan Brewster had practically made a career of Greece. Born in Athens during World War I, the son of an American expatriate teacher, he had graduated from Athens College, the American-sponsored secondary school, and then Wesleyan. He spoke, read, and wrote modern Greek fluently, although for some unexplained reason he was reluctant to use his Greek in his contacts with Greeks. After a year as an instructor at Robert College in Istanbul, Brewster started his diplomatic career as a Foreign Service clerk in the Athens legation in 1940, and became an officer in 1945. Following tours in Ankara, Istanbul, and Beirut, he returned to Athens in 1947 for five years, the last three with the ECA foreign aid mission. He then had tours in Paris, the Department, and Berlin. Brewster returned to Athens in 1961 and served for four years as political counselor. In 1966 he took over the Greek desk in Washington, which he relinquished in 1969. He tried to get himself reassigned to Athens again at that point (as economic counselor or anything else) but ended up instead as political adviser to Admiral Rivero, the American NATO South commander in Naples.

A man lacking in verbal ability and decisiveness, Brewster had the reputation of being a worrier, an old maid who couldn't make up his mind. His knowledge of Greece was of course vast, but he had probably damaged his career by specializing too much in one country. In 1967 he was finally promoted to class 1 after a nine-year wait; had he not made it that year he would have been retired prematurely the next, an outcome that would not have disappointed some of his colleagues, owing to the intense competition for senior positions in the Foreign Service.

Brewster's views on Greek politics were known to be conservative. When he visited Athens in March of 1967 to reconnoiter the situation prior to the upcoming parliamentary elections scheduled for May, the joke went the rounds of Athens that his real purpose in coming out was to register himself on the electoral rolls so that he could later send in an absentee ballot for Constantine Karamanlis, Greece's conservative prime minister for the eight years prior to 1963. Brewster apparently had little faith in any Greek politician or faction other than Karamanlis, and he thought the solution to everything would be for the ex-premier to end his self-imposed exile in Paris and to return to lead his ERE party to victory in the elections. Brewster even stopped off in Paris to see Karamanlis on his way home from Athens, but to his chagrin the meeting was declined by Karamanlis, who, standing on prideful protocol, thought he rated a visit from a higher-ranking American official after the years of U.S. neglect of his person.

Whenever he was criticized for some unenlightened aspect of our policy toward Greece, Brewster would complain that it was the fault of his principal assistant, **Marion Mitchell**, a career FSO, who made no attempt to hide her pro-junta sympathies. He just couldn't control Marion, Brewster would lament. His inability to keep her under discipline said a great deal about

Brewster's own character: people asked, if she isn't following your orders, can't you have her transferred?

My own background with Greece went back some years, but I had had no recent experience there. I had lived in Greece for some three years as a child, from 1936 to 1939, while my father was the American consul in Thessaloniki. After the war, in 1946, my father was assigned as DCM in Athens, and I spent eight months of that year there. I spent part of the time at Athens College, a larger part wandering around the city and countryside, and a month working for the Allied Mission for Observing the Greek Elections, as "district secretary" in Tripolis, which meant interpreter, mess officer, administrative officer, and jack-of-all-trades to the chief observer for the Peloponnesus, Colonel Xan Fielding, a British war hero who had spent two years fighting with the Greek guerrillas against the German occupation. Paddy Leigh Fermor, Fielding's wartime buddy who had engineered the famous exploit of kidnapping the German Air Force commander in Crete, General Kreipe, lived with our group at the hotel, and I spent most of the month listening to their war stories and perfecting my Greek. This job was not obtained through nepotism but rather through another form of corrupt practice: childhood friendship with Bruce Lansdale, with whom I had grown up in Thessaloniki and who had been seconded to the Observer Mission by the U.S. Navy to be personnel officer and chief recruiter of local talent for the mission. He hired me and sent me to Tripolis to help out Fielding.

Except for occasional brief visits I had been away from Greece for nearly twenty years when I was assigned to the Embassy in 1966. Because I had learned the language as a child, my Greek was fairly fluent though still not fully mature. Mark Twain famously quipped that Wagner's music is "better than it sounds." In my case my Greek sounded better than it was. The local employee who ran the Embassy's Greek language classes was kind enough to assign me a personal tutor, with whom I conversed for an hour a day most days prior to starting work, and this was invaluable. I had not followed Greek politics closely during recent years, but I had a feel for the country and its people through prior residence there. Also, connections with Greece had been maintained through my brother Mike, a Princeton professor who spends part of nearly every year in Greece. His wife, Mary, was originally Greek, and his scholarly specialty is modern Greek literature. He is perhaps the best-known translator into English of the best modern Greek poets and has published many novels set in Greece and works of nonfiction under his real name, Edmund Keeley.

SETTING THE SCENE

FIRST IMPRESSIONS

I arrived in Athens on July 31, 1966, and reported for duty at the Embassy the following day. When I learned that I was to be responsible for reporting on external rather than internal political affairs, I was dismayed to realize that I knew perhaps less about the Cyprus problem than I did about the domestic politics of Greece. In the afternoon of the first day my boss, Kay Bracken, walked into my office, slapped a telegram down on my desk, and said, "Draft a reply to USUN and the Department saying this is all very well but it doesn't take care of the Turkish right of intervention under Article Four of London-Zurich, so it won't wash in Ankara." Then she walked out.

I hadn't the foggiest notion of what she was talking about and was no more enlightened after reading the telegram, which presented details of someone's counterproposal to someone else's scheme for a "final" solution to the dispute between Greece and Turkey over Cyprus. By asking a few judicious questions of John Day, the Embassy's previous Cyprus "expert," I was able to discover that Mrs. Bracken was making reference to the Treaty of Guarantee, which was part of the London-Zurich accords that had brought independence to Cyprus, Article 4 of which had been interpreted by the government of Turkey as conferring on it the right of unilateral military intervention in Cyprus to uphold the constitutional rights of the Turkish Cypriots against encroachments by the Greek Cypriots.

I had no hope of becoming as expert on the Cyprus problem as either Kay Bracken or Ambassador Talbot, but I set out to learn a lot in a hurry, at least enough to draft sensible cables. Once I had briefed myself on the problem, I found that it did not occupy me full time, for the Cyprus issue was fairly quiescent that fall, with the Greek and Turkish governments engaged in a "dialogue" designed to compromise their outstanding differences on the issue. I had plenty of spare time to look about and observe the political setting in which the Embassy found itself.

The first thing that struck me was the Embassy itself, especially its staffing. Most of the senior officers appeared to be very close to retirement, having chosen Athens as a pleasant post in which to serve out the final years of their careers. In fact, all but one of the eight senior officers of the mission either retired or otherwise left government service during the next three years: the ambassador, the DCM, the political and economic counselors, the consul general, the defense attaché, and the head of the military mission. It did not seem propitious that Washington had staffed the place with a group of people on their last legs, so to speak.

The one exception was the CIA station chief, Jack Maury. In 1977 his job at CIA headquarters was liaison with the U.S. Congress.

The second thing that struck me about the Embassy was that, as in many other overseas missions, its State Department contingent was vastly overshadowed and outnumbered by the military and intelligence components. There were several thousands of American military personnel stationed in the country who were not part of the mission, but the Joint U.S. Military Assistance Group Greece (JUSMAGG) had a couple of hundred officers and men, even though their sole task seemed to be to go over with their Greek counterparts the mail-order catalogue of U.S. military hardware to help make up shopping lists.

Despite the staff-cutting genius of former ambassador Ellis Briggs, a notorious enemy of large missions, the military attaché section of the Embassy still numbered about forty. (The chief attaché, apparently ignorant of Briggs's reputation, had made the mistake of starting his introductory session with the newly arrived Briggs as follows: "Mr. Ambassador, you'll be pleased to know that here in Athens we have the largest attaché operation outside Germany, Japan, and Korea . . .") During my first three weeks I made several futile attempts to penetrate behind the steel gates that protected the attaché offices from casual visitors and finally decided that they didn't want me going through there because I might discover that they had very little work to do and consequently spent a good many days taking advantage of their government-subsidized memberships of the golf course in Phaleron. With the exception of one officer who acted as liaison with King Constantine, the reporting of the attaché office produced practically no intelligence nor any other product of value during my four-year tour in the Embassy.

The civilian intelligence setup was something else again. It is of course impossible for an outsider to estimate the number of American intelligence officers operating in a given country, but there were certainly hundreds in Greece. They were not all involved in Greek affairs, however, for Athens was used by the CIA as a sort of regional headquarters for all sorts of activities involving the Soviet Union, the Communist Balkans, the Near East, and North Africa. Athens was a "privileged sanctuary" where the living was good and the natives friendly. How many were directly involved with Greece it was impossible to tell, but they certainly vastly outnumbered the reasonably small Embassy Political Section, which numbered six officers when I arrived, including the Political/Military Section. In subsequent years the various staff-cutting programs decreed by the Department cut the section by 50 percent—the first cut justified by balance-of-payments considerations, a second on grounds of efficiency, and a third to reduce the overall U.S. "presence" abroad.

The CIA was also cut, but no one knew by how much, and even if they had taken an equivalent proportional cut, the State Department political affairs contingent would still have been outnumbered thirty or forty to one. The CIA, unlike the military, did produce some useful intelligence, with, however, some strong biases, of which more later on. At the same time that the number of State political officers was being cut, the number of CIA officers for whom the Embassy provided direct cover was increased in exactly the same measure, so that the overall number of bodies present in our section never changed; only their agency allegiances did.

The CIA's working habits and arrangements in Greece were (with one minor exception) identical to those I had observed in all of the other countries in which I have served, namely, our intelligence people were solidly entrenched with the group in power, working hand-in-glove with them through extensive and fairly open liaison arrangements as well as more private deals, while they ignored the outs except to try to penetrate the organizations of the extreme Left, subvert them, factionalize them, expose them, or otherwise disrupt their capabilities. Thus the CIA was in bed with the palace, the army, the Greek intelligence service, the rightist party, the conservative business community, the establishment in general. The "apostate" group of Right-Center politicians then in charge of the government was practically the CIA's creation. The CIA's relations with the Center Union and the liberal political forces in general were nearly nonexistent, and anything or anyone to the left of George Papandreou (at a guess half of the Greek body politic) was considered the enemy and fit only for annihilation or at least castration, figuratively speaking.

Now, this was not a new phenomenon to me. In country after country where the United States has purportedly vital interests the CIA works in close alliance with the ruling regime, most often a right-wing authoritarian elite of some sort, sometimes monarchical, sometimes military, in a few cases civilian at least in facade. It is a veritable anomaly that the career Foreign Service officers, the pure diplomats who represent the State Department abroad, are not the ones who carry on the important relations with these foreign regimes. Having little or no resources other than their brains and personalities, they necessarily take a distant backseat to their cousins from the CIA. At the same time the CIA people neglect the opposition, whether friendly or unfriendly, in their single-minded concentration on those who hold the levers of power at the moment. This explains why they are so often caught pantsless by unpredicted coups. They have been working so hard with the regime in power to prevent its overthrow by hostile forces that they of course miss the attempt that turns out to be successful. (The coups they help thwart are of course countless.)[1]

There are obvious explanations for this state of affairs, other than the bias toward conservative governance. One of the most basic is simply that many people are lazy, and most CIA officers would really rather be diplomats. It takes a great deal of work to maintain one's cover, to penetrate often clandestine opposition movements and organizations, to gather the really hard-to-come-by intelligence that can be obtained in no other way, and to preserve one's objectivity by treating all worthwhile intelligence neutrally rather than playing up what one has purchased from one's ideological bedmates. It is also a great deal more glamorous for the station chief to dine and otherwise amuse himself in the company of kings and prime ministers, to hobnob with the power elite (as the diplomats are supposed to do), than to grub around in the sometimes unpleasant, sometimes dangerous lower depths of the unwashed opposition.

I am not here proposing that it is unnatural for representatives of the U.S. government to be working closely with the leaders of very friendly regimes. What I am trying to point out as curious is that since World War II this function has been nearly totally usurped from the diplomats by the CIA. The latter can be expected to argue that there are good and legitimate reasons for these arrangements, that it is much better for a friendly monarch, for example, to deal privately with an intelligence liaison type on a man-to-man, highly informal (and somewhat clandestine) basis than to limit his exchanges to chats with the American ambassador, which are necessarily generally formal, official, and on the record. In my experience this is not much better than rationalization after the fact. The important point is that an ambassador cannot ordinarily give the monarch a private radio communications system, or an executive jet plane to tool around in, or even an Italian sports car. He doesn't have the chips. He can of course recommend an aid program for the monarch's country, but that comes along with a bunch of auditors who try to ensure that the money is neither wasted, stolen, nor diverted to personal baubles.

There is an understandable though pernicious tendency for the CIA's operatives to want to maintain in power all those foreign rulers and political leaders who cooperate closely with them, who facilitate their intelligence work, and who generally look favorably on the activities of the CIA. The State Department suffers from a similar tendency toward overrating foreign leaders who lend support to our international policies, but this is perhaps half legitimate. The important distinction may be illustrated by pointing to the practice of the CIA of seconding American public relations advisers to assist foreign potentates who suffer from decidedly bad images in improving their evil reputations. We care about their images because some of the dirt rubs off on us through too close association with them. Isn't this merely a matter of helping our friends? It all depends on how one defines a friend; in my experience the CIA defines "friend" of the United States as "someone friendly to the CIA," which of course gets us into all sorts of highly anomalous relationships.

To conclude, I should like to stress one of the consequences of this curious reversal of roles. While the CIA operatives are hobnobbing with the power elite it is usually left to the career FSOs in the Political Section to try to keep tabs on the opposition, on the political outs. This is not easy to do, for the FSO's resources are limited to shoe leather, a clever line of chatter, a strong stomach, and some paltry representational funds. Also, he has to be careful not to get too visibly close to the opposition—which in most countries is considered anything but loyal—else he risks being declared persona non grata by an angry regime. The CIA operative, despite the "danger pay" bonus he collects owing to his "dangerous" profession, rarely risks such an untoward reaction, even if (and this really happened) he is caught rifling the prime minister's safe, for the prime minister is as often as not in our pocket; rather, we have purchased him by filling up his.

In most of the situations I am here referring to, the political "ins" are the conservatives, which means that the "outs" are by CIA definition "leftists," i.e., to the left of the rightists in power. An FSO who chooses to cultivate the opposition risks being labeled "soft on leftists," "overly sentimental about democratic ideals," or otherwise some kind of security risk who merits being placed under surveillance himself by his CIA colleagues. They justify such surveillance on the basis that he may inadvertently or intentionally blow a friendly spook's "cover." In my experience FSOs uniformly go out of their way to protect the cover of their CIA colleagues, often at the risk of being considered spooks themselves. The nadir of this anomalous predicament for me was that in Greece my CIA friends tried to discredit me with the opposition to the junta by letting it be known in subtle ways that I was really a CIA type under very deep cover. Needless to say, with a few people this tactic was successful. And no doubt my strong feelings on this subject, as expressed above, were influenced by my unfortunate personal experience.

THE POLITICAL SITUATION

The internal political situation in the fall of 1966 was outwardly calm but still unsettled, with a general malaise pervading all Greek political factions and the Embassy itself. The "apostate" Stephanopoulos government had been in power since September of the previous year, after the crisis of the summer of 1965 had been temporarily resolved by the installation of a government made up of forty-five defecting deputies from George Papandreou's Center Union party, supported in parliament by the votes of the ninety-nine conservatives of the ERE party plus eight Progressives, giving Stephanopoulos a highly precarious one- to two-vote margin in parliament. What amazed everyone in the fall of 1966 was that the Stephanopoulos government had survived so long, that the economy had stayed in reasonably good shape, with the recent trend of a 7–8 percent annual GNP growth rate maintained through 1966, and that absent was the civil strife and turmoil that had characterized the 1965 summer as a consequence of the king's ouster of George Papandreou in a constitutional dispute over who had the right to name the defense minister.

The Stephanopoulos cabinet had a few "strong" personalities in it, such as the premier himself, Mitsotakis, Costopoulos, and Toumbas, and a few capable younger men, such as Tsouderos and Rendis, but the bulk of the ministers (and there were fully forty-five of them, since each apostate had had to be bought off with a ministerial portfolio to make it worth his while to desert Papandreou and the Center Union) were second- and third-rate politicians who had demonstrated their venality by having agreed to being bought off in order to ensure the toppling of Papandreou. It was true that a number of the apostates had deserted Papandreou on principle, considering him and his son Andreas dangerous demagogues who were leading the country to ruin, but most of the apostates had been purchased pure and simple. In the rough-and-tumble sessions of parliament of that period the Center and Left deputies taunted the apostates by shouting "How much?" at them whenever they appeared.

The crisis of 1965 had left a bad taste in everyone's mouth, which accounted for the general malaise. The loyalist centrists were bitter over having been forced from power after they had achieved their first genuine electoral majority since the war in the elections of 1964. The apostates were grabbing while the grabbing was good, but most of them were aware that they had sealed their political dooms by defecting from the Center, and they desperately wanted only to hang onto power long enough to build their personal retirement funds. The conservatives were frustrated by the position in which they found themselves of being the parliamentary support of a government made up of defectors from their chief opposition party, but they feared elections any time soon because they despaired of beating the Papandreous in another contest. The Left was maneuvering in typical fashion, hoping that the political crisis could be exploited to discredit the two major bourgeois-nationalist parties as much as possible and to disillusion as many Greek voters as possible into becoming protest supporters of the Left.

It was difficult to tell how much of this malaise rubbed off on the American mission. Most Greeks blamed primarily the king for having created, or at least having failed to resolve satisfactorily, the crisis with Papandreou in 1965. There were stories that the Embassy, the CIA, someone—in any case, the "foreign factor" that was the Greek euphemism for official U.S. government involvement in their domestic political affairs—had helped engineer the defections from the Center Union, had bought off the deputies to abandon Papandreou. Most Greeks were unable to believe that the Americans were no longer calling all the important political shots in their country, that things had changed drastically since the days of Peurifoy and the other ambassadors who had literally made and unmade Greek governments during the Truman Doctrine and civil war periods, using the power of the purse to back up their actions, since U.S. government financial, economic, and military aid were the sole props that kept all Greek governments from collapsing in those days. All U.S. aid except for military hardware had ceased since 1963, and beginning with the Kennedy administration and the advent of Ambassador Labouisse the Embassy had tried to take a backseat role and avoid giving even the appearance of dictating to the Greeks about their internal political affairs. Talbot had continued this tradition, but it was next to impossible to persuade the average Greek that things had changed and they were now going to be treated as mature, capable people who could handle their own affairs without foreign tutelage.

Certainly the Embassy was concerned that the 1965 crisis had not really been resolved and that the day of reckoning between King Constantine and George Papandreou had merely been postponed. No one had any really good ideas about how it ought to be resolved, but it was evident that elections would one day have to be held (they were due again in any case in 1968, four years after the previous elections). They could not be postponed forever, but everyone hoped that they could be delayed as long as possible, that stability would reign in the meantime, and that something would turn up to help resolve the situation and keep it from becoming explosive again.

My personal view at the time was that the king had made a grave error (whether on his own or on someone else's advice I did not know) in not going to elections immediately in the summer of 1965 and thus turning over to the people the job of resolving the constitutional issue that had arisen between himself and George Papandreou. It seemed evident that the reason he had not done so was that he feared the decision would go against himself and that Papandreou would have been returned to office triumphantly with renewed majority support. But even admitting this, it seemed to me that Constantine had merely aggravated the dispute and hardened feelings on all sides, and that when the day of reckoning finally came, as come it must, his own defeat would merely be magnified, and perhaps to such an extent that the continuation of the monarchy itself would be placed in question.

I was among the embassy officers who made trips through the countryside that fall trying to gauge the sentiments of the people toward the king and the principal political factions, to get an idea of how elections might come out if and when held. My impression, which did not diverge from that of the others, was that very few people had changed their minds since 1964, that the supporters of Papandreou were still his supporters, that monarchists still supported the king, that conservatives could be counted on to vote conservative, and that elections in 1967 or 1968 would most likely return a verdict similar to that of 1964, in which Papandreou had carried 53 percent of the electorate and a healthy majority of parliamentary seats, as against 35 percent for the conservative ERE and 12 percent for the cryptocommunist United Democratic Left (EDA). It appeared that Papandreou's enemies had good reasons for wanting to postpone elections as long as possible in the hope that something would happen to erode the old premier's support among the populace.

One aspect of the Embassy's posture that fall deeply disturbed me. It was that the Embassy seemed to have very bad relations with the Center Union party, one of the two bourgeois-nationalist parties of the country and the one that appeared to have the support of a majority or at least a near majority of the electorate. The bad relations doubtless could be blamed on both sides, but since I was in the Embassy I was concerned to understand how this situation had come about.

For one thing, the Center Union politicians were engaged in a boycott of embassy receptions and social affairs of all kinds, an action they justified on the basis that they refused to associate with any of the apostates who had cooperated in the king's effort to divide and destroy the Center Union party. The apostates made up the government in power at the time, so it was obvious that a number of them would always be included in any embassy function; the apostates were the government to which we American diplomats were accredited, after all. Nevertheless, it seemed to me that an effort could have been made to get together socially or otherwise with the Center people, perhaps by inviting them separately and as a group. We enjoyed excellent relations with the apostates and with the conservatives.

I decided that I would make a special effort to get to know some Center people, since no one else in the Embassy seemed to have very close or extensive contacts in that part of the Greek political spectrum. It was perhaps that the Center blamed us at least partly for what had happened to them in 1965, but I had not been in Athens then so could perhaps, as a newcomer, escape the obloquy. It turned out to be easier to get to know Center-Right than Center-Left people, since the Embassy's relations were especially bad with the Center-Left, which brings us to the case of Andreas Papandreou, the son of the party leader and the chief personality on the Center-Left.

THE PHENOMENON OF ANDREAS PAPANDREOU

It was not hard to tell that no one in the Embassy (with one exception), or in Washington for that matter, had any use at all for Andreas (as he was universally referred to), and the feelings seemed to be reciprocated; but the reasons were not all that easy to understand. The one exception was a junior economic officer who had been Andreas's student at the University of California at Berkeley, where Andreas had chaired the Economics Department. This officer had stopped seeing Andreas after the summer of 1965 because, he said, such contact was obviously frowned upon by the senior officers of the Embassy.

My first awareness of the anti-Andreas animus that pervaded the U.S. government had come during my very scant briefing in the Department prior to departing for Athens. The then Greek desk officer had handed me a large file folder of background material on Andreas prepared by the CIA. Among other things, it purported to prove that he had been a fellow traveler, if not worse, for many years, since his student days; that he had engaged in corrupt practices during his membership in his father's government, such as throwing juicy contracts to a friend who was a city planner; that he was morally sinful in that he had carried on an affair with the city planner's wife; and that he was generally a most reprehensible individual who posed a serious danger to U.S. interests in Greece.

At the time I did not so much resent this effort to brainwash me about a person I had never met as I was somewhat astounded by the attempt to discredit one individual in this fashion, an individual who, if guilty of all these sins and crimes, would not be likely to beguile an innocent but fairly experienced officer like me for very long. I undertook a project to understand this peculiar relationship between the Embassy and Andreas, for it was surprising that mutual hostility could be so great with someone who had been an American citizen for some twenty years, who had made an outstanding reputation as an economist at several American universities, finishing as chairman of the Berkeley Economics Department, who in American politics was a Stevensonian Democrat who had worked actively in Stevenson's presidential campaigns, who had come to Greece at the behest of the conservative prime minister, Constantine Karamanlis, to establish an economic research center designed to attract a first-class team of economists who would undertake the task of economic planning for Greece, and who had stayed on at his father's request to enter politics and bring his considerable talents to the Center Union cabinet of 1964–65. It seemed to me that on the surface, at least, one would have expected the Americans to have done their utmost to cultivate Andreas, to consider him a most worthwhile American asset at the very heart of one of the two great nationalist parties of the country, to try to capitalize on his long association with the United States to reap whatever benefits could accrue from such a relationship.

It was apparent that relations had at one time been good, when Andreas had first arrived in Greece. He had had a number of friends in the Embassy. Then things had gone very sour, dating apparently from Andreas's entry into Greek politics. A serious study of the deterioration of this relationship would make a fascinating monograph in itself, but here I can offer only a few summary observations. They are taken from a memorandum I wrote to Ambassador Talbot on March 10, 1968, analyzing our policy predicament and proposing an entirely new approach.

I speculated in that paper that one reason Americans hated Andreas was that he had formerly been an American and that his anti-American statements gave him the appearance of a turncoat, a traitor. I then tried to account for his anti-Americanism. One reason could have been that his former status as an American handicapped him in Greek politics; some Greeks even considered him an American agent who had been infiltrated into Greece, or if they did not believe it, they spread the story to discredit him and to try to keep him from succeeding his father as party leader over the heads of many other senior Center politicos. Perhaps Andreas struck anti-American postures to prove that he wasn't an American stooge.[2]

Once the Center Union was in power, Andreas came to feel that the U.S. government's involvement in internal Greek affairs was too great and derogated from Greek sovereignty. He observed that the Greek military and the palace, both closely allied with the Americans, acted as totally independent power elements, that is, independent from the elected government. Even more important, the Greek CIA (KYP), which Andreas supervised as minister to the prime minister in his father's government, appeared to be an appendage of the American CIA station, and it was believed that KYP had been used to help defeat the Center in its electoral campaigns against the conservatives over the years. Andreas tried to rectify this situation by bringing KYP under government control, and a direct clash with the interests of the American CIA ensued. (For obvious reasons I did not mention it in my memo to Talbot, but a CIA officer in Athens once candidly admitted to me that under the Papandreou government American CIA operatives had been placed under surveillance, which was new treatment for them in Greece, and to which they took violent exception. This surveillance is perhaps understandable in view of the discovery by the Papandreou government that KYP regularly tapped the phones of cabinet ministers, on whose behalf no one knows.)

Andreas also resented the failure of the U.S. government to support Greece in the Cyprus dispute with Turkey, a dispute that reached crisis proportions during the Center government's tenure. The U.S. government's posture of neutrality between Turkey and Greece is quite understandable and even commendable, but each side felt it was the side of right and justice and expected the backing of its great Western ally. By the same token, the United States resented what it felt had been obstructionism and lack of cooperation on the part of the Papandreous in the American effort to obtain a resolution of the Cyprus crisis in 1964. The extremely prideful Dean Acheson so resented what he considered the Papandreous' sabotage of his Cyprus mediation mission of 1964 that he labeled them in print "the old fool and the young rascal," a crack that was then picked up and spread by former ambassador Briggs, thereby giving away his own prejudices—he who had declared the 1961 elections to be fair, the same elections that Papandreou called a fraud and that caused him to launch his "unyielding struggle" against Karamanlis. Andreas and the Center people had long felt that the Americans favored their conservative ERE rivals (Briggs, for instance, referred in print to the "good" Karamanlis after attacking the Papandreous). If the Americans had been prejudiced against the liberals when they were out of power, some Americans insisted that following the Center victory in the 1963 and 1964 elections the Embassy had established close working relations with them, as it had with their conservative predecessors. But for various reasons these relations went sour and got even worse after the king drove Papandreou from power.

I quote one other point from my memo:

> Andreas engaged in demagoguery, opportunism, political pragmatism, or whatever one wants to call it, by taking anti-American and anti-NATO positions calculated to appeal to the left-of-center voters whom he hoped to convert into the Center Union. This was a calculated effort to wean away from the far left party (the EDA) and entice into the fold of the Center a group of people who had genuine anti-American feelings. I suppose Andreas calculated that the right-of-center spectrum included within the Center Union was closed to him because rival Center politicians had this area "locked up." So he decided to make his push on the left-of-center, and his anti-American positions went very nicely with this effort.

Andreas had found another basis for appealing to the Greek leftist voter. As a result of the Communist domination of much of the wartime resistance to the Nazi occupation of Greece and of the subsequent Communist-led rebellion against the royal government, many Greeks had become "tainted" by prior association with the Communist movement. Government security authorities labeled these people as belonging to one or another category of Communist (nominal, dedicated, dangerous, and so forth), which created for them an inability to obtain documented security or police clearance (a so-called white paper) needed to find employment, to obtain licenses and permissions of various kinds, to gain access to higher education, and to obtain many other things that are considered rights by most citizens but that were made into privileges to be denied to present and former "Communists." Those labeled leftists were treated as thoroughly second-class if not third-class citizens, and they voted for the EDA because the extreme Left party was the only one that promised to lift the stigma one day.

Andreas offered the prospect of lifting it even sooner, for he had a chance of coming to power now, he didn't approve of the policy of establishing two sorts of Greeks, the acceptable and the "untouchables," and he promised to lift these severe restrictions on former leftist activists. Thus they might have voted for him and his picked candidates in droves. (The suffering of these people was brought home to me long after the coup when I learned that the daughter of our cook, though very bright, could not obtain admission to any educational institution beyond the secondary level because her father had once, years before, been an EDA neighborhood organizer; a case of "the sins of the fathers . . ." with a vengeance.)

Others have speculated differently than I. Some say the Americans simply couldn't transfer their love from the ERE to the Center Union. Others allege the CIA tried to recruit Andreas and he refused, thus earning the CIA's hatred. The U.S. military supposedly got most upset over Andreas's anti-NATO remarks in his campaign speeches. However, contrary to the impressions of some, Andreas never proposed that Greece ought to leave NATO.[3] He argued that an alliance like NATO should be two-sided, with support by Greece for the interests of the alliance to be reciprocated by NATO's support for Greece on the Cyprus issue—but how could he ignore the plain fact that Turkey was also in NATO? Another line was that Andreas had gone out of his way to attack the Greek "establishment" (he even coined a new word in Greek for this term), who then retaliated by filling the ears of their American friends with anti-Andreas gossip.

Two incidents that played a large role in the bad relations between Andreas and the American mission were those involving Vincent Joyce and Laughlin Campbell. I am unable to give an objective account of what actually happened in these two incidents, for I have only the contradictory versions of interested parties: Andreas's version from himself on the only occasion that I have talked with him, and the versions of CIA partisans of Campbell and Embassy partisans of Joyce on the other hand. In both cases Andreas had bitter disputes with officers of the American mission, and he succeeded in making enemies of the official Americans even stronger than might otherwise have been the case.

The Joyce incident arose over the Papandreou government's decision to terminate the right of the U.S. Information Service to feed one of its propaganda news broadcasts directly into the Greek government's domestic radio service, a privilege that had been ended for the British after they had used it to broadcast material critical of Greek policy in the Cyprus dispute. The Greek government then terminated all such privileges for the foreign propaganda services. James Vincent Joyce, a brilliant but abrasive and somewhat erratic USIS public affairs officer, got into a shouting match with Andreas over this decision, which (to make a long story short) resulted in the Greek government's declaring Joyce persona non grata when the dispute became public knowledge in Athens through a press leak. I had served with Joyce in Amman some years earlier and could understand how he could have rubbed a Greek government official the wrong way. Andreas was equally capable of exacerbating a personality conflict and losing his temper with an American official. There was a lot of talk about the hostility toward Joyce being based on the fact that he had a Turkish wife, but this was never the relevant problem, I believe.

The essence of the dispute was that Joyce and the American mission thought our close ally Greece ought to accord us special privileges in our operations on its territory, while the Papandreou government felt that some of our activities were derogations of Greek sovereignty and ought to be modified. The Voice of America arrangements involved reciprocal benefits: we had installed important propaganda broadcasting facilities on Greek territory, and we permitted the Greeks partial use of these facilities for their own broadcasts. It does appear to me that Andreas's government was justified in ending the practice of our feeding our material directly into its news broadcasts as though they were locally produced official materials. Moreover, the decision taken by Andreas, on behalf of the Papandreou government, was not directed solely against the United States but was merely an extension—demanded for the sake of consistency—of an action taken against the British broadcasting service, and the French as well.

Laughlin Campbell was the CIA station chief prior to Jack Maury. I do not know the CIA's official version of the incident in question, except that it disputes Andreas's version. The latter is that Campbell tried to persuade Andreas to help enlist his father in support of an electoral scheme called the "kindred party system" that the CIA had cooked up for use in Greece (or copied from a French election system). This scheme would have had the

Council of State separate all political parties into two categories, "nationalist" and "nonnationalist," for example, and the initial allocation of all parliamentary seats in each district would be to one or the other category. The final allocation of seats would then be among the parties of the winning category according to their proportional voting strengths.

The transparent effect of this scheme would have been to obliterate the "nonnationalist" (a Greek euphemism for Communist) left, since at its best the Left had never been able to win more than a quarter of the votes and would thus have won no seats at all. The "kindred party system" was also allegedly designed to build a strong Center so that it could replace the EDA as the principal opposition party in parliament (the EDA had finished second to ERE in the 1958 elections). But the scheme clearly favored the right-wing ERE party of Constantine Karamanlis, which could easily have dominated the "nationalist camp" made up of itself and the liberals, thus ensuring another electoral victory and continued rule by ERE. In essence the plan was to create a "nationalist front" to defeat the Communists, to organize the Center into a reasonably strong opposition party, and to re-elect the ERE.

The plan had no appeal for George Papandreou. His primary objection to the proposal was that it was undemocratic, and would have meant that the Center was accepting a second-place finish before the race had even begun. The old man thought it would tend to force voters out of the Center and into the extreme Left, thus guaranteeing that the Center would continue in minority status and that Karamanlis's party would continue to rule. The liberals also felt that it would lead to an unhealthy polarization of the political forces in the country.

According to Andreas's account of this incident,[4] Crown Prince Constantine had first enlisted his aid to arrange a meeting with his father, George, but the latter had flatly refused to go along with the "kindred party system." Next Laughlin Campbell asked for Andreas's help in arranging an appointment with his father because, he explained, he had offended him on some earlier occasion. Andreas said he was willing, but if the purpose was to ask him to accept the kindred party system he was sure to get an immediate negative reply: "He is not about to commit suicide to please you." Campbell replied angrily (according to Andreas): "Go tell your father that in Greece we get our way. We can do what we want and we stop at nothing."

While these remarks attributed to Campbell are hardly credible, the important thing is that when Andreas next visited Washington he went to the White House to see his friend Carl Kaysen, deputy to McGeorge Bundy, and complained about the role of the CIA in Greece, especially in the elections of 1961, which the Center Union felt had been rigged against them with American assistance. Andreas also talked with Phillips Talbot, then the assistant secretary of state for the Near East and South Asia, who in typical fashion listened carefully but—according to Andreas—gave no indication of his views. Not long after this Washington visit by Andreas, however, Laughlin Campbell was transferred out of Greece and replaced by Jack Maury. My own view is that the CIA's bitter animosity toward Andreas Papandreou and the Center Union in general was irretrievably reinforced by his intervention against their station chief in Athens. If there is one trait that is characteristic of the CIA, it is that its members stick together against the rest of the world, and the agency gives unswerving support to its own personnel, at least in public, no matter what they do. It should not be surprising that in certain places CIA officers have more cordial (if still wary) relations with some of their Communist mission counterparts than they do with their supposed American colleagues in the same embassy who work for rival agencies such as State.

The conclusion of my March 10, 1968, memorandum to Ambassador Talbot was that Andreas was supersensitive and inclined to react violently against what he regarded as prejudice against him by the American mission,

> rather than shrugging it off as natural antipathy in view of the threat he posed to established interests, American and Greek. Andreas does not have the thick skin that most professional politicians grow. But I have also long felt that Andreas's power and prominence were created by his enemies, who have displayed the same sort of paranoia.
>
> Does this account for the passion of the hatred of Andreas? If he were not so hated perhaps he would not have so many adherents. As the Arabs say, "The enemy of my enemy is my friend." . . . One might propose to write Andreas off, label him Public Enemy Number One, and do our damnedest to eliminate him as a political force in Greece. The difficulty with this course is that we may simply succeed in making him a hero to the mass of the Greek people who will thereby become even more convinced in their anti-Americanism. The villain of one country is almost inevitably the hero of another.

But I am getting ahead of my story, for this memorandum to Ambassador Talbot was written nearly a year after the coup, at a time when Andreas, released after spending nearly eight months in jail and permitted to go abroad, had set himself up as the head of the Panhellenic Liberation Movement (PAK in Greek) and was devoting himself to overthrowing the Papadopoulos junta. A year and a half earlier, in the fall of 1966, my concern was that the American mission appeared to have cut itself off from all but the most hostile relations with the Center Union party, one of the two chief nationalist political forces in the country and the party that seemed destined to win the next parliamentary elections.

Thus it was a much more serious matter than mere personality conflicts between an irascible Andreas and some short-tempered and arrogant American officials. Relations between mission and party were so bad that we even lacked useful information on what was going on inside that party. Suffering from bad relations locally, an embassy is in trouble; lacking intelligence on the situation, it is hopelessly unable to function. The Embassy, the CIA, and the military were equally to blame. The CIA is normally supposed to keep in touch with the political "outs," but the CIA was not on speaking terms with the liberals. The Embassy might have been deemed to be more sympathetic to the liberal forces—sympathetic enough at least to lend them an ear—but no apparent effort was being made to contact them.

Ambassador Talbot had exactly two meetings with George Papandreou, the dominant political figure of that day in Greece, during the nine months preceding the coup that I served at the Embassy. At one of these meetings Andreas acted as interpreter for his father; other than this occasion Talbot had no contact with Andreas during that period. One explanation would be that DCM Anschuetz was supposed to keep in touch with Andreas. They had been "friends" and were perhaps still so in a very guarded sense on both sides. Anschuetz had two or at most three meetings with Andreas during the same nine-month precoup period (initially the critically important preelectoral period). Their talks on these occasions, sought out in each case by Anschuetz, were doubtless wide ranging, but from Anschuetz's point of view they were designed, in addition to getting a line on Andreas's thinking and activities, to urge Andreas to pursue a course of greater moderation, to soften his attacks on the king, the monarchy, NATO, and the Americans, and to get him to cease heating up the electoral attack against his political opponents on the Right. Anschuetz doubtless genuinely believed that a calmer debate would be better for all concerned, but especially for those on the defensive: the king, the Right, the United States of America.

THE MONARCHY

My effort to understand the Andreas phenomenon that fall was strictly informal—I am inclined to say unauthorized, for no one, least of all me, was encouraged to delve into such matters. I did undertake a more formal study of the opposite pole—the monarchy—at the suggestion of my boss, Kay Bracken. I don't know now, nor did I know then, whether she was really interested in what I might prepare on the subject of the Greek monarchy, or whether she merely wished to give me something to do to keep me occupied and out of trouble. A better motive on her part was most likely to educate me, and that was worthy. The evidence tends to suggest that my education was what it was all about, for she never made any use of what I wrote, and when I tried to reclaim my paper from her files after she had left the post a year and a half later, I found that my study had disappeared.

I do, however, recall the general theme and tenor of what my fairly superficial examination of the history of the Greek monarchy revealed. It was that the monarch had been a nearly constant cause of disruption and turmoil in the Greek body politic since the first monarchy of King Otto had been imposed on the newly independent Greeks by the great powers in 1832. That was of course the era when European politics were dominated by Prince Metternich. Not only was republicanism abhorred, but a government was not considered in any way legitimate unless it was headed by a monarch. The first king had been thrown out by the Greeks, while the second (originator of the present line) had tried to rule as a more or less constitutional monarch.

The modern era in Greek politics dates from the 1909 military revolution that brought the great Cretan statesman Eleftherios Venizelos to power. From that date until 1946 the Greek monarchy had been the central issue in Greek politics, with the people dividing between the royalists and the liberal-republican Venizelists. After Venizelos and Constantine I had split during World War I over which side to support, there had been constant ups and downs for the monarchy, with frequent abdications, deposings, plebiscites rigged and unrigged, military coups (generally by the Venizelist officers), dictatorships, royalist restorations, and finally the royally sanctioned Metaxas dictatorship of the pre–World War II period.

The most noteworthy thing about the recent history of Greece, however, had been the apparent resolution of the "regime question" (as the Greeks euphemistically call this dispute) in favor of a working constitutional monarchy (the Greeks' term—they have their own for everything—is "crowned democracy"). The 1946 plebiscite on the return to Greece of King George II (I had served as a junior employee on the allied mission that monitored this plebiscite and declared it to be reasonably honest) had resulted in a 60 percent positive vote (68 percent of those voting) for the king's return, and the verdict was generally accepted (except by the Communists), especially after the more popular King Paul had succeeded his brother on the throne in 1947. During the subsequent two decades there were still plenty of die-hard antimonarchists in Greece, but the royal issue no longer dominated Greek politics as it had for so long previously, and in fact was rarely an issue at all.

Unfortunately, this situation was not to last, partly because King Paul's queen, Frederika, had a penchant for involving herself in domestic politics. First the royal couple quarreled with Karamanlis in 1963 over a royal visit to England, and the dispute was instrumental in the departure from power of the longtime conservative premier and his subsequent self-exile to Paris. Then in 1965 had come the constitutional crisis between Constantine II and George Papandreou, which had propelled the issue of royal political intervention to the very center of the Greek political stage once again. Unfortunately for the stability of the country, the next following parliamentary elections were bound to present themselves as essentially another plebiscite on the monarchy, and this time it looked as though the vote might well go against the king. Such was the conclusion of my study, which I fear was not welcome reading in the Embassy, although the judgment seemed self-evident and unarguable to me at the time, as it still does today.

TRIALS AND NEGOTIATIONS

Two of the major events of the fall of 1966 were unrelated but nearly contemporaneous trials of major political significance. In Thessaloniki was held the trial of the assassins of the EDA pacifist deputy Grigorios Lambrakis, and of the police officers who had been implicated in this episode (the whole story is accurately told in the popular film Z). The assassins were convicted and sentenced to moderate prison terms, and the police officers received even milder punishments.

In Athens at nearly the same time was held the trial of twenty-eight regular army officers accused of treason and conspiracy for allegedly having organized a clandestine, pro-Andreas Papandreou conspiratorial group in the army known as ASPIDA ("Shield"). This trial went on for some weeks and resulted in the conviction of some officers and the acquittal of others. It was generally felt that these trials had to be got out of the way before the country could proceed to elections, since both trials stirred strong passions on the Right, Center, and Left. But a problem remained. Certain liberal politicians, headed by Andreas Papandreou but including some leading apostates as well (even Mitsotakis was mentioned), were accused of complicity in the ASPIDA affair, and their political opponents demanded that they be tried as well. They could not even be indicted, however, for as deputies they benefited from parliamentary immunity so long as parliament remained in session.

In early October Cy Sulzberger set off a storm of controversy in Athens with a barrage of columns about Greece in the *New York Times*. Sulzberger's wife was of Greek origin, and they were both close to the Greek royal family, so people in Greece took it quite seriously when Sulzberger wrote in one of his columns that if King Constantine thought his country was headed for disaster he would not hesitate to suspend the constitution and resort to an "extra-parliamentary solution" (the Greek euphemism for a military coup or dictatorship under royal sponsorship). It was equally clear from Sulzberger's columns what would constitute such a disaster, for the American columnist displayed his strong anti-Papandreou prejudices by labeling the father the "greatest demagogue" of Greece and describing his son as "extremely arrogant and ambitious." Everyone took it as fact that Sulzberger had based his column on an interview with the king, whom he regularly saw on visits to Athens. In a subsequent article Sulzberger denied that he had met with King Constantine to discuss a dictatorship.

In December serious negotiations toward an attempted resolution of the long political crisis were undertaken by the contending forces, mainly through private discussions among leading newspaper publishers—Eleni Vlachou representing the conservatives and Christos Lambrakis representing the George Papandreou liberals—and the king's political adviser, Dimitrios Bitsios. It was evident to politicians of all factions that parliamentary elections eventually had to be held; there was no other solution. The disagreement was only over when and how and under whose direction. George Papandreou, then in his seventies, was desperately eager to be prime minister one more time; he was obviously strongly motivated to try to prove at the ballot box that he had been right in his 1965 dispute with the king, and he was supremely self-confident that he still commanded the loyalty of the majority of the people. Papandreou was therefore susceptible to any reasonable proposal from the other side that would lead to the elections he had been demanding publicly and privately since July 1965.

Papandreou and Panayotis Kanellopoulos, leader of the conservative ERE party, agreed through intermediaries to support a caretaker government of nonpoliticians headed by John Paraskevopoulos, a banker, who would serve as prime minister for about five months with the joint parliamentary support of the two big parties and would then preside over elections. Paraskevopoulos was acceptable to Papandreou because he had presided over a caretaker government in 1964 and had conducted what Papandreou considered fair elections, since he had won them.

There were two political factions that were most displeased with this arrangement. One was the apostate group, who felt that the king had simply pulled the rug out from under them after having used them for his own purposes for a year and a half. The Stephanopoulos government resigned the minute the Paraskevopoulos scheme was disclosed, for it meant that the ERE party had abandoned them. They felt they faced certain political defeat, although they somewhat gamely organized a new party called the Liberal Democratic Center and proposed to contest both the Right and the Center in the forthcoming elections as a party located between the two ideologically. The prospects for the apostates seemed quite dim, however, as they were detested by the centrists as traitors and disdained by the Right as opportunists.

The other faction that was unhappy was Andreas Papandreou's left-of-center grouping within the Center Union. He nearly broke completely with his father over the Paraskevopoulos deal and was supported in his intransigence by about forty Center deputies—not enough, however, to defeat Paraskevopoulos in parliament. What Andreas disliked most about the scheme was the evident agreement of his father with Kanellopoulos that if neither of their parties obtained a majority in the next elections they would join together in a coalition government to be headed by Papandreou. Andreas, more militant and unwilling to compromise merely so that his father could be prime minister again, thought that this aspect would disillusion the followers of the Center Union and would prevent the absolute majority victory to which Andreas and his cohorts looked forward. He also doubtless thought his own role would be a minor one in such a Right-Center coalition. Things were eventually patched up between father and son, and Paraskevopoulos took office as planned.

Part of the patching-up process was apparently a deal between George and Andreas that in return for the latter's support of the Paraskevopoulos government in the confidence vote in parliament, Andreas would have the right to choose a large number of the Center candidates for deputy in the forthcoming elections. This was a significant gesture, for it would permit Andreas to project a larger number of his left-of-center adherents as candidates, especially for the seats occupied by the formerly liberal apostates, who, it was believed, could be easily defeated. The obvious result would have been a larger Andreas contingent in the Center party and in the new parliament.

Elections were anticipated for May of 1967 under a new electoral bill to be presented to parliament for approval. Otherwise the Paraskevopoulos government was to take no major initiatives but to act as a genuinely caretaker, nonpolitical government. As I went off with my family and the Lansdale family for a skiing holiday in Yugoslavia over New Year's, it seemed that the political crisis had finally been resolved.

In January it became evident that perhaps things had not been so well resolved. The promise of elections in May nearly immediately created a heated pre-electoral atmosphere in the country, with the politicians of all factions off and running hard for office. The actual electoral campaign in Greece is supposed to last at most forty-five days between the dissolution of a parliament and election day. But the contending factions had for so long been frustrated in their desires to have at each other before the people that they could not wait for the dissolution of parliament and the actual setting of an election date to have a go at each other.

The Embassy was at pains, naturally, to try to gauge the probable electoral result and how the contending forces would sort themselves out both before and after the elections. The Embassy's greatest concern, it seemed to me at the time, was over whether or not the Papandreous would be able to win an absolute majority and thus confront the king with what would obviously have been a popular defeat for him. If the Papandreous achieved less than a majority victory, it was assumed that there would be a coalition formed of the two big parties, and the Papandreous would presumably be restrained by their need to keep the support of the conservative ERE party.

Ambassador Talbot at this stage posed to his DCM, Norbert Anschuetz, the question of what forces or elements there might be that could act as a restraining influence on Andreas Papandreou should his party come to power after the elections with majority parliamentary support. Anschuetz was the person in the Embassy who knew Andreas best, which is why this task was assigned to him. The startling aspect of this assignment was that Anschuetz was asked to put his analysis in writing. He made no effort to conceal that he found the task most disagreeable. During the year that I served with Anschuetz in Athens it was one of the very few pieces of writing he produced, that is, a work of serious political analysis, not counting letters to his friends. His secretary said she had the best job in the Embassy.

Anschuetz's analysis covered a lot of territory in order to come to the conclusion that there would be absolutely no restraining influences over Andreas should his party come to power with majority support. The obvious implication was that this would be a most dangerous occurrence, filled with dire consequences for the United States. The slogans Andreas had been projecting had most sinister connotations, in the Embassy's view: "The King reigns, the People rule"; "The Army belongs to the Nation"; "Greece to the Greeks." These were popular slogans designed to win votes from the people, but they were variously interpreted by fearful Americans to mean that Andreas intended to abolish the monarchy, pull Greece out of NATO, remake the army in his own image, play footsie with the Communists, and even worse things if such could be imagined. The Anschuetz analysis came to the stark conclusion that we faced disaster if Andreas won the election.

I did not agree with this analysis nor with the conclusion, both as concerned Andreas's true intentions if the Center Union returned to power and on the specific question posed by the ambassador as to what restraints might exist over Andreas's behavior. But I kept quiet because I did not feel capable of arguing with someone presumably as expert as Anschuetz, and my views were not invited. I believed there would be one significant restraining influence, and that would be the Greek Army, which had an officer corps of some ten thousand men known to be nearly solidly right-wing, royalist, and conservative, who could be counted on to exert maximum pressure on Andreas to keep him from even contemplating anything so drastic as eliminating the monarchy or pulling out of NATO. Andreas would find it simply impossible to impose such decisions on the army even had he wanted to, I thought. The ultimate army sanction would of course be the threat of a military coup.

The supposed experts felt that the army could not be counted on to be a restraining influence because once in power Andreas and his cohorts would be able to manipulate the military, through transfers, retirements, promotions, recruitment, and so forth, to transform it from the solidly pro-West, pro-American, pro-NATO bastion it then was into a personal power instrument of Andreas himself. This prospect appeared to me ludicrously impossible, especially in view of the ASPIDA case, which demonstrated that the organizers of the alleged conspiracy had been able to recruit only a small handful of the ten thousand officers into their purportedly pro-Andreas group: only twenty-eight officers had been indicted, and some of them had been acquitted. Unless a second term in power would have permitted the Left faction of the Center Union to engineer a dramatic increase in the recruitment rate of officers to its banner, it would have taken Andreas decades to make a dent in the military ranks, no matter how hard he worked at it.

AN ALTERNATIVE: U.S. INTERVENTION?

Though I was never privy to the discussions at the time, there were proposals floated in February within the Embassy for a possible massive intervention in the forthcoming elections, principally with money to give extra support to conservative candidates, designed to elect enough of them to keep the Center Union from winning an electoral majority.

Documentary evidence of what was being considered is now readily and publicly available in volume 16 of the State Department serial publication

Foreign Relations of the United States (*FRUS*), the volume that covers Cyprus, Greece, and Turkey from 1964 to 1968. The documents reporting this intervention plan (nos. 255, 259, and 261) have been redacted in part, but the intent is clear.[5] The Embassy's proposal was definitely stimulated by Anschuetz's analysis and conclusion presented above, which focused on the alleged impossibility of restraining Andreas Papandreou should he and the Center Union gain control of the government through elections. One argument cited in support of this scheme was the great success such an intervention had achieved in Ceylon in 1965, where a conservative party had been assisted in order to defeat and drive from power the allegedly extreme leftist Bandaranaike party. Perhaps someone in Washington was prescient as to what the ultimate effect of a similar intervention in Greece might be: in 1970 the Bandaranaike party won an overwhelming victory in Ceylon, driving our clients from power most ignominiously.

I can now provide one additional document that confirms what happened in Washington. Probably the CIA in Athens worked up the intervention proposal, but it was endorsed by Ambassador Talbot on February 11, 1967, and forwarded to the State Department by an embassy telegram. The caption at the top of the letter Talbot received in response, "Roger Channel," was a designation used primarily by ambassadors abroad to discuss CIA matters confidentially with the State Department, in messages normally not shared routinely with the CIA itself. John Owens, the Greek desk officer, drafted the letter, it was cleared with a Mr. Denney in the Bureau of Intelligence and Research (INR) that manages liaison with the CIA, and signed by William J. Handley, a deputy assistant secretary in the Near East Bureau. (Handley was a close friend; he had been our ambassador in Bamako, Mali, in his previous assignment, and went on to become an outstanding ambassador to Turkey starting in 1969 while we were still serving in Greece.)

ROGER CHANNEL   16 MAR 1967

The Honorable
Phillips Talbot
American Ambassador
Athens, Greece

Dear Phil:

By now Jack Maury has undoubtedly told you of the 303 Committee's decision not to support a limited covert political action program in the forthcoming Greek elections. While Jack has probably told you of the proceedings of the 303 Committee—which he attended but at which no one from NEA or INR was present—I thought it might be helpful to fill you in on the factors leading to the committee's decision. Deputy Under Secretary Kohler met on March 14 with George Denney and Bill McAfee from INR and John Owens and me to explain the decision.

As Jack has probably informed you, there were two meetings of the committee, on March 8 and 13. Prior to the first meeting, Stuart Rockwell and John Owens, together with Tom Hughes and Bill McAfee, had met with Foy Kohler to present our conflicting positions. We, of course, strongly supported the action program (despite the same misgivings shared by you) as the best of the alternative courses open to us. INR had argued against, basing their arguments on the danger of a compromise, the question whether intervention would be effective, and the feeling that the unfavorable trends in Greece taken advantage of by the Andreas Papandreou forces would not fade away simply because of his defeat in one election.

Following their second meeting, which ended in a kind of stalemate, with Vance (who was absent due to sickness) opposed to the program and Walt Rostow and Foy holding strong reservations, it was decided to refer the problem to the Secretary and the President for a decision.

Foy saw the Secretary Monday evening and discussed the problem at length with him. It was the Secretary's decision not to approve the plan, based both on the danger of a security compromise and the general feeling that we should be out of the election business, except in those cases where there was a clear threat of a Communist takeover. Undoubtedly the Secretary's thinking was influenced by the recent exposes concerning CIA activity in the United States and abroad. Further, the Secretary had strong reservations about the utilization of Greek-Americans in such operations, and this feeling was shared by Foy, who noted that we had long ago decided to avoid becoming entangled with Greek-Americans in Greek politics.

In our discussion with Foy I stressed the danger of a military takeover if the trend towards Andreas seemed irreversible, citing your letter of February 28 in which you noted that the King had for the first time asked what our reaction would be in the event of the imposition of a dictatorship. However, it was Foy's position that the prevention of such a development should be through diplomatic persuasion and not by a covert operation.

There appears little hope of reversing the decision, and unless there is a sudden and unexpected worsening of the situation I do not recommend that we make the effort, in view of the Secretary's opposition. Incidentally, because of the Secretary's decision, it was decided not to refer the matter to the President.

Foy specifically asked me to write you and let you know of the committee's thinking. He particularly wanted you to know that it was the heavy weight given your recommendation that made the negative decision so hard to make. The committee was fully aware of your original reservations in regard to the proposal and of the fact that you reached the decision you did only after the most careful study and with the greatest reluctance. They were also impressed by your determination to supervise every step of the operation.

I did want you to know, Phil, that we gave the proposal the old college try, but given the present climate as regards covert operations, I am not too surprised that we were unable to obtain a favorable decision.

All the best to you and Mildred.
Sincerely,
William J. Handley

I have no idea how Talbot and his senior colleagues in Athens reacted to this rather firm turndown by Washington. Nevertheless, the negative decision taken in Washington did not arise out of any solicitude for Andreas Papandreou. The most senior official engaged with the Greek situation at that time reportedly said that "something" had to be done to prevent Andreas from coming to power, for an Andreas victory would be disastrous. This attitude was certainly reflected in the Embassy; an unfortunate incident of that period will serve as illustration.

Three

THE AUTHOR GETS INVOLVED

ANDREAS'S MARCH 1 SPEECH

Two embassy officers—John Day and Richard Helgerson, the USIS information officer—decided to attend a speech given by Andreas Papandreou to the Foreign Press Association weekly luncheon in Athens on March 1, 1967. For the convenience of the correspondents present, mimeographed copies of the speech were distributed to the guests during the luncheon preceding the speech. After according the text a quick perusal and consulting together, Day and Helgerson decided it was so anti-American that it would be improper for them to sit through Andreas's speech. So they walked out of the luncheon and returned to the Embassy.

Their departure did not of course go unnoticed—every move by the "foreign factor" becomes a major political event in Greece—and the story was the lead item in all the newspapers the next day, with a great deal of comment. It was rumored that the walkout had been intended as a deliberate provocation of Andreas to bait him and to show the public at large that the U.S. government disapproved of him. It was also rumored that Day and Helgerson had merely carried out the orders of Anschuetz, who was up to one of his usual "snake-like" tricks. I believe that Day and Helgerson, although they both personally had no use for Andreas, to put it mildly—they were, in fact, leading advocates of the anti-Andreas posture of the Embassy—were genuinely motivated by a feeling that they shouldn't sit through that sort of speech. Diplomats have a habit of walking out of things to show their own sense of impropriety as well as their displeasure.

I do know that they did not consult Kay Bracken by phone before walking out of the luncheon (she was available at her office in the Embassy), and she was quite annoyed with them for having failed to do so. She thought it was an action that unnecessarily involved the U.S. Embassy in the local political conflict and created unfavorable headlines (the columns of the rightwing press were of course filled with praise for the American diplomatic walkout). Since I was out of town on a trip, Mrs. Bracken asked my wife, Louise, to arrange a luncheon date for her with a journalist friend of ours who wrote a column for *Ethnos,* the leading pro-Andreas paper, to permit her to mitigate the damage to the extent that she could. (This columnist had earlier let us know that he planned to write a blast against Mrs. Bracken in his paper; we had dissuaded him and then arranged for them to meet, hoping that personal contact would defuse some of the hostility.)

This March 1 speech by Andreas is worth summarizing, not because it provoked the walkout (although that incident was a major event of that political season in Greece, strange as it may seem in retrospect), but because it included the major themes then being injected into the pre-electoral political campaign by Andreas, with their specifically "anti-American flavor," and a summary will therefore give a firsthand view of what it was that was frightening the Americans, without as yet offering a final judgment as to whether those fears were justified.

Papandreou began by citing the February 24 disclosure in the Athens press of the testimony by General Tsolakas at the ASPIDA trial, which Andreas said confirmed the view of the democratic camp that the alleged "conspiracy" of ASPIDA had been a "frame-up." This was followed, Papandreou continued, by a judicial request, processed through the Paraskevopoulos government, for the lifting of his own parliamentary immunity so that he could be brought to trial for high treason in connection with the ASPIDA affair. The Center Union deputies had unanimously decided to vote against the lifting of his immunity because the motivations were political rather than judicial, Andreas charged. In analyzing the significance of the ASPIDA case, he claimed it showed that in Greek political life "the cards are stacked, the deck is fixed. In this light it is not surprising that the Right has been almost continuously in government for over 30 years, even though it represents a minority of the Greek electorate. To achieve this remarkable feat it has employed a variety of methods."

After detailing these techniques, Andreas launched into a discussion of American involvement with Greek politics. "The cards are stacked in Greece for an additional reason. Greece, ever since it became a free nation, has been under the tutelage of one or more friendly powers. The sponsor nation has always seen fit not only to direct political developments within Greece, but also to shape its foreign policy, more or less independently of vital Greek interests. Since the Greek civil war the United States has replaced England as a sponsor nation." Andreas proceeded to detail postwar American involvement with Greece, the aid given, the participation in the process of government formation, the close connections with the palace and the Right, the support for a "strong" king in Greece, "in other words, for a constitutional practice which contrasts sharply with the corresponding practice in the crown democracies of the West."

Andreas explained that American policy in Greece is not monolithic, for there are at least three distinct American agencies in Greece: the State Department, the military mission, and the CIA. But altogether, he said,

> American policy in Greece has displayed the basic characteristics of the cold-war foreign policy which has dominated the world scene since the death of Franklin D. Roosevelt. This policy has been characterized by some insensitivity to the needs and the problems of the allies of the United States, especially so in the case of small nations. . . . Greece, as a developing nation, a nation barely emerging from a semi-colonial status, is extremely sensitive about its national independence, its freedom to chart its own international political course, its right to pursue freely its own national interest without placing in quandary its allied relationships. We do not raise the question concerning the participation of Greece in the NATO alliance. But at the same time we demand that Greece be recognized as an independent nation, which pursuing its own particular interests *has chosen* to be a member of the Western Alliance. Greece refuses the status of a poor relative, of a satellite. It insists on its right while executing its obligations as an ally, to determine its own course. . . . But above all, Greece insists that its allies cease interfering in its internal political affairs.

Speaking, he said, as someone who had spent twenty years as a member of the academic community of America, Andreas then offered some thoughts which may give a clue to the peculiarities of American foreign policy.... It has always been a source of surprise for me, how a country which is making democratic progress on the internal front—with the outstanding exception of the race question—could blunder so much in foreign policy as it has in the case of Vietnam, Latin America, and even in its relations with its NATO allies. One has the feeling that somehow it has never felt secure, that it has never been satisfied with a reasonable allied relationship, but that it was always driven to establish complete dominance in the affairs of allied states. It has been said quite often that America became a world power so suddenly that it did not have the time to adjust to its new role. But all this is quite superficial. The reason lies far more deeply than this.

Papandreou explained that in a deeply pluralistic society such as the United States, democratic process requires a balance of power among organized internal forces and groups, but that in foreign policy this balance is absent because the average American displays little interest in foreign affairs. This situation allows three forces to dominate foreign policy:

First, the Pentagon, which with the advent of the Cold War shaped American foreign policy as a policy of containment of the Soviet Bloc. It gave primary emphasis to strategic considerations in all dealings of the United States with other nations. Second, the CIA, which, as an outgrowth of the Office of Strategic Services which functioned during the Second World War as the key war intelligence unit—expanded beyond all expectations, assumed responsibilities and functions way beyond the initial purpose of the organization, and established an independence from the control of the government that made it possible for it practically to chart a parallel foreign policy for the United States. Last, but not least, the American investors abroad and the exporters to the world market played an important role as a pressure group in the formation of American foreign policy. Under the circumstances it is not surprising that a military, bureaucratic, intelligence-oriented, and business-dominated foreign policy failed to keep pace with democratic developments at home.

It does not come to us as a surprise to learn that America is going through an internal upheaval. The Negro problem is one cause, but there is probably a deeper cause, which underlies the conflict around the Negro problem and the foreign policy problem.

It is that America is not living up to American ideals. And it is felt mostly by the intellectuals and by young people who come straight from the history books, who have been imbued with democratic principles, who found the War of Independence and the Declaration of Independence a glorious period in their past, who have made a faith out of national independence, national integrity, self-determination for a nation, and the equality of people. For them American presence in Vietnam is an error of the first degree, and American involvement in the internal affairs of other nations intolerable.

After alleging that the United States had relegated Greece to semicolonial status, had tried to link Greece, Turkey, and Iran in order to strengthen NATO's southeastern flank (by giving these three countries nearly half of its military aid budget), and had tried to force a solution of the Cyprus problem in the context of the NATO alliance, Andreas charged that "the disclosures that are going on now in America concerning the role of the CIA in foreign policy should leave no doubt as to what we mean when we insist that Greece should belong to the Greeks."

He then alluded to the efforts of President Kennedy to "subjugate the Pentagon to civilian authority" and discussed the difficulty of accomplishing a similar thing in Greece, where whenever the Greek people tried to assert their constitutional rights the army would threaten to intervene to establish a military dictatorship. The army, he said, had been purged since the Greek civil war so that "at the top level, officers who belong to the junta, the paramilitary organization known as IDEA, have come to hold the key positions. In our view the King needs no praetorian force. The constitution is his shield, the constitution which no party challenges in Greece. The army is a part of the administration and as such fully subject to the authority of the duly elected government. It should be nonpartisan, stay out of politics, and be concerned with its exclusive task of protecting the integrity of the nation from external enemies." Andreas accused the army of having taken several recent actions internally that constituted intervention in the forthcoming elections, with no relation to external dangers.

He called the decision of the government to proceed with the prosecution of political personalities such as himself for involvement with ASPIDA an act of desperation, of sheer panic, to prevent the democratization, modernization, and development of the country.

> It discloses a decision [on the part of the establishment] to use terrorist techniques for altering the election results or even to bypass them altogether in a move which might lead to an open dictatorship.

For the sake of the nation and the Greek people, we should like to hope that the forces that influence political developments in Greece today will choose to display some judgment, that they will make an effort to understand the true dimensions of the great peaceful revolution that is under way in our country, of the maturity and the determination of the Greek citizen.

For Greece this is its greatest hour, the turning point in its contemporary political history. The option is between social and political stagnation in the context of a semi-colonial civilization or a great step forward in the founding of a new, free, independent, progressive society, a full member of the European community of nations. The people, we know, have opted for the second. They will fight for it. And they will win.

Somewhat anticlimactically, Papandreou closed his speech with a challenge to the king and prime minister to carry out the free elections they had promised, while implying that plans were already under way to hold fraudulent elections in the style of most underdeveloped nations, a course the Greek people would never permit.

The objective observer would have to conclude that if nothing else, this speech by Andreas Papandreou was prophetic. Its language was often harsh and perhaps hyperbolic (in the fashion of Greek campaign speeches), and the tone no doubt "anti-American" (or only anti–U.S. government?), but had Senator William Fulbright or Senator Eugene McCarthy given a speech with very similar themes at the National Press Club in Washington the same month, no one would have been at all surprised and certainly no one would have walked out. In fact, had Papandreou given the speech in Washington, it would not have created a huge fuss (in Greek a *megali fasaria*). Why, therefore, the extremely sensitive reaction on the part of American diplomats (who might have been mildly encouraged to see the State Department and the USIS getting off nearly scot-free while the brickbats were thrown at the Pentagon, the CIA, and the business community)?

The difference was that this was Andreas Papandreou speaking, and the territory on which he was speaking was Greece. He was a former American citizen, a man with a personal and direct knowledge of the American scene, and official America in Athens simply couldn't abide such words from such a source. To them he was Tokyo Rose or Lord Haw Haw, not a Greek politician running for office on a reformist platform. And he was speaking in Greece, which the American military felt was a special territory they had invested years of energy and billions of dollars turning into a close ally with whose military forces cooperation could not have been better. They were fond of saying that they didn't even have to ask for overflight clearance. They said blanket clearance had been given in advance, which was not quite true.

Greece was CIA territory as well, for the closest of liaison arrangements existed with the Greek intelligence services that we had created. The American "services" felt free to operate in as many ways as can be imagined without local interference. In fact, they were freer there than they ever could be at home, where enemies with evil intentions might be equally free to expose them to public scrutiny. Greece was—and this is what Andreas was really saying between the lines—a vast and friendly American military-intelligence base in a most strategic location.

As for the business community, conditions for the foreign investor had always been ideal, although less ideal under the Papandreous than under their predecessor Karamanlis. The Greek American businessman-operator Tom Pappas liked to complain that the Papandreou government had insisted on renegotiating the deal he had worked out with Karamanlis on behalf of Esso on terms more favorable to Greece, but he had an even stronger complaint about the instability: "I had to buy five governments in four years to get this thing through!"

What did they fear would happen if Andreas came to power? That he would renegotiate contracts? Of course. That he would curtail the activities of the CIA in Greece? Probably, as well as making the Greek services more independent and responsive to Greek government direction. That he would pull the country out of NATO, throw the American military out, and close down their bases? Highly unlikely, since any actions in this direction would surely bring down on his head the wrath of practically all of the ten-thousand-man Greek officer corps as well as earn him the hostility of the majority of the Greek electorate, which was firmly wedded to the country's NATO and U.S. alliance ties.

Andreas stated quite openly that there was no intention of calling into question Greece's NATO ties. He merely wished to transform the alliance relationship so that Greece got as much out of it as it was expected to put into it. For one thing, he thought Greece ought to be supported by NATO in its dispute with Turkey over Cyprus, since "justice" lay with the Greek cause (self-determination for the Greek Cypriots). This was totally unrealistic, since Turkey was also in NATO and had just as much claim to NATO support regardless of which side justice lay on (for Turkey it lay in the sanctity of treaties, specifically the London-Zurich accords). NATO could not take either side, and worked hard to keep the two allies from coming to blows.

But Andreas's tone did appear to indicate that he was appealing to the left-of-center and even leftist voters with his attacks on American attitudes and policies. Was he not playing into the hands of the Communists; would they not come to manipulate him and dominate any government in which he played a leading role once he had counted on their support to propel himself into power?

It was my analysis at the time that Andreas was attempting to broaden the electoral appeal of the Center Union party by pulling in the floating protest vote that had always existed in Greece and that tended to vote with the Center when it was strong and looked like a winner, but with the extreme Left (the cryptocommunist EDA party) when there was no other realistic choice but the Right. This was a legitimate electoral tactic and posed no real danger, for this leftist element within the Center would be a decidedly minority fraction, could not dominate the party, and was not under Communist discipline in any case.

But Andreas had a secondary motive as well for wooing the leftist protest vote, and that was to broaden and increase numerically his own personal base within the Center party in order to position himself favorably for a challenge to take over the party leadership when his father died or retired.

The Center-Right was closed to him, as it was already well in hand for Mitsotakis and other Right-Center politicians who had been much longer on the scene. Andreas's best tactic was therefore to build up the strength of the left-of-center by pulling in new voter support, while at the same time shifting the entire Center Union party somewhat toward the Left, where he held the commanding position. Only in Greece, it appeared, a mild reformism that in America would hardly stir the most liberal supporter of the Democratic Party was regarded (by American observers at least) as a dangerous radicalism and demagoguery that could not be tolerated.

A POLICY ASSESSMENT

In early March of 1967, sometime after Andreas's speech, my boss, Mrs. Bracken, asked me to prepare a draft paper to be submitted to Washington in fulfillment of the regular requirement for an "Annual U.S. Policy Assessment for Greece." This report was by that time nine months overdue and had been repeatedly postponed because it was felt that fast-breaking developments in Greece would outdate it as it was being written. I do not know why Mrs. Bracken asked me to prepare a draft of this paper—the major contribution to it was ordinarily made by the internal affairs political officer—but perhaps she thought I had more time than the others or at least could produce a draft more quickly. The Department had been pressuring us for some weeks to get the paper in. It was not a propitious time to prepare such an assessment, for the elections were only two months away, but we could procrastinate no longer. I decided to draft the paper with my own ideas, while realizing that my views would not meet with acceptance up the line. I tried to tailor them sufficiently so as not to outrage my superiors, but the draft I submitted was clearly quite unacceptable.

The seventeen-page draft had the following summary statement:

> 1966 was on the whole a very good year in U.S.-Greek relations, certainly better than anyone could have reasonably predicted at the beginning of the year. By contrast with earlier years there were no serious crises in our relations, and there was much greater internal political stability than was expected. As we move into 1967, however, the prospects are far from bright. Greece is facing elections in May, but few observers believe that the elections will resolve the dilemmas that remain from the events of July 1965 surrounding the fall of the Papandreou-led Center Union government. No party is expected to gain a majority in the elections, a result that could prevent the formation of a stable government, although an ERE-EK [Center Union] coalition might be able to assume power for a while. The greatest danger to the American position in Greece is that Andreas Papandreou, who has recently assumed a violently anti-American stance, will come to power by one means or another or will wield dominant power in a Center Union government. Because of this danger it is important that we take steps to dispel the image of the U.S. as the exclusive ally of the conservative ERE party in Greece, and at the same time explore the possibility of mitigating Andreas Papandreou's anti-Americanism. The U.S. can still count on a vast reservoir of good will in Greece, but this could be dissipated if we are projected as partisans of one political camp in an increasingly polarized domestic political scene.

In reading this paper over now, I am struck by the impression that its author must appear incredibly naïve to have thought statements that cast the U.S. role and image in Greece in such an unfavorable light could ever have been presented to his superiors as a serious proposition. Instead of placing the blame for all of our difficulties entirely on the shoulders of Andreas

Papandreou—as I was quite aware the Embassy was determined to do—I more than implied that we might also be at fault for taking extreme sides (note the words "exclusive ally" and "partisans") in Greek domestic politics.

A second impression is that the depiction of Andreas Papandreou accorded much more closely with the attitude of my superiors than it did with mine. The explanation is that I did not present this draft with the idea that it would be adopted and sent in, but I hoped it would force the senior officers of the Embassy to face up to the implications of their own attitudes toward Greek domestic politics and especially to the consequences of their fervent hatred of Andreas Papandreou (that I shared neither their animosity nor their fears will appear shortly).

A few of the points made in the body of my draft Annual Assessment are worth recalling. In the "Prospects" section I noted that some quarters doubted the elections scheduled for May 1967 would be held then: "An effort to postpone them, except for causes which were universally accepted as valid, would probably result in serious domestic violence on the part of the political left and center, which would feel that the postponement was a device to keep them from taking power legitimately." After doubting that any party would win the elections, I considered the possibility of an absolute majority victory by the Center Union: "Should the King, the military, or anti-Center political forces generally, seek to prevent the Papandreous from coming to power, the country would be plunged into a serious political crisis and the United States would be faced with most difficult choices, that is, we would have to decide whether we could cooperate with an unconstitutional regime in Greece, to put the problem in its straightest terms. If a Papandreou-led Center government were permitted to take office, the prospects for U.S.-Greek relations would not be all we could wish." The paper went on to discuss Andreas's anti-American stance, the difficulty the United States would have in dealing with him, and possible explanations for his unfriendly posture.

"The critical question for the near-term interests of the United States in Greece," I wrote, "is whether or not Andreas Papandreou is irredeemable." The United States did not face the danger that domestic Communism would take charge of Greece, for the EDA's voting strength was somewhere between 10 percent and 15 percent of the electorate and was weakest whenever the Center was strong. Nor would an ERE victory pose any danger: "The danger for us is not that the right might win, but that the U.S. has become so identified with the right that we would find it most difficult to work with governments controlled by anti-right parties." I explained this identification as arising mostly from the fact that the Right had been ascendant during most of the period of our close cooperation with Greece since the war, and that the ERE pursued pro-NATO and pro-U.S. policies that we found comfortable.

The United States no longer played the intimate role in Greek affairs that it had formerly, but most Greeks were not aware of the change, or refused to believe it, and in any case all Greeks seemed to accept the involvement of the "foreign factor" so long as it worked for their side and against their political enemies. I then returned to the subject of Andreas and speculated on the effect of his coming to power in succession to his father. I suggested that while opinions among American officials about Andreas differed, it might be wise "to explore now whether it is possible to re-establish a cordial relationship with Andreas. It would be unwise to write him off as hopelessly irredeemable or to imagine that he can never come to power."

The "Conclusions" section of the paper examined the implications of several possible developments. An unjustified postponement of the elections would cause a crisis, I thought, and the imposition of an unconstitutional government, dictatorship, or "extra-parliamentary solution," whether instigated by the palace, the military, or conservative political elements influencing both, would place the United States in a grave dilemma, "for Greece is a European country, a NATO ally, a nation with a long democratic tradition (not a Latin American, Asian or African country lacking in democratic traditions and used to authoritarian regimes); U.S. recognition of and acceptance of an unconstitutional regime in Greece would be most difficult to justify."

An electoral victory by the extreme Left was so remote a possibility that it did not merit discussion, I thought. An ERE victory achieved without fraud would be an acceptable, even desirable outcome. Inconclusive electoral results would produce prolonged instability unless an ERE-EK coalition could be formed, which would be a favorable development from the U.S. point of view, though it might not last long. An EK electoral victory was possible, though most observers doubted it. It posed difficulties for the United States discussed earlier and was therefore a contingency to which we should be giving serious thought "because it is something that we can perhaps prepare for."

The final "Recommendations" section proposed that we make clear to the king "in a polite but firm manner that any deviation from the Constitution to impose a political 'solution' on the country (which is a euphemism for preventing the Papandreou-led Center Union from winning a popular election or from taking power if elected) would pose grave problems for the United States, which would find it most difficult to recognize an unconstitutional government in an allied country. Pass the same word in military and right wing circles."

My second recommendation was that we curtail or "sanitize all American activities in Greece which help create the impression that we meddle in the country's internal affairs, pull the political strings, or like to throw in the weight of the 'American factor' on one side or another," and especially that we try to disassociate the United States from exclusive identification with the fortunes of the ERE party. Third, I thought we ought to attempt to reestablish cordial relations with the Center Union, "both as insurance in case of a possible EK electoral victory and to mitigate the hostility to the United States of the left-of-center forces which look to Andreas Papandreou for leadership." I thought that we should also try to establish cordial relations with Andreas himself. Other proposals were that we keep lines of communication open to all noncommunist politicians and groupings in the country; and I concluded with several suggestions on ways to improve our image in the country, to capitalize on what I felt was still a deep reservoir of goodwill among the Greek people for our past assistance and present continuing support.

My final recommendation read as follows: "Encourage whatever Greek government is in power to pursue rational and progressive economic and social policies which will strengthen the country's democratic base, raise the standard of living of the people and make more efficient the country's public and private institutions so that Greece will be better able to stand on its own, to compete in the modern world, and to contribute to our mutual alliance."

I have quoted extensively from this paper, not because I consider it a brilliant analysis of our situation in Greece in March of 1967 (although I am not ashamed of it as a draft), but rather because it gives a good idea of what the issues of that day were as I saw them, and by indirection as others saw them also. As I tried to make clear in introducing this Annual Assessment, I did not make these several recommendations because I thought they would be accepted but because I thought they were precisely the areas of action that our policies were neglecting. As should be evident, the most serious problem for the United States—the possibility of a Papandreou electoral victory—I thought we were failing to face up to at all.

My draft—which never went to Washington in any form—disappeared into Mrs. Bracken's in-basket, and two days later (I probably finished the draft under pressure of this deadline) I went to Nicosia for a one-week familiarization visit and on-the-spot examination of the Cyprus problem, followed by a week attending a Foreign Service Institute executive management course in Beirut, and a week's visit to Ankara and Istanbul, the other "end" of the Cyprus dispute. I returned to Athens in early April and submitted an "Impressions of Cyprus" report to Mrs. Bracken.

The Cyprus problem is outside the scope of this memoir, despite the fact that it occupied most of my time in that period, but I cannot pass over this paper without citing one small aspect of it that demonstrated some foresight (these occasions are infrequent enough to merit attention). After giving my impressions of the island and the situations of the two warring communities, I listed six recommended courses of action. The second was to "fire" Grivas, that is, get him off the island somehow and back to Athens, since he was an irritant to the Turks and a hothead who was capable of creating a major incident that could set off another war. General Grivas, the EOKA hero who had led the *enosis* struggle (for union with Greece), was then the top Greek military commander on the island, in the position of commander of the Greek Cypriot National Guard and all the mainland Greek forces on Cyprus. Seven months later he did create a major incident, as we shall see. I tried to push the idea of getting Grivas off the island in April, but got nowhere; I was given to understand that the United States had acquiesced in (if we had not actually encouraged) his return to Cyprus after the crisis of the winter of 1963–64 so that he, a fanatical anticommunist, could act as a counterweight to Archbishop Makarios on the Greek side, since we feared that the archbishop was "playing around" with the Soviets and with such "pro-Soviets" as Nasser. Apparently it would not have been consistent behavior if we had now promoted Grivas's departure.

On my return to Athens Mrs. Bracken gave me back my draft Annual Assessment and proposed that I rewrite it and this time include some material provided by the labor officer and the Economic Section. The redraft, which is dated April 11, a month after the first draft, reads very much like the earlier version, with mostly the same language, so it is difficult to tell whether Mrs. Bracken had expressed any views about it. The principal changes and additions resulted from updating, for in the intervening month there had been some significant political events, including the downfall of the Paraskevopoulos "service" government and its replacement on April 3 by an all-ERE government under Kanellopoulos. It will be handy to quote or summarize these changes, for they will bring the account of internal political developments up through early April.

> Paraskevopoulos was unable . . . to carry out his limited mandate of getting a new electoral bill adopted by the Parliament to institute the simple proportional system and of then holding elections. His government fell as a result of an ERE-EK dispute over the issue of the electoral bill, essentially because the EK attempted to add to it an amendment that would have extended Andreas Papandreou's

immunity from prosecution (for involvement in the ASPIDA affair) through the elections, a proposal that the ERE party adamantly opposed as unconstitutional. King Constantine attempted to form a successor government in various ways, and when George Papandreou declined to cooperate in the formation of an all-party government the King gave his mandate to ERE leader Kanellopoulos, who formed an all ERE government.

If he carries out his declared intentions, Kanellopoulos will lead the country to elections in late May or early June of this year. Some right-wing political forces would like to see the elections postponed.

This draft then made the same point as the earlier one about the likely untoward result of an electoral postponement and proceeded to analyze the prospects as before. One change was that the possibility of an EK-ERE coalition following elections was now deemed "slight." Important factions in both the ERE and the EK now strenuously opposed this idea.

Another change was the new climate created by the king's extraordinarily inept action of permitting one party to control the government during the elections, contrary to the Greek tradition of having nonpartisan (or at least nonpolitical) "service" governments conduct elections.

The King's action of giving the mandate to the ERE party and at the same time of giving that party the right to dissolve Parliament and hold power during the electoral period may have a decisive effect on the outcome of the elections. The Papandreous are sure to exploit this issue, as they have already begun to do by labeling the King the true leader of the ERE party and by making the monarchy itself a central issue in the electoral campaign. The EK might exploit antimonarchist sentiment so successfully that they could gain an absolute electoral victory. On the other hand, the ERE is doubtless counting on the advantages of holding power during the electoral period to cut down the EK's voting strength and at the same time to build an ERE victory psychology among the populace. Control of the government also gives the ERE opportunities to influence the election outcome by the granting of favors, by pressure tactics, by placing people friendly to ERE in key positions, and even by outright electoral fraud. But a victory by the EK remains a possibility and on balance recent events have probably enhanced the position of the Papandreous, assuming that the elections will be held and will be honest.

A few changes to the earlier draft bear the marks of having been made by Mrs. Bracken—for example, a statement that in the 1964 elections "some voters under Communist discipline obeyed orders to vote for EK candidates," and the remark that some official American attitudes toward Andreas resulted "from experiences with him during his previous period in government," presumably a reference to disputes such as the Vincent Joyce episode. Another addition (obviously my own) was that "the accession of the Kanellopoulos ERE government to power has made post-electoral cooperation between the two major parties a much less likely prospect than before." And a further significant updating stands out: "The fact that the role and institution of the monarchy have increasingly become the central campaign issue has an important bearing on the possible electoral outcome. The center and liberal forces are by tradition at least mildly antimonarchist, and recent events have made the EK even more so. The ERE is traditionally monarchist. The coming elections will be viewed by many voters as close to a plebiscite on the monarchy. Unfortunately the King will probably also have to regard it so, especially if the EK wins a majority."

Except for the addition of some recommendations in the labor and economic fields, the final section of the paper read the same. There was one slight revision, in the paragraph on relations with Andreas: "Attempt to influence Andreas himself to take public positions and to pursue policies which are not hostile to the U.S. and to NATO by proving to him that such a program is harmful to Greece."

Like the earlier version, this draft was never used in any report that went to Washington. Typical of many such exercises, the Annual Assessment was OBE (bureaucratese for "overtaken by events"), namely by the military coup of April 21, 1967.

Rather than reject it outright or revise it herself, Mrs. Bracken took the easy bureaucratic course and "sat" on it until it was no longer relevant.

I do not believe it would ever have been adopted as written by me, for the point of view that underlay it was entirely alien to the thinking that held ascendancy in the Embassy at that time. The only productive effect it had was to crystallize my own thinking by requiring me to put my thoughts down on paper in advance of the important events that were to ensue later that month.

PREPARING FOR ELECTIONS

The redraft of that paper was typed up ten days before the coup. What were the concerns of the Embassy at that time that were not fully reflected in that rather formal required report? One that was of special concern to everyone, it seemed to me, *was* covered in the draft assessment: the election was rapidly becoming a pure confrontation between the Papandreous and the king, and it was increasingly taking on the character of a plebiscite on the monarchy. The implications of a Papandreou victory were obvious and enormous: a vote of no confidence in the king, a repudiation of his role in and after the July 1965 constitutional dispute with George Papandreou, and a humiliation that would have been disastrous for a politician but probably fatal for a modern king. If the king were alone and isolated, it would have perhaps only meant the end of the monarchy, with a whimper rather than a bang. But there were powerful monarchist elements in Greece—the right-wing party, the army, the establishment in general—that simply would not permit the monarchy to disappear, since they considered it a major, even essential bulwark against the forces of radicalism (from their point of view) or of reform (from the point of view of their opponents).

The Embassy, the CIA, all those interested in Greek politics, in fact, were obviously and necessarily trying to predict the outcome of the forthcoming parliamentary elections. There were no public opinion polls that could help, analyses tended to be highly impressionistic, partisan, and even emotional, and there were no sound guidelines in the heated atmosphere of the day, so predictions varied widely. Some dreamers thought that Kanellopoulos's ERE could pull it off, but some of his most ardent supporters (e.g., Eleni Vlachou, owner of *Kathimerini* newspaper) felt the situation was doomed and that the ERE (and the king) would go down to ignominious defeat. The Center Union was confident, predicting victory. They had the psychological edge because they had won the previous election, had been denied its fruits, and were coming back as the insurgents, tasting blood, with the king apparently on the run and resorting to desperate measures such as giving the mandate to the ERE party so that they could rig the election in favor of themselves.

There was no Gallup Poll–type organization in Greece, and the USIS polls eschewed Greek domestic politics, concentrating on attitudes toward U.S. policies and other such "psychological" concerns. A couple of years after the coup, a Greek who claimed to know told me that the CIA had conducted a private pre-electoral poll and had discovered to its dismay that the ERE had lost ground since 1964. The poll allegedly indicated that the ERE vote had fallen more drastically than any of us believed, down to 20–25 percent of the electorate, which would have meant a shattering EK landslide. My Greek informant claimed that it had been this poll that had encouraged the CIA to "trigger" the coup (though personally ardently pro-American, he was firmly convinced, as were and are most Greeks, that Papadopoulos acted at the instigation of the CIA). I have no independent corroboration of this tale, but hindsight leads me to make two observations now: (1) it would have been surprising had the CIA not taken the precaution of conducting a preelectoral poll to see how the electorate was trending; and (2) if the results of such a poll were as bad for the ERE as my informant alleged, I have no doubt that the CIA would have suppressed the poll, which may be the reason why I never heard about it at the time.

Although I cannot confirm the existence of this poll, those embassy officers and private individuals who to me appeared to have the soundest understanding of the Greek electorate anticipated the same outcome. They began in April to predict a Papandreou victory and many of them a majority victory, that is, a result that the king and his supporters could never accept. Many observers said they thought the results would be very similar to those of the last parliamentary elections: 53 percent Center Union (EK), 35 percent ERE, 12 percent EDA. Our own very limited soundings in the countryside indicated, as I have noted, that most voters' views had not changed since 1964. My personal prediction for the forthcoming elections, based more on intuition than on knowledge, gave the Center Union an increased percentage over 1964, that is, perhaps 55 percent to 60 percent of the votes (in this the CIA and I may have been in agreement).

In mid-April Kanellopoulos, having failed to obtain parliamentary support for his government, dissolved parliament and proclaimed elections for May 28. Of course, the electoral campaign had really been in progress since December, when, with the fall of the Stephanopoulos government, the country had been headed toward elections by one path or another.

An interesting aspect of the electoral mood was that if ERE's supporters were demoralized by what they regarded as the last-ditch efforts of the king and the Right to control the electoral result by giving the powers of government to Kanellopoulos for the electoral period, the Left was no less demoralized by the inroads that Andreas Papandreou was apparently making in the ranks of their traditional supporters. Like many western Communist parties (for example, those of Italy and France), the Greek Communists had turned somewhat conservative, especially as far as parliamentary elections were concerned: they liked to hold onto the seats they had, which meant jobs, patronage, prestige, and electoral success that proved to their adherents and foreign mentors that they were doing their job and at least holding their own in a democratic, parliamentary climate. A drop in EDA voting strength from 15 percent to 12 percent, for example, meant to everyone, at home and abroad, that the Communists were falling down on the job.

What was happening in the electoral campaign of the spring of 1967 was not that Andreas Papandreou was falling into the hands of the Communists but rather that EDA voters were flocking to Andreas's banner and threatened to give him a massive, personal electoral victory. My evidence is not personal, but straightforward reporting by those "American services" charged with following the affairs of the Communist party of Greece. That party's leaders were furious over the defections to Andreas that were resulting from his "center-left campaign" (my term). It appeared to them, as it did to disinterested observers, that the EDA would lose seats in the new parliament. They were making no deals with Andreas, nor with anyone else in the Center Union. This year, unlike 1964, they were contesting every seat in every electoral district; they were not instructing any of their disciplined adherents to vote for Center candidates, as they had in 1964 in districts where they had no chance themselves and thus decided to try to diminish the number of seats won by the Right.

The air was filled with coup talk in April of 1967, and with good reason. In what follows I make no claim to prescience; had it not been for the reporting of our intelligence services I might have had a vague premonition of a coming coup, but I would not have had the foreknowledge so necessary to any intelligent advance analysis of such significant events. The gossip became louder following the desperation maneuvers that brought the Kanellopoulos government to power. The most elementary analysis would have disclosed that one strong possibility was a majority Papandreou victory and a consequent possibility was that the king would decline to accept the result. In anyone's parlance this would amount to a coup d'état, although the Greek penchant for political euphemisms would have provided various fig-leaf expressions to disguise the shameful deed.

The intelligence reporting available to the Embassy indicated that planning for a coup was far advanced in the highest echelons of the Greek military. General Spandidakis, the chief of the National Defense General Staff and highest-ranking officer (the king was commander in chief by constitutional prerogative), had directed the preparation of a plan for a military takeover of the government with all the trappings—code name, unit maneuvers, declarations of intent, and so forth. This was to have been a coup ordered by the king, to be carried out in his name, and motivated by a desire to preserve the monarchy in the face of the attacks being mounted by its enemies (namely, Andreas and company). Our intelligence reporting—as one would expect in reports prepared by coup experts—dealt far more with details of the plans for carrying it out than with the political content of the action, that is, with what the new ruling group would do once they were in power, and what next steps it might lead to. In other words, we knew a great deal about who would take over and how, but little about what they would do with the power once it was theirs.

Following dissolution of the parliament in mid-April, the electoral campaign got under way in earnest, but the political exchanges of the precampaign skirmishing had already achieved a high degree of rhetorical rancor. Perhaps the most inflammatory—and therefore most often quoted—remark had (allegedly) been made nearly two months earlier. Andreas was accused of having declared in a speech that if the king refused to abide by the election results following a Papandreou victory, the adherents of the Center Union would gather in a mass rally in Constitution Square and swear in the new government without the king. This was a bold and perhaps insulting challenge to the king, a dare to him to try for a constitutional "deviation," a threat to call out the street mobs to prevent the monarch from overturning the election results. After the actual coup, people who wished to justify the coup used this remark against Andreas: they claimed that Andreas had himself threatened to overthrow the constitution if he could not get his way otherwise. It became somewhat tiresome in subsequent months to point out that Andreas had not threatened to have the people swear in the government if they lost the election (as a result of alleged fraud, for example) but to do so only if the Center won an absolute majority and the king refused to accept the fact.[1] I learned much later that it was highly doubtful that Andreas ever made the statement attributed to him.

I endeavored, without entire success, to track down exactly what Andreas had said on this occasion, since it became such an oft-repeated justification for the coup after the fact. First I asked Aleko Tzinieris, our longtime Political Section press analyst, to research the newspapers of the time. He reported back that according to the press Andreas had stated in a speech on February 21, 1967, that following elections the winning party "could go ahead and set up a government without consulting the King." Aleko's written report to me continued:

> In fact some of the accounts even quote him as suggesting that if the winning party does not get an absolute majority but only a plurality it can form the government without consulting the Palace. He cited the precedent of a party in Denmark which did not receive a majority, yet its leader set up the government without even calling up the King on the telephone. He, therefore, never seems to have made it conditional upon the King's refusal to swear in the new

cabinet. Another much criticized point in his speech was his position that the proclamation of elections was for the government rather than the King to decide.

I retained lingering doubts, for it had been my impression that Andreas's remarks, whatever their true content, had reached the public through stories in the right-wing papers attacking him, and that the business about the mob swearing in the new government in Constitution Square was a canard dreamed up by an unfriendly critic and presented as what he thought Andreas would like to do. I thought it might be interesting to have Andreas's version, so I wrote to him in the spring of 1971 asking for the exact quotation, if he could recall it, as well as the context. I noted that the business about the swearing-in in Constitution Square had somehow been made to carry the implication that Andreas was advocating a "popular front" of the Center Union and the EDA, which together would form a majority sufficient to swear in the government without the king's blessing, even if the Center Union by itself had not obtained a majority in the elections. I asked if he had not been anticipating an absolute majority victory by the Center Union, which would have meant "you were saying that if the King refused to accept that verdict and permit the Center Union to form the new government that the people would ignore him and swear the government in themselves."

Papandreou replied to me on May 6, 1971, in the following terms (I quote from his letter):

> This whole issue arose in the "question and answer" period following a speech I gave on February 21, 1967, at the King George Hotel. The translation of the speech (titled "Economic Planning and Private Initiative") is to be found in Appendix I of Stephen Rousseas's *The Death of Democracy* (p. 185 in the original edition).
>
> Someone asked me, I believe, whether we would be sworn in by the King if we won in the forthcoming elections. I answered that the King's role, under our Constitution, was that of a symbolic Head of State, and that the King did not have an alternative to inviting the party with absolute majority to form government. Then I proceeded to make some comparisons with *practices* in Denmark, which has a constitution formally most similar to that of Greece. I told the audience that Jens Otto Krag, following his (relative) victory in elections that had been held recently (in reference to the time of my speech), had announced his victory and the composition of his cabinet on

television. I added that the Danish King was a member of Krag's audience. I used this example to point out that there were differences in the "practice" of the two royal establishments. I *never* spoke about Constitution Square, etc. My only point was that the King in Greece had transgressed his constitutional rights.

And you are quite right, of course, that I anticipated an absolute majority victory for the Center Union, which made all the questions of collaboration strictly academic.

I am sorry not to have the quotations you need. I do remember that I gave a statement to the press in rebuttal of the various unfounded charges. You could find it in *Ethnos* anywhere between the 22nd and the 25th of February 1967.

I am afraid that it is next to impossible to clear up this question satisfactorily, mainly because the alleged statement was in the form of an answer to a question from the floor and the exact wording was therefore transmitted by journalists—some of them decidedly hostile to Andreas—rather than quoted from the approved text of a formal speech. Perhaps it is not important what Andreas said or was reported to have said, although these disputes over constitutional prerogatives were at the heart of the political controversy in Greece during the period 1965–67.

My personal conclusions are that (1) Andreas *was* challenging the king to dare to do anything but accept the verdict of the electorate in the forthcoming parliamentary elections; (2) the king and his royalist supporters *were* correct in believing that Andreas wanted to make the monarch a purely symbolic figurehead devoid of any political powers; and (3) the story of the mob in Constitution Square was the figment of a rightist journalist's imagination.

George Papandreou, who deserved his reputation as the greatest crowd-pleasing political orator of the day (a skill much admired in Greece since classical times), had scheduled the opening blast of his personal electoral campaign war for Sunday, April 23, in Thessaloniki. It would have been St. George's Day, the name day of the party leader. Huge crowds of Center Union adherents were expected to pour into the northern city to help the "old fox" get things off to a rousing start. The police and security authorities alleged later that they had expected trouble—riots, if not worse. At the very least there would have been the reverberating chants of "Pa-pan-dre-ou! Pa-pan-dre-ou!" and the thunderous cheers for the party slogans that would have been heard all the way to Athens: "The king reigns, the people rule"; "The army belongs to the nation"; "Greece for the Greeks!"

The Rolling Stones gave a concert in Athens about that time, and we took our teenage daughter to hear them. At the end of the performance a large group of young people surged toward the bandstand, as rock fans are wont to do. The large number of policemen in the stands and on the field (it was in a football stadium) viciously beat the kids with sticks to drive them back, using much more force than appeared necessary, since the young people were not intent on rioting but rather on touching the Stones. Our *Ethnos* journalist friend who was with us remarked of the police, "They're practicing for the coup. That's the way it will be when it comes."

Four

THE DAYS BEFORE THE COUP

PRESENTIMENTS AND ALARUMS

About April 17, I began to be seriously concerned that we were inevitably headed toward a coup d'état of some kind in Greece, and it was my firm conviction that such a development would be a genuine disaster for the United States in Greece. What set me off on the train of thinking that culminated in an attempt to affect our policy decisions later that week was not a sudden illumination, but a period of brooding stimulated by a single telegram from Washington that I had been given the privilege to read, even though it was a highly classified personal message dated April 3 to Ambassador Talbot from Deputy Assistant Secretary of State Stuart Rockwell addressing high-level policy issues.

The full text of the Rockwell cable is given below, and I hasten to add—for the reader and anyone else interested—that my publishing it here is not a violation of any national security laws or regulations, for in 1997 it was declassified and obtained by Greek journalist Alexis Papahelas under the Freedom of Information Act, and he kindly gave me a copy of the original document when I helped him with his book on the junta period. The text was subsequently published in the aforementioned *FRUS* volume 16, but having a copy of the original document allows me to make what I consider an interesting deduction.

According to the Handley-to-Talbot letter of March 16 cited earlier, the king had first broached with Talbot the idea of imposing a dictatorship at a meeting prior to February 28 and had sought the U.S. reaction. Now Talbot had met again with the king at the latter's request, on March 29, and Constantine had again solicited his views on what the reaction of the United States government would be to a resort to an "extra-parliamentary solution" (which is how the king phrased it, though it could only come about through some kind of coup d'état). Because this was doubtless a highly sensitive matter, Talbot understandably did not report it to Washington by telegram, but rather in a letter to Dan Brewster in which he included his suggestions about how to respond to the king. An enclosure with this letter was a "memorandum of conversation" detailing his latest talk with the king. At the time I did not see those items, but it was clear from the State Department's response (which I did see) that he did communicate in precisely that fashion, which had the effect of limiting distribution severely at the Washington end, and in the Athens embassy as well. These items were of major importance, not only because they contained the ambassador's considered views about the current situation in Athens but because they included a couple of memoranda prepared by John Day (no doubt guided by Norbert Anschuetz) entitled "The Problem of Andreas Papandreou" and "Brakes on Andreas in Power," the conclusion of which was "In sum, we see no really reliable brakes on Andreas." These studies no doubt echoed the views expressed by Anschuetz in a memorandum he had provided Talbot as far back as November 2, 1966, analyzing Andreas's policies and prospects.

In its response the Department referred to two letters from the ambassador dated March 30 and 31. The full text of the March 30 letter has been published in *FRUS* volume 16 (Document No. 265), but the editor described that of March 31 in a footnote as "not found." The "memcon" enclosed with the March 30 letter was also "not found" by the *FRUS* editor. My guess is that the letter of March 31 from the ambassador may have transmitted the two John Day memoranda and included Talbot's suggestions for how to respond to the king.

The Department's telegram responding to the letters was sent on April 3, 1967, the date on which the Greek government was put by the king into the hands of Kanellopoulos. It was drafted by Dan Brewster, the office director for Greece, cleared by John Owens, the Greek desk officer, and signed off for dispatch by Stuart Rockwell. Note especially the last sentence in paragraph 2, which was apparently added by Rockwell, as it was inserted in Brewster's original draft (with a different typewriter font) before he signed off on the telegram. That is the sentence that "drove me up the wall." It in effect canceled all the rest of the Department's position, and it was cruelly unresponsive to the king's request for advice. The following text is identical to Document No. 267 in *FRUS* volume 16.

FOR AMBASSADOR FROM ROCKWELL

1. Your two letters received over weekend and given very careful study. You are to be highly commended for manner in which you handled first session with King. We hope that there will be continuing dialogue. Gratified in [sic] meanwhile to see that King has offered mandate to Canellopoulos thus providing time for political parties themselves to work their way out of impasse. We concur with points you propose to make orally (ref March 31 letter). We recommend that points one, two and four be made strongly and in whatever detail you consider advisable at time.

2. We would be inclined to warn more strongly against possible constitutional deviation. Depth of Greek feeling against such a move should be more carefully weighed by King. Andreas as QTE martyr UNQTE with Lambrakis machine standing fully behind him would be very formidable opponent. As matter of principle, of course, U.S. would be opposed to extra-parliamentary move. You should stress point that U.S. reaction to such move cannot be determined in advance but would depend on circumstances at time.

3. Finally, strong statements along lines paras 6 and 7 most desirable. We are glad that lines of communication are open to you and hope that King will feel free to communicate directly with you whenever he wishes to discuss his problems.

4. Letter follows.

RUSK

With his addition to this message Rockwell indicated that he didn't want us to be totally negative regarding a possible coup, but he did want us to leave the king hanging, not knowing how we would react until after the fact. What was the king supposed to do? Go ahead and do or not do what he wanted, after which we would tell him whether we agreed or not? We knew what the "circumstances" were. Everyone knew what the circumstances were. They would not change before the king would have to make his decision, whatever that might be.

Talbot met with the king on April 8, and it was clear from his reporting telegram to the Department that he had intelligently and skillfully adapted or tailored his instructions from Washington to soften the blow that Rockwell's insertion would have delivered to the king, though he kept his remarks consistent with the message he was told to deliver. The king's response to Talbot was that his presentation left many questions unanswered. In fairness to Talbot, I here quote from his reporting telegram (Document No. 269, FRUS).

> I gave King Constantine five-part answer Saturday evening to his question of March 29 whether he could count on United States support should he be forced to undertake a constitutional deviation. I reassured him of continuing United States interest at highest level in Greece's difficult situation. I said we share his concern over policies that might be adopted by government with Andreas Papandreou as leading figure but believe certain restraints could operate to keep such a government from at least some of extreme measures Andreas now advocating. I expressed our agreement with the King's hopes that current difficulties can be overcome through parliamentary processes. I stated the inability of USG to give advance assurances of support to King and noted our traditional opposition to dictatorial solutions to constitutional crises. They are wrong in principle and rarely work yet create many new difficulties. A dictatorship in Greece might cause short-term upheavals, leading to more repressive measures, and to coalescence of opposition forces which in turn could be penetrated and dominated by international Communist agents. Adverse international reactions would not be limited to the Communist apparatus but would include supporters of democracy. Considerable criticism could be expected in United States. Finally, I restated as a guiding principle of United States in Eastern Mediterranean our policy to encourage progress and stability in Greece and to maintain close relations with Greece.
>
> The King responded with thanks, but felt many questions remained unanswered.

My only comment today is that King Constantine was a lot more intelligent than he has ever been credited for being. He realized he had been given a nonanswer.

In spare moments in that period I mulled over what I would do if presented with these problems. I had not been presented with them, and no one had asked or would probably welcome my opinions. But I was seriously troubled and decided that I ought to at least try to get the senior officers to focus on the problems that concerned me and that I thought ought to concern them. It would have been useless to talk to Kay Bracken, who was of course preoccupied, and even if I got through to her there was no guarantee that she would pass my thoughts on to Anschuetz and the ambassador, where the powers of decision really lay. So I decided I would write a memorandum to her, making it as brief as possible, but pulling no punches.

On Wednesday and Thursday, April 19 and 20, Bruce Lansdale, the director of the American Farm School in Thessaloniki, was in Athens on one of his regular business trips to make personal contact with Greek government officials. Bruce was my oldest friend in Greece; we had grown up together as children in Thessaloniki before World War II, when his father had directed the YMCA and mine had been the American consul (we had lived at the Farm School in those days). Bruce's schedule was so busy that I had only a brief opportunity to talk to him privately on Wednesday, so to get more time with him on Thursday I offered to drive him to the airport in my old VW Bug. We had about half an hour on the way out and then another twenty minutes waiting for his flight back to Thessaloniki to be announced. To my mind Bruce was the American who best understood Greece and the Greeks—he had been running the Farm School for some fifteen years by then. He might not have been aware of all the political intrigues that were discussed along the Athens cocktail party circuit, but he had an unfailing grasp of how a Greek would react to events, particularly a Greek peasant, but in an essentially democratic society such as Greece (in the sense that it is relatively classless) the thoughts of the peasant are not so far removed from those of the Athenian salon intellectual. I wanted to try out my thoughts about the situation on Bruce.

"I'm sure there's going to be a coup," I began, and his response was, "So am I. What is the Embassy going to do?"

My response was: "I wish I knew." I then told him what was bothering me, and was considerably elated to find that he agreed with nearly everything I said. Thus encouraged, I drove back to the Embassy, shut my office door, plopped myself down in front of the typewriter, and on page after page of yellow-lined legal paper produced the following draft memorandum to Kay Bracken. It was dated April 20, 1967. I reproduce it here in its entirety:

SUBJECT: THE PRESENT POLITICAL CRISIS

I feel compelled to offer these thoughts on the present political crisis because I sincerely believe that the direction in which we are heading is extremely dangerous at a minimum and potentially disastrous for American interests in Greece. Specifically, it seems to me that the odds very heavily favor the imposition of a dictatorship as the resolution of the present crisis; and I fear that a dictatorship "solution" now will ultimately end in another Dominican Republic disaster for us at best, and at worst in another Vietnam. Three aspects of the present situation need to be examined: the chances of a "dictatorship" solution, the time of it, and the consequences that might flow from it.

Chances

It appears almost inevitable that a dictatorship will be tried. Important political elements—the Palace, the ERE hard core, the military, the conservative establishment—are determined that they will not permit the Papandreous to come to power. It seems more and more likely that the Papandreou-led Center Union can win an absolute majority in the May 28 elections. They might achieve this on their own, or they might achieve it with covert EDA subsidization. Even if the EK gained only a plurality victory, they might try to form a government with EDA parliamentary support but not EDA participation in the government. The small parties are likely to be all but wiped out under the present electoral system. The ERE is very unlikely to win a majority, unlikely as well to gain a plurality, and in my view has little chance of forming a government by picking up stray small party candidates and by engineering defections from the EK. An ERE-EK coalition government after the elections is a possibility, but appears to be growing less and less likely because of partisan hardening on both sides during this campaign period.

The above has to do with how the elections might turn out. But for the present purpose what is much more significant is how those who think in terms of a dictatorship "solution" *think the elections will turn out.* The point is that there is a serious risk that the Papandreous will win an absolute majority. The King, the military, the ERE hard core, and others who would consider a dictatorship a way out know this quite well, and there is a good chance that they will act on the belief that there is a serious risk of a Papandreou victory. There would be two ways to prevent a Papandreou victory: open electoral fraud, which would have to be on such a scale that it would be obvious to everyone, or the postponement of elections. Either of these tactics would sooner or later—probably sooner—lead to a dictatorship, for in both cases the center and left would react violently, the government would in turn use strong suppressive measures, and the outcome would inevitably be dictatorship. The more likely event—postponement of the elections—would in itself amount to a constitutional deviation and would merely be the first step toward a dictatorship.

What we therefore have in prospect is the imposition of a dictatorship *prior to* the elections, for those favoring a dictatorship would clearly want to impose one before a Papandreou victory, not in response to one. The pro-dictatorship group is capable of stimulating violence prior to the elections to create an excuse for postponing elections and moving into a dictatorship. A simple device would be to arrest Andreas Papandreou, which would lead to violent demonstrations, to repression, to more violence, to postponement of the elections, etc.

Timing

The elections are 38 days away. The pro-dictatorship group would probably not want to wait till the last minute. Therefore the next three weeks appear to me to be the critical period. The moment would come when the pro-dictatorship group makes up its mind that a Papandreou electoral victory cannot be prevented. No matter how circumspect the EK is in order to avoid creating excuses for the imposition of a dictatorship, the anti-Papandreou group can easily convince itself that the EDA will secretly subsidize pro-Andreas candidates to put an EK with a strong leftist faction in power. EDA might well do just that, in order to bring about a crisis, to force a final and irrevocable EK-Constantine confrontation which the Communists would hope would eliminate the monarchy from Greece, their first major victory in this country since 1949. The EDA would not have the same reasons as the EK for fearing a dictatorship, for the EDA could go underground, having as it does disciplined cadres who could keep their organization more or less intact against the day when the dictatorship would fall and the Communists could emerge to take charge in a chaotic political environment.

The pro-dictatorship group would be unlikely to give us much or any advance warning that they were moving to a constitutional deviation. They could guess that we might be opposed to the idea, and they would therefore wish to present us with a *fait accompli*, assuming that we would eventually have to accept the *de facto* situation. We might wake up one morning, say three weeks from now, to find a dictatorship already installed and functioning. Then we would be in really bad shape, because we could hardly reverse the course events would have taken, and we would have to try to live with an unconstitutional regime in Greece. The fact that we were opposed to a dictatorship—if we are so opposed—would not do us much good with the opposition, for everyone in this country would assume that it was either our idea, or we had encouraged it, or that at least we had condoned it. And the fact that we had remained silent prior to the imposition of a dictatorship would not excuse us in the eyes of most Greeks. They would take that as tacit assent. But even more would believe that we were solidly behind the dictatorship, because as you well know most Greeks find it hard to believe that we do not manage the internal politics of the country, particularly the roles played by the Palace, the ERE, the military and the conservative forces generally, in other words, those who would have been responsible for establishing the dictatorship. What all this adds up to is that if there is a dictatorship we are going to be saddled with responsibility for it whether we opposed the idea or not. The only way out of this dilemma that I can see is that we must at all cost prevent the establishment of a dictatorship.

The only force adequate to stop the imposition of a dictatorship is, in my view, *active intervention by the United States now*. They will not necessarily listen to us, but there is a good chance they will. They need us, in the sense that they need the backing of American military power and of NATO for their security against external dangers, and they need American and NATO military assistance for their own forces, which under a dictatorship would need to be strong for internal security reasons as well as for protection against external threats. We can survive without Greece. This relative balance of needs gives us tremendous leverage, and no one in Greece knows that better than the Palace and the military establishment. If we told those favoring a dictatorship flatly that such a "solution" to the present crisis would be unacceptable to us, I think there would be a very good chance that they would not try it. And I cannot see any other way of stopping a dictatorship now.

It is not sufficient to tell the King that our attitude toward a dictatorship would depend on the circumstances. This is much too vague, and would be an injustice to the King. What "circumstances"? The King might well misread the signal. He might take such a statement as implying willingness to go along if he could present adequate justification for it. If we took such a line with him I think it would be grossly unfair to him later to show our disapproval by refusing to accept and recognize a dictatorship. It would be a tragedy if a dictatorship were imposed in the mistaken belief that the USG thought it was OK although not too happy a solution and then we pulled the rug out by declining recognition.

I personally can think of only one "circumstance" that would justify our acceptance of a dictatorship in Greece, and that would be the threat of a Communist takeover from within or from without. This prospect appears to me to be very remote today. A dictatorship, however, could set in motion forces that would eventually lose Greece to the Communist camp.

It needs to be emphasized that we must make our position clear *now* on how we stand on the dictatorship question. If we are opposed, we must do our utmost to get that idea across now, before a dictatorship is attempted, and before elections, even if they are held. If we don't care whether there is a dictatorship or not, or if we actually favor one, then there is no problem for the present. But we should be examining very carefully the probable long-term consequences of a dictatorship in Greece.

Consequences

The Metaxas dictatorship does not provide a perfect historical analogy for several reasons: World War II terminated it, the dictator died more or less on the battlefield, having become a hero for saying no to the Italians, and the Greek Communists were new to the game and hence made many mistakes. Nevertheless, there are relevant historical lessons. The Metaxas regime succeeded in suppressing most liberal and progressive political activity, in fact practically all political activity, but the Communists were able to go underground, keep their organization going, and the occupation provided them a good opportunity to extend their organization, arm themselves, obtain foreign support (British mainly), train their cadres, so that by war's end they were the best-organized and strongest single political element in the country. They made a premature effort to take control, and were eventually defeated. The lesson is, however, that the dictatorship did not get rid of the Communist threat, but probably contributed to its strength, so that the Communists emerged nearly victorious when the dictatorship eventually went the way of all dictatorships. These are facts of life, and although circumstances may change, the same eventual outcome could develop out of a dictatorship today. Only this time it could be much worse, for the Center would probably be willing to join with the Left, and instead of the approximately 30 percent support for the rebellion in 1944–46, we might now have 60 percent or even 70 percent in active revolt against a dictatorship.

I don't know whether the administration can stand another Dominican Republic at this point, but I doubt that there is any enthusiasm in Washington for another such experiment. I suppose we could live with a dictatorship in Greece, as we do in many other countries. It would certainly be a setback for us in world opinion and NATO. We might even successfully avoid direct involvement. But I sincerely believe that we would not be able live with the aftermath of a dictatorship, with what would succeed it when it inevitably fell. I think a dictatorship "solution" would be an attempt to combat inevitable historical forces which are alive in Greece today, and would be doomed to defeat because it would be contrary to those irresistible forces. This could get us into a philosophical argument over the degree to which men are able to overcome, guide, control historical forces the way they are able to dam or divert rivers. At any rate, I don't see a potential dictator in Greece today of the stature needed to fight history much less to defeat it. It seems to me we are neglecting one of the oldest and best adages of diplomacy: discover the inevitable and then exploit it to your advantage. A dictatorship is not inevitable in Greece, but the pressure for profound social, economic, and political change appears to me to be irresistible, and it is this force which will win in the end. We should be exploiting it to our advantage.

Who is it who is exploiting this force? None other than Andreas Papandreou. And in the aftermath of a dictatorship it will be Andreas, or someone very much like him, who will come out on top. And then where will we be, we who will be held responsible for having established the dictatorship in Greece? I would think we would be pretty well out of Greece.

A dictatorship would produce a resistance movement not at all to our liking. It might initially be led by liberals and progressives, but the Communists would surely cooperate, and they have a way of dominating underground and clandestine groups and movements. This is the danger of a dictatorship, for I don't think one could last for very long, and its existence and actions would only serve to alienate even more people into the ranks of the opposition, the ranks of the resistance movement.

What is the alternative to a dictatorship? I think it is to ride out the forces at work. At the very worst what we would get is Andreas Papandreou. This might be most unpleasant, but it might not be lasting. Andreas himself worries me because he displays traits of paranoid personality, unpredictability, vindictiveness, instability, but his programs are another thing altogether. I think we have been overhasty in judging his program to be bad, as well as in equating his demagogic campaign statements with his programmatic beliefs. There is a serious need for many of the domestic changes advocated by the Papandreous, in education, in the economy, in agriculture. Keeping the army out of politics is certainly something that Americans can sympathize with. It is doubtless a fact that the army leadership has been strongly pro-conservative since the war, although not in some earlier periods of Greek history. What is wrong with the EK's desire to water down the pro-ERE purity of the military establishment? We wouldn't want to see that army become an exclusive EK province either, but could we not count on conservative elements in the army to resist successfully an EK effort to dominate the military establishment completely? As for the monarchy, I am afraid the institution is on the way out now; a dictatorship would save it only temporarily, and would probably assure its demise. The monarchy's best chance of survival is to adapt to the times, which in Europe means by becoming a-political.

As for the Papandreous' international policies, it strikes me as curious that when De Gaulle pulls out of NATO—because we refused to help him obtain a national nuclear deterrent and declined to grant France status equal to Britain's and ahead of Germany's within the alliance—we declare that it's all for the good, for the alliance has been cleansed of its anomalies and now we're stronger than ever. [This had been the theme of a talk to embassy officers some days earlier by Harlan Cleveland, our ambassador to NATO.] Yet when a Greek politician proposes that Greece take a somewhat more independent stance with regard to NATO and to his country's almost purely Western ties we get most upset and wonder whether the man isn't really a Communist. France is showing her independence because she is now able to stand on her own, has the economic and political strength to cut some of her apron strings to mother NATO. Perhaps Greece is ready to demonstrate some maturity as well, to become less of a dependent client and more of a self-sustaining member of the European community. I think it would be a serious mistake for us to go down fighting against inevitable trends in trying to maintain the comfortable postures of the last twenty years.

P.S. I have discussed these general ideas during the past two days with Bruce Lansdale, who among Americans I know has the best understanding of the Greek mentality. Although I cannot speak for him, I know that he agrees with the point of view expressed above.

The postscript was a not terribly subtle effort to beef up my demarche with the big gun of a recognized expert outside the Embassy, much as a young scholar will fill the preface to his first published book with the names of senior academic colleagues who have gone over his manuscript for him. Talbot, Anschuetz, and Bracken knew Lansdale well, and they all had great admiration for him, especially Talbot, who did not claim to have the longstanding knowledge of Greece and the Greeks that the others had and who therefore leaned on the expertise that local American residents like Lansdale could provide him.

Two retrospective comments about this April 20 memorandum are perhaps in order. The first is that the coup and resulting dictatorship I was anticipating was of course what came to be known as the "Generals' coup," the one that never took place because it was preempted by the "Colonels' coup" of Papadopoulos and company, about which I had no foreknowledge at all. The second is that the noteworthy thing in my approach was the emphasis on *timing*. I was proposing that we face up to the implications of a dictatorship now, prior to the elections, for it seemed to me self-evident that the coup would occur before the elections and not after them. The Embassy's analysis and reporting up to that time had been to the effect that a coup was a possibility if the Papandreous won a majority victory in the elections, a result that would be unacceptable to the king. It was my reasoning that those bent on a coup would determine this to be the probable result before the elections were actually held and would move to impose the dictatorship in advance, before a Papandreou victory had made it clear what the real motive for the coup was.[1] I therefore thought it was incumbent on the Embassy to face the issue immediately, to do something to stop a coup before it took place. Mired in typical bureaucratic inertia, the Embassy seemed inclined to delay facing up to the issue until the crisis actually arrived, until we knew what the electoral results were and what our (and the king's) options might then be.

Of course I was off on the timing. I wrote that we might wake up one morning—three weeks hence perhaps—to find the dictatorship already installed. I finished the draft memorandum at about 6:30 P.M. on Thursday, April 20, and locked it in my office safe with the intention of having my secretary type it up the following morning.

Louise and I then went to a cocktail party at a Greek friend's apartment in Kolonaki Square, the host a ship owner's lawyer. The guests were the usual establishment types with the usual talk: how was the ERE doing, wasn't it awful what Andreas had said about swearing in the government in Constitution Square, there'd surely be trouble in Salonika on Sunday. We decided to stop by Vladimiros's restaurant, perched on the side of Lycabettus Hill, for dinner. I wanted to talk to Elias, the proprietor and a friend of my brother Mike, to find out if possible what the political Left was thinking, especially what its attitude was toward Andreas, whether they were going to fight him all out or secretly subsidize his candidates to try to bring down the Right. "Vladimiros" was a Hellenized Russian name that this strangest of all Athenian characters had deliberately affixed to the restaurant to display his political sympathies. Under a full reddish beard his maitre d's costume was a khaki military uniform without insignia, for he claimed to have fought with the Communist guerrillas during the German occupation, and he now presented himself as an adherent of the extreme Left party, the EDA.

Vladimiros had a mixed clientele heavily inclined toward the diplomatic community, Western, Eastern, and neutralist, with a scattering of tourists who could find their way up the hill, and Greeks of all Athenian descriptions.

The better I got to know Elias, the more I began to believe that he was an intelligence operative, but it was impossible to fathom for which side he was working. He seemed to be on excellent terms with the Russians, but the restaurant was also frequented by American CIA types. I thought he was perhaps working for all sides, for his own account. The restaurant changed ownership after the coup, Elias shaved off his beard, down to a neat mustache, and his costume changed from khakis to corduroy slacks and a blue Shetland sweater. Some weeks later he disappeared from his usual haunts, and the rumor was that he had taken to the hills to organize a new guerrilla movement to overthrow the junta. But the next time I saw him it was on the stairway of the Hellenic-American Union, and when I asked him what he was doing he said, "Perfecting my English. One never knows, you know!" He then disappeared into the mass of English-language students leaving the building after class.

That evening, April 20, Elias assured me that he thought Andreas was doing a good job, was using the right tactics, looked like a winner, but personally he was going to stick with the EDA, and most of his colleagues on the Left would do the same. We talked to him for about an hour after dinner and then drove home to the suburb of Halandri at about 12:30 A.M. and went to bed.

WASHINGTON WEIGHS IN

By a strange coincidence, at nearly the same time we went to bed (and six hours after I had locked my memo in my safe at the Embassy), in Washington the State Department dispatched a telegram to the Athens embassy with an important policy proposal. It was dispatched at 6:51 P.M. Washington time on April 20; it was received at the Embassy during the night and was not read until the following morning. The telegram, addressed to Ambassador Talbot, suggested that he call on EK leader George Papandreou and propose to him a compromise agreement to resolve the current political impasse with several components. These were (1) all sides should cool the rhetoric; (2) the king would assure George that Andreas would not be arrested; and (3) George would assure the king that if he won the elections he would appoint only "people of mutual confidence" to sensitive posts in Foreign Affairs and Defense, and would not carry out a widespread shakeup of the armed forces leadership. Talbot was asked for his comments on this proposal, and was also asked to take no action in the absence of further instructions.

Years later, when I saw a copy of this telegram as sent from Washington (in *FRUS* volume 16), I learned that it had been drafted by John Owens, the Greek desk officer, and his boss, Dan Brewster, the office director, signed off by Lucius Battle, the assistant secretary for the Near East (since April 5, 1967), and approved by Stuart Rockwell, Battle's deputy, and by Under Secretary Nicholas Katzenbach, the number two official of the Department. This was no doubt a high-level effort by the Department to deal with the crisis in Greece. Unfortunately, it suffered the usual fate of bureaucratic initiatives taken too late: OBE—"overtaken by events."

Five

THE COUP

THE COUP OF APRIL 21, 1967

My first knowledge of the coup came from my son, Chris, who burst into the bathroom where I was taking a shower and informed me that I wouldn't have to go to work that Friday morning, because the schools were closed, the buses weren't running, and Kifissia Boulevard was filled with tanks moving toward Athens. "Oh my God!" I said, and hurried to get ready to go to work.

The story of the April 21 coup in Greece has been told in many places and does not bear repeating here except for a few vignettes that may illuminate U.S. policy problems at the time. I drove to work in my old Volkswagen Beetle and had no trouble negotiating the various roadblocks and diversions until I reached the main intersection of the Kifissia and Alexandras boulevards in Ambelokipi, a few blocks north of the American chancery. There, soldiers under command of a captain had blocked all the streets with tanks and armored personnel carriers, and no one was permitted to pass, with very few exceptions. The few exceptions were officers in uniform. And as I stood there arguing with the captain—on my own behalf and for a few diplomatic colleagues similarly blocked—I was more than a little dismayed and annoyed to observe a number of our service attachés and senior military mission officers passing through the roadblock in their chauffeured limousines and receiving smart salutes from the Greek soldiers, which they naturally returned. No civilians were getting through, not even full-fledged ambassadors of NATO countries. It struck me as curious at the time that those in charge of a military coup appeared to have no fear of foreign military officers, but for some reason they did not want civilian diplomats to reach their chanceries. The attachés did not offer to pick us up in their cars, so we waited and argued.

The discussion with the captain became quite heated. As one of the few diplomats at the roadblock who spoke Greek, I carried a large part of our side of the argument. I encouraged all the arriving diplomats to descend from their cars and to join the civilian phalanx with which we were confronting the troops. Our principal argument was that we were diplomats and had to get to our embassies, coup or no coup; in fact, it was even more important that we get to our offices that morning, so that we could inform our governments of what was going on. This line had no appeal to the captain, who simply kept repeating that he was under orders to let no civilians through. At one point the soldiers pushed us back from the intersection toward the nearest apartment building, and a few colleagues decided they should perhaps go home and wait things out after they observed some bloodstains on the sidewalk nearby. (The coup has always been advertised as "bloodless," and with the exception of a very few victims it was very nearly so, at least initially. Most successful coups are in fact bloodless, while the unsuccessful ones often are not.)

One of the civilians stopped at the roadblock was our own CIA station chief, Jack Maury, who returned home after a brief effort to talk his way through. He, too, had noticed that non-Greek officers in uniform were getting through, so he used his head and broke out from an old trunk his Marine Reserve colonel's uniform left over from the war. (Having gained some weight, he split some seams putting it on.) On his second try at the Ambelokipi roadblock, now in uniform, he made it through to the Embassy. I reached the Embassy shortly thereafter, when the captain in charge of the roadblock finally relented and let all the diplomats through in a one-time lifting of the gate. Once inside the ring of tanks and soldiers, we had no difficulty making it the rest of the way to our offices.

On arriving at the Embassy I discovered that the first American diplomat to learn of the coup had been, strangely enough, the ambassador himself. In the middle of the night, Dionysos Livanos, the nephew of Prime Minister Kanellopoulos's wife, had awakened Talbot at his residence (two blocks from the chancery building) to tell him that soldiers had taken his uncle away "for his own protection." But Livanos said he feared it was a military coup because he had seen some tanks in Constitution Square. He added that his aunt was hysterical and had asked if the ambassador would please come along to the prime minister's apartment in Kolonaki nearby and assure her that everything was going to be all right. (Like many other people, she and

Livanos had assumed it was an American-approved coup.) Talbot agreed to do so, but stopped off at the chancery first to send a "flash" telegram to the State Department. The ambassador dictated the text to a code clerk, a cable that contained all the information he thus far had; but in the urgent confusion, the code clerk ran together in one sentence what Talbot had meant to be sent as two. The cable as received in Washington read: "UNDERSTAND PRIME MINISTER HAS JUST BEEN SIEZED [sic] BY MILITARY ELEMENTS AND TANKS IN CONSTITUTION SQUARE. TALBOT."

The telegram was sent at 3:27 A.M. Athens time and received in Washington at 8:34 P.M. It was immediately distributed to the Executive Secretariat Operations Center (S/S-O) and to the White House, DOD, CIA, USIA, and NSA. The code clerk, as above, had misspelled "SEIZED." A senior watch officer in the Department's Operations Center telephoned the Greek Office director, Daniel Brewster, at home and read him the cable. Brewster was puzzled by the brief text because the picture it presented to him was one of the aged and dignified prime minister being surrounded by a large military force including tanks in the principal square of downtown Athens. He wondered (as he explained many weeks later), What was the prime minister doing in Constitution Square in the middle of the night? Why did they need to use tanks? Is he putting up some resistance? Before heading in to the State Department, Brewster told the watch officer to send a cable to Embassy Athens with the following text: "WHO SENT EMBTEL 4729? WHERE IS AMBASSADOR TALBOT? RUSK."

It had crossed Brewster's mind that the cable from Athens had perhaps been sent by a drunken code clerk or by a duty officer who thought this would be a funny joke.

When he arrived back at the chancery, having comforted Mrs. Kanellopoulos and heard from her an account of her husband's arrest, Talbot read Brewster's cable and was highly indignant, for he was not aware of the run-on sentence in his original cable, which he had dictated and which would not be typed up as sent until much later in the day. Talbot shot off an answer to the Department as follows: "I SENT EMBTEL 4729. I AM IN MY EMBASSY. TALBOT."

ASSESSING THE COUP

Everyone in the Embassy that morning was of course busy trying to find out as much as possible about what was happening. Solid information was scarce, for the city was sealed tight, all telephonic communications had been cut off, and the radio was playing nothing but martial music and an occasional announcement by the coup group. (The local American Armed Forces Radio station switched to twenty-four-hour-a-day rock and roll.) It was a situation familiar to any modern diplomat who has had experience of military coups, but that made the effort of gathering intelligence and achieving understanding no less frantic. One of the least commendable offerings came from our labor attaché, who on arrival at the chancery insisted that his good trade union contacts were certain it was a Papandreist coup, that is, a leftist coup. This made absolutely no sense and was rightly ignored. From the early public statements of the coup group, we realized that this was a rightist takeover, and the identities of the principal perpetrators—two colonels and a brigadier—indicated that this was not the anticipated Generals' coup, although that coup's leading planner, General Spandidakis, had joined the coup group as an individual once it had gotten under way.

The coup crisis merely aggravated an unfortunate tendency that already existed in the Embassy's upper echelons, namely, that we had—unlike most bureaucracies—too many Indians and not enough chiefs. The earlier parts of this account have perhaps indicated my feeling that our senior officers were not giving enough attention to the policy implications of the situation we were passing through. One explanation was that they all behaved like first secretaries, political officers whose job it was to report on developments to the Department of State and perhaps analyze their hidden meanings. Policy was apparently something to be left to Washington. We were all just reporting officers. John Day was the second secretary, whose only job was to report on internal political developments, but Kay Bracken saw that same role as her own, as did the ambassador. And so did Anschuetz. Although he rarely wrote anything down, he still prowled the town in search of a reporting officer's tidbits, as though he were still Peurifoy's man in the Political Section rather than the number two man in the American mission, the minister-counselor. I was guilty of involving myself in internal reporting, which was not my job, but my self-justification was that what I was covering was what all the others were inclined to ignore. In any case, on April 21 we suddenly all became full-time reporting officers, with Talbot himself donning his old mantle as chief foreign correspondent of the *Chicago Daily News* and firing off a slew of cables with all the information we could gather as fast as it came in.

As there appeared to be plenty of reporting talent engaged in that task, in that and subsequent days I took on (unasked) the job of talking with the growing body of American and British journalists who rushed into Athens to cover the story. The senior embassy officers had all along been reluctant to talk with press people.[1] They feared the press, feared leaks, feared exposure, and did not trust any journalist to do an honest job or to honor their confidence. In this attitude they were typical of a great many Foreign Service people who have no use for the press and a great deal of fear of it. My approach has always been that it should be of supreme interest to American diplomats how the countries they are serving in or working on are covered in the American press, for that coverage molds public opinion, circumscribes what the State Department can and cannot do, and influences Congress more than any other factor. In other words, foreign correspondents are going to file some kind of story, for it is their job and that's how they earn their living. If an FSO doesn't care what they write, then he should have nothing to do with them. But if he does care, he should be just as cooperative as possible, in fact go out of his way to be helpful. But a Foreign Service officer runs perhaps no greater risk than to deal directly with the press, because the punishment for unauthorized leaks, for having given something to the press that someone else thinks the press should not have had, can be severe indeed.

No one in Embassy Athens would even see the correspondents who camped out in our lobby downstairs, and the correspondents would not be satisfied with USIS "press" officers (they are never satisfied, for they rightly judge that the people who know the score are the embassy political officers). During the week after the coup I spent hours and hours with the American correspondents, giving them what I could and trying to help them do the best reporting job they could, without violating our own standards of secrecy. They naturally kept pressing for a meeting with the ambassador, to get from his own lips a statement of what the U.S. attitude toward these events was. Talbot declined to meet with them for at least a full week, by which time most of them had left town to rush to the next trouble spot. By that time we had received some guidance from Washington that Talbot could lean on in trying to explain the American posture toward the new Greek government.

My draft memorandum to Mrs. Bracken (detailed in the previous chapter), completed the evening before and now reposing in my safe, had of course been "overtaken by events." I regretted this, most of all because I felt it contained some analysis that was still relevant to our situation postcoup, but I had no doubt that it would now be impossible to get anyone to pay attention to it, caught up as they all were in the task of keeping Washington informed of the fast-breaking developments. I considered forgetting about it, but then I decided that I would try to get Mrs. Bracken to read it if she had a few spare moments. I gave it to her with the explanation that it had been written the day before but might still contain some ideas that would be useful now, despite the intervening coup. She put it into her in-box, and it was then returned to me four or five days later with the inscription at the top: "Noted. KB."

She never mentioned the memo to me nor anything discussed in it, but I presumed she had meant to indicate that she had at least read it. There was certainly no intimation that she had passed it up the line to Anschuetz or the ambassador. One of my bosses in the Department once explained to me that the written notation "Noted" is the most useful expression for dealing with paperwork in a bureaucracy. It meant absolutely nothing: it indicated neither agreement nor disagreement and was therefore neutral; but it covered the writer to the extent that one could never be charged with having completely ignored the paper in question; one had taken it into account in some fashion; one had "noted" it. Mrs. Bracken's "Noted" almost made me laugh out loud when I saw it: she had learned the same technique, perhaps from the same boss.

Everyone was preoccupied with his or her own thoughts and reactions. Anschuetz was vastly amused by the turn things had taken, and he advised Kay Bracken and John Day that he was ordering from the Hilton Hotel nearby a cooked crow, a meal that they could share now that he had turned out to be right. A few weeks earlier he had casually mentioned to them that his good friend Nick Farmakis had told him confidentially that a military coup was coming, only it wouldn't be by the generals we were keeping our eyes on but by some personal friends of Nick's in the army, some colonels. No one except Anschuetz had taken this report at all seriously, for Farmakis (whose name means "poison" in Greek) was a known braggart and a somewhat sinister behind-the-scenes operative, the only deputy in the parliament who described himself as a "fascist" and someone who had been openly proclaiming the need for a military dictatorship to anyone who would listen to him. He was considered so unreliable an informant that his prediction had not even been reported to Washington. Day and Bracken had discounted it entirely as wishful thinking on the part of Farmakis, and now Anschuetz was having his revenge.

Most of the inside information we received about the coup group during that and subsequent days came from Farmakis, who was personally close to Colonel Papadopoulos and had assumed the function of press spokesman for the new regime. He apparently wanted to maneuver himself into the post of foreign minister, or elsewhere in the cabinet, but his unsavory reputation as a business fixer and political fanatic reportedly precluded his having a more prominent official role. Within weeks he was moved back behind the scenes, where he remained. It was characteristic perhaps that no matter what group came to power the ubiquitous Anschuetz had a special pipeline to their inner core—for what it was worth after the fact.

Most Greeks, and many non-Greeks, are firmly convinced that if the United States (or some of its "services," a euphemism for the CIA) did not actually install the Papadopoulos regime, we at least had foreknowledge of it and had given our advance approval for the "constitutional deviation." I cannot conclusively resolve this issue—though I have tried many times to formulate a reasonable position—because I do not have access to all of our government's files. Jack Maury certainly gave every appearance of being as much in the dark as I that Friday morning at the Ambelokipi roadblock, but those committed to a conspiracy view of history and of these events would argue that of course the head of the CIA station would have had to give the appearance of knowing nothing and of having slept through it all.

I am personally convinced that Talbot, and hence the State Department, had no foreknowledge, although he was as aware as everyone else in the upper reaches of the Embassy of the planning for the Generals' coup. The exchange of telegrams presented above between Talbot and Brewster should be fair evidence on this score. Assuming that Maury was unaware—busy as he was keeping watch and reporting on the Spandidakis group working on behalf of the king—is it not quite possible that lower-level officers of the CIA in Athens had learned in advance of the Papadopoulos coup and said nothing to their superiors? Yes, it is possible. As explained earlier, the CIA had a very close liaison relationship with the Greek intelligence service (KYP), and the key perpetrators of the Colonels' coup had served in the KYP and had worked with their American counterparts over the years, notably Papadopoulos himself, Makarezos (one of the central triumvirate), Roufogalis, Hadjipetros (who became KYP head after the coup), Ioannides, and others. The Greek CIA was a largely military outfit, and the coup planners were officers whose principal orientation had been toward the intelligence field.

But let us consider two aspects of this question. If one were Papadopoulos, a colonel who had spent many years conspiring and planning a military takeover of the government, who knew that a generals' takeover was in the offing, who was aware that his own action would be totally contrary to the firmly hierarchical disciplinary traditions of the Greek armed forces (and carried out without the king's authorization), who could not be sure what the reaction of the American government would be to his action prior to its successful execution, would such a person dare take *any* American official into his confidence? Would he not fear an exposure that would not only kill his plan but also subject him to a trial for treason perhaps? Would it not be preferable to present the American government with a fait accompli, which it would have no choice but to sanction?[2]

Then, from the point of view of a putative CIA officer who had received advance information about the coup from Papadopoulos or one of his associates, would he fail to pass on a report to his superiors about it? In intelligence work careers are made by obtaining and passing on just such critical information as that, by being the key man in a fast-breaking situation, and by having developed the essential channel that no one else can exploit. Still, what if one were a CIA officer who sympathized with the Papadopoulos group, who knew about their plans, and yet feared that his superiors in the CIA and the American government generally might not approve of this particular group taking over (a bunch of unknowns, lower ranking, not the king's men)? What would one do in that case? Would one pass on a report, risking the failure of the coup, the arrest of the officers implicated in its planning, the destruction of a carefully nurtured chain of contacts in the Greek military and intelligence services?

I do not know the answer. What I do know is that the American CIA station in Greece was filled with Greek American officers who shared a hatred for Andreas Papandreou and all he stood for, who were right-wing in orientation and totally committed to the Papadopoulos coup once it occurred, and who have remained its ardent defenders ever since. This does not answer the question, but it perhaps says something relevant to the subject.

Jumping forward to forty years later, a noteworthy piece of information on this question became available in 2007 with the publication by Doubleday of *New York Times* reporter Tim Weiner's book *Legacy of Ashes: The History of the CIA*. In a rather brief section on Greece at the time of the 1967 coup, this passage appears on page 331:

> Yet the colonels had taken the CIA by surprise. "The only time I saw [CIA Director Richard] Helms really angry was when the Greek colonels' coup took place in 1967," said the veteran analyst and current intelligence chief Dick Lehman. "The Greek generals had been planning a coup against the elected government, a plan we knew all about and was not yet ripe. But a group of colonels had trumped their ace and acted without warning. Helms had been expecting to be warned of the generals' coup, and when a coup occurred, he naturally assumed it was this one, and he was furious." Lehman,

who had read the overnight cables from Athens, "tried to cool Helms off by pointing out that this was a different coup, which we had no line on. This was a new thought."

Andreas Papandreou was arrested as part of the coup group's roundup of potential activist enemies, most of whom were "certified" leftists or Communists of several categories (KYP and the CIA had them all labeled and catalogued as "dangerous," "committed," "sympathetic," or "nominal"); but the coup was not, initially at least, justified by the danger Andreas posed to the Greek body politic. The coup group broadcast the story that there had been an imminent danger of a Communist coup—one recalls the allegations about the police uniforms, the stores of small arms, the seventy truckloads of EDA party files and materiel, the various "proofs" that never saw the light of day because they never existed. But a few months later this justification was abandoned when it was realized that such a story wouldn't wash even with the Americans (much less the Europeans), who had become a bit more sophisticated about the strengths and weaknesses of the Communists in Greece and elsewhere. The Communist movement in Greece was decapitated by the arrest of some eight thousand of its leading personalities on the day of the coup and in the next few days, in accordance with the NATO plan called "Prometheus." The Greek opposition likes to allege that Papadopoulos had executed the plan in carrying out his coup, although they fail to acknowledge that a NATO plan intended to deal with an attack against Greece by a Communist neighbor, Bulgaria for instance, would hardly call for the arrest of the country's prime minister, by tanks in Constitution Square or otherwise, his defense minister, and most of the members of his cabinet, the cutting of all telephonic communications, and so on and so on.

It is possible that Papadopoulos adapted parts of the so-called Prometheus plan—for example, the arrest of large numbers of allegedly dangerous Greek "subversives" who might have formed an internal fifth column during an invasion of Greece by a Communist state—for convenience's sake in executing that portion of his takeover of the country. But this is far from proving (as Andreas and others have charged) that NATO had in being plans for the military takeovers of the governments of all the alliance members, which I simply do not believe.

One of the Embassy's most urgent needs was for biographic information on the key military officers who had perpetrated the April 21 coup. Washington was begging for anything we could provide on the major personalities, as well as for our assessment of what it all meant, and we were somewhat desperate for any background data we could scavenge on Papadopoulos, Pattakos, Makarezos, and the others. We needed to find clues as to the political orientation of the group that had suddenly taken charge of our NATO ally's government. Had the coup been engineered by the senior generals of the Spandidakis group, our intelligence situation would have been quite good: we had a lot of data on those officers, we knew their orientation thoroughly (basically rightist, royalist, and pro-American), and the leading personalities were well known to our own senior officers of JUSMAGG (Joint U.S. Military Assistance Group Greece) and the attaché office, who had worked with them intimately for years.

We turned first to our military attachés, who had among their prime assigned functions the collection of biographic information on key Greek military personalities. They came up with practically nothing of value on the officers in question: they had in their files the standard forms on a number of them, but these contained mainly information about their previous military assignments, dates of promotion, medals, and other decorations, whether they sipped Scotch whiskey or liked American cigarettes, but nothing on their politics. The American military in Greece liked to believe that the Greek army was apolitical—despite its long prewar history of intervention in politics and despite the universally acknowledged rightist/royalist bias of the officer corps—so their bio data sheets were hardly informative. The most they would say about a Greek officer's orientation was "pro-US, pro-NATO," which almost went without saying.

JUSMAGG was hardly more helpful. The officers of our military mission took quite seriously the admonitions they doubtless received to avoid any involvement in Greek internal affairs, so much so that they went out of their way to avoid political discussions with their Greek colleagues. Nevertheless, we hoped to find some data from the reports prepared on all Greek officers who had undergone training in the United States. Included in JUSMAGG's files were a great many of the senior officers of the Greek armed forces, whom we had been training for some twenty years in Greece and in the United States. But what we discovered in the days following April 21 was that few of the officers in the coup group had received U.S. training, which was a good indication that they were not outstanding officers, since we naturally selected only the best for our highly sought-after stateside courses and military schools. One explanation was that their English was poor (neither Papadopoulos nor Makarezos spoke English, and Pattakos made frequent gaffes in subsequent months by depending on his own inadequate English in talking with foreigners), and only officers competent in English could go to the States for training.

In desperation we turned to the CIA station for bio data on the leaders of the new regime. The number two CIA officer proudly showed us a report from January 1967, which though brief and not too informative did identify a group of army officers who were plotting a coup, and a Colonel Papadopoulos headed the list. This had been a group (it turned out later on) whose acronym designation was EENA, a subgroup of the dominant IDEA fraternity of the Greek army. From the report this sounded like a fairly serious group, and it was quite distinct from the plot headed by General Spandidakis, about which there was so much CIA reporting in the months preceding the coup.

The very curious thing was that there were no further intelligence reports on the Papadopoulos group after January. One would have thought that in the coup-talk atmosphere prevailing in Athens at that period, Washington would have instructed the CIA station to dig up all it could on this middle-level officer group about which we knew so little. It is of course possible that the CIA knew a great deal about these officers, since a number of them had had KYP assignments and had worked in tandem with our own intelligence officers. I found it extremely peculiar that all of the CIA's attention had become focused on the Spandidakis group after January and none at all on Papadopoulos, at least from the evidence of the CIA reporting that I saw at that time.

I checked this out later at the State Department with the analyst for Greece in INR (Intelligence and Research), who presumably had access to all the important intelligence reaching Washington on this and other subjects (except of course for such reports as the CIA and other intelligence services did not choose to disseminate to his level of the State Department, which I believe would be rare). This INR analyst, a Greek American by the name of Charilaos Lagoudakis, had been in the job for a couple of decades and knew Greece better than anyone else in the Washington bureaucracy. He too had been struck, in the early months of 1967, by the sudden cessation of information on the Papadopoulos coup group, about which there had been considerable reporting prior to that time. When I asked Lagoudakis if he had seen any evidence of official U.S. government foreknowledge of the April 21 coup, he showed me a memorandum that he had sent to his boss, Philip Stoddard (head of the Greece-Turkey-Iran section of INR/RNA), on February 6, 1967. Its subject was "the right-wing conspiratorial group in the Greek armed forces," and it read as follows:

Since June 19, 1965, RNA has seen some 15 CIA reports from various sources on the so-called "Rightist Greek Military Conspiratorial Group." The latest report was dated January 23, 1967. These reports state that the "conspiratorial group" is ready to stage a military coup when, in its view, a dictatorship would become necessary as the only alternative to Center Union control of Parliament. Some twenty names of active and retired officers are mentioned as key members of this military movement, prominent among whom are Lt. Col. D. Papadopoulos [the leader of the April 21 coup; the initial D. is wrong] and Lt. Col. D. Stamatelopoulos [original founder of the conspiracy and later a rival to George Papadopoulos from outside the regime who sniped at it regularly in articles published in the rightist paper *Vradyni*]. The "conspiratorial group" reportedly has existed since late 1963, but was presumably dispersed by Papandreou upon his accession to power in February 1964. Papadopoulos reportedly said in December 1966 that "once a dictatorship is established, it will seek US support in order to implement social and economic measures which can deter the present tendency toward the left." The first meeting of the "group" since the fall of the Stephanopoulos government allegedly was held on January 4, 1967; Col. Papadopoulos was the principal speaker.

We have no information on this "conspiratorial group" from non-CIA sources, and the available CAS [Controlled American Source] information is very sketchy. Inasmuch as army and Palace circles are reportedly concerned about the possibility of a Papandreou victory in the May elections, it would be useful to have further information on this rightist group, which may now be preparing for a possible coup. Perhaps discreet inquiries by CAS and the Political Section might be in order.

Copies of this memorandum went to the Greek Office director, Dan Brewster, and to the Department's office for liaison with the CIA. Lagoudakis followed up with requests to the CIA for further information on this group, but nothing reached him prior to the April 21 coup d'état. One wonders today whether further information became impossible to obtain because the conspiratorial group went into action to prepare the coup and imposed secrecy, or whether later information was obtained and was either suppressed or at least not disseminated to normal recipients of such intelligence reports. My own speculation was that the Papadopoulos group went into operational mode in February and cut off contact with whatever source had been reporting to the CIA.

I believe that the evidence provided by Tim Weiner's 2007 book about the CIA confirms the supposition that the CIA, from Director Richard Helms down to the lower echelons (e.g., Jack Maury in Athens), remained in the dark when Papadopoulos preempted the generals. It was another classic "intelligence failure."

COUP VIGNETTES

In the spring of 1971, while writing the first draft of this book, I received a letter from Malcolm Thompson, the Embassy's politico-military officer at the time of the coup, in which he recalled some of the atmosphere prevailing in the chancery at that time. He wrote:

> Episodes that stick in my memory are: (1) the sending of John Day back to Wash. to try to find out what the Dept. wanted and his return more confused than ever (!); (2) my sneaking into Gen. Eaton's office across the hall from the Amb. (with Eaton's permission) to read his copies of the cable traffic since the juicier items were removed from the regular reading file; (3) the apparition of Kay rising from that couch in her office after a night on duty; and (4) Amb. Talbot's continuing admonitions to all of us not to become involved or to discuss the issues with our Greek friends! What an incredible and absurd way to react to a crisis situation. A sort of "hear no evil, see no evil, speak no evil" philosophy.

The scenes that stick in one's memory vary from person to person. I recall being approached in an offhand manner by John Day late on the afternoon of the day of the coup: "There's a friend of ours down in the lobby, Leo Lagakos. Says he wants asylum in the Embassy. Of course that's ridiculous. We can't give him asylum; he's a Greek." Day wanted me to talk with Lagakos, since he was too busy himself. My first reaction was to the surprising view of Day: who but a Greek would be seeking asylum in the American Embassy on a day like that?

Of course, it is true that the U.S. government takes a very cold-blooded and selfish attitude toward the question of asylum, observing the principle that if the asylum seeker is of value to the USG (for example, a defecting high Soviet official) then of course we grant him asylum (and safe conduct to the United States for thorough interrogation—"debriefing"), but if he is simply a poor soul who has fallen out of favor with his own government and is headed for the gallows, we take him in under our extraterritorial wing only if he is being pursued by an angry mob that threatens to tear him limb from limb, and then only temporarily.

Leonidas Lagakos was a Center Union deputy from Sparta, the youngest deputy in the recently dissolved parliament, an adherent of Andreas Papandreou and a wealthy man-about-town. He was a bachelor who had the distinction of appearing in public (usually at the Hilton Hotel) with a different glamorous but not entirely pretty girl every week, but he also spoke English, French, and German with native fluency even down to the latest popular slang phrases. I knew him only slightly, from having escorted an American congressman-elect who knew Leonidas on an evening on the town with him.

Leonidas came up to my office and explained that he was afraid to go home (he lived with his mother in an apartment house he owned on Alexandras Boulevard near the Embassy). He had observed his place surrounded by police, who he assumed were looking for him and would arrest him (as they had many other deputies of the Andreas camp) on sight. He wanted to spend the night in the Embassy until he figured out how and where he could go into hiding. I talked him out of this idea with the argument that his presence in the Embassy would soon become known to the police via their spies, who could be assumed to be among our employees, and then he would find it impossible to leave for the "duration" (of what, I did not say).

As we considered alternatives, he finally hit on the idea of moving into the apartment of one of his girlfriends, who could harbor him for a few days at least: "Her father's a general and probably in on the coup," Leonidas explained, "so they'll never look for me there." His logic escaped me, but I concurred. He left the Embassy after dark, and when I saw him again some days later in Kolonaki Square he said he had hid out with that girl and now everything was all right, as he had "squared himself" with the police. He remained at large throughout the subsequent months, rather ashamed that he was one of the few Center-Left deputies who had not been arrested (status symbols change drastically following a coup). Despite his reputation as a lightweight, I grew very fond of Leonidas, who from then on was always an available source of the latest political gossip and of the wildest possible theories to explain the erratic behavior of the new government.

Ambassador Talbot reacted quickly and efficiently to the sudden events on April 21, and dictated reports of his actions in a flurry of telegrams to Washington, some of which have been published in *FRUS* volume 16. He talked by phone with King Constantine, whom he found "blazingly angry" and who stated that "incredibly stupid ultra-right-wing bastards, having gained control of tanks, have brought disaster to Greece." The king confirmed that he had already sworn in a new government, but only after wringing a concession from the coup leaders that it be headed by a civilian. He also asked if U.S. Marines could be landed in Greece if necessary and how long it would take helicopters to reach the Tatoi Palace in the Athens suburbs to evacuate his family if needed.

With the aid of General Spandidakis and Nick Farmakis, the ambassador, accompanied by General Eaton, met with the new prime minister, Judge Constantine Kollias, and Spandidakis, the new vice premier, at 10 P.M. that evening and obtained several assurances: that those arrested would not be physically harmed, that order would be maintained, that Americans and American installations would be protected, and that the new government would be responsive to the orders of the king. The new leaders asserted that Kanellopoulos and the other ERE ministers who had been taken into custody would be released that night or the next day, as would George Papandreou, though not Andreas. Talbot and Eaton registered a strong complaint that American-furnished equipment had been used to overthrow the constitutional government of Greece. His interlocutors claimed that the coup had been prompted by a grave Communist threat to Greece, and argued that had the military not acted another Vietnam might have occurred. Earlier in the day Talbot had met with Margaret, Andreas's wife, and her father, Mr. Chant, who had come to the Embassy to plead for American intervention to save Andreas's life. The ambassador assured them that he had already done so and would by every means discourage the Greek military leaders from any resort to violence or bloodshed.

King Constantine never signed the decree suspending key articles of the 1952 constitution, in contradiction of the new government's action of publishing the decree in the *Official Gazette* as though it had been signed. The king was quite unhappy with the coup: when two of the officers who led it met with him at his Tatoi Palace after the takeover to advise him that they had acted in his name, he dismissed them from his presence with a curt order to send him "his general," that is, Spandidakis, his senior-ranking commander.

Constantine did not personally know the officers who had pulled off the coup (except for Pattakos), and he did not want to deal with lower-ranking types like colonels. He was also most angry that his longtime military aide and confidant, Major Arnaoutis, had been beaten up by coup officers who had placed him under arrest. The king demanded the release of Arnaoutis, then went to downtown Athens to confer with his political adviser, Dimitrios Bitsios, who could offer him neither solace nor advice, since Constantine could not find him (on hearing that a coup was under way, Bitsios had sought refuge in the British Embassy). There was also a report that the king visited the headquarters of the British intelligence service near Kolonaki Square. Constantine finally reached the Pentagon (as the headquarters of the Greek army in Athens was commonly known), where he was dismayed to find all his senior officers behaving in a cowardly fashion, lamely explaining that there was nothing they could do to resist the coup and suggesting that the king accept it as irreversible.

Constantine was perplexed and disturbed. He conferred repeatedly with Talbot and with the British ambassador, but neither gave him any encouragement to try to turn the coup around. It was said that the queen mother, Frederika, advised her son to accept the inevitable and to go along with Papadopoulos and his gang, distasteful as it might be. Constantine was present for the swearing in of the new cabinet, which, as he had insisted, was headed by a pro-palace civilian, Constantine Kollias, a judge. Kollias, however, was never anything but the most abject figurehead who took all of his orders from the coup group. Constantine was photographed with the new government, and when the picture was published in the press early in the next week it signaled his acceptance of the regime, although he continued to remind all callers privately in subsequent months that he had never signed the decree officially sanctioning the suspension of constitutional rights and guarantees.

I recall how we suspended part of our military aid. General Eaton met with the ambassador on the day of the coup, April 21, and expressed some concern that a shipload of tanks was about to arrive at the port of Piraeus to be turned over to the Greek army as part of our military assistance program. Since American-furnished tanks and other weapons had just been used to overturn the constitutional government of our ally, Eaton and Talbot agreed that it would not help the public image of the U.S. government locally or at home (especially at home) to have another batch of U.S.-origin tanks parading through the streets of Athens at this juncture. Talbot proposed that the ship in question be diverted to Turkey and that another shipload of tanks and other heavy weapons destined for the Greek forces be offloaded in Italy and stored there pending further clarification of the situation in Greece.

Thus began, as an emergency measure and with our own public image the sole consideration in mind, the policy of the partial military assistance suspension that remained in effect from the day of the coup until it was finally lifted in its entirety in September of 1970. In subsequent weeks this suspension policy was reexamined, and it was decided that its continuation might provide some political leverage we could use to get the new government to perform in ways we favored, in general to encourage it to restore constitutional, representative, democratic government to the Greek people.

Most of the executive branch in Washington, and especially the military, came to regret this suspension policy, for it later proved as difficult to reverse as it had been easy to impose in the heat of the coup crisis. It required years of exchanges of telegrams, memoranda, staff studies, presidential examination, argument and counterargument, and finally a National Security Council decision to reverse a "policy" that had been reached with very little consideration by Eaton and Talbot in a conference lasting only a few minutes, since the proper course of action at the time was obvious to everyone: "We don't want those U.S. tanks paraded through the streets of Athens right now."

On the day of the coup those of our Greek employees who showed up at the chancery were told that they needn't work that day but should return home and await developments. The following day, a Saturday, we were officially closed, although it was of course one of our busiest days of that year. Our loyal and able Political Section press briefer and translator, Aleko Tzinieris, reported for duty, and we decided to reestablish our regular routine by beginning the day with Aleko's review of the Athens press for the members of the Political Section assembled in Kay Bracken's office. Tzinieris began by reminding us that strict censorship had been imposed on the entire press and that the number of papers to be reviewed was somewhat diminished, since the two EDA papers had been shut down by the new regime; the conservative publisher Eleni Vlahou had stopped publication of her two papers because she declined to publish under a regime of censorship; and the apostate paper, *Eleftheria*, had not appeared since the coup, its editor, Panos Kokkas, having fled the country while the coup was in process. Kokkas, a slippery operator with friends in every camp, had been one of the very few people to receive enough advance warning to slip through the hands of the police and out of the country without being arrested.

Aleko suddenly stopped talking and then literally broke down, began weeping, clutching his sheaf of notes and newspapers to his chest, and, with great sobs interrupting his lament, recalled that he had worked for the Embassy for twenty years the coming month, having been hired away from the office of the British Information Service by the American aid mission set up to implement the Truman Doctrine, and now it had all come to this, the imposition of a military dictatorship, with the American Embassy apparently condoning it. How could we stand by and see this done to the Greek people? What had all our aid to Greece amounted to if it was going to end in this? Now the junta had just published a decree saying he would have to take his bird-hunting shotgun to the police station and turn it in. Where would it all end? Aleko said he simply couldn't continue and asked to be excused. Kay Bracken thereupon displayed one of her toughest sides and, with no feeling for the sensibilities of this longtime employee who was now so clearly ashamed to be associated with the official American establishment in his country, proceeded to argue with him that it was not our fault, we were not to blame, it was the fault of the Greeks themselves that their democratic system had collapsed, had been unable to weather the strains, and what were we supposed to do about it?

Six

REACTING TO THE COUP

"OUR PRESENT DILEMMA"

This scene upset me emotionally to such a degree that I was unable to concentrate on my work for the next hour. But later in the day I gathered myself together and set down on paper my first reactions to the coup, in the form of a memorandum to Mrs. Bracken, since I despaired of obtaining her undivided attention long enough to hear me out, busy as she was reporting developments to Washington. The memo was entitled "Our Present Dilemma" and opened as follows:

> I think you would agree that we now find ourselves in a most unsatisfactory situation, with a disastrous government in power, and no favorable alternative in sight. The adverse consequences for the United States that will flow from a military dictatorship should be apparent to all, and since I tried to set them forth in my draft memo of April 20 which I gave you yesterday, I won't repeat them here. Whether we like it or not, we are going to be held responsible by most Greeks for having installed this dictatorship, or at the very least for having acquiesced in it. Our only hope of salvaging something now would be to assist in toppling this government or at the very least to make it clear to all Greeks that we wholly disapprove of it.

The memo went on to say that we had two means of bringing down the government or of showing our disapproval of it: nonacceptance and withholding our military aid. I said I did not agree that no question of "recognition" existed, for although the chief of state remained unchanged, the new government was clearly unconstitutional. We could continue to recognize Greece as a state (this is the usual French formula), with our ambassador accredited to King Constantine, but we need not accept a regime that had installed itself, apparently over the opposition of the chief of state. We could restrict our relations to the king alone and inform him outright that we could not accept a military dictatorship; this would strengthen his hand in dealing with it, perhaps to the extent of assisting him to get rid of it. As for military aid, it was within our discretion to withhold it, and we could advise the king that we would be unable to continue it to the new regime.

"I cannot go along with the argument," I wrote, "that we must accept this government because we need to have 'contact' with it in order to influence developments. We will not influence developments, but will only play into their hands by acquiescing in their assumption of power. What may look to us like exercising influence over the government will look to the Greeks like working hand in glove with it."

I closed by suggesting that the best alternative would be for the king to install a civilian, apolitical, technicians' government responsible to himself, which would maintain all constitutional liberties except the franchise and which would hold elections one year hence, a year to be used to cleanse the political life of Greece of the poisons that had infected it.

My initial reactions to the coup were formulated on the basis of what we could learn about the backgrounds and orientations of its leading perpetrators and on my analysis of their first public declarations about their intentions and programs. I dismissed their claim that they had acted to prevent a Communist takeover of the country as the purest of propaganda, but I did accept the anticommunist credentials that they were thereby attempting to confirm. They were obviously pro-U.S., pro-West, pro-NATO. But what else were they?

I formed a very low opinion of their stature as individuals. We had very little information on which to base a judgment of them as potential political leaders—nothing about their social perspective or economic philosophy, for example—and not much as to their brains or capacity for leadership. All we had to go on, really, was their military records. Preliminary bio data indicated that they were not to be numbered among the outstanding officers of the Greek forces. In Greece the officers commanding the highest respect were those who had shown valor in combat and who had demonstrated an ability to command troops. There were many officers still in the services who had made outstanding records during World War II, in the Greek civil war, and in Korea.

Papadopoulos and most of his associates in the coup group were a lesser breed, officers who had tried to advance their careers through political intrigue, through plotting, by working in intelligence and personnel, backroom types who did not command the respect of their colleagues because they had not shown the ability to command and because they had not obtained advancement through brave acts on the field of battle, in World War II, the Greek civil war, or Korea. Many had very right-wing records, some had served with the notorious collaborationist "X" gangs during the German occupation, some, like Papadopoulos himself, had taken off their uniforms during the war and gone to school to try to get a better education than that provided by the military academies. Papadopoulos's matriculation at the Polytechnic was commendable from one point of view—the desire for higher education is certainly not denigrated by Greeks[1]—but it did not endear him to his military colleagues, who considered that the proper course for a soldier was to carry on the fight against the fascist powers in the Middle East or from the mountains of Greece.

Because the coup leaders were not men who commanded the respect of their fellow officers, I felt they would be able to rule only by intimidating the rest of the officer corps and the populace in general, not by obtaining their trust and support. The coup group's early public declarations indicated that they considered themselves a revolution. They had not seized power to prevent chaos from descending on the country—although that is what they said—but because they despised politics and politicians of all camps, because they believed that the Greek army was the only group fit to rule the country, the only clean and uncorrupt force. They displayed a disdain for their own countrymen; their public statements indicated that they did not believe the Greeks were capable of democracy.

I formed the impression that we were here facing not a temporary cleansing operation but rather a movement that regarded itself as permanent, a group that was not bent on preparing the country for civilian rule again one day but rather intended to stay in power for many years, for a generation perhaps. The programs they proclaimed themselves determined to carry out (including the political education of the Greek people) would take at least a generation if they could be accomplished at all. Since I did not think they were men who could ever win the allegiance of the Greek people, I saw nothing but trouble ahead, a permanent dictatorship that would not be acceptable to the people, who would eventually rise up to throw them out;

civil war would again erupt in Greece, with the United States definitely on the wrong side this time.

Our immediate problem was of course to determine what their relations would be with the United States, and ours with them. Although they counted on the alleged threat of a Communist coup to win themselves immediate acceptance by the Greek people, I thought they were probably counting on American fear of Andreas Papandreou to gain at least our acquiescence, with the CIA and the American military giving them wholehearted support for their own bureaucratic reasons. The Embassy's reporting in the very early days about public reaction to the coup was to the effect that there had been absolutely no popular resistance (after all, it *had* been bloodless, had it not?); there seemed to be general acceptance, or at least apathy, and general relief in some quarters. This seemed to me a very superficial analysis. There certainly had been relief expressed by some Greeks, but these had been diehard rightists who had been looking for any safe port in the face of their expected electoral defeat by the Papandreou forces; a military coup was certainly better than Andreas, according to them. Among nonpolitical Greeks apathy was the most common reaction. But liberals and leftists were outraged.

On Sunday, April 23, I recorded for Mrs. Bracken a summary of the reactions I had heard from a cross-section of my Greek friends and contacts, ranging from an apostate cabinet minister to my barber and including a journalist, a businessman, a lawyer, my landlady, a taxi driver, and other, generally sophisticated people. I listed the following as widely held opinions in Athens:

> (1) Bitterness at the Americans, whose tanks and guns were used to effect the coup. (2) The belief that the Americans condone the coup as being "good for Greece" if they didn't actually instigate it. (3) The conviction that King Constantine is behind or with the coup. (4) The belief that the coup leaders represent the ultra–right wing ideologically. (5) Shame and hurt pride that Greece "has now descended to the level of Guatemala." The analogy of Guatemala is cited specifically by many people, apparently because of the well-publicized involvement of the CIA with the overthrow of a regime there. (6) The conviction that the coup will only play into the hands of the Communists, who will ultimately profit from the hatred for the king, for the conservatives and for the Americans. (7) The belief that an underground resistance movement will soon begin to manifest itself. (8) Disgust with everything and everyone.

I noted also that the saddest aspect was to observe so much hurt pride "among a people who depend on their pride to sustain themselves through all adversities."

OTHER REACTIONS

I have focused thus far on my own reactions. What were the reactions of the other elements of the American mission? The CIA people were careful to keep their cards close to their chests, but it was not difficult to detect in them a decided admiration for the authors of a successful coup—a sort of professional camaraderie that was reinforced by the fact that some of the leaders of the new regime were alumni of the Greek intelligence service, the KYP, which our CIA had created and trained and worked with. In later years Andreas Papandreou liked to remark in his speeches that so far as he knew Papadopoulos had been the first professional intelligence operative to have propelled himself into a prime minister's job via a coup.[2]

The American military in Athens tended to display a certain reticence about expressing any views on matters political, usually insisting that their job was military assistance pure and simple. But at the time of the coup and subsequently they displayed a sensitivity toward any criticism of the new regime. They're military officers, aren't they? What's wrong with that? I found myself often having to state that I had nothing against military officers so long as they stuck to their military functions but that I definitely did have questions that I thought were legitimate when they installed themselves in place of a government. The American military were inclined to view Papadopoulos and his cohorts as fine, upstanding officers, patriotic, pro-Western, pro-American, honest and efficient, worthy of our support. My own view of Papadopoulos was that he was something else besides, that is, a fanatic who thought he was the savior of Greece, who had convinced himself that he alone was destined to rule Greece and was the only person in Greece capable of leading her out of the morass in which he thought she was then mired.

It is a truism about the Greeks that each one thinks he would make a better prime minister than the next fellow, and there are many coffeehouse conversations that begin with the pontifical phrase "If I were prime minister I would . . ." A man who thinks he could rule the country better than the incumbent prime minister is not only very common in Greece but could at worst be charged with blind egotism. However, a man who, like Papadopoulos, thinks he is the *only* Greek capable of being prime minister is by definition suffering from a degree of megalomania that borders on insanity.

In the early days after the coup the American military in Greece took a backseat. Perhaps they were more influential in Washington, where the Pentagon doubtless played a major role in policy making. But in Athens they deferred very much to the ambassador and the Embassy, except when the subject of military aid came up; and this subject increasingly became an irritant to JUSMAGG because our policy prevented them from engaging in any joint planning with their Greek military colleagues, and they were constantly placed in the embarrassing position of having to explain to the senior Greek officers why we had suspended a significant portion of our military aid. American officers in this position seem to be particularly sensitive to social slights: they came to us constantly with woeful tales about how some Greek general had turned his back on them and refused to talk, how the senior Greek officers were boycotting their receptions to show their displeasure over our military assistance policy, how General Angelis had barked angrily at General Eaton and blamed him for everything, when Eaton all along had been begging for a reversal of the aid-suspension policy. Most of the American officers suffered through their uncomfortable relationships like good soldiers; a few were so fanatically proregime that they went so far as to whisper around town that there were some Communists among the embassy officers who were hostile to the Greek regime.

JUSMAGG was only nominally under the ambassador's jurisdiction, for General Eaton's actual boss was EUCOM, which meant General David Burchinal. The latter took the position from the very beginning that the new regime in Greece was pro-U.S., pro-West, pro-NATO, anticommunist, and composed of fine Greek officers, so what was all the fuss about? Let's give them their military aid and get on with our jobs. EUCOM looked with great favor on what had happened in Greece, at the time of the coup and consistently throughout the following years. Burchinal's telegrams struck me as slightly ludicrous, because they took such a simplistic view of what was at stake in Greece (literally, these are good guys so let's help them or the bad guys will take over), and also as dangerous and highly out of line, since I did not think it was EUCOM's job to be analyzing the internal political situation in Greece and to be recommending U.S. government policies to Washington.

The American whose reaction was the most important of all, at least in Athens, was of course Ambassador Talbot. As Townsend Hoopes wrote of Talbot's mentor Dean Rusk, he had "a knack for arguing by dubious analogy."[3] I recall that Talbot was fond of making comparisons among the personalities of the various countries of the region over which he had had jurisdiction in the State Department, the Near East and South Asia bureaus.

Thus, he would refer to Zulfiqar Bhutto as "the South Asian Andreas Papandreou," and in another context he would note that Andreas was behaving in Greece just the way Bhutto had in Pakistan. This struck me as wrongheaded at the time, for the differences between Bhutto and Papandreou were at least as significant as their similarities, never mind the differences between Pakistan and Greece, but I then had no idea how pernicious an effect this determination of policy on the basis of analogy rather than analysis could have.[4] The thing that Bhutto and Papandreou had most in common, from Talbot's point of view, was that they caused trouble for the United States. From his perspective they were simply troublemakers, so it was perhaps not so necessary to try to understand their political roles within the contexts of their quite different countries.

But this analogy carried over into Talbot's reaction to the April 21 coup. He immediately concluded that this event found its explanation in the observation that "Andreas Papandreou was clearly too rich for Greece's blood." According to Talbot, the former Greek American economics professor had brought on the coup single-handedly simply by being an indigestible element in the Greek body politic. Talbot had made a bow in the direction of his own professed liberal American sympathies by referring to "the rape of Greek democracy" in his first long telegram to Washington analyzing the April 21 coup, but apparently he thought that the chief rapist was the politician then in enforced residence at the Pikermi Hotel and soon to be moved to the Averoff Prison, rather than the colonel sitting in the Prime Ministry telling Kollias what to do.

Talbot's most unfortunate analogy was to view the April 21, 1967, coup in Greece as a manifestation similar to the 1960 coup in Turkey, the aftermath and working out of which had been within his purview as Near East–South Asia assistant secretary. In pouncing on this analogy he was crucially abetted by Kay Bracken, who had been his subordinate in Washington as head of GTI, the Greece-Turkey-Iran office. They were viewing the Greek coup in the most optimistic light possible when they compared it to the 1960 military takeover in Turkey, for the Turkish military had stayed in power only eighteen months, had prepared a new constitution within one year, had had it ratified by the people and placed into effect shortly thereafter, and had held elections and installed a coalition civilian government six months later. If the postcoup situation had developed in a similar fashion in Greece, the United States would have been most fortunate indeed.

But the Turkish analogy being promoted by Talbot and Bracken impressed me as wholly misleading and therefore dangerous. The Turkish military had intervened in politics to eliminate from power the Menderes regime because it had become autocratic and was wrecking Turkish democracy and threatening to implant itself permanently in power as a dictatorship. The Turkish military, carriers and longtime defenders of the tradition of the Atatürk social and political revolution, had intervened to *preserve* the Turkish democratic state, to uphold the Turkish constitution, and to prevent autocracy. They threw out those bent on rigging the elections, banned them from politics, and held honest elections that brought the political opposition (Inönü's RPP) to power.

Papadopoulos and company, by way of contrast, had intervened to prevent elections from being held, they had torn up the Greek constitution, and they had then installed their own authoritarian and dictatorial regime, which they clearly (to my mind, at least) intended to make into a permanent institution. What is revolutionary and what is counterrevolutionary in politics obviously depends on one's perspective, but the essential difference between the Turkish and Greek military interventions was that the latter was antidemocratic while the former was designed to preserve a democratic system. This seemed to me such an elementary and self-evident difference that I could not understand how Talbot and Bracken could be so blind to the realities. I still do not understand it except to note that they must have felt so relieved that things had gone as well as they had in Turkey in 1961 that they were hoping a similar result could emerge in Greece in 1967 or 1968. What they hoped to see they began to see as reality—a case of wishful thinking.

Aside from the problem of "policy making by analogy rather than analysis," what most influenced the senior officers in the American mission in Greece in April of 1967 was that they were paralyzed in advance by their fear of the coming to power of Andreas Papandreou. They could see no viable alternative to his victory in the scheduled May elections, and they could not face the prospect of his electoral triumph. The coup intervened to prevent this horrendous event, and they were profoundly relieved. This euphoric relief precluded them from making an objective analysis of what was happening because their psyches were overwhelmed by fear of what might have happened.

Furthermore, all the senior officers—Talbot, Anschuetz, Maury, Bracken—suffered from the psychological disposition natural to bureaucratic executives of being extremely defensive about their own past policy decisions. All four of them had been intimately involved with our policies toward 1960s Greece leading up to the coup, and an objective observer might have analyzed those policies to show that they led inevitably to a coup d'état that would be presented to the United States on a platter and that the United States would have to accept gratefully since all other "solutions" had become either impracticable or unacceptable. Could these four people have sat down in April 1967, looked back over the prior five to six years, and tried to understand how we had gotten ourselves into such an awful predicament, a predicament that found us not merely forced to accept a military coup d'état in Greece but actually forced to *welcome* it since no conceivable alternative was in the least bit attractive to us?

This was above all a time for a fresh look at U.S. policy toward Greece, but only a brand new team at the top could have been expected to take an honestly fresh look. Could any one of those officials, for example, have made a dispassionate analysis of the phenomenon of Andreas Papandreou at that stage?

On Sunday, April 23, Louise and I had lunch with Admiral John Toumbas, foreign minister in the Stephanopoulos apostate government, and his family at the Royal Yacht Club in Tourkolimano. Toumbas had been a war hero. After his destroyer was torpedoed off the Turkish coast during the Second World War, causing the loss of his bow section, he had closed enough watertight doors to make the rest of the ship reasonably seaworthy, and had then backed his ship all the way across the Mediterranean to Alexandria. Following retirement he had entered politics as a liberal. He was a longtime Venizelist who had been expelled from the navy for participation in an antiroyalist plot in the mid-thirties but had reentered the service with the onset of the war at government (Metaxas) initiative. He considered the April 21 coup a disaster for Greece, for the United States, for NATO, all this despite the fact that he was violently opposed to Andreas Papandreou, a sentiment that had accounted for his split with George Papandreou and for his having joined the apostate government. We had developed a personal relationship with Toumbas because he was a close career navy friend of retired admiral Vasillis Kyris, the stepfather of my brother Mike's wife, Mary.

Toumbas ostentatiously seated Louise and me in the places of honor at the table, whether out of diplomatic courtesy alone I do not know, but I believe it may have been out of admiration for the United States, which he believed had not yet accepted the coup, since we had engaged in no public act of obvious recognition up to that time. Perhaps he was hoping that we would not recognize the new regime. At any rate he was extremely proud that the Royal Navy was still holding out, as he knew from his close friends in the active duty officer corps. During lunch word came to him from a colleague that the navy had finally capitulated and was now going to support the coup. Tears filled Toumbas's eyes, and he stopped eating and pushed himself away from the table. So it was all over, he said in French, the navy has gone along! This meant that the king was going along too, for the navy was extremely royalist, more so than any other service, and if they had given up then that meant the king had given up. What will happen to us now? Admiral Toumbas was devastated.

I recount this vignette because it goes to show that the success of the April 21 coup was by no means instantaneous: two and a half days later its opponents such as Toumbas were still hoping that there would be resistance from loyalist military elements and that the king would not acquiesce. He even hoped, apparently, that the Americans would refuse to accept the coup!

The fact is that the Papadopoulos coup was pulled off with a good deal of technical brilliance, as coups go, with very little bloodshed and—most important of all—no intra-army fighting at all. The explanation is that Papadopoulos preempted the Generals' coup, and his timing was superb. He launched his takeover just after a meeting in Athens of all the top military brass, gathered from all over the country, and the takeover was timed to catch all the senior commanders on their way back to their provincial posts or just after their arrival at home. These senior commanders were well aware of the Generals' coup being planned by Spandidakis, and they were also aware that the chief of the General Staff had just ordered a delay in its execution. But when the messages ordering the carrying out of the Papadopoulos coup arrived at the various military unit headquarters, the generals receiving them assumed that Spandidakis had pushed the button and they reacted accordingly, that is, loyally—they supposed—to Spandidakis and to the king. When they woke up to the realization that a batch of colonels had taken over, it was too late to do anything about it, except to go along, especially as that was what the king gave the appearance of doing.

MAC THOMPSON'S ATTEMPT

After the luncheon with Toumbas I stopped by Malcolm Thompson's house in Psychiko. I was disturbed by the course our embassy had embarked upon, and I wanted to trade thoughts with him, for Mac Thompson was my only colleague in the Embassy—at least on the political-executive side—who saw things at all the way I did and with whom I could have a sympathetic exchange of ideas. Mac showed me a memo to Mrs. Bracken that he had written the previous day and that his wife had just typed up. He intended to give it to our boss the next day in the office, with a copy to DCM Anschuetz. In the spring of 1971, when I was writing this book, he sent me a copy of the memo, with the following comment: "Not bad as I re-read it now considering it was done in haste the day after the event. . . . I don't know whether

Anschuetz ever saw it. He never mentioned it. I know the Amb. did not. Kay gave it back to me 3–4 days later without comment."

It is a six-page paper that examines in systematic fashion the problem of U.S. policy toward Greece following the takeover by "a relatively small extreme rightist group within the Army." As factors bearing on the problem, Thompson listed U.S. non-involvement in the coup and lack of foreknowledge, despite which (he wrote) at least half the Greek people would believe we had engineered it or had done nothing to prevent it. The extreme Right (which he estimated at 10–15 percent of the Greek people) would welcome U.S. acquiescence in a military dictatorship.

Although faced with a fait accompli, the United States still possessed a number of options (leverage) that could determine the continued success or failure of the new regime, including the withholding of the military assistance program, diplomatic action (recall of ambassador, condemnation in UN and/or NATO), and a presidential or other official U.S. government statement condemning the change of government by a nondemocratic process. Thompson noted that a failure to exercise any of these or other options would be regarded by the overwhelming majority of the Greek people as "acceptance of the present government and the means by which it came to power." Another factor to be considered, Thompson wrote, was that a U.S. failure to dissociate itself from the dictatorship would cause the United States to suffer a serious ideological defeat in the eyes of the free world and particularly in the emerging nations of Asia, Africa, and Latin America. The Communists would be handed a propaganda weapon to be exploited in connection with Vietnam and elsewhere to depict the United States as an "antidemocratic" and "imperialist" force in the world.

The memorandum then proceeded to analyze, in an entirely dispassionate manner, three possible courses of action, with the five or six advantages and disadvantages of each course listed. (Henry Kissinger did not invent the technique of choosing among "options.") The first alternative would be to support the new government and to seek through exertion of influence on the king and military leadership to moderate its policies and steer it in a more constitutional direction. The objective of this course would be to reestablish the control of the king and the former military leaders or officers of their caliber and outlook, and ultimately to bring about a return to civilian control and elections.

Thompson's second alternative read, "Maintain hands off, aloof and critical attitude while privately informing military leadership that unless it steers more moderate course and otherwise behaves U.S. may be obliged to suspend military aid and take other measures to reduce its support of present

GOG."⁵ The third alternative was to take immediate and forceful action to bring about the overthrow or dismissal by the king of the present military government, restoration of the constitution, and appointment of a service government to conduct elections as soon as practicable (two to six months). The first of the steps to be taken under this option (if the recognition issue had already been passed by) should be official condemnation of the coup and the announcement of a suspension of relations from Washington (by the president or secretary of state) followed by a cutoff of all military assistance and other forms of aid to Greece. If the situation required it (Thompson deemed this unlikely), we should be prepared, at the request of the king, to take appropriate military action to remove the leaders of the coup from power.

The lists of advantages and disadvantages concerned mainly the efficacies of these several courses of action, which groups in Greece and internationally they would appeal to or displease, chances of success, effect on NATO and U.S. installations in Greece, and various other considerations, including ideological and propaganda concerns. Did space permit, they would merit repetition here in full, for the remarkable thing about this paper is how intelligent the analysis is, especially when one considers that it was written in haste one day after the coup. Few analytical policy memoranda written in the heat of a crisis merit close rereading years after the event. A second remarkable feature of this paper is its boldness, not only in recommending forceful action to overthrow the regime, but also in advocating lesser courses that would have cost Ambassador Talbot his job; it takes a brave Foreign Service officer to suggest the necessity that his boss give up his post in the higher interests of U.S. foreign policy!

Thompson's conclusion did not mince words:

> The first alternative, that of tacit approval of the present government, ties the U.S. to a losing cause, since dictatorships inevitably fail. Such a course of action will do great damage to the U.S. position as leader of the Free World. Regardless of the evolution of events in Greece, we cannot afford the cost. The second alternative is essentially a delaying tactic. It bears the grave danger of allowing the situation to pass beyond the point of return before any action is taken. It also is a compromise on an issue where history has shown there is no middle ground. To be effective it requires quiet, behind-the-scenes diplomacy—an almost impossible task in the present explosive situation. It also leaves us vulnerable to charges from the

left of supporting the present regime since it is a policy that cannot be publicly enunciated.

This leaves overt U.S. intervention the best alternative. Although the most dangerous, it is the only one with a chance of saving democracy in Greece, be it under a Constitutional Monarchy or otherwise, and at the same time preserving the U.S. image in the Free World. In the long run it has the best chance of maintaining the ties of friendship that have bound the American and Greek people for over a hundred years. It is also a course of action for which we possess the power tools (political, economic, and military) necessary for execution. If we act quickly and decisively, the odds on success are good. In all likelihood once we make our position unequivocally clear, we could expect the support of our NATO allies. Finally, it is the only course of action consistent with America's democratic heritage.

The course the U.S. government ultimately adopted was a mixture of Thompson's first and second alternatives; he and I were the only people in the entire American mission who advocated the third course. Marion Mitchell of the Greek desk in Washington drafted the Department's basic paper that explained the policy we adopted then and followed for months and years afterward. According to her paper, we faced three choices following the Papadopoulos coup: (1) we could break relations; (2) we could embrace the new government; (3) we could recognize it and work with it, attempting to influence it to return the country to a democratic regime. The choice to be made was of course obvious (according to Marion): cutting ourselves off from any contact with the new regime would be a ridiculous policy, for we would then be able to exercise absolutely no influence in Greece; and to embrace it would have been contrary to our principles. Alternative three of the Mitchell scheme was the only sensible course. The option of encouraging the replacement of the Papadopoulos gang with something more to the liking of the mass of the Greeks and the Americans was apparently never considered, or if it was, it was discarded as impracticable or at best very risky.[6]

That Sunday after the coup, Malcolm Thompson and I decided that since we were unlikely to get anywhere with Kay Bracken we would wait a couple of days in the hope that Anschuetz would read Thompson's analysis, and we would then seek a meeting with him to discuss it. Anschuetz appeared to be the one senior officer who might possibly be sympathetic to our approach.

A DRAFT TELEGRAM

On the afternoon of Monday, April 24, Kay Bracken suddenly darted into my office and handed me a draft telegram to Washington that she had just prepared (with whose help if anyone's I do not know). She said if I had any comments I wished to make on it to please give them to her within ten minutes, as the ambassador was anxious to get the cable on the wire to Washington. I read it hurriedly and dashed off my comments on the typewriter, marveling at the haste with which we were proceeding on such critical questions.

Mrs. Bracken's draft recapitulated the Embassy's contacts with the new regime since the coup, with some nearly incredible aspects. For example, it was noted that in his initial call on the new authorities Friday evening, principally to protest the continuing restrictions on the movements of U.S. citizens, Talbot had addressed Kollias as "Sir" and Spandidakis as "General" instead of using their new ministerial titles (such care not to accord recognition!). Anschuetz's contacts with Farmakis had been on the basis of "existing personal relationship," the cable assured Washington, and were for the purpose of eliciting information, not for establishing a formal relationship. General Eaton had called on Spandidakis to explain about the status of our MAP (Military Assistance Program): currently arriving shipments were being offloaded onto a U.S.-controlled dock and held in our custody, "a very temporary measure pending sorting out of situation." The CIA had established the mission's sole contact with any of the coup instigators to that date.

The draft cable then discussed problems arising from the lack of contact with the new regime, such as how to handle the upcoming visit of the director of the international division of the National Park Service! Talbot argued that while other countries could stall on having dealings with the new regime, the American Embassy's "pervasive relationships at technical as well as political levels" required prompt adoption of a policy. The ambassador proposed to continue normal working relationships at lower levels, and as for higher-level contacts, "I believe we must either prepare to resume them or oppose this regime by suspension of mutual security and other cooperative programs." The latter course, according to Talbot, would be of value only if there were a possibility that it would bring down the regime. A somewhat murky passage of the draft then stated: "I cannot now see consequences of collapse of this regime under pressure, but assume this would occur only if the King, under pressure of American disapproval, were to rally some military elements to oppose Pattakos's tanks. This presumably would mean civil war, in which King's support in civilian population might be mobilized primarily by far leftists, thus in effect making the King 'captive' of Communists." Talbot's conclusion was that we should work out a modus vivendi with the new regime, as the king would need to do (and was then in process of doing), if the United States and NATO were to maintain a presence in Greece and if there were to be any hope of a restoration of constitutional government. Talbot then proposed three conditions we should lay down in return for being willing to work with the new regime: that we not raise a question of recognition but explain the problem of proving to the American public that the regime's objective was to return to constitutional processes as quickly as possible; that we educate them about the effect American public opinion has on MAP appropriations and also enlist their help in educating international press opinion as to their good intentions; that "we utilize the dialogue regarding long-term MAP planning as a means of pressuring the government by installments to formulate and announce their program of evolution toward a constitutional regime."

This was not the only telegram of the period in question that dealt with critical policy decisions about the new regime, but it is illustrative of the Embassy's posture in its concentration on appearances rather than realities (public opinion and promises rather than performance), in its unwillingness to face up to the really hard issues (for example, just what kind of regime were we now dealing with?), and in its plain wrongheadedness (the analysis that ended up with the king, supported by the Communists, fighting against Pattakos's tanks left me breathless).

My comments on it to Mrs. Bracken began with this statement: "I appreciate the opportunity to comment. For what it is worth, I disagree wholly with the policy recommendations set forth in the draft." My counterproposal was that we arm the king with the weapons of firm American disapproval of the regime and a decision to suspend U.S. MAP so long as it remained in power and to encourage the king to work with the senior officers of the army to overturn the coup, reassert army discipline, and restore civilian government. I argued that the army leadership was loyal to the king rather than to the new colonels and that the king by so acting could rally not only the army behind himself but the whole population—Right, Center, and Left.

While admitting that such an attempt would be hazardous, and might if it failed cost the king his throne and us our relations with this dictatorship government, I thought the risks worth taking

> because I sincerely believe that if the King accepts this government he will lose his throne eventually anyway. His acceptance of this

government will eventually turn practically the whole population against the monarchy, which would disappear in the aftermath of the dictatorship's fall, and fall it inevitably must. If we think that dictatorship government can be preserved permanently in Greece, then the proposed policy paper makes sense. But I don't think a dictatorship can last here for very long, and by very long I mean even ten years. We *must* think in long-range terms now. Longer than ten years.

I then discussed the risks for the United States of the course I advocated, namely, that it might cost us our relations with the regime if we failed.

This to me is not a grave matter, because in the long run this government will not be around and we still will be, and Greece needs the U.S. much more than the U.S. needs Greece. Failure to move *against* this government will, however, cause the U.S. to be identified with the dictatorship, and when it falls we will fall too. Someday constitutional democracy will be restored to Greece. In the elections that follow that restoration the king, the United States, and the Greek army will all be candidates. And how the three behaved during the last ten days of April 1967 may well determine the fate of those three candidates in the elections. I think our chances of being voted down (and out) in those elections will be very high if we now fail to move against this government and by that failure become identified with it in the eyes of all Greeks of all partisan persuasions.

My final comment concerned the effect on the U.S. world image of our acceptance of yet another right-wing, unconstitutional, repressive regime in a friendly country.

MAC AND I TRY AGAIN

The following day, April 25, Thompson and I asked for a meeting with Anschuetz. He strolled into Thompson's office at about noon and said, "I believe you gentlemen wished to see me?" As Thompson recalled in his letter to me in the spring of 1971: "I certainly do remember our session with Norb. He standing by the window twirling his gold watch charm and surveying us with that look of utter disdain. What a scene." Not knowing whether or not Anschuetz had had a chance to read his paper, Thompson began with the analysis contained in it. After two or three minutes the DCM began fidgeting, walking back and forth in front of the window, obviously most uncomfortable. I interrupted Thompson, thinking that our time was running out, and launched into a pitch of my own along the lines of the memo quoted immediately above. I had not talked for more than five minutes at most before Anschuetz excused himself, saying he was late for a luncheon date, and he hastened out the door of Thompson's office. We shrugged at each other with weary resignation and went back to our work, such as it was.

It was at about that time, if I recall correctly, that Ambassador Talbot dispatched John Day to Washington in an attempt to have him communicate orally to the Washington policy end what he felt he was failing to get through by cable. Talbot was also totally perplexed as to what line Washington wished him to take vis-à-vis the new regime, and he hoped that Day would be able to elicit from Brewster, Rockwell, and company some guidance as to what we should be doing. Day's return from Washington the following week brought very little illumination other than confirmation that the State Department was as confused in person as it appeared to be at the end of the telegraphic channel.

The meeting with Anschuetz had discouraged me but it did not shut me up. On April 25 I sent two additional memoranda to Mrs. Bracken commenting on the central policy problem, and I then began to give copies to Anschuetz as well, on the basis that our discussion that day had legitimized my sending my thoughts directly to him rather than via my boss. The first paper addressed to them that day presented four additional considerations that argued for a policy of trying to topple the government rather than trying to work with the dictatorship to change its nature or its policies. The first consideration was that the coup leaders were shaky still (I alluded to a CIA report about Spandidakis's concern over the American reaction to the coup), and American disapproval would be enough to make them cave in, whereas if we waited until the regime had consolidated its position our ability to influence the situation would decline.

My second point was that by accepting and trying to work with the dictatorship we would be backing a losing horse. The third was that the recommended policy of working with the regime would not work: even if we forced the coup group to announce a program of evolution toward a constitutional regime, they would never implement it.

> The regime needs our approval now, but once they have obtained it our leverage will gradually disappear. . . . To ask the dictators to restore a constitutional regime would be to ask them to put their

heads on the block, for any successor government would declare them to be traitors and would act accordingly. Is there a single historical example of a dictatorship that has remained in office for an indefinite period and then voluntarily surrendered power to a constitutional successor? I know of none. Dictatorships are abolished only by war, assassination, suicide or the natural death of the dictator, by an internal coup in which one general or colonel replaces another, or by popular revolution. They do not abolish themselves.

My final point had to do with Vietnam, where we had acted forcefully to have a constituent assembly elected, a constitution promulgated, a president elected, and so forth, in order to legitimize the government and to show that we were fighting there to preserve a free and democratic regime.

To condone the imposition of an unconstitutional, unpopular, illegitimate regime in Greece, an allied nation where only twenty years ago we committed ourselves to assist in the fight for a free and democratic country, would be to suffer an intolerable setback in our effort to justify the Vietnamese war in world opinion. The opposition to the war in Vietnam among our allies, among the neutralist nations, and among a segment of the American people—and this opposition is the greatest threat to a resolution of the problem satisfactory to us—arises from the conviction that we are not really fighting there to sustain a free and democratic regime, but that we are fighting to maintain in power an unpopular, military, oppressive though anti-Communist regime that would collapse without our support. The damage to our position in Vietnam that would be caused by our acceptance of such a regime in Greece should rule out any consideration of a policy of acquiescence here.

With John Day in Washington a larger share of the reporting on internal developments fell to me, although, as I noted earlier, our normal surfeit of political reporting officers in the higher reaches of the Embassy meant that the burden was shared among a number of people. I still had plenty of time to bombard my superiors with unasked-for advice. I sent Bracken and Anschuetz a second memo on April 25 with some thoughts on what might be done if the coup could be reversed, as I had all along been advocating we try to bring about. This was a somewhat speculative operational plan that does not merit examination today, except in passing.

I recommended close consultations with our NATO allies to work out a common policy. I proposed that the king restore the army to the control of officers loyal to himself.

Mrs. Bracken penned a marginal query: "How do you do this when they were retired within 24 hours?" My answer, unstated at the time, would have been: they were obviously not all retired, as the king's abortive countercoup in December demonstrated.

The king would then install a civilian government of technicians and bureaucrats to hold office until elections were held a year later. I then discussed a reformed electoral law.

Marginal comment by Bracken: "What does this mean? Ayub's Basic Democracy system?" Note the Pakistan analogy again.

Its effect would have been to bar the precoup politicians from the next election, allowing a new crop of leaders to emerge, with the incidental advantage of making the election something other than a plebiscite on the monarchy and a judgment of the Greek army and the United States, permitting all three of these elements to accept its results with equanimity. My final proposal concerned the Communists and how to deal with them in the preelectoral interim period, my point being that the best course would be not to drive the Greek Communist leadership underground.

I concluded as follows: "These ideas are thrown out without a great deal of reflection because there is not time now. But something along these lines has a much better chance of saving Greece for the West, I believe, than does the present dictatorship."

Mrs. Bracken wrote a comment at the bottom of this memo in her standard purple ink: "RK—we agree re disadvantages of dictatorship but what next must be feasible without bloodshed. KB."

I am not proud of this memorandum, and it strikes me today as an effort forged in desperation, an attempt to compromise my own best hopes with what I thought my superiors might buy, but I was trying anything to get them off the track they were on and onto some path that was headed in the right (to my mind) direction. I was no longer thinking clearly, it seems to me now, but was rather jumping from instrument to instrument, like a maniacal one-man band, trying his damnedest to attract some attention.

Seven

DEALING WITH THE NEW GOVERNMENT

A CALL ON KOLLIAS

With John Day in Washington attempting to explain things to Rockwell and Brewster, it fell to me to accompany the ambassador (at his request) on his first formal call on Prime Minister Constantine Kollias on the morning of Wednesday, April 26. Because the king had attended the swearing in of the new cabinet and been photographed with them, Washington had apparently accepted the inevitable and decided to carry on more or less normal relations with the coup regime. It pretended that no gesture of recognition was needed, as the king still sat on his throne and the ambassador was accredited to the king.

Because my spoken Greek was not yet adequate to fulfill the role of official interpreter (although I had no difficulty in following the Greek side of the conversation), we took along Stephen Calligas, the Embassy's longest-serving local employee. Prior to and even after the McCarthy period and its resultant paranoia about security, Calligas served as interpreter for a succession of American ambassadors in Athens for their most sensitive conversations with Greek leaders. Stephen was the proverbial soul of discretion; had anyone ever accused him of repeating an embassy secret, even to his wife, he would have fainted dead away and gone straight to the corner of heaven reserved for loyal local employees of American embassies.

As it turned out, Stephen did not do the interpreting that day, for Prime Minister Kollias had with him his own quite competent man. While I sat poised to take notes, Ambassador Talbot and Kollias exchanged the usual stiff pleasantries indulged in by two personalities conscious of their roles but lacking any human content in their mutual relations. They had met only once before that day, a brief encounter on the evening after the coup.

The amenities completed, Kollias turned to business. Sober of mien, he asked the ambassador if it was true that the American Sixth Fleet was on its way to Phaleron Bay. No, replied Talbot, not so far as he knew; in some perplexity, he asked why the prime minister wished to know. Because, said Kollias, a rumor was circulating in Athens that the American Sixth Fleet was on its way to Piraeus and on arrival would order the resignation of the government headed by Mr. Kollias. With his somewhat inexpressive smile, Talbot responded that this rumor was of course ridiculous. Regardless of where the Sixth Fleet was at that moment, which he did not know, it was not going to intervene in Greek internal affairs, and the prime minister could rest assured that there was nothing at all to this story.

Visibly relieved, Kollias relaxed. Only when the tenseness went out of his body could one see how much his hands, clasped on his desk in front of him, were shaking. "Excellency," he said, "would you be willing to issue a denial of this rumor in the name of your embassy?"

Thinking quickly and most adroitly, Talbot replied, "Mr. Prime Minister, you know as well as I do that there are a great many rumors circulating in Athens these days, more than the usual number. If I started issuing denials of rumors, there would be no end to it, and the rumor that would then be believed would be the one that I had not heard about and had therefore not been able to deny. That is a losing proposition, Mr. Prime Minister, I assure you."

"I can see your point," responded Kollias. "But would you have any objection if I issued a denial?"

"None at all," said Talbot, "but I think the same strictures would apply in your case. And you might just give it more currency by denying it."

Kollias said he understood the ambassador's point quite well, but the situation he had to cope with was that a large group of people at that very moment were standing on the broad sandy beach at Phaleron Bay, some with binoculars, waiting for the fleet to come in to depose the government. And according to the rumor, these people were preparing to guide our marines up the hill to the Parliament Building, where the prime minister and the ambassador were meeting. The ambassador, he added, could understand what anxieties such a situation might give rise to, even if it had no basis in fact.

The conversation turned to other subjects—the intentions of the new government, the justification for the coup, the composition of the cabinet, relations with the United States, our Military Assistance Program, NATO, and I do not recall what else. I kept notes assiduously, knowing that as soon as we got back to the Embassy I would have to draft the reporting telegram to Washington on this important first official conversation with the nominal leader of the new regime. But I could not get over the shaking hands of the prime minister and his obvious concern about the intentions of the U.S. government toward his government. I kept thinking: But they are so afraid! They have absolutely no confidence. If the ambassador said "Boo!" old Kollias would collapse behind his desk and have a heart attack!

I did prepare the reporting telegram, a rather long one. Washington was obviously hanging on our every word, for this indeed had been our first high-level, direct, *official* contact with the new regime. I reported the conversation exactly as it had occurred, and to his credit Ambassador Talbot approved it as submitted to him, with only minor revisions and no deletions. My exact recording of Kollias's concern about the Sixth Fleet rumor must have made Washington wonder—if nothing else had made them wonder up to that time.

The ambassador had been guarded in his response to Kollias about the Sixth Fleet. In fact, a Sixth Fleet task force group was then in Greek waters, undoubtedly brought there a day after the coup as a result of the king's request on April 21, when he feared for his life and asked for a possible evacuation lift for himself and his family if that became necessary. It was then in "Greek waters"—the Aegean—but definitely not headed to Piraeus to overthrow the new Greek government. It was available in the area, however, if and when needed.

I must interject at this point my serious surprise and distress that this important reporting telegram was not included in volume 16 of *Foreign Relations of the United States,* covering our relations with Cyprus, Greece, and Turkey from 1964 to 1968. I can think of no reasonable explanation for this omission, which certainly violated the congressional insistence that these volumes provide a "thorough, accurate and reliable documentary record." This telegram provided irrefutable evidence that five days after the April 21 coup the Papadopoulos regime was still on extremely shaky ground and could have been overturned with minimal effort.

In Athens on April 26, 1967, Talbot, in his characteristic fashion, gave no sign that Prime Minister Kollias's apprehension about a Sixth Fleet intervention had made any particular impression on him. That it had a huge impact on me is evident from the short memo I wrote to Mrs. Bracken (copy to Anschuetz) the following morning (April 27), when the full import of the Kollias conversation hit me. I give it here in full, mixed metaphors and all:

> Subject: U.S. Posture Toward Coup
>
> I feel as though I am beating a dead horse, but the more people I talk with, Greeks and non-Greeks, the stronger my conviction is:
>
> 1. that we could topple this regime with no more than a flick of the finger. To wit, a strong statement disapproving, and a clear refusal to accept, this government, would be like blowing a puff of air on a house of cards. A mere rumor that the Sixth Fleet is heading this way has them quaking in their boots.
>
> 2. that because Greeks feel it would be so easy for us to force the resignation of this regime, guilt-by-acquiescence will be much, much greater. Since they believe it would be so easy for us to get rid of it, they must conclude that we are happy with what has happened.
>
> 3. that even beyond the question of the hatred we will reap later on for having accepted this regime, we are missing a golden opportunity to gain the lasting love and loyalty of 90 percent of the Greek people, who cannot themselves dispose of this regime but who would be eternally grateful to us if we would do so. Such opportunities occur for few nations and at few times, and once rejected they are not repeated.

Mrs. Bracken read the memo that day and returned it to me with the following purple-ink notation at the bottom: "RK You cannot topple a regime in these circumstances unless there are forces ready to assume counter coup posture. As the King told the Amb he has now lost confidence that senior cmdrs or others King might know would go along—he is in how many divisions has the Pope state. If anyone could figure out divisions & whether substitute in these circumstances would not be continuation same kind dictatorship see nothing to do except pressures on this govt to behave. Do you have any ideas on military situation?"

Granted that this was nearly a week after the coup and that every senior embassy officer was tired and overworked, this comment strikes me as a singularly inarticulate analysis of the issues at stake. Just what was I supposed to know about the military situation? If, with thousands of American military in the country and hundreds of civilian spooks, it was I who was supposed to know how many divisions the king had on his side, then our intelligence was spectacularly lacking in the areas that counted.

Norbert Anschuetz dropped his (carbon) copy of the above memo on Ambassador Talbot's desk at the conclusion of one of their discussions that day, unbeknownst to me. This gesture apparently communicated to the ambassador his first hint that there was any disagreement at all among the officers of the Embassy about the policy we had been pursuing since April 21 (to say nothing of the period before April 21). On Friday, April 28, his secretary told me that the ambassador would like to see me.

I asked, "About what?"

She did not know, but said with a smile, "The DCM showed him your memo. Maybe about that." She explained what memo she meant, and I went into the ambassador's office an hour later not knowing what his reaction to my dissent would be.

I do not recall the details of the conversation now, but he opened with something like the following: "You say here with a flick of the finger. Just what does that mean?"

I explained that I believed it was still not too late for us to turn the situation around, to get the government back into the hands of the king, the army back under the control of its senior generals—in effect to overturn the coup. Unemotional as always, Talbot gave no visible reaction to my somewhat aggressive presentation, not so much as a raised eyebrow. I went back over the arguments contained in all of my memoranda of that week, since I assumed that Talbot had seen none of them. I went back as far as the long April 20 memo analyzing the situation on the eve of the coup and predicting the event, though three weeks off on the timing.

Talbot was fascinated by questions of timing and asked to see that paper, as well as the other memoranda, whose content I tried to cover as best I could in that half-hour conversation. When I remarked that I had mulled over the ideas in the April 20 memo for nearly a week until the conversation with Bruce Lansdale had finally stimulated me to set my thoughts down on paper, Talbot said dryly: "Next time you have a bright idea, don't wait a week before passing it on." I did not give the response I should have (one of those killing phrases that one thinks of only after the conversation has terminated): "But what good would it have done? Kay never passes anything on to you!"

At the ambassador's request I delivered copies of all of my "policy papers" of that week to his secretary, and he took them home to his residence for perusal at leisure over the weekend. On the following Monday his secretary returned them to me without comment. To this day I have no idea what effect they had on Talbot, but there is nothing unusual in that, for he hardly ever reacted in any way to anything. (The only time I ever saw him really broken up with major laughter was at a staff meeting after a visitor from Washington recounted an anecdote about the extreme discomfiture of a rival ambassador—I believe it was Toby Belcher in Nicosia—a case of the purest schadenfreude.) I suspect, however, that Talbot was more than a little annoyed with Kay Bracken for having failed to inform him of the dissents bubbling up from lower down in the Embassy ranks. He may not have been interested in my views or at all affected by them, but he probably did not like the idea that he wasn't being kept fully informed of what was going on within his own mission. I suspect further that Anschuetz's motive in dropping a copy of my memo on the ambassador's desk had been to sow a little dissension between Talbot and Bracken—always a worthwhile endeavor—in such a way that no blame could be attached to him. Anschuetz's cleverness commanded admiration, but only from a certain distance.

A POSTMORTEM

From that point on I did not discontinue my efforts to influence the course of our policy, but I suspended for a time the bombardment of memoranda upon my bosses. About a week later, on May 6, I tried to sort out the guilty parties in a Memorandum to Myself entitled "*Post-Mortem* on Responsibility for the Military Dictatorship in Greece." Needless to say, this memorandum was in one copy only, which went into my files without distribution.

> It is well known that history is usually written by the victors, practically never by the vanquished, and only occasionally by disinterested observers, and then long after the event. The history of recent events in Greece that will be written soon will in most cases probably blame the Papandreous for having created a political impasse that made the imposition of a military dictatorship necessary and inevitable. I believe otherwise. The responsibility falls on many people, most of all the following, and in descending order of importance.
>
> (1) The military officers who successfully pulled off the coup d'état, for having plotted for ten years to impose a military dictatorship under their own leadership on Greece, for having willfully and

premeditatedly conspired to commit treason and overthrow Greece's democratic and constitutional regime.

(2) The IDEA clique of senior Greek officers who conspired exactly as did those in (1) above and who are less guilty only because the others preempted their plot in the end, but who in one sense are more guilty because they held more senior positions and thus had greater responsibility for upholding and defending Greek institutions.

(3) King Constantine, for having authorized planning for a military takeover of Greece to prevent a return to power by the Papandreous and for thus having sanctioned in advance what happened. His sole displeasure was that it was middle grade rather than the most senior officers on active duty who pulled it off. The king was also guilty of innumerable political blunders in dealing with the Papandreous and with their political opponents and of having helped create the impasse that encouraged others to terminate democracy and impose a military dictatorship.

(4) The king's advisers, for having given him such bad advice.

(5) The conservative establishment of Greece, for having displayed a willingness to sanction any "solution" that would prevent a return to power by the Papandreous. Their lack of devotion to democratic principles and procedures makes them almost as guilty as those who directly violated them by imposing the dictatorship.

(6) The United States Government, which, fully aware of the plotting to impose a military dictatorship and fully aware of the determination of powerful elements in Greece—the monarchy, the army, the conservative establishment—to use any means to prevent the Papandreous from returning to power, failed to take steps in advance to make clear to these elements that a military dictatorship would be unacceptable to the United States, the only action that could have been taken in the late pre-coup stages that had a chance of preventing the coup from taking place. A failure to act to prevent a crime can be as reprehensible as the criminal act itself. This failure of American policy is attributable to the inertia that characterized the American officials most influential in shaping U.S. policy toward Greece, who had as well a perhaps subconscious hankering for the dictatorship "solution," since the alternative of a Papandreou electoral victory was too horrifying to them to be accepted as a possible risk.

(7) The Papandreous, for having stooped to demagoguery in their ambition to regain power and thereby having given their opponents what they believed was adequate justification for overthrowing Greek democracy.

(8) The Greek Communists, for merely existing and thus establishing the possibility of their cooperation with the Papandreous in order to return the latter to power and thereby providing an excuse for the coup plotters to use to justify their action.

It is interesting that it is the *last* point, the Communist threat, that is now being used by the military dictators to justify their rape of Greek democracy.

In retrospect, I would have to make one addition to this list of villains and at least one revision of the nature of the blame. The omitted person is Constantine Karamanlis, who in his anger and vanity sat out the whole business in Paris and did not lift a finger to help the Greek people, who had honored him by electing him prime minister of their country three times. After his tiff with the royal family in 1963 and his party's defeat in the parliamentary elections that fall, Karamanlis had turned his anger against the Greek people and said in effect, "If that's the way you're going to treat me, then the hell with it." He quit Greece in a display of anger, allegedly using an assumed name (a rumor that turned out to be false), and refused to return until the Greeks begged him to come back and rule over them once again, but strictly on his own terms, as a sort of benevolent dictator.

The honorable course for Karamanlis in the months before the 1967 coup would have been to come back to Greece and lead his party in the electoral campaign. This would have been the only thing that would have put any heart into his demoralized ERE party and permitted them to make a respectable showing, although it is doubtful that he could have led the ERE to victory over Papandreou. What Karamanlis could have succeeded in doing, however, would have been to cut the Center Union's margin down sufficiently so that the elections would not have resulted in a Papandreou landslide, and that might have forced the old man into agreeing to an EK-ERE coalition. But the important thing for the thesis of this book is that the presence in Greece of Karamanlis at the head of his party would have had a dramatic impact on the pre-electoral climate, perhaps enough to keep the generals from plotting the coup that the colonels preempted (because the generals would not have felt a takeover to be necessary to check Papandreou).

Karamanlis thus bears some responsibility for the coup on the basis that he did not lift a finger to offer any help in the dangerous climate that he was quite aware was coming to dominate the Greek political scene. It was often said of George Papandreou—and he candidly admitted it himself—that he was great in the opposition but a poor political leader once in office. He was an indifferent and querulous administrator whose great political forte was his impassioned oratorical attacks in parliament on the governing party for its sins. Karamanlis was the opposite: a skilled administrator, tactically adept, but petulant to the point of immobility when he was not sitting in the seat of power. Instead of going into an honorable opposition when he lost an election, he refused to play the game any longer and simply walked off the playing field and went home. It is regrettable that some political surgeon had not figured out a way to join Karamanlis and Papandreou together so that they could perform a Siamese-twin act.

Now, four years after the coup, the major revision I would make in the postmortem concerns the performance of Andreas Papandreou in the preelectoral campaign, specifically his insistence on trying to make the king the chief political opponent of the Center Union in the election. It is true, as the Center charged, that Constantine's action in handing the government over to Kanellopoulos, leader of the ERE, to rule during the campaign and then conduct the elections (instead of the traditional service government) made the king in effect the head of the ERE party, for only an ERE victory would have satisfied (and protected) the king at that point. But Andreas's attacks on Constantine were as unwise as they were unnecessary. He stood on his principles—no forgiveness for what the king had done to the Center Union in July of 1965—and he was also making an obvious electoral appeal to the left-of-center and other antiroyalist voters; but the important thing is that he frightened the royalists and conservatives generally so much that they were willing to resort to extreme measures to thwart Andreas, and in thwarting him they destroyed Greek democracy.

It was believed that George Papandreou, at the time of the formation of the Paraskevopoulos government, had promised the king that the Center would not make the monarchy an issue in the forthcoming electoral campaign. Old George was a very shrewd political strategist, and he knew that the monarchy and the king's behavior were issues for many Greek voters whether he said anything about them in his speeches or not. He knew that the Center would get the antiroyalist vote no matter what. So why make it an issue? Andreas, certainly less wise (his adherents would say more principled), insisted that the king was the enemy and had to be attacked. Evidently George could not restrain his son, though he tried. In parceling out blame now, in retrospect, I would have to exonerate George Papandreou almost completely, for he was playing the game wisely and fairly. Not so Andreas, who for all his virtues displayed a signal lack of political skill in making the grievous miscalculation that his anti-Constantine campaign was the path of light and truth. Unfortunately, he played into the hands of his enemies, who were also the enemies of Greek democracy.

A more minor revision I would make today concerns the senior officers who commanded the Greek armed forces at the time of the coup. Not only were they guilty of preparing, on behalf of the king, the Generals' coup that the Colonels preempted, but they were singularly lacking in courage and loyalty when confronted with the Papadopoulos takeover. Is there anything they could have done on the morning after the coup? I do not know, but the description one recalls of their behavior when the king went to the Athens Pentagon to confront the Colonels—their plea of helplessness—makes one wonder about the caliber of the entire Greek officer corps of that era.

My brother Mike came up with another sort of postmortem about a year after the coup. Reflecting back on Talbot's performance in Athens in 1967, he remarked that while it is true that an ambassador is generally little more than a messenger boy working for an official telegraph agency, there are occasions—few and far between—when an ambassador has a once-in-a-lifetime opportunity to be something more, to act decisively and personally to rescue his country from a disastrous situation. Such an opportunity had been presented to Ambassador Talbot in April of 1967, my brother said, and clearly he had flubbed it: "There he was with a golden opportunity to do something to earn his salary, and what he did was sit on his butt and do nothing."

I cannot fault that judgment, for Talbot was sitting in the position to have done something about the Greek situation in 1967, prior to the coup in advising the king, at the time of the coup in overturning it (presuming that he had been unable to prevent its occurrence), and failing that, at least in preserving the good name of the United States in Greece and in the world. Through being unwilling to take any risks at all he in fact jeopardized our entire position in Greece, the full consequences of which of course fell to his successors, as is always the case with a bureaucracy. One's mistakes do not come back to haunt one; they haunt one's successors.

A VISIT BY NIXON

Our first VIP visitor after the coup was Richard Nixon. I was assigned as his escort or control officer, most probably because no one else cared for the job.

Although he was then already gearing himself up for the 1968 campaign for the Republican presidential nomination (by traveling around the world and getting his name in the papers), he had been all but counted out of politics for the past five years, and no one gave him much of a chance to make a comeback. His visit to Athens had originally been scheduled for a date that fell immediately after the coup, and on learning of the coup Nixon had telegraphed the ambassador offering to postpone his arrival if Talbot thought it best, or to come ahead if Talbot thought he could contribute something helpful in the new situation. Talbot suggested postponement, and when Nixon arrived in Athens in mid-June (accompanied by Pat Buchanan, his press agent and later his speechwriter), Talbot had departed for Washington on consultation to be followed by home leave. Nixon and Buchanan stayed at the residence in the ambassador's absence.

For about two and a half days I stayed at Nixon's elbow, trying to make things run smoothly. I was not at his elbow the *whole* time, obviously; among other things, he had lunch at Tatoi alone with Constantine and Queen Anne-Marie. Nixon was a remarkably easy visitor to handle, except for one facet: Buchanan apparently had no authority to make the least decision by himself, but had to check out everything with the boss, even permission to pay for a cable of greetings to a convention of Young Republicans meeting in some place like Topeka, the cable costing all of three dollars, if I recall correctly. Nixon impressed me as a person who made all the decisions affecting his life by himself, the big ones as well as the minutiae. I wondered if, were he ever elected president, he would be capable of delegating any authority.

Anschuetz was the chargé in Talbot's absence and decided to host a reception where Nixon could meet some of the key figures in the new regime as well as some prominent political figures from the precoup days, all gathered together in Anschuetz's garden. The guests naturally split into two hostile groups, having nothing to do with each other, not even exchanging greetings. There was some anger at Anschuetz for having placed them all in an uncomfortable situation, but only a man of Anschuetz's personality could have pulled it off. It was the first, last, and only occasion under American auspices at which members of the regime and a significant number of the leading ex-politicians appeared together; ever afterward opponents of the regime would telephone the Embassy's protocol office when receiving an official American invitation to make sure that no members of the "junta" would be present before they would agree to attend.

Following the reception Anschuetz hosted a small stag dinner—about ten guests—for Nixon. Talk at the table was entirely dominated by Anschuetz's friend Spyros Markezinis, the Progressive Party leader, who held the floor with a two-hour nonstop monologue that exhausted everyone, Nixon included. The following day I escorted Nixon to the Acropolis, where he joined Art Linkletter, who was filming some material for his TV show *House Party*. They were longtime friends, and Nixon earned the benefit of exposure to Linkletter's millions of viewers.

Nixon also called on several of the regime's leaders. The most memorable meeting was with Brigadier Stylianos Pattakos, the interior minister and tank corps commander who had played such a key role in the coup. Pattakos had built himself a reputation as a somewhat genial, somewhat sinister clown who constantly put his foot in his mouth but who also had the endearing quality of candor. He was the Spiro Agnew of Greece. For this occasion he used an interpreter, which kept down the number of his gaffes. Nixon had doubtless met a great many peculiar political personalities in his travels about the world, but the alternately bluff and ingratiating Pattakos evidently startled the sophisticated ex–vice president.

As an example of the dialogue that often caused Nixon to give me an unbelieving sidelong glance (he wondered afterward if the interpreting had been accurate, and I assured him it had been), I will cite an exchange on the subject of press freedom. Noting that some two months had passed since the coup and that it was apparent that complete tranquility and public order reigned in the streets, Nixon wondered if the new regime could not lift some of the restrictions on the press, which at that time was strictly controlled to the extent that editors had to check out their page makeup, placement of photographs, size of headlines, and so forth with the government censor.

"Censorship was not my choice," said Pattakos to his visitor. "It was the freely taken decision of the press people themselves."

"How was that?" Nixon asked. "That is not what I have been led to believe."

"You have doubtless been lied to, Mr. Nixon. I will tell you exactly how it came about. Just last week I called together all the journalists, editors, reporters, publishers, everyone, in my capacity as minister of the interior, and I said, Gentlemen, the entire matter is up to you. You alone shall decide whether we shall have censorship or not. Now I offer you the choice. Either we have no censorship at all and anyone who steps out of line goes straight to the detention camp on the island of Yiaros, or we have censorship and the censor decides what gets published and everyone stays out of trouble. Mr. Nixon, they voted for censorship, I assure you."

I could not keep from chuckling at this, for Pattakos himself was chuckling, but Nixon, when he heard the translation, did not see the joke. I had to explain to him that the junta had incarcerated thousands of alleged leftists,

Communists, and others on the already notorious Aegean prison island of Yiaros. In the car after the interview, Nixon commented to me, "That man doesn't pull any punches, does he?"

Prior to his departure from Athens, Nixon held a press conference at the airport. I warned him that there would be representatives of the junta there posing as journalists who would try to get him to say something favorable about the regime that they could exploit in the local press to show American support for the government. Highly experienced at this sort of thing, Nixon handled himself expertly and stressed several times the need for an early return to constitutional norms and civil liberties, as well as democratic elections. But at one point he let fall the remark that it appeared to him that "something had to be done" in April 1967, meaning that the political situation in Greece had been so troubled that some extraordinary action was inevitable, and of course this resulted in streamer headlines the next day in the progovernment press together with high praise for Nixon's declaration "in support of the April 21 revolution."

SHIFT OF FOCUS

The Arab-Israeli crisis that developed in late May and early June, leading to the Six-Day War, naturally turned the attention of senior Washington officialdom concerned with the Near East–South Asia area entirely away from Greece, preoccupied as they were with that much more dangerous crisis. From that time on, moreover, the relationship of Greece to the Near East situation came to dominate all consideration of U.S. policy toward Greece, and the justification for our acceptance of the Papadopoulos junta came to be founded on the need to bolster the "southeast flank" of NATO in view of the turbulence in the Near East, to give us a secure forward base for possible military intervention in the eastern Mediterranean, and all the other arguments that have become so familiar from official State Department verbal output since the summer of 1967. This refocusing of our policy toward Greece was probably especially pronounced in the mind of the new Near East–South Asia assistant secretary, Lucius Battle, who had formerly served as ambassador in Cairo and who therefore naturally looked at Greece with somewhat Near Eastern eyes.

Yet this changed perspective persisted long after Battle's departure from that post, and was especially pronounced after the Nixon administration came into office in January 1969 and Joseph Sisco became the assistant secretary for NEA. But it was less a matter of changed personalities than that the policy dovetailed so conveniently with the Pentagon's desire to continue close military cooperation with the Greek regime. This tactic, or rationale, was cleverly designed to disarm liberal members of Congress who combined an anti–Greek junta stance with a firm commitment to all-out U.S. support for Israel. These critics of the Greek junta were in effect advised to mute their objections to U.S. policy toward Greece if they did not wish to jeopardize U.S. efforts to maintain a strong and secure base from which a U.S. military intervention in the Near East could be launched to rescue Israel and thwart the Russians. No one in either branch of government apparently had the perspicacity to question whether any Greek government—including that of Papadopoulos—could abandon Greece's long-standing neutrality in the Arab-Israeli dispute and destroy its relations with the Arab states, where Greek interests were paramount, by permitting the United States to use Greek territory to support a military intervention on the side of Israel. No Greek government, when the chips were down, could agree to such a drastic change in policy. (The same was true of Turkey, our other eastern Mediterranean NATO ally.) Thus, the Pentagon was insisting on its need to preserve a friendly launching pad that it could never hope to use in the most likely contingency of all.

Eight

ANDREAS PAPANDREOU AND PROSPECTS FOR DEMOCRACY

ANDREAS IN DANGER

There had been a great deal of concern in the hours immediately after the April 21 coup, among both Andreas's family and friends in Greece and his friends in the United States, that the clearly anti-Papandreou group that had seized power might move immediately to execute him. President Johnson has been quoted as having been startled to be suddenly inundated with phone calls and telegrams and visitors demanding that he instruct Embassy Athens to intervene with the Greek junta to save Papandreou's life. Johnson knew who Papandreou was, for he had arranged the well-known attempt to solve the Cyprus crisis in the summer of 1964 through a face-to-face meeting in the United States between Inönü, head of the Turkish government, and George Papandreou (who was accompanied to the United States by his son), an effort that was abortive and that left a bitter taste about the Papandreous in the mouths of American officialdom concerned with the Cyprus problem because they considered that the Papandreous had been obstructionists.

As the hours turned into days and weeks, the fears of a summary execution of Andreas receded and the new concern was that he would be tried for treason by the new regime. Immediately after the coup, Ambassador Talbot had intervened with the junta to express the hope of the U.S. government that all the people they had arrested, including Andreas Papandreou, would be treated properly and that there would be no summary executions. Like

Johnson, Talbot was surprised if not dismayed that the most urgent telegraphic traffic he was receiving from Washington, officially and privately, did not carry instructions on the attitude to be taken toward the new regime but consisted mainly of appeals on behalf of Andreas. He expressed some surprise that everyone was focusing on this one politician, who was now clearly *hors de combat* at the very least. Fairly soon it became apparent to everyone that summary execution was not going to be a problem, in the case of Andreas or the other detainees, based on the assurances that had been received from the Kollias government that they would behave in a civilized fashion.

My own view was that even short of summary execution, the manner in which the case of Andreas Papandreou was handled by the junta would have an important bearing on our relations with it at the time and in the future, for Andreas was no ordinary Greek politician but a personality with many prominent friends in the United States, particularly in academia and in political circles. On May 1 I sent a memo to Mrs. Bracken referring to two editorials that had been summarized by USIS in its report on press reaction in the United States to developments in Greece. Both had appeared in pillars of the American journalistic establishment.

The *New York Times* wrote that if the military rulers of Greece had any concern for world opinion they would call off their apparent plan to try Andreas Papandreou for treason, for a junta that had seized power and imposed a state of siege against the obvious wishes of the king was in a poor position to try anyone else for unconstitutional behavior.

The conservative *Washington Star* said that should Andreas be brought to "trial" on a charge of treason under prevailing conditions, it would be a mockery of justice, for a fair trial was the one thing that Andreas could not hope to get at the hands of the right-wing army group that had taken control in Athens. The paper noted that there is such a thing as treason against the state as well as treason against the rights of an individual in what is presumed to be a civilized society. "Our hope is that the new military leaders in Greece will understand that they, too, are on trial in the tribunal of world opinion, and that the verdict will depend in substantial degree on whether the trial of Papandreou is to be a fair trial in any meaningful sense of the term, or simply an inexcusable act of vengeance."

My memorandum went on to urge that we make clear to the Greek government at the highest levels and on an urgent basis that judicial action against Andreas in the prevailing circumstances would be ill advised both for itself and for its relations with the United States and the rest of the world. I echoed the reasoning in the two editorials and added the comment that it seemed the regime had already prejudged the case against Andreas and that after all that had happened the regime would feel it had to return a verdict of guilty in order to justify the coup. In an official announcement confirming the escape from Greece of Paul Vardinoyannis, a somewhat controversial Center politician from Crete who along with Andreas had been accused of involvement with ASPIDA, the Greek government said that his action "has fully confirmed his guilt and the guilt of his fellow accused politicians."

I suggested a number of arguments that we could use with the junta, including the effect on U.S. and world opinion, the fact that Andreas was no longer a threat and could be safely released, and the inadvisability of setting a precedent with treason trials, and I closed as follows:

> If necessary, we should go so far as to face the coup leaders with the facts regarding treason, to wit, that a successful act of treason (such as their own) is promptly labeled a "popular revolution" by the traitors who take power, whereas an unsuccessful effort to acquire power by conspiratorial or other illegal means (which is what the ASPIDA conspirators are accused of) is promptly labeled treason by those who thwart the would-be conspirators. In other words, there are all sorts of treason, but only unsuccessful treason is so labeled. The fundamental difference between EENA and ASPIDA is that one succeeded and the other did not. It ill behooves a gang of traitors to start pinning the label on others, and it sets a dangerous precedent which their successors will be only too happy to exploit.

A copy went to Anschuetz. Neither he nor Bracken responded in any way to my demarche, so far as I can recall. On May 5 I followed up with a rather emotional piece stimulated by a reading of the CIA station's examination of the prosecution case against Andreas, freshly disseminated throughout the U.S. government.

> I think it is imperative for us to send a comment to the Department on this CAS [Controlled American Source] report, lest senior officials be misled by it. It states in the introduction that "In the opinion of CAS the case is persuasive but not conclusive" against Andreas Papandreou. This is an outrageous statement. The evidence presented is practically all hearsay, it is a pure rehash of the testimony used in the military ASPIDA trial, it says a lot about what certain officers did and said, but nothing about anything Andreas may have

done. It accepts statements by a braggart like Captain Bouloukos as the basis for convicting the person he is bragging about knowing.

At the very worst one could accuse these officers (and Andreas, if he was involved) of having tried to advance pro-EK officers into key positions in the Army and of trying to thwart a rightist military coup against the Papandreou government. With the acknowledged existence of rightist conspiratorial organizations within the Army such as IDEA and EENA, it was nothing more than prudent for a pro-EK group of officers to take steps to protect themselves.

A report such as the attached, with the comment prefaced to it, is a shocking piece of work. It is highly immoral to associate ourselves in this way with a travesty of justice.

Again, there was no response from Anschuetz and Bracken. An embassy political section has the right (duty, in fact) to submit comments to the Department of State on CIA reports with which it disagrees. That is the course I was urging, and I did so on only two or three other occasions in Athens. Ordinarily a misleading or biased CIA report is so blatantly obvious that it can be safely ignored, but this report on the ASPIDA indictment was malicious as well as misleading.

My reaction to the purported evidence against Andreas was more instinctive than well reasoned, but some months later the entire frame-up was exposed to the public. As recounted by Papandreou in his book—and his account accords with published reports at the time of the incident—

> the indictment made reference to only one piece of direct evidence against me. A high school friend, whom I had not seen for years, Andreas Vachliotis, had made a deposition according to which *I had told him* of my plans to organize a military coup, dethrone the King, and take Greece out of NATO. Vachliotis's testimony supported that of Kyriakos Diakoyiannis, a journalist friend of his.
>
> A few days later this piece of "evidence" disappeared into thin air in a dramatic way. Vachliotis and Diakoyiannis escaped to America. They gave a press conference in Washington, announcing that they had perjured themselves under pressure from the secret police and KYP. *Ramparts* magazine published their complete statements.[1]

Andreas then quotes excerpts of Vachliotis's recantation alleging that KYP had framed Andreas in order to destroy him.

BITS AND PIECES

Among the unused studies and abortive memoranda in my files is a long draft dated May 5 and entitled "Status and Prospects of Greek Democracy." It was apparently commissioned by Kay Bracken, who suggested that I put some of my oral views on future prospects in writing. The first page shows some changes in her handwriting, but thereafter the paper was apparently abandoned as a thoroughly bad job. It holds little interest today except to note that I tried to lay out a twelve-month program for the restoration of full democracy to Greece—not that I was optimistic this would happen, but the idea that it was even within the realm of speculation is somewhat astounding.

On May 10 I indulged in a bit of serious irony in a memo to Mrs. Bracken about a CIA report:

> It is more than a little ironic that this whole unhappy chapter of Greek history we are living through began because King Constantine feared that the Papandreous were tampering with "his" army, and by means of things such as the ASPIDA conspiracy (allegedly) and the transfer and promotion of officers they were trying to place pro-EK officers in key positions. Now we have Pattakos planning to promote and transfer officers to benefit those "who could be counted on to support the coup leadership in any showdown with the King."
>
> The present group is planning to do exactly what the Papandreous were accused of attempting. The difference is that the present group will succeed in transforming the army into a personal instrument (not necessarily loyal to the King) because they *are* the Army. The Papandreous would not have succeeded because they would have been working *against* the Army, not within it. And once Pattakos and company succeed in making the Army a personal instrument of their power there will be no way to undo their work, and we will simply have to learn to live with Army rule.

With hindsight it is now possible to say that Colonel Papadopoulos, the chief conspirator, devoted his very formidable energies during the six months following the coup to exacting preparations to counter the anticipated effort by the king to oust his group from power. By retiring certain officers, transferring others to safe spots, locating his own men in key units, and generally creating a vast spy system of officers who reported to him directly on the reliability of their superiors in each major unit, Papadopoulos was able to thwart the king's countercoup attempt in December. That failed attempt then permitted Papadopoulos to purge the armed forces of all higher-ranking officers not thoroughly loyal to the April 21 coup group, and there is no doubt that today the armed forces are his personal instrument. Yet nothing is permanent, and if he is ever deposed it will of course be by that very same instrument.

O. K. Marshall, our defense attaché, simply didn't like Papadopoulos and the other coup colonels, and for this reason he suffered less than his colleagues from a peculiar blindness that afflicted all the senior American military officers in Athens. As Papadopoulos proceeded to purge the Greek army's senior ranks in successive waves, our military representatives would solemnly report to the weekly country team meeting chaired by the ambassador that the officers being (prematurely) retired were mostly "deadwood" and their replacements were among the finest officers in the Greek services, a great improvement over those they were replacing. Six months or a year later, of course, some of the recently promoted would in turn be cashiered, and our officers would again report that the deadwood had been weeded out and young geniuses moved up to take command.

They would simply not admit, not face the fact, that Papadopoulos and his gang were carrying out a systematic purge of the Greek armed forces to remove all those who were opposed to the April 21 "revolution," including all those whose loyalties might be primarily to the king. I became so exasperated with our self-deception that at one staff meeting I blurted out, "Now if this year's deadwood was last year's geniuses, and this year's geniuses are going to be next year's deadwood, what are we going to do when there's no more deadwood to promote?" On analysis this statement doesn't make much sense, but it was perhaps more polite than what one might have said, which was that some number of our own American officers might fall into the category of deadwood on the way out.

Another bit of evidence that I had now shifted my efforts from trying to persuade my superiors to get rid of the junta at once to proposing programs that would bring back a normal democratic system gradually is a short draft I prepared on May 16 entitled "Possible Formula for Evolution Toward Resumption of Political Activity in Greece." The details are no longer of interest, but I was now thinking in terms of a two-year program, the first year to include preparation, ratification, and promulgation of a new constitution, with elections for both executive and legislature to follow one year after the promulgation of the constitution. I am also today startled to find a passage speculating that the regime might hold a Gaullist-style referendum on a new constitution with the format "Either you vote yes for the Constitution which will lead to a restoration of normal political life in the country, or you vote no and reject the Constitution which would mean an indefinite continuation of the present regime in power." A year and a half after this was written, Pattakos told press and public that the Greeks had two choices in the constitutional referendum scheduled for the end of September 1968: "Either you approve the constitution by voting yes or we'll rule without a constitution." A classic instance of a political Hobson's choice.

Mrs. Bracken apparently found something worthwhile in this effort, for she gave it back to me with the notation: "RK. Re political, Amb. wants variety of formulas (basket of ideas) with pros & cons that he can use in various conversations."

Thus encouraged, I expanded my paper on May 18 to a large basket of seven possible schemata for arranging a return to democracy, with long lists of advantages and disadvantages for each. Three of these proposals were labeled "Turkish Plan," "Korean Plan," and "South Vietnamese Plan," so I fear I was falling into the fallacy of thinking by analogy myself. Needless to say, none of these seven plans was ever adopted by the American Embassy, much less by the Greek government.

This account perhaps gives the impression that a large part of my work was not being put to any good use during this period. That is incorrect, for my primary responsibility was still Cyprus, about which there was a considerable body of noncontroversial reporting, but mainly I have focused here on unused items because they are the more interesting ones. For example, in late May I prepared a long draft cable attempting to give guidance to USIA in Washington on how to cover Greek developments on VOA broadcasts. The Greek government was upset by some of the items we had broadcast, and of course we were vulnerable to their pressure because of the vast VOA facilities that were implanted on Greek soil. My draft telegram, which was not used, tried to reconcile our wish to preserve unhampered our valuable facilities while still presenting objective and complete reporting on the Greek scene in order to maintain the credibility of VOA as a source of news.

A proposal that I made privately to Mrs. Bracken, not in the draft telegram, was that we establish a clandestine "Voice of Free Greece" on a small ship in international waters in the Mediterranean to take over the role of keeping the Greek people informed of the truth about what was happening in the country and about U.S. attitudes toward the regime; in other words, the things we were having difficulty broadcasting over the VOA. This suggestion was never seriously taken up.

While he was in the United States on consultation and home leave in the summer of 1967, Talbot gave a background briefing at the State Department on the Greek situation. It was not for attribution, or even for publication, but someone present took careful notes that were transmitted to a Greek journalist in Athens. This journalist (an acquaintance of mine) was subsequently arrested, and on his instructions the notes on the Talbot backgrounder were buried in his garden by his family. When the journalist emerged from prison a couple of years later, he unearthed the notes. They were duly published by an Athens liberal newspaper as a supposedly secret embassy report to the State Department analyzing the Greek situation as of June 1967. It was not such a report, and USIS suffered no qualms of conscience over issuing a denial of its authenticity.

But for me the published notes had a strange ring of reality, for there was Talbot searching for analogies in all directions, with special attention to the danger that Papadopoulos might turn out to be a Nasser (for many years "Nasser" had been his nickname in the Greek army because of his inveterate plotting) and Greece might end up, if we weren't careful, under Soviet tutelage much like Egypt, if by our own actions we drove the regime out of the Western camp so that it had nowhere else to turn but to the Communists. This analogy about incipient Nasserism has plagued all rational analysis of the Greek problem ever since, which is somehow curious, for it flies in the face of three very elementary contrasts:

(a) Nasser's 1952 revolution that overthrew King Farouk was overwhelmingly supported by the mass of the Egyptian people, whereas Papadopoulos has never been able to build any significant, much less mass, popular support in Greece.

(b) Papadopoulos has used U.S. support as a major prop to keep himself in power, whereas Nasser played up U.S. and general Western hostility to himself to win the undying love of the Egyptian people. The Egyptians are an ex-colonial people with a natural antipathy for the West, whereas the Greeks are a Western people with an unquenchable desire to become full-fledged members of Europe.

(c) Egypt is a neutralist nation for which the West was not an available source of arms supply because of Egyptian hostility to Israel. Nasser had to get arms from the Soviets to keep the support of his military. Greece is a member of NATO, very well equipped with Western arms, and the one thing that might cause the Greek armed forces to throw Papadopoulos out would be if he tried to cut the country's ties with the West and turn instead toward the Soviets.

In late August King Constantine went to Canada and the United States, partly to take in the America's Cup races off Newport and partly to assess for himself in Washington the attitude of the U.S. government toward the junta with which he was trying to work in Athens. The races were interesting, but Washington was entirely depressing for the king. He arrived in Washington coincidentally and for him unfortunately just after Vachliotis and Diakoyiannis had held their press conference revealing their perjured testimony against Andreas Papandreou in the ASPIDA case.

Constantine got the runaround in the executive branch, where he was seeking minimal support for a stand against Papadopoulos and his gang, and on Capitol Hill he received a lot of reluctantly given sympathy from liberal senators, who could not forget that he bore major responsibility for the crisis of 1965 in Greece—if not single-handed responsibility then at least more than 50 percent. They challenged him to defend the oppressive government in Athens, and he made the classic (and well-publicized) remark "It's not my government!" This remark did not go unnoticed by Papadopoulos, but it apparently made no discernible impression on Talbot. It struck me as an indication that perhaps the king had become so disillusioned that we could work with him on a plan to remove the junta and then try to find a solution more to his liking as well as ours.

MEETING MARGARET

Andreas Papandreou's wife, Margaret, was an American citizen, as were their four children, all born in the United States. Andreas had had his citizenship lifted when he ran as a candidate for parliament in 1964, an act that on the basis of the law in effect at that time automatically lost a naturalized American his citizenship. But on the basis of her own status as an American (and that of their children), Margaret had turned to the American Embassy for help in that time of greatest peril for her husband following his arrest as part of the April 21 coup.

Despite the Papandreous' friendship with Anschuetz, Margaret received little help from the Embassy and not even much sympathy, although, as mentioned earlier, Talbot had intervened with the junta regarding treatment of Andreas. The Embassy refused to deliver to Margaret mail that had been sent to her through official channels by prominent friends of Andreas in the United States such as John Kenneth Galbraith. Margaret has recounted in some detail her painful experiences of that time in her book *Nightmare in*

Athens,[2] so there is no point in repeating an account here. But she was generous and cautious enough to avoid any mention of my wife or me by name in her book, knowing that it would have had a decidedly negative impact on my Foreign Service career, since as of 1971 Andreas is still the U.S. government's number one enemy on the Greek scene. But some coverage of our relationship with the Papandreou family is in order in this memoir in view of the central role that Andreas played in the events of that period in Greece.[3]

In mid-August Mrs. Margie Schacter, a close friend of Margaret Papandreou who had been living with her and helping to look after the family while her husband was in Averoff Prison, called on me at the Embassy. We had met briefly at a cocktail party. It became obvious from her conversation that she and Mrs. Papandreou thought there was absolutely no one in the American Embassy with the least sympathy for their situation and they were hoping that I might at least provide a channel of communication for them to this establishment that represented the United States government in Greece. Up to then their point of contact had been Norbert Anschuetz, until his transfer to Washington earlier that summer. Although (as I learned later on) Mrs. Papandreou had found Anschuetz to be less sympathetic and helpful than she had hoped on the basis of their prior friendship, he had at least been willing to receive her, and he sat very close to the ambassadorial throne.

I agreed to Mrs. Schacter's suggestion that I drop by Mrs. Papandreou's house for a drink and a chat. At that point I had never met either Andreas or Margaret Papandreou. My wife, Louise, accompanied me to Mrs. Papandreou's, as did my brother and sister-in-law. (One falls easily into adopting Greek customs: a personal invitation can without offense be translated into an invitation for the whole family.)

Her conversation was rather guarded, but her main interest was obviously in obtaining any information she could on what the intentions of the Greek regime were with regard to her husband: would he be tried, when and in what manner, would the trial be open to the public (many friends and lawyers had promised to come from the United States and Western Europe, if the trial were open, to ensure that it was fair), was there any chance he would be amnestied or otherwise released? I could not enlighten her very much on any of these aspects, and I am sure her sources of information were much better than my own, but people in Greece—even the most sophisticated—have a tendency to believe that the American Embassy knows everything that is going on in the country because it is involved in everything. We all went out to dinner at the Rotunda restaurant in Philothei, a favorite spot for Center politicians. The date was August 15, 1967.

From that time on for the next four months, Louise had fairly frequent contact with Mrs. Papandreou, and I saw her occasionally also. I thought it important to keep in touch with her for a number of reasons, but mainly because she was an American citizen who felt that the Embassy had neglected her, if not worse, because of its animosity toward her husband. I also thought it worthwhile to keep up to date on her plans, as there was a great deal of interest in the Papandreou case in the Congress and the U.S. public, and we had frequent official and private inquiries to answer.

I was certainly aware that the U.S. Embassy frowned upon any sort of contact with the Papandreou family, except for a willingness to service her routine requests for consular assistance. Nevertheless, I made up my mind that we should try to do what little we could for Mrs. Papandreou, regardless of the opinions of others. Perhaps it was foolhardiness, but I was sensitive to the criticism that had been leveled at the Embassy by friends of the family, including some very prominent American figures, for its unsympathetic attitudes. In retrospect I am sure that Louise and I did the right thing, though I cannot now imagine that there is anything I could have said at the time to my superiors that would have persuaded them to encourage us in the course we undertook. I thought that in the long run the U.S. government would be the beneficiary, even if only to the extent of diminishing some of the hostility that the entire Papandreou family was bound to feel for the official American representation in Greece. Clearly there was no one else willing or able to play a role of this kind.

On September 7 we invited Margaret to dinner at our house, along with my brother Mike and his wife, Mary. We offered to lend her some books for Andreas's reading in prison, and she came over on a subsequent occasion to choose them. I recall she later reported that Andreas especially enjoyed two books by Bertrand de Jouvenel. The prison censor rejected some books because their titles indicated (erroneously) that they might be about Communism; for example, Veblen's *Theory of the Leisure Class*. Once in a while Louise dropped by Margaret's house for coffee and a chat. She appreciated the fact that Margaret never tried to involve her in discussions of embassy politics or personalities during these occasions.

On October 15 Margaret again had dinner at our house, and Bruce Lansdale and his wife, Tad, also attended (they had never met her before). The Lansdales had declined a dinner invitation from the Talbots, with whom they were staying, in order to attend ours. Word of this got back to Mrs. Talbot by a devious channel, and the news no doubt displeased her. Bruce was very moved by Margaret's story of her tribulations, and he later called Louise from Salonika to inquire how he could get some free Farm School milk to her for her children.[4]

Our contacts with Mrs. Papandreou did not go unnoticed by the Greek security service, nor by our own CIA. Our first inkling of this surveillance came from a chance remark by the widow of a former CIA official in another post who was working for the JUSMAGG in Athens. Louise first met her in a dentist's office, where she asked to have her son go ahead of ours because she was late for work. Some days later she phoned to invite our son to a birthday party. When Louise asked her address, she replied, "I live next door to the Papandreous, and you know where that is, don't you?" She did indeed live next door, and doubtless kept an eye on who visited the house.

A couple of weeks later, after we had had Margaret for dinner at our house a second time, Louise was having lunch in the Embassy cafeteria and the number two man in the CIA station wandered in and asked if he could join her at her table. After a few pleasantries he asked her what her car had been doing parked outside the Papandreous' house the previous afternoon.

"What business is that of yours?" she responded. "Are you tailing my car?"

No, he explained, a Greek police report had "happened" to cross his desk and he had "recognized" our CD (Corps Diplomatique) license plate number in the report.

"I was there having tea with Mrs. Papandreou," Louise said. "Do you feel that I shouldn't have been there?"

"Well," the CIA man said, "they're rather a controversial family, aren't they?"

Louise's retort was that nonetheless Mrs. Papandreou and her four children were American citizens about whom many other Americans in the States were expressing concern. She added that she had gone to see Mrs. Papandreou openly, and if she had had anything to hide she would not have left her car parked outside a house that she could reasonably assume was under police surveillance.

When Louise told me of this encounter, I immediately took the matter up with Mrs. Bracken, acting on the assumption that the CIA would pass the report on to her as well. I had the distinct impression that the CIA frowned on what we were doing (though I had been keeping Mrs. Bracken informed of our few encounters) and by tactics rather lacking in subtlety wished to intimidate us into stopping it.

I presented to Mrs. Bracken (in a written note dated October 19) my rationale for maintaining these contacts and noted that Mrs. Papandreou's main interest seemed to be to get her husband out of Greece by any possible means and then to go to the United States. I also reported her morale as having improved recently, especially after she had succeeded in having her telephone service restored (the government had cut it off for a time). The Greek regime had recently p.n.g.'d a Danish diplomat, Ib Alken, who had many close contacts with centrist figures in Athens, and I thought they might be preparing to try something similar with me, although they would have hesitated to take such action against an American, I felt. I suggested to Mrs. Bracken that if the regime should complain or inquire, officially or unofficially, about my contact with Mrs. Papandreou, I hoped that our response would be that since she and her children were American citizens, and in view of the great interest in the United States in her husband's case, the Embassy deemed it advisable to have one of its officers keep in touch with her.

Mrs. Bracken took it up with the ambassador and then told me not to initiate any further contacts with Mrs. Papandreou, but to wait for her to call. (This is a way of saying, "If you get into any trouble, you're on your own, son.") Otherwise, she and the ambassador felt, I "might impair my usefulness to the Embassy." Mrs. Bracken said I should tell Mrs. Papandreou that if she had any business to take up with the Embassy, she should see the consul general. I didn't do that, but I obeyed orders and let Louise carry the ball, although I saw Margaret occasionally after that at her request.

SPECULATIONS

In the summer of 1967 Norbert Anschuetz was transferred to Washington and was replaced as DCM by Roswell McClelland, whom I had known slightly some five years earlier when he had served in Dakar and I in Bamako in West Africa. On September 5 I wrote up "Some Thoughts on Prospects for and Means of Restoring a Democratic Regime to Greece," addressed in Kay's absence to the acting political counselor, George Warren, who that summer had replaced Malcolm Thompson as politico-military officer and number two man in the Political Section. He passed the paper on to McClelland, who found it interesting, but it stopped short of the ambassador. It made what I considered were some bold predictions—for example, that Papadopoulos and company would not restore a normal democratic regime "soon" (that is, within two years) but were thinking more in terms of five or ten years as needed "to carry out the aims of the revolution." Under pressure of foreign and domestic opinion for some movement toward normality, I thought, they might move eventually in the direction of a "single-party system," that is, a sort of democratic facade to permit their self-perpetuation in power.

I speculated about how the junta might proceed to try to legitimize itself through single-party elections of an executive and a rubber-stamp parliament. I was skeptical about our ability to influence the direction in which things seemed to be moving, and I thought the junta would probably succeed in installing itself permanently no matter what we or anyone else (including the Greek people) desired. Through logical analysis I tried to counter the proposition that a "transitional" regime (then figuring greatly in local speculation) under someone like Karamanlis could be worked out. I expected instead further polarization into pro- and antiregime camps, and I concluded with a highly pessimistic rundown of what we might do if faced with a "single-party solution," none of the options being seen as recommended: to oppose its establishment, to accept it as the lesser of evils, to work with friendly elements within it, to try to mount an opposition to it. All options seemed guaranteed to lead to disaster.

Ambassador Talbot had invited Prime Minister Kollias and some of the other leading figures in the junta government to dinner on October 3, and he asked me to draft an appropriate toast. I sweated over this task for some hours and finally came up with 643 carefully crafted words that I thought would accomplish the assigned objective of being reasonably friendly but engaging in a fairly subtle lecture about the virtues of democracy, with allusions to the ideal of Athenian democracy that had inspired the founders of the American republic, and by a circuitous route arriving at a closing toast to the health of His Majesty, Constantine, King of the Hellenes. I was quite proud of the product, but apparently it did not appeal to Talbot, for the toast he gave was a rambling extemporaneous lecture that sounded more like six thousand words.

In mid-October we faced the Department-imposed task of drawing up a "six-month assessment" of the performance of the new regime and our relations with it. We all pitched in on it. I prepared a couple of draft sections as my contribution, and part of the material I prepared was actually used. I wrote sections on accomplishments, problems, and prospects of the "National Government" and on "how will the regime react to foreign criticism?" The regime's performance had definitely been mixed, and one of the ways I thought it might try to build popular support would be "to whittle away at the power of the monarchy" in an attempt to appeal to the considerable portion of the Greek populace that was antimonarchist.

Nine

THE COUNTERCOUP

PLANNING THE KING'S COUP

On November 14 a childhood friend from Salonika, Argini Goutos, and her husband, Michael, arranged a meeting for me at their house in Kifissia with George Mavros, the leading Center Union party personality then still in circulation (George Papandreou had been almost continuously under house arrest since the coup). Others present that evening were my wife, Louise, Mrs. Mavros, and Bruce Lansdale.

The following morning, November 15, I wrote a three-page "memorandum of conversation" reporting the substance of George Mavros's remarks (with copies to the ambassador, the DCM, the economic counselor, and, in Washington, Dan Brewster and Charilaos Lagoudakis). It is appropriate to mention at this point that this was precisely four weeks prior to December 13, 1967, the date on which King Constantine launched his countercoup against the Papadopoulos junta.

Mavros "has a fairly specific action plan," my report began,

> for extricating the country from its present political difficulties. The king would play the key role by getting the government back into his own hands and then installing a transitional government. According to Mavros's plan, the king (having gotten his family out of the country) would go to Salonika with Prime Minister Kollias on December 13 (he was specific as to the date), would there rally the

Army commanders in the north to his side. On presentation to the government of the Mitrelias draft constitution, the king would announce to the country that he had accepted the resignation of the Kollias government.

The Pattakos-Papadopoulos-Makarezos crowd would have no choice but to capitulate to the king's action, for they are aware that most of Greece's military strength is in the north and would side with the king if they tried to make an issue of it. If they tried to hold out, they could not do so for long. In his announcement the king would thank the coup group for their services to the country but would declare that their task had been completed with the submission of the new constitution. He would also declare a general amnesty for all people connected with the coup and for all of their victims (people imprisoned as a result of the coup).

According to Mavros's plan the king would then install a royalist military government made up of the most senior generals who have been retired in recent years, before and after the coup, and who have had no connection with the coup (he mentioned several names including Gennimatas). This group would rule for a certain length of time, maintaining martial law, press censorship, and the present restrictions on civil liberties. When the time was ripe the king would replace the military government with a civilian all-party government made up of outstanding people, both politicians and able non-politicians, including Karamanlis, Kanellopoulos, George Papandreou, in other words, all prominent Greeks willing to serve their country. This transition government would stay in power for a while and would prepare the country for a return to elections.

On the question of elections, Mavros thinks a drastic reform is needed so that able people will be willing to enter politics without having to indulge in the normal, dirty politicking that the old Greek system required. He outlined a scheme under which the people would simply vote for a party list, and each such list would be headed up by 25 or 30 people of high intellectual caliber and moral stature who would be assured of election because of their positions high on the list and would thus not have to indulge in vote-buying, succumbing to special interests, and corruption to get elected.

Mavros said that the Americans should play a role in all this by giving the king their full support, both now to encourage him to act as set forth above and at the time the king dismissed the present government. Mavros said that he and a large group of prominent people are actively pushing this plan and urging it on the king. He assumes that the junta is aware of this effort but feels they cannot do much to stop it, since the people involved are too numerous and too prominent and are not plotting to overthrow the government but only to have it replaced. (This seems a somewhat subtle distinction for the likes of Papadopoulos to accept.) Mavros believes that all important politicians would be prepared to declare publicly their support for the king's action. This would help rally the people to accept the plan.

The remainder of the memo reported Mavros's critical remarks about the Mitrelias constitution-drafting committee, the Litton contract, the junta, and foreign press coverage of Greece, and about the United States for ruining its standing with the Greeks through failing to denounce the coup. He stressed his desire to avoid bloodshed and thought the Papadopoulos junta ought to be pardoned after they had been deposed.

I found Mavros's scheme an intriguing one, but wondered about its chances of success. If a large number of people were openly talking about it and urging it on the king, word of it would surely reach the junta, which would then take countermeasures to thwart it. Louise and I drove back home to Athens from Kifissia with Bruce Lansdale, who labeled it pie-in-the-sky.

Two days later Lansdale, back home in Salonika, sent me a letter containing a characteristically indirect comment on the Mavros plan in the form of one of the Hodja stories he was fond of retelling. Nasreddin Hodja is a semimythical Anatolian villager whose adventures display a combination of homely wisdom, foolishness, and earthy humanity—in sum, peasant philosophy of a special Near Eastern–Balkan sort. To understand the story one must know how yogurt (*yaourti* in Greek) is made in the home: by adding a "starter" dollop of yogurt to a bowl of boiled milk, wrapping the bowl in flannel to keep it warm overnight while the milk ferments, and thereby producing a bowl of new yogurt, the bacteria necessary to the process having been provided by the "starter." Yeast is also usually added to speed the fermentation process. "Dear Bob," Bruce wrote,

> One day, my friend Hodja was walking down to the pond with a bucket of yeast, of the variety they use to make *yaourti*. His curious neighbor saw him and asked what he was up to.
>
> "Oh," said Hodja, "It's simple. I'm going to throw this into the pond and the whole pond is going to turn into *yaourti*."

Well, the neighbor knew, and everyone else knew, that this was impossible. But who dared tell the great Hodja it was crazy? And besides, with Hodja, you always stood a chance of being made a fool of.

So the neighbor just hid behind a tree and watched as Hodja threw the bucket of yeast into the pond and stood there and waited, and waited, and waited. And nothing happened. He looked rather disgustedly toward heaven, shrugged his shoulders, and walked up the hill toward home.

Seeing the complete failure, the neighbor came out from hiding and attacked Hodja. "Now you knew perfectly well that this wouldn't work, Hodja," he lectured pointing his superior finger.

For a moment Hodja looked downcast, but then he turned to his neighbor with an enormous satisfied and rather contented grin—

"But wouldn't it have been wonderful if it *had* worked!!!"

Do you suppose that our friend George of the other evening may be throwing *yaourti* in the pond? You may want to share this with the Ambassador if you think it's appropriate and he needs a second of *Hodjasophia*.

Sincerely,
Bruce
November 17

I did share Bruce's letter with the ambassador. He sent it back to me the next day with a characteristically noncommittal notation at the bottom written in the green ink he always used: "Thanks, indeed."

Our most recent contact with Margaret Papandreou had been on November 1, when Louise and I had had dinner at her house, along with Margie Schacter and Margaret's closest Greek friends, Tito and Kiveli Zographides, who were to become our close friends in subsequent years. On November 21, in the midst of the Cyprus crisis, Margaret invited us to stop by for a drink. Margaret disclosed that she knew about the king's planning for a countercoup and noted that George Papandreou was in accord with the king's plan (confirming George Mavros's claim that the leading politicians of all parties were behind the king). Margaret offered to arrange a meeting for me with George Papandreou, who was temporarily not under house arrest, but it did not work out. After conferring with the elder Papandreou, Margaret reported back that he would agree to talk with me, trusting me on her say-so, if the Embassy wished to have his views on the current situation for its information. I passed this offer on to my superiors but was not instructed to follow it up.[1]

CRISIS IN CYPRUS

November 15, the day that I had written the report on Mavros's scheme for the king's takeover, was also the day that the 1967 Cyprus crisis began.

When I wrote this book in 1971–72, I made no attempt to cover this major event in Greek-Turkish and Greek-U.S. relations, primarily because I had no access to the key documents relating to the Cyrus Vance peacekeeping mission of November 22 to December 3, a signal early case of successful "shuttle diplomacy" that prevented the outbreak of war between our two NATO allies. At that time the cable traffic among Athens, Ankara, Nicosia, Washington, London, Paris, and New York was still highly classified, perhaps as many as a hundred documents reciprocally captioned "VANTO" and "TOVAN" between Vance and Washington. (Most of the key documents are now available in volume 16 of *FRUS*.)

Fortunately, that story has now been told, in a book by Parker T. "Pete" Hart, our ambassador to Turkey at the time.[2] Hart was able to obtain access to the key documents, though he had to take notes rather than make copies, as they had not yet been declassified. It is a thoroughly well-researched, well-written, and reliably accurate account, which was enhanced by interviews of many of the principal actors on all sides by the author.

During the period November 15–December 3, I was almost wholly caught up with the Cyprus crisis, all day every day, and even during my hours of sleep. I spent most of the nights sleeping in my office in the chancery, the first week as embassy duty officer and the second because Cyprus was my responsibility.

The crisis actually began in September when Papadopoulos made an ill-fated and ill-advised attempt to resolve the Cyprus dispute with Turkey by means of a poorly prepared, crash "summit meeting" of the Greek and Turkish prime ministers on both sides of the Evros River border between the two countries in Thrace. Papadopoulos apparently believed that sheer force of will and desire would solve the problem, but when he discovered that the Turks were not about to compromise their demands to accommodate him, his dreams of glory went up in smoke. The Turkish side learned from this episode that the Greek junta was in an extremely weak position, totally lacking in popular support, frightfully eager to earn some laurels by solving the Cyprus problem, desperately afraid of any military action that might be unsuccessful and might thus cause the Greek Army to turn against them. The Turks proceeded to capitalize on this situation to their own advantage, as one would expect and could hardly criticize.

The hotheaded General George Grivas, commander of the Greek forces on Cyprus, provided the Turks with the opportunity to take advantage of their relatively more advantageous position. On November 15 he attacked two Turkish Cypriot villages—Kophinou and Ayios Theodoros—with massive force, on the pretext of pushing a Cypriot police patrol through the villages, and killed a number of Turkish Cypriot villagers. The crisis quickly heated up to near-war proportions, and by November 22 it looked as though the Turks were determined (and prepared) to invade Cyprus to enforce their will.

Talbot was obliged to hoist storm signals despite his reluctance to bother Dean Rusk with a problem, and Washington became energized just in time to save the situation from complete disaster. President Johnson hurriedly dispatched Cyrus Vance from New York in a presidential jet to Ankara, with hardly any advance briefing, and Vance proceeded to work with very little sleep for ten days in the three affected capitals to achieve an ultimately successful resolution. The Greek government had to bring the aged but able right-wing retired diplomat/politician Panayiotis Pipinelis into the cabinet as foreign minister to rescue them from war, and they had to agree to the Turkish demand that all illegal Greek forces be withdrawn from Cyprus in return for a Turkish promise not to invade the island.

The significance of this episode for the internal situation in Greece was manifold, but we can limit ourselves to the observation that it showed everyone, from the king down to the last taxi driver, that the junta was by no means as strong as it seemed. Papadopoulos and his group had displayed a cringing readiness to accept humiliation from the Turks in order to avoid having to engage them militarily, for they feared that the upshot of a military defeat would be their own demise.

All this encouraged the king to think that the junta had lost face and stature and could be easily dislodged. Constantine had himself played an important role in negotiating the solution constructed by Vance. But unfortunately, he also thought he had learned the lesson that the junta was weak as well as incompetent and did not enjoy the confidence of at least an important segment of the senior officer corps of his army. What he did not realize was that the junta was very competent and well organized in one vital area: grabbing the reins of government and holding on to those reins even in adversity.

Constantine had also been encouraged to make his move at this time by the strong anti-junta statement issued from Paris by the former conservative prime minister, Constantine Karamanlis, published in *Le Monde* (and in Greece after some dispute between the right-wing press and the government) at the end of November. Karamanlis was criticized in some quarters in Greece for attacking the government when it was down, and while it was reeling from Turkish blows at the very height of the Cyprus crisis; but the principal effect of the Karamanlis statement was to reaffirm the conviction that the junta was in a weakened position and could be toppled with a slight push.

The king had been increasingly frustrated ever since April by his own inability to exercise any important influence over the junta. He kept determining to take a stand on this or that issue, but in the end he had caved in every time because he could see no alternative to going along with their demands. In early December he felt he was facing a decisive issue: the desire of the government to retire a large body of senior military officers who were known to be loyal to the monarch and not entirely dependable from the junta's point of view. The king decided he would finally take a stand on that issue, but Papadopoulos kept pressing him for his signature to the retirement decree.

Constantine decided he had to make his move prior to the publication of the annual army retirement list in January. Despite his stalling tactics, he would eventually have to approve some kind of retirement list, and it was bound to include the names of a great many senior officers personally loyal to him, those key commanders he would need to count upon in any countercoup attempt. Talbot was at least as aware of this situation as anyone else, but he made no great effort to discuss the king's problems with him, try to counsel him, or even get an accurate fix on the king's thinking at that critical juncture. Besides my report from Mavros four weeks earlier, there had been subsequent indications (mainly from our defense attaché, Colonel Marshall) that planning for a countercoup was under way among some senior commanders in the North. Still Talbot procrastinated. It was only on the very eve of December 13 that the king himself took the initiative by taking Talbot into his confidence, telling him briefly of his plans and asking that he pay him a visit at Tatoi early the following morning.

CHECKMATE OF CONSTANTINE

Earlier the junta had tried to intimidate the king by showing him a security report that listed his movements hour by hour and minute by minute, whom he talked with, what was said—an extraordinarily insulting dossier on a chief of state, but perhaps typical of those who had been trained in an intelligence service. The king proceeded to launch his countercoup, more or less along the lines of the plan outlined by Mavros. He had obtained the agreement and support of the leading politicians, such as George Papandreou and Kanellopoulos, in writing—their letters were found by the junta in the palace after the countercoup failed—and there was no doubt about the loyalty to his cause of the senior generals who were supposed to execute the countercoup. But, as is well known, it was carried out in a most inept fashion.

Constantine did take Prime Minister Kollias with him to Salonika (as Mavros had outlined). He also took his entire family, instead of sending them out of the country first, along with their pets and nursemaids, the queen's obstetrician, the queen mother, various aides, God knows how many trunks—two planeloads altogether. He might as well have asked the junta to take inventory for him. Prior to the departure of the king's flight north, Talbot came to call on him at the Tatoi Palace, as the king had requested, a meeting that was duly recorded by the junta.

If Papadopoulos and company had any doubts about the king's true intentions in flying north, they were dispelled in short order when a royalist general arrived at the Greek Pentagon bearing a letter from His Majesty, the commander in chief, to General Angelis that relieved Angelis of command of the Greek armed forces and appointed in his place the general bearing the king's letter. After reading it, Angelis called in his guards and had his caller placed under arrest. This episode may strike the reader as a curious act of formalism—protocol, almost—on the part of the king, an unnecessary preservation of the forms of courtesy, but I am inclined to believe that his intention was to make it easy for General Angelis, to give him an opportunity to save his skin by obeying the king's order and turning his command over to his designated successor. General Angelis sided with the junta, of which he had not been an original member, and he has sided with them ever since.

The government allowed Constantine to proceed with his countercoup attempt, making no effort to stop him, but they were somewhat concerned about how involved the American government was in the king's attempt. Had the ambassador's call on the king at Tatoi just before the countercoup meant that Talbot had given the signal for it to proceed after receiving word from Washington? This made little difference so far as the success or failure of the king's effort was concerned—it was destined to fail, since Papadopoulos had laid his own plans carefully—but Papadopoulos was apparently worried about what this might mean about the American government's continued acceptance of his regime.

At noon we received word that Papadopoulos, by now having installed himself as premier in succession to the defecting Kollias, wished the ambassador to call on him. There was not much Talbot could do; he could not avoid the issue. He had no idea how the king's attempt was faring, for we were singularly lacking in useful intelligence that morning, but he decided he must face the music. He took John Day along to take notes and made his way nervously down to the prime ministry. This meeting proved to be the most uncomfortable half hour of his entire mission to Greece, as he was interrogated by Papadopoulos and his cohorts about how much he knew about what the king was up to, whether he was behind it and, if not, then what was he doing conferring with the king at Tatoi that morning, and just whose side was he on anyway? Talbot parried their thrusts as best he could, but whether or not he realized it at that moment, his further usefulness as the American ambassador to Greece was all but wiped out that very day—that is, at least so long as the junta remained in power. The junta never trusted him again, considered him implicated in the effort to oust them from power, and had no use at all for him from that day forward. He remained in the job for another thirteen months, but with decreasing effectiveness, if one can make a meaningful distinction between inertia and paralysis.

I recall that I had a rather emotional reaction to the king's abortive countercoup attempt. Kay Bracken was full of disdain for the impetuosity and stupidity of the young king. I carried no royalist banner myself, but I argued with her that we had to offer him what support we could, that he simply had to succeed, otherwise we would be stuck with Papadopoulos for the indefinite future, with no restraint on him possible and with no means of exercising any influence on the government's course. It was perhaps tragic but indeed a fact that after April 21 we had placed all our eggs in the king's basket. We had counted on him to exercise a moderating influence on the junta, and we had furthermore counted on him to rescue us by throwing the junta out if things went really sour. "Kay," I said, "he simply has to succeed! If he fails now we have had it, and I mean that!" I do not recall her answer, but "Oh, pooh pooh" would not be too far off.

It was apparent that the king was using up all the assets that he and we possessed for affecting the future course of developments in Greece, for all the senior pro-American and pro-NATO officers who had not been implicated in the April 21 coup were now involved in the king's attempt; if they failed they would at the very least be eliminated from power, and they might even be killed. (In the event none were, fortunately.) The king's coup failed because these officers were too trusting: they knew who in their commands were Papadopoulos's spies and placed them under arrest when the countercoup started. But these arrested officers immediately pledged allegiance to the king and to the countercoup and were thereupon released and ordered to return to duty. They promptly turned around and, according to Papadopoulos's plan, arrested the senior officers, all the king's men, and that was the end of the countercoup.

My assignment on the day of the countercoup was principally to keep in touch with our consulate general in Salonika and keep them advised of developments in Athens. I was also to try to find out from them what was going on in the north, where all the action presumably was occurring. As it turned out, there was very little action anywhere and total silence at our consulate in Salonika. The junta had immediately cut all normal means of communication with the north as soon as the king had left for the north; but we did have our emergency single sideband. The only trouble was that no one was listening at the other end.

I worked all morning in the code room trying to get a rise out of Salonika. As we learned long after the event, it turned out that the consul general, Bill Hamilton, had gone off hunting in Yugoslavia, as was his frequent wont, without informing the ambassador, as required by State Department regulations. He was thus out of the country during the entire time that the major event in northern Greece since at least the Italian attack on Epirus in 1940 was taking place in his consular district. (Salonika was Hamilton's preretirement post.)

His deputy, Walter Silva, had taken off for Athens that morning by car, had just slipped through Larissa a short time before the king landed there to declare the countercoup, and was apparently lodged somewhere in Athens, totally oblivious of the events then shaking the country as it had not been shaken since April 21. He showed up at the Embassy the next day, December 14, sheepishly wondering why the PX at the American air base was closed, since the main purpose of his trip to Athens had been logistic—to replenish the larders and liquor cabinets of our colleagues in the northern outpost of the American mission. I told him to console himself with the observation that some people had probably also slept (or something) through the French Revolution as well, and if they had enjoyed themselves, not to worry—living through history and being aware of it can often be painful.

I have said that the countercoup was clearly a failure from its very start, from the moment that Constantine took off from Tatoi Airfield encumbered with all the baggage that even a modern king must carry into battle, but this failure was not obvious to us in the Embassy as the afternoon of December

13 progressed into the night. We were truly desperate for information on the progress of the king's effort. A sort of wake developed in Kay Bracken's office in the evening, running on after midnight. A chief mourner was Colonel O. K. Marshall, the army and defense attaché, who was a personal friend of the principal officers involved in the king's effort and who had predicted certain and early victory, based on his reconnaissance earlier that month to all the Greek army units in the north, a tour doubtless monitored by the junta and something that had contributed to their suspicion that the Americans had instigated the whole affair.

Another mourner was the assistant military attaché, whose job it had been for some years to keep in close touch with the king. They played squash together and had developed a genuine friendship, and this channel of contact had been most useful for keeping a line on the king's thinking without getting the ambassador involved on an official and highly public level. This American officer volunteered to drive north in his car to try to reach the king (who was believed to be in Kavalla at that moment), to try to find out how the thing was progressing, and to report back to us if he could find some means of doing so. We had, of course, highly sophisticated communications installations in Greece, but what we needed right then was something very simple: a telephone or a radio between the king in Kavalla and his officer-friend in Athens. The ambassador vetoed the officer's trip to Kavalla, since he was so well known to military people in Athens as the king's friend that he would never have gotten through the inevitable junta checkpoints blocking all passage to the north.

At that point I volunteered to undertake this mission, arguing that I was quite unknown to most of the military. I had a quite obscure gray VW Beetle without a diplomatic plate that I might just manage to get through on one excuse or another, perhaps a courier run to our consulate in Salonika. My offer was tentatively accepted, and I was advised to go home and get some sleep and return early in the morning, since it was likely to be a very long drive.

I went home and to bed, and when I returned to the Embassy at about 7 A.M. I was informed that the king had fled to Italy, was then in Rome with his entire entourage, prime minister, queen mother, wife, obstetrician, pets, trunks, and all, and it was all over. I was dejected and felt let down. I simply did not want to think about what we had done, what the king had done, how we had permitted such a fiasco. My despondency was doubtless made up in part of disappointment that I would not be making that dash to the north after all, but it was not the missing out on an adventure that most depressed me; it was the fact that the trip was now not necessary, that in less than twenty-four hours the king had first raised my hopes and then dashed them completely with his failure. Once again we had been Overtaken by Events.

The day after the king's flight to Rome I had a brief private session with Ambassador Talbot. As always, the timing of events fascinated him.

"You remember that conversation you had with Mavros? He called it for December 13 and December 13 it was. How did he happen to hit on that date?"

"That was the date he mentioned," I said. "I don't know. The king thinks thirteen is his lucky number, so he probably chose the date, and as I recall it had to do with the date the Mitrelias Committee was supposed to submit the new draft constitution. That was scheduled for December 15, and the idea was that the king would go to Salonika a few days in advance and receive the text and then accept the resignation of the Kollias government."

"Yes, I know all that," said Talbot, "but if Mavros knew the date and you knew the date, why everyone must have known the date!"

"That's right," I said. "That's right! Everyone knew the date. Obviously."

On Monday, when mail deliveries resumed, I received a short note from Bruce Lansdale, mailed from Salonika on Thursday: "Dear Bob, Sorry about that yogurt yeast. Maybe a different kind will work better. Bruce."

I did not bother to pass this note on to the ambassador; he probably didn't understand how yogurt is made in the home.

AFTERMATH OF FAILURE

The biggest loser from the failure of Constantine's countercoup attempt was not Ambassador Talbot or the U.S. government but of course the king himself. He lost what face he still retained after his inept interferences in politics of the previous two years. The lowliest character of all in the Greek antipantheon is the incompetent bungler who botches up any job he undertakes. One could forgive a chief of state's political biases, but one could not excuse his ineptitude.

Among the highly anomalous aspects of the king's uncoup (in which I include his failure to give Talbot even a full day's advance notice of what he was about to undertake) was the fact that he had chosen the unluckiest day of the Greek month, the thirteenth. It was not quite *the* unluckiest, which would have been a Tuesday the thirteenth (like our Friday the thirteenth): it was on a Tuesday that the Byzantine Empire fell to the Turks, or something like that. In 1967 December 13 fell on a Wednesday. In Greece, as elsewhere, thirteen is supposed to be an unlucky number. Surely Constantine's education and training had been Hellenic enough for him to know that the highly superstitious Greeks would be prepared to declare in advance a failure any dangerous enterprise undertaken on such an inauspicious day; only a nut would try to pull off a coup on a thirteenth day of the month. Unless the nut were Constantine.

But there were contrary explanations: Constantine had tried to fool the junta by scheduling his effort on a day—December 13—when they would never expect it (unless they had been listening to Mavros). Furthermore, Constantine thought thirteen was his lucky number: his birthday fell on the thirteenth, he was the thirteenth "Byzantine" king of that name, he had been married on that day, or he had come in thirteenth in his first sailing race, or something. In any case, he considered thirteen lucky. He was obsessed with it: the royal automobile license plate was number thirteen. But such is fate that he has now gone down in history as a *goursouzis,* a man with the evil eye on him, a man who is unavoidably unlucky; for this term of derision and contempt—pinned on him now by his enemies—means a man who may bet all he wants but who always loses.

Margaret Papandreou was understandably concerned over what effect the king's failure would have on her husband's situation. We had last seen her on December 9, shortly before the king's move, when she had come to dinner along with the Zographides. On December 19 she appeared at our house at about 9 A.M. in an agitated state, worried that Papadopoulos might take some drastic action against her still-imprisoned husband now that the countercoup had failed. She asked Louise if I could give her any encouraging information or advice. I went to see her that evening. She wasted no time, asking for my assessment of what Constantine's aborted ouster attempt would mean in general and specifically for Andreas. I do not recall exactly what I told her, except that my analysis turned out to be incorrect in certain important respects. I did not want to give her any false hope that the December events might lead to her husband's release from prison. I told her I thought Papadopoulos had now measurably strengthened his position, for he had got rid of all the royalist elements in the army leadership and in the government, and he would henceforth be able to rule the country just as he saw fit, with no restraining forces exerted against him.

I had no idea what decision with respect to Andreas this might lead him to. Perhaps Papadopoulos would feel so self-confident that he would decide he could afford to let Andreas go, as he no longer posed any threat, or he might want to distract people's attention with a big show trial of the ASPIDA people. But, I speculated, it would be difficult for him to try Andreas and the others for treason without also trying the officers who had just assisted the king in his countercoup effort, and Papadopoulos would probably not want to risk stirring up dissension in the army by putting a whole batch of distinguished senior generals in the dock. In sum, I did not know what would happen, but the most dangerous thing was that Papadopoulos was now supreme in power and could do more or less as he wished.³

My analysis was wrong in that Papadopoulos and his gang would continue to feel quite insecure even after the December events, and their shakiness would not be dispelled for another month to six weeks. For one thing—and this was important psychologically—Greece's principal allies, led by the United States, did not accord instant recognition to the new government headed by Prime Minister Papadopoulos. The situation was quite different from what it had been on April 21 in that now the chief of state had fled the country, and the junta had promptly and illegally installed a regent in his place, General Zoitakis, the man who before April 21 had made Papadopoulos privy to the Generals' coup and had thus permitted him to preempt the plan.

Despite his considerable experience in diplomacy, Ambassador Talbot nearly blew the question of recognition. On December 14 the Embassy received a call from the Prime Ministry that the prime minister would like to receive the ambassadors of the principal NATO allies of Greece, including Ambassador Talbot. I was in the ambassador's office when the message came in and was horrified to observe that Talbot's immediate reaction was to accept the invitation. I pointed out that his meeting with the prime minister would be tantamount to recognition and would be broadcast as such. Talbot hesitated and then said it would not necessarily mean that, as he could make clear to Papadopoulos at the time. Trying to think quickly and in some desperation, I suggested that I call the other Western embassies to see what their plans were, since it would be best if all the NATO embassies concerted on a single policy and acted consistently on this. Talbot readily agreed.

I called the British, French, Germans, and Italians and found, as I had expected, that none of these ambassadors had any intention of meeting with the new self-appointed prime minister. To do so would mean recognition, and they were without instructions on this score from their foreign ministries. They were of course eager to know what the Americans were planning to do. I tried to cover my embarrassment by saying that we were pretty much in the same situation as they were (which they could interpret any way they liked, but at least it didn't make us look as stupid as we would have if I had said that my ambassador was considering accepting the invitation).

As it turned out, we stalled on the recognition issue for several weeks. Not until almost a month later, January 12, 1968, did the Embassy resume "informal" top-level contacts with the Greek government, when Talbot called on Foreign Minister Pipinelis. And it was not until about January 23 that we formally granted recognition and resumed full diplomatic relations, as Talbot announced following a second, official call on Pipinelis. Had the ambassador gone off half-cocked that December 14 to see the new prime minister by himself, he would have made himself the butt of ridicule by the Athens diplomatic community, perhaps lamely explaining afterward that of course he had not meant to accord recognition by his action, but wasn't it important to find out what was going on? An unfriendly critic might have added that it was also important to try to square oneself with the new regime, which thought he had been in cahoots with the king or perhaps even the instigator of his ill-advised escapade.

Ten

ASSESSING THE COLONELS' REGIME

THE *FDR* FIASCO

In mid-February, a few weeks after the Embassy had resumed normal relations with the Greek regime, Ambassador Talbot enthusiastically accepted a proposal by the local American military that he invite Colonel Papadopoulos, the new premier, to a luncheon aboard the Sixth Fleet carrier *Franklin D. Roosevelt*. The American military sold the idea to him as a means of reingratiating himself with the junta, to counter their displeasure with his performance in connection with the king's coup. The ambassador and the prime minister would break bread together aboard the American carrier, and they would be friends ever after.

I pointed out to the ambassador that while this scheme might be of some benefit in making Papadopoulos less suspicious of him, and therefore more amenable to accepting his advice, it would have the decidedly adverse effect of totally undercutting the posture of "cool but correct" relations with the Greek government that we were supposed to be maintaining as the cornerstone of our policy. I anticipated that the luncheon would be heavily publicized in Greece and abroad as an embrace by the U.S. government of the new Greek regime. My argument was countered with the observation that only official U.S. Navy journalists and photographers would be aboard the carrier, so we would be in control of any publicity that might arise out of the function. As a former newspaperman Talbot should have known better than to swallow that.

Papadopoulos eagerly accepted the invitation and brought with him to the luncheon the two other principals of the coup group, Brigadier Pattakos and Colonel Makarezos. There was extensive photographic coverage of their visit to the ship by the official U.S. Navy photographers, who, with their usual efficiency, provided full sets of large, blown-up prints within a few hours for delivery to the high-ranking Greek guests. Naturally, these pictures were plastered all over the Athens papers in their very next editions, under banner headlines proclaiming the shipboard visit a momentous occasion in the history of the April 21 Revolution, as it surely was, since it signaled the official and indisputable embrace of the junta by the U.S. government. The backlash in the U.S. Congress and the American press, led by the *New York Times,* was equally vehement, with severe criticism of Talbot for having permitted himself to be so used. The fact that the ship in question, the *FDR,* carried the name of the father of modern American political liberalism aroused special bitterness in that it had served as the bed on which the Greek junta had been embraced.

Ambassador Talbot lamely replied to the criticism (privately) that of course we had not anticipated the way in which the regime would make propaganda capital out of the visit, a visit that was moreover quite routine: it was traditional for Greek defense ministers to pay courtesy visits to major ships of the Sixth Fleet visiting Athens. Talbot's critics in the Greek opposition couldn't stomach that answer. It was true that Papadopoulos was defense minister, but how could anyone overlook that he was also the prime minister—and the obvious difference between a routine visit by a civilian defense minister of a normal political cabinet under a parliamentary regime and this unprecedented gesture toward a group whom the king had tried to get rid of only a few weeks before?

One interesting aspect of this episode (an episode that still rankles many Greeks, for whom it remains a classic instance of diplomatic ineptitude) is that the great enthusiasm the Papadopoulos regime displayed in giving massive publicity to the event is proof positive of their desperate hankering after American acceptance and support. At that time, and for many months afterward, the members of the junta continued to feel terribly insecure in their ministerial chairs and went out of their way to play up and exaggerate any small sign of American benediction.

ANDREAS RELEASED

Margaret Papandreou and her four children were facing a bleak Christmas season, with husband and father in Averoff Prison, Papadopoulos riding high (apparently) down at the Prime Ministry, and the future very much in doubt. To cheer them up a bit, Louise delivered to them a fat American frozen turkey to roast for their Christmas dinner. We then drove north to Salonika through a raging snowstorm that our Citroën negotiated successfully despite the blockage of most highway traffic for a couple of days. We were joining the Lansdale family for a skiing vacation in Austria. We gave up the idea of driving beyond Salonika because of the icy road conditions ahead in Yugoslavia, and continued instead by train to the unfashionable (and thus inexpensive) resort of St. Johann im Pongau (the wrong St. Johann).

On Christmas Eve we watched the news on Austrian television, and were surprised and delighted to see a film clip of Andreas Papandreou with his family outside their house in Psychiko, greeting friends and well-wishers and smiling and hugging his children. He had been released just before Christmas as part of a general amnesty decreed by Papadopoulos that resulted in the departure from jail of some hundreds of political prisoners.

I took this at first to be a gesture of generosity and moderation, which of course it was, but subsequent analysis back in Athens led me to believe that it was more a part of Papadopoulos's campaign to win recognition and acceptance from Greece's Western allies, who were highly sensitive to the question of the regime's treatment of political prisoners. Andreas had a lot of friends in the West, and it helped smooth things along to let him out of jail.

This action also disposed of the problem of what to do with him, specifically whether to bring him to trial for treason on the ASPIDA charges. The case was a flimsy one at best, and a show trial with less than solid evidence would certainly not have helped the regime's image abroad. That Christmas Papadopoulos even amnestied the army officers who had been convicted back in 1966, prior to the coup, for implication in the ASPIDA affair. Greeks said he could do no less, since he was not planning to act against the king's countercoup officers beyond discharging them from the army, though with full pension rights preserved. There were also stories, which I could never confirm, that the ASPIDA officers had originally been members of Papadopoulos's EENA conspiracy group, which in the 1960s had split into left and right wings, the leftists going into ASPIDA, the rightists staying with Papadopoulos and now occupying the seats of power. In other words, according to this version, Papadopoulos was now merely freeing ex-comrades in conspiratorial arms.

Following our return to Athens from Austria, Louise and I were invited by Margaret Papandreou to their house for dinner so that her husband "could meet the only Americans who had been kind to her," as she expressed it, during all the time he had spent in Averoff Prison. I was eager to meet Andreas after all this time, and it no longer seemed improper. Since he had been amnestied, all was forgiven, and he was back inside the pale if not yet in the parlor. Andreas said he had enjoyed our turkey very much and was highly appreciative of our help to his wife and children during the previous four months.

We talked for several hours, the only conversation I had with him during my four-year tour in Athens. It helped me come to some of the understandings that are apparent from the points of view presented in this memoir. He told me his versions of the Vince Joyce and Lock Campbell episodes, traced the checkered history of his relations with the official American establishment in Athens, recounted his prison experiences, and gave his analysis of Papadopoulos, Pattakos (who had called on him frequently in prison), and the other junta leaders, much of which is now recorded in his book, *Democracy at Gunpoint: The Greek Front*. It was fascinating, for it was all then new to us.

Andreas also talked about his plans for the future. He hoped to obtain permission to go abroad, where he planned to resume his teaching career, for he had to earn his living and support his family (he had no private wealth, and his father, despite his half century in Greek politics, had never amassed much wealth). He said nothing directly about any political plans, but from a number of things he said there was no doubt in my mind that should he succeed in getting out of Greece, he would engage in whatever anti-junta activities he could find the time for outside of his academic duties.

Andreas also disclosed that he and Margaret had called on Ambassador and Mrs. Talbot at the residence a couple of days earlier, while he was still anxiously awaiting a response from the Greek government to his request for a passport. This information surprised me, for I was certain that Talbot would have reported his conversation with Andreas to Washington by cable, yet I had not seen any mention of it, no reporting telegram, in the Embassy reading file. The following account of the Talbot-Papandreou meeting is drawn from a number of sources, with the contradictions noted.[1]

The meeting was arranged at the request of the Papandreous and came about through Margaret's suggestion, although in his book Andreas says it was his father's idea. Andreas offered the ambassador genuine thanks for the kind treatment by the Embassy of his wife and children during his incarceration. Margaret had not yet told him the truth about how she had been treated, for she feared that he would fall into a rage and launch some sort of verbal attack against the Embassy, which might have jeopardized their chances of getting out of Greece. Andreas assumed that Louise and I had been acting on embassy instructions in "looking after" his family. The truth was—as I have already explained—that we were given absolutely no encouragement to have anything at all to do with the Papandreous. Even longstanding precoup friends of the family, such as our economic officer, Ed Cohen, a former student of Andreas's at Berkeley, felt inhibited from maintaining even the most distant of relations.

Talbot accepted Andreas's expression of thanks on behalf of the American Embassy. He was doubtless vastly relieved to find that neither Mr. nor Mrs. Papandreou apparently harbored any feelings of ill will toward the Embassy, despite what he very well knew was the nearly absent official interest in the family's welfare once it became clear in the days immediately after April 21 that Andreas would not be summarily executed. Talbot was as eager as the Greek government to know what Andreas's plans were and was profoundly relieved to learn that he hoped to resume his academic career.

Andreas naturally said nothing to Talbot about any plans for resistance activities abroad. He was certainly not candid with Talbot—he did not tell "the whole truth"—but I believe this was understandable. One reason for his call on Talbot, I thought, was to make sure that the Americans would not place any obstacles in the path of his departure—for example, by telling the Greek government that it would be unwise to let him go. This is somewhat ironic, for many Greeks believed that Andreas was released from prison and allowed to leave the country as a result of official American pressure on the Greek government to that end. There had been no such pressure, although Talbot *had* tried, and had succeeded, just after the April 21 takeover, in obtaining assurances that Andreas would not be executed; and much later on he had interceded with the Greek authorities when Margaret had difficulties with her permit to visit her husband in Averoff Prison.

With his normal paranoia about the attitude of the official American community toward him, Andreas would have feared a contrary sort of pressure on the question of his departure from Greece. Talbot promised Andreas speedy issuance of a U.S. visa once he received his new Greek passport and was pleased by his decision to go to the United States to resume his academic career. According to Talbot's report to Washington, they had a long discussion about the current situation in Greece, and Andreas expressed support for the U.S. posture toward the regime of working with it step by step to restore a constitutional and elected government in due course.

Once when I mentioned to a colleague my hunch as to what the real motive had been for Andreas's final call on Talbot—that he wanted the Embassy to think his sole interest was in resuming his academic career abroad, so that the Embassy could confirm this impression to the Greek government should they inquire—my colleague was shocked at my statement. Apparently he thought I shared the Papandreous' fears about what the Embassy might do. I wasn't sure what Talbot might do, but I believe I was accurate in assessing the motives of the Papandreous on this occasion.

Suppose Andreas had had the temerity to tell Talbot the whole truth, confidentially, namely that his main reason for wishing to leave Greece was to free himself to work his damnedest to bring about the downfall of the junta by organizing a broad-based international resistance movement, and that his second order of business (after touring Western European and Scandinavian capitals) would be to go to Washington in order to lobby in the halls of Congress and within the executive branch for a drastic change in U.S. policy toward the junta (precisely what he did do when he left Greece). Would Talbot have kept his confidence, would he have extended his noninvolvement to cover Andreas's hoped for departure?

Margaret Papandreou explained the January 8 call on Talbot in the following terms:

> At this point Andreas and I decided to pay a visit to Talbot at the Embassy to see if we couldn't get some of the burrs whirred out of the machinery that had stopped the passport in its forward progress. We decided (a) to be nice to him and thank him for what he had done for us, (b) to practice not gagging when we expressed the sentiments under (a), (c) to show little interest in Greek affairs, except on a high analytical level, and (d) to show inclination toward a return to teaching. I arranged the interview through McClelland of the political section, and on Saturday, January 12 [sic], we had a tete-à-tete with the ambassador at noon at his residence—with ouzo—which had the atmosphere of two boxers sparring lightly in the gym while saving their heavy punches for the real fight later. On the following Monday night, Andreas was handed his passport by Pattakos himself and wished "good luck—to you and your family." The thing we had dreaded, a demand for a written renunciation of politics, did not come up. If it had, our only way out of Greece would have had to be the illegal one.[2]

As an illustration of Margaret's feelings about the Embassy, after weeks of frustrating contact by herself, relatives, and friends with Talbot, Anschuetz, and others following Andreas's incarceration, I cite the following passage from her book (268–69), a scene in which Walter Heller and Margaret are discussing the planned exposure in the United States by Vachliotis and Diakoyiannis of their perjured statements against Andreas in the ASPIDA case, an operation that Margaret was trying to carry out with great secrecy.

> Heller says: "Well, I told Kay Bracken about this story. I thought they should know what kind of methods were used to get Andy."
>
> I didn't move. I stared at him for several seconds. The rapid, steady torrent of information we had been exchanging stopped like the abrupt end of a summer storm.
>
> "Oh, Walter," I finally burst out, "you've been in government service too long—or something. You think of the Embassy as an *ally*. All along it's been one of our greatest enemies, refusing to understand anything Andreas was doing, and fighting him at every point. They know the dirty methods that have been used; they don't want others to know that they know. Now I *am* afraid."
>
> "I don't think Kay has any desire to make things rougher for you. But I'm sorry. I thought this would help."
>
> "It isn't that any of them have personal animosity toward me, though they may have toward Andreas, but they are all part of a machine and in the end become the cogs that grind out the policy. And the policy is not very favorable toward us, nor toward the Greek people, I am afraid. Well, anyway, it's done."

According to Andreas's account of his January 8 meeting with the ambassador,[3] Talbot did most of the talking and apparently indulged his penchant for analogies, for he likened George Papandreou to Mossadegh of Iran (not a very flattering comparison to throw at old George's son). Andreas wrote that this meeting took place before he had a promise of a passport from Pattakos and that Talbot, knowing Andreas had received many offers of academic positions in the United States, said he was authorized to give him a visa should he want one.

As I later learned, Talbot happily sent off a long cable to Washington reporting his conversation with Andreas. Two or three days later Andreas obtained permission to leave Greece and received his passport personally from Brigadier Pattakos, within whose jurisdiction such matters lay. Pattakos took the precaution of secretly tape-recording his conversation with Papandreou on that occasion. In response to the jolly brigadier's question as to whether he had been mistreated in prison, Andreas said not especially,[4] except for being kept in solitary. Asked about his plans (would he try to mobilize public opinion abroad against the regime? for example), Andreas responded that he would seek to regain his health, he would pursue an academic career, and he would be "true to himself." Asked by the brigadier if he planned to return to politics, Andreas said, "If the Greek people want me to return, I will." They then discussed the regime, its policies, and its future—disagreeing on all scores, of course—and Pattakos gave him his passport and wished him luck. Andreas, Margaret, and the children hopped aboard the first available plane for Paris before the junta could change its collective mind.

When I finally was able to read Talbot's cable reporting his farewell conversation with Andreas, I was more than distressed by its substance and tone, for more reasons than one. Not only had Talbot chosen to pass on to Washington Andreas's words of thanks for the Embassy's help to his family, but he had taken credit personally for what had been done. He gleefully reported that Andreas planned to stick to an academic career and had no political plans. Had he cared to inquire or shown me the cable prior to dispatch, I could have corrected Talbot's impressions before he put himself on record in that manner, which was only asking for trouble. I am afraid that my gut reaction was, If that's the way he's going to be, then let him ask for it; I wash my hands of it. And in the aftermath I was relieved that we had not had our dinner meeting with Andreas and Margaret until after they had seen Talbot at his residence, so that none of the misunderstanding, deception, or whatever it actually had been could be blamed on me.

In fact, we didn't talk about our dinner with Andreas and Margaret with anyone, which the following incident may help to explain. A few days after the departure of the Papandreous from Greece, we were invited to lunch by the Shan Sedgwicks. He was a retired *New York Times* correspondent with a Greek wife who, like Sulzberger's, was close to the royal family. The guests were a virulently right-wing, pro-junta group, mostly elderly retired types like former American ambassador to Taiwan Karl Rankin. Throughout the lunch they all ranted and raved against the U.S. Embassy for having "allowed" Andreas to escape from Greece, suggested it would have been much better had his demise been arranged in prison, and so forth. Louise and I bit our tongues, fearful that someone might uncover the fact that we had just recently dined with the monster.

Talbot's cable returned to haunt him almost immediately after it was dispatched. On his arrival in Paris, Andreas gave a press conference in which he blasted the junta with both barrels. It was then apparent to everyone that he had no intention of installing himself in some academic backwater of the

United States where he would quietly pursue research in econometrics and, thoroughly chastened and cleansed by his term in jail, keep his views on the junta to himself. It became clear that he intended to organize what forces he could abroad in a resistance movement with the aim of toppling the Papadopoulos junta with any means available.

Pattakos, doubtless stung by criticism from his colleagues for having been so stupid as to let Papandreou out of the country and thus beyond the junta's control, immediately put out a statement to the press claiming that Andreas had promised him he would not engage in politics abroad. He even offered to play his taped recording of their final conversation for the press, but on reconsideration decided against this course, probably because it would have merely confirmed that the wily Andreas had made a fool of him.

Someone else who looked quite foolish at this point was Talbot, with his naive prediction that Andreas was going to be a good boy from now on and could be counted on to behave. On Talbot's instructions the USIS in Athens put out a partial version of Andreas's last conversation with the American ambassador in which Papandreou allegedly gave his blessing to the American policy of trying to work with the regime in Greece. This was transparently designed to cut the ground out from under Andreas and make him out to be a liar, a hypocrite, a rat, or some combination of all three.

As anyone could have predicted, Andreas immediately replied from Paris with a violent counterattack, the full text of which is given in his book.[5] Andreas alleged that Talbot's motive in putting out his version of their conversation had been to try to prevent Andreas from being an effective voice in the United States during his forthcoming visit there. Andreas referred to the "pernicious role" of the American Embassy and other American agencies in Greece and mentioned their *Gauleiter* representatives. He charged that the Embassy was trying "to assist the junta in their unholy task of enslaving the Greek people and destroying in Greece all sense of human dignity.... After eight months of complete isolation in the hands of the totalitarian regime in Greece, I could hardly have approved of the U.S. Embassy's maintenance of 'correct relations' with the tyrants of Greece."

It is possible that once they were safely out of Greece, Margaret had told her husband the truth about how she had been treated by the Embassy while he was in jail. This would help account for the rage Andreas displayed in Paris over Talbot's effort to discredit him. Talbot was quite upset about being called a *Gauleiter*, but he doubtless chalked it up to Andreas's deep-seated anti-Americanism, which his jail term had apparently done nothing to moderate.

"DEAR CHARLEY"

On January 15, 1968, I wrote a letter to Charilaos ("Charley") Lagoudakis, the intelligence and research analyst for Greece in the State Department:

> I am sure you are as aware as I am of the ironies in the present situation, but just between you and me and the lamp post, here they are.
>
> Last winter and spring, as the country was preparing for elections, there were fears about the true goals and intentions of the Center Union, and Andreas Papandreou specifically, and great trepidation about what would happen should the Center Union win the elections. Among other things, it was feared that a victorious Center Union would overthrow the regime, abolish the monarchy and send the King into exile. Furthermore, the Center Union was accused of wishing to purge the armed forces in order to turn them into instruments of their own political power, to ensure military support for the Center. Also, the Center leaders were called demagogues, that is, politicians who make wild promises to the people that they can never hope to fulfill, in order to gain the people's support and votes. Lastly, there was fear that a Center victory would be merely the first stage in an eventual Communist take-over of the country.
>
> Today the King is in exile. The monarchy is dead as a political force. There is a good chance that we may eventually have a republic here, in other words, a final overthrow of the regime. The armed forces are now being purged of all loyalist-royalist elements so that they can become a pure instrument of the present regime, in other words, a political tool of the government. As for demagoguery, the junta could give a few lessons to Andreas Papandreou in how to gain popular support by making outlandish claims and promises of glories to come if people will only support them.
>
> And finally, the question of a first stage leading to an eventual Communist take-over—I leave you to contemplate the prospects of this development, if you can still keep from smiling.

HARASSMENT CONTINUES

The harassment by the Greek security services and the American CIA continued. On January 29 Margie Schacter telephoned Louise to inform her of the near-fatal automobile accident Tito Zographides had suffered a few days after the Papandreous' departure from Greece. She suggested that Louise meet her at the Papandreou house in Psychiko, where she was going to be engaged in packing their household effects, to hear the sad details of the accident, and discuss what we might do to help Tito. Louise drove there on a dark, rainy afternoon in our old VW, which carried a "foreign mission" rather than a diplomatic plate. Louise left the house with Margie a half hour later, dropping her off near the main boulevard to catch a taxi into town. The following morning DCM McClelland called me into his office and told me that our car had "again been reported parked outside the Papandreous' house." He instructed me to tell my wife not to go there again. At the time the house had been empty for two weeks, ever since the Papandreous' departure for Paris on January 15.

Like many wives of Foreign Service officers, Louise gets involved in various welfare activities that American women are encouraged to be active in abroad, or were before they were "liberated" in 1971. Louise enjoys such work and did it without being told or asked. On February 5 she and Mrs. Bonte Duran, an American married to the United Nations resident representative in Greece, visited an Orthodox priest named Father George, who had recently been released from detention. They had heard that he was ready to resume his program of feeding poor children in his parish of Perama, a near-slum area next to the port of Piraeus that was crowded with refugees from Asia Minor who traditionally voted for leftist candidates. In years past Father George had been helped by USIS wives, who gave him monthly donations of sugar that they collected at their meetings. The Welfare Committee of the American Women's Organization of Greece (AWOG, honorary president Mrs. Talbot) had also assisted Father George's programs in the past. Mrs. Duran and Louise were members of this Welfare Committee. Other generous organizations, such as Church World Service and the U.S. Sixth Fleet, had made donations to Father George. The Swedish Evangelical Church had built him a day care center in Perama, from which, however, the Greek government now barred him.

Mrs. Duran and Louise listened to an emotional report from Father George, a man of limited education (not uncommon among Greek parish priests) but a very large heart, which they then recounted—doubtless equally emotionally—to the next meeting of the American wives on the Welfare Committee. The wife of CIA's number two, present at the meeting, took copious notes. The next day her husband went to the ambassador and reported that the American wives were getting involved in politics, and left-wing politics at that. The ambassador wisely passed the buck to his wife, who not only decreed that Perama and Father George were henceforth out of bounds, but took the rather extreme precaution of disbanding the entire Welfare Committee and ordering the appointment of a whole new batch of wives, entirely contrary to the semidemocratic or at least honorable procedures that normally prevail in such organizations. Louise, having tracked down what had happened, later confronted the CIA man and asked him what evidence he had that Father George was a "Communist," which was the apparent basis of the entire imbroglio. The deputy station chief said that Father George had always voted for the cryptocommunist (as we liked to term it in the Embassy) EDA party.

How he knew how the man had voted, in a country supposedly dedicated to the secret ballot, he did not explain. Furthermore, voting for EDA was obviously the only sensible course for those who lived in Perama—priest, peasant, or proletarian—as anyone who has spent some time there can attest.

THE MEANING OF FASCISM

On February 23, in an effort to educate some of my colleagues about the nature of the regime we were working with, I prepared and circulated a memo on "The Meaning of Fascism." The new DCM, McClelland, and Mrs. Bracken were at that time inclined to argue that "the coup leaders feel their revolution has its own legitimacy." Thus, accepting the fact that this had been no mere power grab but something that was trying to present itself as a genuine revolution, just what sort of revolution was it? My memo tried to make a subtle point, without a direct statement that would have antagonized everyone (that is, by calling the regime "fascist"), by quoting an encyclopedia article on fascism after the following introduction of my own:

> Since April 1967 I have heard the term "fascist" bandied about in many conversations, and in many cases I believe the term has been misused or has been used without a full understanding of its meaning in the context of 20th Century history. Some people tend to associate "fascism" with extreme right-wing conservatism, rule by the entrenched power elite, a reactionary ideology, aggressive military expansionism, anti-Semitism, and the dictatorships of Mussolini and Hitler. I think this is only partially accurate. More correctly "fascism" as we have experienced it historically has the following general characteristics: authoritarian government and dictatorship,

rule by a single party with a mass base of supporters but with power vested in a very small elite, extreme nationalism, militant anti-Communism, regimentation of life, anti-individualism, "corporate" organization of the state, anti-Semitism, emphasis on efficiency in government, a somewhat progressive social program appealing to underprivileged groups, political alliance with vested interests, anti-intellectualism, racism (in Germany), a revolutionary as well as counter-revolutionary origin, demagogic appeals to prejudice, the demand that the individual subordinate himself to the nation, opposition to parliamentary democracy, emphasis on police state methods, bellicosity in foreign affairs, and appeals to Christian virtue. Because the ideological base of fascism is vested in emotion rather than in a rational program, it is flexible and easily adapted to different national conditions. And because fascism was the direct cause of the tragedy of World War II, fascists no longer advertise their ideology as fascism.

The encyclopedia article (*Columbia*, 2nd ed., 1956) followed. It does not appear to me now that I was making my point with any great subtlety, for my list of the characteristics of fascism was a reasonably accurate description of the programmatic content, such as it was, of the April 21 "Revolution." But I apparently did not make my point, for the DCM sent me back his copy of the memo with the notation: "Helpful refresher at this juncture in Greece's political life. RDMcC." I was trying to say that what we were doing was giving our support to a fascist regime in a NATO ally, and the DCM labeled this a "helpful refresher"!

FRICTION AT THE EMBASSY

KAY LEAVES, I CONTINUE

I believe this is an appropriate place to slow down if not to stop this memoir, because I begin to get the feeling "More of the same!" Kay Bracken, having been passed over by Talbot for the DCM slot, had decided to retire to Florida. She offered to stay on till summer, until a new political counselor arrived, but her offer was declined and she left Greece in February. A farewell gathering in her stateroom on the ship she took home out of Piraeus was made memorable by the vicious verbal attack she made on Talbot, which no one could help overhearing. The stateroom was quite small, and there was no neutral corner into which Talbot could escape from her wrath. The rest of us turned away in embarrassment. Kay was extremely bitter at the ambassador; the grounds were personal, for I never detected any disagreement that they might have had over policy. Kay may have felt that she had received a promise of the DCM job. As noted earlier, the fact was that Mrs. Talbot wanted a married DCM whose wife could assist her socially, that is, in entertaining Greeks, diplomats, visitors, and others at home, and the ambassador had bowed to her wishes.

On March 7 Talbot asked us all to give him our "horseback hunches" on how we thought things would develop over the following six months in several fields: constitutional progress, political activity, public administration, the economy, what Talbot liked to call "the politics of demilitarization" (still in pursuit of new analogies, he had just read a book on how other countries had worked their way back from military coups), and the restoration of constitutional government. It would be of only mild interest to detail here my predictions of that day, but they were on the whole quite pessimistic. I guessed that a constitutional referendum would indeed be held about September 15 (it was actually held on September 29), as promised by Papadopoulos. I doubted that political activity would be permitted in connection with the plebiscite or at any other time soon. I thought the "brain drain" out of Greece would accelerate. I predicted economic difficulties for 1968 but doubted that these would be translated into political problems for the regime. I threw in a wild guess that the new constitution would not be promulgated until April 21, 1971, that is, four years after the Papadopoulos coup. I concluded that the government would only reluctantly move in the direction of restoring constitutional government, and it would move as slowly as possible. Today such a statement seems self-evident, but at the time it flew in the face of the foundation of our entire policy toward Greece, which was to prod the regime to move rapidly toward a restoration of constitutional, representative, democratic government.

The above ambassadorial exercise set me off on a train of thinking that came to involve a reexamination of our entire policy posture, and two days later, on March 10, 1968, I launched a determined effort to get the senior officers of the Embassy to face the facts as I saw them. The first salvo was a nineteen-page memorandum entitled "Some Thoughts on Our Present Predicament," which I addressed to the ambassador through George Warren, the acting political counselor following Kay Bracken's departure. I have quoted from this memo earlier in the present memoir the portion giving an analysis of the Andreas Papandreou phenomenon. (The full text of this memo is the first item in appendix B.)

This memorandum so "shook up" George Warren that he gave it to the DCM, Ross McClelland, rather than the ambassador, a perhaps understandable instance of buck passing, since he did not want to be thought responsible in any way for my views, even for forwarding them. Some days passed, and I heard nothing from the ambassador or anyone else about what I conceded was a bureaucratic "bombshell." The first person who spoke to me about it was the new CIA station chief, Jack Maury's replacement, who approached me at a cocktail party hosted by his deputy and said, "About your memorandum, do you think we could talk sometime about that?"

I was quite startled, since I had intended my memorandum for the ambassador's eyes (as well as George Warren's, McClelland's—I had sent a carbon copy directly to the DCM—and my Political Section colleagues'), but

I said, "Sure, whenever you like." I went to see him the next day and discovered without surprise that what was bothering him was my account of the Lock Campbell–Andreas Papandreou incident, as well as my assertion that one of the reasons for the split between Andreas and the Embassy had been Andreas's efforts to curb the CIA in Greece and to bring the KYP under Greek government control. He did not contradict the versions presented in my paper, but tried to "put things in perspective."

My memorandum had apparently created quite a stir in the CIA station, for the next person who mentioned it to me was a more junior CIA operative who did not work in the chancery but rather in a separate office downtown (he liked some of my ideas, curiously enough), and I wondered how my paper had made its way down there. I worked myself into a state of annoyance at this point, for it seemed to me wholly wrong that I should be discussing the paper with CIA people before the ambassador had even seen it, so far as I knew. If Talbot had desired to show it to them to get their opinion on it, that was fine with me, but this unauthorized lateral distribution bothered me quite a bit.

I took the matter up with McClelland, who agreed with me that what had happened was improper. He said he had passed my paper on to the ambassador, but that he was preparing an answer to it himself. It was my suspicion that a CIA man who worked in my section of the Embassy had taken the copy of my memo that I circulated to my Political Section colleagues and had delivered it to his CIA boss, the station chief, without asking my permission, presumably justifying himself with the argument that I had made "allegations" about CIA operations in Greece that they were entitled to know about. But a couple of days later George Warren, my temporary boss, came to me and apologized and said it had been his fault. He took full responsibility for the fact that the CIA had received my paper before the ambassador had.

I must say that I never fully trusted Warren again, for I was never afterward sure whom he was working for, despite the fact that he was a career FSO. Either he had given a copy of my paper to the station chief without telling me—which would tend to confirm his divided loyalties—or he had been ordered to cover up and take the rap for the CIA man who was working in our section, which was equally revealing of the same situation.

I never received any comment from the ambassador on my paper, and I followed up with some comments on our "One Year Assessment" (one year after the coup) on April 26, which I sent to the ambassador and DCM and circulated in the Political Section. Stuart Rockwell, the deputy assistant secretary of state in charge of Greece, arrived in Athens about that time, and I stated my dissenting views to him in a general meeting of the senior officers as well. On May 3 McClelland sent me a fairly sharp answer to my policy proposals, disagreeing with them in their entirety. That commenced a series of written exchanges between us, first a twenty-three-page counter-blast from me on May 17, a six-page "chapter 3" response from McClelland on May 31 with a postscript on June 6, and a nine-page "chapter 4" from me to him on June 7. (I am obviously long-winded; McClelland is commendably terse.) This may sound like a peculiar procedure for an embassy, but the purpose of putting all these exchanges in writing was to permit our views to be circulated to other colleagues and considered at leisure. Otherwise McClelland and I could simply have gone to the mat together and settled things with a shouting match, or even, perhaps, more quietly. (The complete texts of all of these memoranda can be found in ppendix B.)

I have given here only a brief outline of this spring 1968 effort to turn our policy toward Greece around, because it would require a memoir as long as this one to tell the complete story, which lasted until July of 1970 and covered the second half of my four-year tour at Embassy Athens. That story would be less interesting in a way because so much of it would be internal, purely bureaucratic, without the background music of the critical events in Greece that we lived through in 1966, 1967, and 1968. I therefore leave most of that story for another occasion with only enough of what I was up to in the spring of 1968 to help account, at least partially, for the reaction to my efforts on the part of the senior officers of the Embassy.

GO ALONG TO GET ALONG

Prior to her departure in February, Mrs. Bracken had called me in to discuss my "performance rating report," which she was required to write as my departing boss. What she wrote was only a useless fragment, but what was significant was what she said to me orally. The gist of her remarks was that perhaps my wife and I would be happier if we did not return to Athens after home leave that summer, since we appeared to find the Greek situation disturbing. I agreed that I did find it disturbing, but I said that I had every intention of returning for another two years, and was in fact looking forward to it. The State Department's personnel system had assigned me to Athens for four years, and I saw no reason to seek a curtailment.

McClelland echoed the same sentiment as Mrs. Bracken when he closed one of his memos to me that spring as follows:

I don't know anybody around here in a position of influence who kids himself that Papadopoulos is not bent on holding onto control for as long as he can in order to carry out his revolution. Since we can't remove him, however, the best alternative in the circumstances would seem to be to deal with him and to try to compel him to be as sincere as he professes to be about returning his country to democracy. Maybe it won't work, but we are not in a position to say so flatly at this stage. Meanwhile I do not regard this as a somehow despicable undertaking. It is simply part of our often difficult job as Foreign Service officers; and whether we happen to find it consonant with some absolute and more desirable political ideal is unfortunately beside the point. If in the end we don't like the heat, we're always free, in the old dictum, to get out of the kitchen, or at least to look for another more congenial one.

I will not here deal with McClelland's substantive point (what the prospects were for the removal of Papadopoulos and what the best alternative would be), for I am here concerned with the personal aspect. My answer to McClelland's sally was to toss his citation of Truman's famous maxim back at him: "It is certainly not I who dislikes the heat in the kitchen," I wrote in my memo replying to his.

I do not comprehend how it comes about that if one expresses internally a position at variance with the official line one is thereby showing that one dislikes (or "can't stand," as President Truman put it) the heat in the kitchen. I can very much stand the heat, I find this kitchen congenial, and I plan to remain in this particular kitchen until ordered to leave it. I regret it if I seem to be adding heat to an already overheated kitchen, but my aim has been to try to make people aware of the true temperature, not to inflate it artificially or pretend that it's really quite cool.

At the time I thought McClelland was expressing his own views only. I now believe that in the passage quoted above he was attempting to project the attitude toward my dissents that he *thought* was held by Ambassador Talbot. McClelland was a DCM quite insecure in his position, since he had been chosen by Talbot primarily because he had been available (after six years in the Department Talbot knew very few people) and had agreed to concentrate on administrative matters and not try to compete with the ambassador in the political policy field the way Anschuetz could not help but do. It was not until June 1970, on the occasion of McClelland's departure from Athens on transfer (to Niger as ambassador) and my own scheduled departure later that month, that he disclosed to me how Talbot had viewed my dissents. I had all along assumed that while Talbot had not welcomed my dissents—his only reaction was to ignore them—he had at least tolerated them and not resented me for being their author.

Just before his departure McClelland showed me the final efficiency report he had written on me as my boss (I was the acting political counselor for the last eight months of my tour in Athens and therefore his direct subordinate). His report was highly complimentary in many respects but had been carefully conceived and drafted to preclude my promotion within any reasonable period of time.

The final portion of the "Officer Evaluation Report" had to do with my potential for advancement in the career service, and McClelland had noted that in the Foreign Service one had "to go along in order to get along," a precept that I had obviously failed to live up to. With my copy of the efficiency report, the DCM sent me a handwritten note explaining in more personal fashion what he thought my problems were. The following is a portion of that note:

> While dissent is certainly necessary and salutary, it has to be evaluated just like any other views. To be taken into account it has to "stack up." To some extent yours did, in other respects it did not, so I think you're being unfair and subjective in feeling that your dissent was stifled. Perhaps Kay B. did so, but I certainly haven't. Also, because dissent is "honest" (and I do not for a minute doubt that yours wasn't) does not necessarily make it all valid. Naturally, you believe you were right; every conscientious advocate does. But someone else has to weigh that against other opinions equally strongly and righteously held. The observation I made about "going along in order to get along" was not merely a cliché. As open-minded and intelligent a man as Ambassador Talbot was, he had *very serious* doubts whether he should ask the Dept. *not* to return you to Athens after your home leave in 1968. This is indicative of how he reacted to your dissent.

It certainly would be, if it were true. Talbot's longtime personal secretary has told me that he always welcomed dissent, or at least gave her that impression. He even complained to her about being surrounded by yes-men with no one available to give him a fresh point of view. Furthermore, she doubts that the ambassador considered asking the Department to transfer me elsewhere, "except possibly as a reaction to RDM's suggestion." Rather than McClelland, more probably it was Kay Bracken who had planted the idea in Talbot's mind prior to her departure; as recounted earlier, she had suggested to me that I might be happier elsewhere than in Athens. As it happened, Talbot did not tell the Department to transfer me and I did return to Athens for another two years: five more months of Talbot, a year under McClelland as chargé, and six months under Ambassador Henry J. Tasca.

PARALLELS WITH PAKISTAN

The second half of my Athens tour had its own problems—I took over internal political affairs and thus became an "insider" trying to change our policy against increasingly formidable odds—but there was one major difference: Kay Bracken's replacement as political counselor was Archer K. Blood, an outstanding FSO whose life I did not make any easier by continuing to insist on my dissents but whose approach to Greece was closer to my own than to anyone else's in the mission. He no doubt thought me quixotic at times, and did not hesitate to tell me so, but on occasion he would support my efforts to bring about policy changes, and when he did not support me he at least provided a buffer of protection within a generally hostile environment. Though Blood was not always an ally, he was a most congenial boss, and it was a pleasure to work with him.

Assigned to Athens for a four-year tour, Blood got himself transferred after a year and a half. He realized that nothing but policy struggles lay ahead, especially after the nomination of Henry J. Tasca to head the Athens post. Blood used his good connections in Personnel in Washington to arrange an early transfer out of Athens and left prematurely to become consul general at Dacca, where he had served previously. It was a job more important than many ambassadorships. As he left Athens in February of 1970, he was looking forward to an exciting tour in East Pakistan, with the planned end of martial law and the proclamation of elections before the end of the year, which he anticipated would be won by the Awami League, based in the east. It turned out to be a good deal more exciting than he had bargained for.

Blood dissented strongly (as did his entire staff) from the policy toward Pakistan adopted by the White House and the State Department when Yahya Khan moved to repress the movement for autonomy in East Pakistan in the spring of 1971. Blood departed Dacca shortly after that crisis broke, doubtless under pressure from the Embassy in Islamabad, but he was given a high American Foreign Service Association award for "constructive dissent" and transferred to Personnel in Washington. I wrote to congratulate him on his receipt of the award, remarking that things must have been even rougher for him in Dacca than they had been in Athens. His reply confirmed that the Dacca experience had indeed been a frustrating one, even more so than in Athens, for in his view the policy issues in the Pakistani situation were much more "black and white" than in Greece.

I am no expert on South Asia, but I see some interesting parallels in the situations in East Pakistan and Greece, although I have earlier warned against the pitfalls of facile but dubious analogies. As to the moral issue involved in the Bangladesh affair, I am sure Blood was right that it was a black-and-white case in which the United States stood on the wrong side of the issue. And although it is also true that our policies in the South Asian crisis of 1971 (from which Blood dissented) were little short of disastrous, in the geopolitical dimension, including the somewhat remote danger of a nuclear confrontation, I do not entirely agree with Blood; for East Pakistan seems to me less a black-and-white case than Greece. In the Bangladesh crisis, which eventually led to war between India and Pakistan, there was intertwined a great-power competition involving three nuclear powers: the United States, China, and the Soviet Union, all three taking sides in this grave crisis. In the Greek situation, by contrast, there was essentially only one great power involved: the U.S. of A. The Soviet Union took a completely hands-off position vis-à-vis the Greek coup and its aftermath.

In the end we lost out in East Pakistan in both the moral and geopolitical dimensions. We chose to support the hopeless cause of West Pakistan against the victorious Indians, who ruled over one of the few near-democracies in the Third World. We lost out completely in the great-power competition for influence in South Asia, with India embracing the Soviet Union as its most dependable ally, West Pakistan turning to China as its best nearby supporter, and an independent Bangladesh indebted to India and the Soviet Union. In the aftermath of the debacle, West Pakistan, our chosen instrument, came under the rule of our old enemy Zulfikar Ali Bhutto, the "Andreas Papandreou of South Asia."

Ironically, the foundations of our misguided and disastrous policies in Greece and Pakistan were quite similar combinations of wishful thinking and hypocrisy. We declined to take a tough line with Yahya Khan and the Islamabad government and vacillated for months on the question of continuing arms supply to Pakistan, on the basis that we wished to preserve our "leverage" with that government in order to influence its policies in the direction of "moderation." We never possessed any real "leverage" concerning Islamabad's behavior in areas of its vital interests—the preservation of the unity of the country—and our policies merely fueled Yahya Khan's intransigence.

In the case of Greece we justified our policy on similar grounds: we wished to maintain our influence with the Colonels in order to encourage them toward moderation and toward restoring democratic, constitutional, representative government. Again, we were flying in the face of their vital interests: to restore such government would have meant their end, and I mean physically. Nothing could be more vital.[1]

That was the wishful thinking aspect of our policies in those two countries. The hypocritical element was that we didn't even use the small leverage we had in favor of the holding of free elections and the honoring of their results, on behalf of the release of those jailed for strictly political reasons, or to try to stop the torture, the killings, and the brutal repression. In truth, we weren't all that concerned to see democracy preserved in Greece or autonomy granted to the Bengalis, and we were worried that any application of our leverage would damage our relations with the authoritarian military regimes that ruled over those supposedly strategic pieces of real estate.

To wishful thinking and hypocrisy I must add a willful blindness to the realities. In Pakistan the original anomaly was that we gave arms to an ally that they were supposed to use to defend themselves against the Soviet Communists, but they accepted those arms essentially to strengthen themselves against their archenemy India. In Greece our justification for arms aid was originally legitimate—to build up Greece's defenses against Communist threats to its security and independence and later on to bolster a NATO ally. In the end those arms were used by a mutinous gang of colonels to overthrow the democratic government of a member in good standing of the "free world" that NATO was founded to preserve, and we looked the other way.

LOOKING TO THE FUTURE OF GREECE

ASSESSMENT OF ANDREAS

In pursuit of these parallels I have moved far afield from Greece, my frame of reference. By way of a conclusion I shall try to answer two questions that seem to be still floating in the air, followed by three observations that might be termed the lessons to be learned from this tale. The first of the two questions really amounts to a personal assessment of Andreas Papandreou.

As I was writing this book in 1971–72, I did not know Andreas Papandreou well enough, from personal observation, to analyze his character or even to give an entirely accurate picture of the image he projected upon the Greek political stage. People often ask, how American was he, how Greek?[1] How much was he an idealist, how much an opportunist? I had the impression that despite his two decades of residence in America Andreas remained essentially Greek. It was as a sojourner that he lived in the United States, not as a true immigrant, despite the evidence that he participated fully in American life, even to the extent of an active involvement in domestic politics on behalf of liberal Democratic candidates.

The first two decades of his life formed him, and these were spent in Greece, in the household of George Papandreou. Yet the two decades in America did change Andreas. When he returned to Greece, he viewed his native land as a critic would, rather than as a lover—not that most Greeks do not also view their society critically, quite aware of its shortcomings, its deficiencies.[2] Andreas was not the typical Greek, in that in America he had acquired the belief that societies can be reformed by human effort, the evils eradicated through political action. He acquired the blend of idealism and pragmatism that is perhaps uniquely American in that these impulses are also devoid of any cynicism. The typical Greek is a great cynic, and if one called him a reformer he would probably be insulted.

Andreas's American traits strained his relations with his father. The father could not comprehend or accept what he saw as his son's dogmatism, inflexibility, reluctance to compromise, stubbornness. These were perhaps his American traits viewed in a Greek political context, where they cast a strange glow. While I do not accept Talbot's gruff judgment of Andreas as "too rich for Greece's blood," it is certainly true that he did not slide smoothly into a perfectly harmonious orbit around his father's political sun. In the last analysis, however, it should be up to the Greek electorate—and not up to Phillips Talbot or George Papadopoulos—to decide who is or is not "too rich for Greece's blood," and to judge whether Andreas Papandreou is savior or demagogue, hero or opportunist, god or devil.

The question of opportunism is a more difficult one, and perhaps here I may be allowed some cynicism: a Greek politician who did not take advantage of his opportunities as well as promote a few he did not deserve would be considered a fool by his electorate and would doubtless be voted out of office for displaying rampant stupidity. Secondly, given that Andreas had decided to become a politician, has there ever existed a politician who was not ambitious (as I believe Margaret remarked in her book)? Andreas was certainly ambitious, but in my judgment he was not an opportunist in the sense of someone who picks up and advocates political causes he does not believe in merely because they seem popular and may help promote his political advancement.

How much popular support did Andreas enjoy in the days of pre-junta democracy? This remains a controversial question some years after the events described in this memoir, and it cannot be resolved because the question was never really tested. The test would have come in the never-held elections scheduled for May 1967, in which Andreas was one of the central personalities and, along with the king, one of the two dominant issues. Had George Papandreou's party won those elections with a majority larger than in 1964, a great deal of the credit for the victory would have had to go to the exertions of Andreas, as well as to the failings of the king. Conversely, a lesser majority would have been laid at Andreas's door. His performance in the parliamentary elections of 1964 was no true test: it was his first effort at the polls, and though he did well, he was running with a famous name, on his father's coattails and in his father's home district (old George could have been elected from anywhere, so he withdrew from Achaia in favor of his son).

My own view is that by 1967 Andreas had succeeded in developing a strong and dedicated following made up of the younger and more "progressive" elements of the Center. He had also made a great many enemies, both in the right-center of his own party and in the Right itself, by posing a direct challenge to the political hegemony of the Greek "establishment" and by setting himself up as a strong challenger to inherit his father's mantle as leader of the Center forces over many other competitors who felt they had much better claims and credentials than he. Perhaps the effect of the entry of Andreas into Greek politics was indeed neutral, in the sense that he made as many enemies as friends, lost as many votes as he won for his party. But there was this difference: he held or brought into the Center many younger people who might otherwise have sought a different home, and the enemies he made were in most cases lost to the Center anyway, being either confirmed rightists or the "apostates" who had deserted George Papandreou in his hour of greatest need and who were therefore no longer welcome in the Center fold.

THE PAPANDREOU FUNERAL

There is absolutely no doubt about old George's popularity with the masses of the Greek people. The proof, if any is needed, was his funeral in Athens on November 3, 1968. Several hundreds of thousands of ordinary Greeks—a crowd so huge that it was impossible to estimate its size with a number—jammed the streets of downtown Athens to pay their last respects to the old political warrior, to shout their defiance of the junta that had cruelly kept him under house arrest and totally isolated during his last months of life, and to demonstrate to anyone who cared to notice that they surely would have rewarded him with one last term of office had they been given a chance in May of 1967. The crowd contained large numbers of the disadvantaged of Greece, but middle-class people, professionals, and functionaries were also there in force—in fact, it was a thorough cross-section. Some of the chanting was organized by party adherents, but the outpouring of emotion was spontaneous and entirely genuine. They shouted anti-junta slogans, demanded to know what had happened to their "No" votes (in the constitutional referendum held that September), called for democracy, praised the fallen leader, and most of all simply chanted, over and over again, "Pa-pan-dre-ou! Pa-pan-dre-ou! Pa-pan-dre-ou!"

The crowd was so large that the police were cowed, afraid to try to stop the antiregime chanting. The crowd might have reacted badly to any interference with the expression of their emotions. They might have overwhelmed the police. Only when they could isolate a small group outside the cemetery did the police move to make a sizable number of arrests, mostly of innocent people who at worst were displaying antigovernment feelings. The service itself, in the Metropolitan Cathedral, was notable for the warm eulogy to George delivered by his political adversary, Panayotis Kanellopoulos, leader of the rightist ERE party. Margaret Papandreou had returned to Athens when George was hospitalized with his final illness, and she was a prominent feature of the mass procession from the cathedral to the cemetery.

Ambassador Talbot attended the service, by official invitation. The only other official Americans there were my wife, Louise, and the VOA correspondent, to whom we had given a lift toward the cathedral when we found him blocked by the crowds. I never made it to the church service itself, for after parking the car half a mile away I found myself unable to work my way through the crowds to the cathedral. I decided to stay in the crowd, for it was there much more than in the church that one could absorb what old Papandreou really meant to the Greek masses. Talbot was flabbergasted by the event and its clear demonstration of the popularity of the ex-premier. I wrote up a full report on the funeral, which Talbot permitted to be cabled to Washington without change, though it doubtless caused some gritting of teeth at the other end of the wire.

I was entirely wrong in one of the conclusions I drew from the event: I thought it might provide a lesson to the Greek masses about their strength in numbers and their ability to demonstrate against the junta with impunity if they did it in a sufficiently large group, despite the deterrent effect of martial law. A junior officer serving temporarily in the Political Section dissented from my view in a memo to me, and he was right: he wrote that he doubted the regime would ever again permit such a large crowd to gather in Athens, and in any case the funeral of a figure like Papandreou was a unique occurrence, not likely to be repeated soon. His judgment was accurate: there has not been a similar demonstration in Greece since 1968, although another funeral, that of the Nobel Prize–winning poet George Seferis in September 1971, attracted some tens of thousands to a much quieter demonstration of opposition and hostility to the junta.

I shall quote at this point Louise's firsthand account of the Papandreou funeral because I believe it presents much that is relevant to this story:

> On Wednesday, October 30, we heard that Margaret Papandreou had been given permission to return to Greece to be at the bedside

of her dying father-in-law. She arrived very late at night and went to stay with Tito and Kiveli Zografides. On Friday we were invited to an informal supper there to see her, but plans were changed when old George took a turn for the worse. That Friday night he died. The government offered the family a state funeral, but the offer was declined. The family asked only for use of the Metropolitan Cathedral for a private service. Margaret was secretly pleased that the date of the funeral, November 3, was the anniversary of the Center Union's victory in the Parliamentary elections of 1963. On Saturday the body was placed in the oldest (and probably smallest) Christian building in Athens, the Byzantine church next to the Cathedral. The Velletris (our labor attaché) attended and said that a steady stream of mourners passed through the church, silently paying their last respects. Saturday evening we were at a Halloween party at the Sirkins (our public affairs officer). I tried to find out if anyone there was planning to attend the funeral and whether crowds were expected. No one had any interest in the funeral; talk centered around how Teddy Kennedy had behaved during a visit to Athens the summer before.

On Sunday morning we drove downtown along Vassillisis Sophias Boulevard toward Syntagma Square. I was surprised and disappointed that there were few people on the sidewalks of the boulevard. Three blocks from the square we saw Walter Kohl, the VOA man, walking and offered him a lift to the Cathedral. As we arrived at Syntagma we saw that it was filled with people and there was no hope of making further progress toward the Cathedral by car. You dropped us off and tried to find a side street on which to park.

Walter Kohl and I found ourselves blocked by a wall of people held back by policemen. He said, "This is as far as we can go." I said, "Show your press pass. I have my passport." We were allowed through and walked down Mitropoleos Street toward the Cathedral. The people were shouting. The VOA man asked what they were saying. "They're chanting Pa-pan-dre-ou the way they used to at election rallies," I said. Every side street was jammed with people; every window and balcony along the route was filled. There were many different chants and shouts, few of which I was able to understand. But I was told later that some of them were: "Sit up old man—this is your election"; "This is your referendum"; "Democracy"; "Freedom"; "Down with the junta"; and "Where are our NOs?" The VOA man said the crowds were definitely larger than they had been at the funeral of King Paul (in 1964), which he had attended.

As we approached the Cathedral we saw many young men holding gigantic wreaths sent from all over Greece and by diplomatic missions in Athens (there was none from the U.S. Embassy). I heard that from Rome the King had cabled a request for a wreath to be prepared in his name, but the junta had intercepted the cable and countermanded it. At the side door of the Cathedral we encountered Leonidas Lagakos (the man who had sought asylum in the Embassy the day of the coup). He told us he was in charge of the door and would let us inside. Talbot was booed by the crowd when he arrived at the church and Kanellopoulos refused to shake his hand inside. All during the ceremony we heard the shouts of the crowd outside: Papandreou, Freedom, Democracy! The crowd inside the church behaved as if they were at a political rally, interrupting the eulogies with applause, especially when Kanellopoulos spoke. One of the speakers was cut off by the Archbishop, who took the microphone away—I don't recall who the speaker was.

When the ceremony ended I intercepted Margaret in the aisle. She told me to come along to the cemetery in one of the official cars, but I demurred, feeling they were for the family and their close friends. I saw Tito and Kiveli there and Kiveli's grandmother (George Papandreou's second wife and a famous Greek actress) in a long black veil. The VOA man took off at that point. You and I had arranged to meet outside the church, but when you didn't show up I decided to join the crowd walking to the cemetery. The crowd was quite orderly, but I thought to myself as I walked along: some day they will describe this as a disorderly mob, but I'll know differently. I kept running into all sorts of friends and acquaintances who were of all shades of political opinion. Though I obviously looked like an American, I sensed no animosity toward me from the crowd. There was none of the solemnity expected at a funeral, but a spirit of defiance and exhilaration. Occasionally there was a scuffle on the sidelines as a knot of policemen rushed in to corner someone they wanted to arrest. Afterwards it was said that some of the Center Union youth group leaders who carried the large wreaths to the cemetery were arrested. A few in the crowd shouted "Zito Andreas!" but they were shushed by others, who perhaps feared goading the police.

The part of the crowd that I was in flowed into Amalias Avenue, and I suddenly found myself next to the hearse. Margaret was perched uncomfortably on the rear trunk lid. Thuggish-looking men tried to push me back from reaching the hearse, but I pressed on, feeling quite safe in a Papandreou crowd. Margaret later told me that the CU youths insisted on surrounding and guarding the official limousines, pushing away the government plainclothesmen. Margaret had been inside the hearse at first, sitting in front, but the frequent and abrupt stops caused the coffin to push against the back of the front seat, so she was urged to move outside and sit on the hood of the car. While doing so, in a moment of emotion, answering the shouts to her of partisans in the crowd, she gave a Papandreou V-for-victory sign with her hand. Newspaper photographers duly recorded this scene, and Margaret came in for a lot of criticism when the papers published the picture for behaving in an "unseemly" fashion at the funeral. Referring to this picture a friend later said to me, "If I didn't know better, I'd say that was you in the foreground, Louise." In fact, it was me.

I spoke briefly with Margaret, who again thanked me for coming. We surged along to the cemetery. I showed my passport at the gates and was allowed inside. I was pushed by the crowd almost to the edge of the grave. I retreated to a cement planter, on which I stood in order to see the speakers at the graveside. In the distance, on top of the Acropolis, was another large crowd. I heard that Andreas's eldest son had gone to the Acropolis to return the Greek flag that his grandfather had been given when Athens was liberated from the German occupation (old George had been Prime Minister at the time). Following the graveside ceremony I encountered Leonidas Lagakos again. He insisted on taking me up to some Center Union functionaries, including, I believe, George's private secretary, to "show them at least one American cared to come to the funeral." Then we went to a nearby hotel to have the traditional Greek post-funeral coffee, and to telephone you where to find us.

Next day began the "numbers game" about how large the funeral crowd had been. We lunched that day with the British Commercial Attaché, who without having been there insisted that the crowd had been no larger than 25,000–50,000. This annoyed you so much that when you got back to the Embassy you raised your own modest estimate (in your telegram) by an additional 100,000. The junta eventually conceded there had been 150,000, but the newspapers and newsmagazines published figures in the vicinity of 250,000–300,000. A few days later at a U.S. election-eve party staged by USIS, I asked Walter Kohl why he had made such a low estimate of the size of the crowd in his VOA report, and why the eulogy (obituary, really) had been so short and mean-spirited. Why had he said there were only 50,000 people there when he had told me the crowds had been much larger than at King Paul's funeral? He showed me the report he had cabled, remarking that he was very limited in the time he could use—less than two minutes of air time in the case of the Papandreou funeral. He didn't explain the basis of his 50,000 estimate of the crowd.

The huge crowd was truly spontaneous. Before the funeral I heard no one making plans to attend nor inquiring of others if they planned to attend. All political organizations, student and youth groups had been banned since the coup, so it would have been most difficult to organize a mass rally of this sort. For months afterwards Greeks would ask each other: Were you there? What street were you on? What were they shouting in your area? What a crowd! Weeks later we attended a small dinner at the home of a Greek professor at Athens College. Conversation turned to the funeral. The host uncomfortably explained that he hadn't been able to go as he had had term papers to correct. The guest of honor, a dignified lady in black, recently widowed, whose Greek-American husband had been a distinguished Professor of Philosophy at Harvard, turned quietly to you and said: "I was on Nikis Street. Where were you?"[3]

WAS GREECE EVER A DEMOCRACY?

With this eyewitness account of the Papandreou funeral we have moved outside our time frame, and I have begun to recount the story of the second half of my first tour of duty at Embassy Athens, something I promised not to do. I proceed, then, to the second of my concluding questions—an equally difficult one—which is whether Greece has ever been a real democracy. The question of whether Greece has a genuine and legitimate "democratic tradition," as I have here claimed, has been the subject of endless debate in the press and elsewhere since the 1967 coup destroyed whatever political system Greece enjoyed at the time and replaced it with what most observers will agree is a species of authoritarianism. Apologists for the Papadopoulos junta are fond of pointing out that fifth century B.C. Periclean Athens was founded on slavery, and that throughout its history Greece has been alternately ruled by forces symbolized by the names Athens and Sparta, by those on the one hand representing civilian dominance, political freedom, and liberalism, only to be replaced from time to time by a group representing militarism, authoritarianism, repression, and severity. These apologists like to charge the Greek regime's foreign critics with a sentimentalism induced by their own classical educations and with a blindness to modern Greek political realities caused by their inability to distinguish between the Athens of the fifth century B.C. and the Athens of the twentieth century A.D.

I have myself grown weary of the constant allusions to the supposedly tragic irony (can there be such an animal?) that this tyrannical regime of the Colonels had been born in the "cradle of Western democracy." My personal view is that there is no need to go back to the fifth century to feel bad about the situation, for by 1967 modern, postindependence Greece had made enormous strides toward becoming a reasonably stable Western-style democracy. Despite certain fundamental deficiencies in the Greek personality and Greek political system—defects so far as a smooth working of democratic processes was concerned—it was my view that given a bit more time, say a decade or so, the democratic foundations would have become so strong, so mature, that they would no longer be in danger of crumbling. The tragedy of the 1967 coup to me was that this proposition would not be tested, for the imposition of a dictatorship would by itself so damage those foundations that it might take additional decades, perhaps a whole generation or more post-coup, to rebuild them.

Now, I would be prepared to make a case that Greek democracy was in fuller bloom in early 1967 than was apparent from subsequent events. The ease with which democracy was extinguished by a military clique and the failure of Greek democrats to fight the army with their bare chests does not prove anything to me one way or the other. It is a tautology to argue that the weakness of Greek democracy was proved by the ease with which it was eliminated. I will admit that there existed one major defect that was perhaps fatal.

One way to define the fundamental requirements for a working democracy (assuming there already exist such things as a reasonably informed electorate and systems of communication free enough to keep it informed) is to say that free, honest, and fair elections must be held at relatively frequent and regular intervals, and that the losers in such elections must accept the verdict of the electorate and permit the winners to rule until the next elections. In the case of Greece, both of these principles were violated in the early 1960s. The 1961 parliamentary elections were apparently not free, honest, and fair but were rigged by the outgoing (Karamanlis) administration—

allegedly with assistance from the CIA—and as a consequence George Papandreou and his Center Union party refused to accept the verdict and launched their "unrelenting struggle." Greek democracy died in the aftermath; rather, it was killed by a gang of assassins organized and led by an obscure (at the time) colonel, George Papadopoulos.

In 1967, I believe, the vast majority of the Greek people accepted these fundamental principles required for a working democracy. One group, however, did not: the army thought they were going to be the losers; they decided they would not permit the expected winners to rule; and they had the guns to impose their decision. Now the question to ask is not, was *Greece* a democracy? Instead we might ask, can *any* country be considered a democracy that has an army that cannot be guaranteed to refrain from using its possession of the dominant instruments of coercion to intervene in the political processes of the nation? When we ask this question, how many countries can be considered democracies?

In her book *Nightmare in Athens*, Margaret Papandreou puts the case quite well for Greek "democracy":

> Democracy, that much abused word, did not have firm foundations in Greece. The democratic spirit, however, was deeply ingrained. The majority of the Greek people called themselves democrats, yet they had never experienced anything remotely resembling a Scandinavian, a British, or an American type democracy. They greatly appreciated the benefits of an open, democratic society—freedom of speech, freedom of press, freedom of assembly, privacy of the home, etc.—without understanding their responsibilities. Most of them had been raised in authoritarian homes, under authoritarian governments, with governmental patronage and favoritism the natural consequence of the Turkish occupation where the local pasha determined who was to get what. Therefore, even the concept of committee functioning was alien to them, as was decision making by consensus. Their concept of democracy was closer to the notion of anarchy: everyone should be free to do whatever he wanted, with no restrictions. They had been learning, however, and were actually at the beginning of a modern democratic society.[4]

Mrs. Papandreou goes on to argue that the Greek's individualism is not an innate characteristic but is rather a manifestation of his need to fight for self-preservation in a colonial atmosphere. To my mind she overstressed the effects of the historical domination of Greece by foreign powers, just as

Greeks tend to overemphasize the hangovers from the Turkish occupation. Both of these influences have played large roles, but to me the point to be stressed is that by 1967 Greece was on the verge of reaching a democratic manhood, if not a full maturity.

DON'T MAKE WAVES

There are, finally, at least three things that stand out in my mind as a result of having relived that period in Athens through having sat for some weeks at a typewriter keyboard in an effort to reconstruct—to recollect in tranquility—the experiences of those troubled but wonderful years. The first observation I have already partially drawn, namely, that despite all its claims about welcoming dissent, the Department of State and the Foreign Service of the United States of America do not suffer gladly the makers of waves. If it is now necessary to prove my point and to explain how this comes about, then this memoir has served no purpose at all.

But the question probably still comes to mind of why it was so difficult for me to penetrate through to the senior officers of the Mission to get any consideration for my views. In looking back, at least four explanations occur to me. In the first place, I was a relative newcomer, only nine months in Athens at the time of the coup, so I was in the position (from their point of view) of trying to tell people who had been working on Greece for five or six years or even longer how to do their jobs. What could I possibly have learned in so few months that would be of any validity that they did not know already, they must have thought. Secondly, internal political affairs were not my job; I was supposed to be concerning myself exclusively with Cyprus and other external questions. In a bureaucracy there is a natural and understandable tendency to pay attention to the views of the person who is responsible for the matter at hand and to ignore any unsolicited advice from "outside" kibitzers. The third reason is almost too obvious to require expression: my views were unwelcome because they went directly contrary to those of the powers that be. Had my arguments supported what the Mission was doing (or not doing), they probably would have been embraced with enthusiasm.

Finally, my superiors were inclined to discount my views nearly 100 percent because they thought I was overly influenced by a sentimental attachment to Greece and the Greeks. They believed that I cared too much about the Greeks' loss of their democratic liberties. For reasons that I still do not comprehend today, I was never able—try as I might on repeated occasions—to convince my superiors that what concerned me most of all was the long-range damage being done to the position of the United States in Greece by our policy of embracing the Colonels, or at least of appearing to do so. For a diplomat this must always be the prime consideration, regardless of whether he likes or despises the people of the foreign nation in question.[5] The problem with diplomacy is that diplomats congenitally view the foreign relations of their own government as relations with a given foreign government and not with a foreign *country* or a foreign *people*. The problem is that governments are transient, a people (one hopes) permanent. Obviously relations must be conducted with a particular government at a particular time, but a wise diplomat, in the modern age at least, allows the nature (but not the existence) of those relations to be influenced by factors such as whether that foreign government enjoys the support of its own people. So much for my philosophy of diplomacy.

To move from the general to the particular, the diminishing but still substantial goodwill enjoyed by the United States in Greece is owed largely to the massive economic and military assistance and political support we have given Greece since World War II. Greeks regarded this as aid to their country and to themselves as a people. Of the successive Greek governments that were the official recipients of that assistance from 1947 to 1967, some were more popular than others, but all were democratically chosen. No Greek faction except the Communists begrudged them the aid. Similar assistance, however, granted to a decidedly unpopular regime such as the one that ruled Greece after 1967 was not viewed with gratitude, for it was seen as a major prop keeping that regime in power and not as help to the people at large and the nation.

To return to the matter of dissent, I should note in passing that under the old Foreign Service regulations the subordinate officer who dissented from the views of his superiors had to take the initiative in insisting that his views be forwarded to Washington. Naturally it was a rare FSO who took advantage of this privilege. The regulations were subsequently changed, and during the period I am here concerned with it was the responsibility of the DCM to see that dissenting views were transmitted, with a clear indication, if desired, that these were the personal views of the officer in question and not the considered opinion of the ambassador, the DCM, the Embassy as a whole, the "country team," or anyone else. This was a decided change, for it transferred the responsibility and the initiative from the dissenting officer to his ultimate superior. I probably need not confirm at this point that not a single one of my supervisors or other superiors in Athens ever forwarded any of my dissenting opinions to Washington, with or without their own comments thereon.

One final point on this subject: it is an old and difficult dilemma faced by every member of a bureaucracy—and those in many other types of organization as well—whether to stay on at one's post and "fight the good fight" or resign on principle (or in disgust) when one strongly dissents from a policy, and perhaps carry the fight to the public. One is torn. One thinks: my superiors will be supremely happy if I quit and go away and shut up and stop bothering them. Then one thinks: I should stick it out, stick to my guns, keep trying; maybe I'll eventually succeed. And, if I leave now, surely someone worse will come to take my place, and that will be a net loss for the cause. This is always a most difficult decision.

A Washington columnist noted some time ago in connection with the Vietnam War that resignations by high government officials on grounds of principle have gone out of style. Why didn't any cabinet or subcabinet officer quit over the Vietnam War? Why did they wait until the administration had changed (from Johnson to Nixon) to speak out about their views, claiming that they had been working to change the president's policies all along? I don't know the answer to this dilemma, but I suggest a compromise: one should stay on and fight so long as one is getting any hearing at all from those with the power of decision, but when one begins to turn everyone else off every time one opens one's mouth, then it is perhaps time to leave. Whether one leaves quietly or noisily should depend—in Stuart Rockwell's phrase—on the circumstances.

My second observation, which comes as much from a rereading of the policy disputes of that period as it does from a reliving of the events, is that policy makers in a bureaucracy habitually overemphasize short-term considerations and neglect the long-term interests of the government (or whatever else) they are serving. To give an example, Kay Bracken used to talk about our need "to preserve Ellenikon." The reference was to the American air base adjacent to the Athens airport (that part of the coast of Attica, the town, is called Ellenikon). It was not a major American base, much more logistic than strategic: the Americans who lived there thought more about PXs than they did about nuclear bombs. But, to use Kay Bracken's bit of shorthand, did we want to preserve Ellenikon that year, for a couple of years, for ten years, or "forever"? The military never thought about that. The CIA thought about it, only they did not call it Ellenikon. Kay Bracken meant: what do we, the United States government, need to do to maintain our position here? What I kept asking was: how long do you want to preserve Ellenikon? Or any position here at all? If for a year or two or five, you are perfectly right—play ball with Papadopoulos or any other two-bit dictator who comes down the pike. But if you are interested in the *long term*, in the position of the United

States in Greece in the next decade or two after *you* have been transferred, with the next generation of Greeks, then for God's sake don't tie your future to the Papadopoulos regime.

My third and final observation is that I am today impressed, if I never was before, with the very central role that Andreas Papandreou played in this entire history, not only my particular history, but the history of Greece in the period in question. I thought I realized it at the time. But in retrospect, in now reviewing those events four years later, I cannot escape the conclusion that Andreas stood at the very center of the melodrama, if that is what it was. But he did not stand there alone: forget the prompters in the wings, the critics in the audience, the spear carriers and the rest of us. The other protagonist, strange to say, was Constantine Rex, to such an extent that if I were looking for an honestly descriptive (if silly) title to attach to this memoir I would have to call it "The King, Andreas Papandreou, and I." I do not think that would be too far off the mark, despite the fact that I had spent only one evening in Andreas's company and my only personal contact with the king was to compete against him in a sailing race in the summer of 1967.[6]

The last word should go to the humorist, never to the advocate. The humorist is Walter Silva, master of the put-down, a man who pretended to be utterly devoid of seriousness, who will be recalled as the very relaxed individual who slept through the king's coup. In 1968, shortly before I left Athens on home leave, Walter and I were sitting in my office chatting. He said something about hearing about, being told about, some memos that I had written to McClelland or Talbot or someone about our policies toward Greece. I said, "Walter, here's my file," and handed him my folder of carbon copies of many of the pieces that have been quoted in this memoir. He sat down at my desk to read them, and I went out to do some errands connected with our impending departure. Several hours later I returned to my office to find the file placed upon my desk, but with a fresh drawing on the file folder's cover (Walter was an amateur artist of no small talent) of a knight in rusty armor, astride a decrepit horse, charging across a plain at a clearly Cretan windmill that showed no fear since it was not even turning.

I close as Don Quixote, with understanding and despair.

Thirteen

FINAL THOUGHTS

POSTSCRIPT

A Greek nationalist, after reading this account, might be compelled to protest that what I was advocating at this critical period of recent Greek political history was nothing different from what my adversaries were engaged in, specifically that I was advocating one kind of intervention whereas they were involved in another kind. Why did I not take the honorable position of arguing for a policy of nonintervention in the internal affairs of Greece, noninterference of any kind?[1]

On principle I could not fault this critic. All I can say in extenuation is that during the period in question the spirit of Cold War competition still dominated international relations, with each of the superpowers vying for influence in the Third World, trying to ensure continued support within its spheres of influence and where possible enforcing conformity within its own power bloc. Interference by one side or the other or both was a fact of life; it would have been unrealistic—a head-in-the-sand attitude, really—to propose that one superpower refrain from trying to exert its influence in Greece or elsewhere. Thus interference was a given, and not only the kind expected of the CIA; the problem, the argument, concerned the purposes and ends to which that interference would be put.

The entire question of the involvement of the "American factor," as the Greeks term it, is a most complex and fascinating one. Greek politicians nearly to a man—and they are not as unrepresentative of average Greek thinking as the Papadopoulos junta would have us believe—have never taken a position against American involvement in the affairs of Greece. They all want it, but they want it exerted on their own behalf and to the detriment of their political enemies. Even the most ardent opponents of the junta regime have never ceased hoping the Americans will eventually come to their senses and step in to throw the junta rascals out. The Greek junta itself only complains about American interference when they fear it is going to be exerted against themselves, to force them somehow to restore a democratic regime sooner than they would like.

What I have presented in this memoir as Ambassador Talbot's do-nothing-ism, he would probably have explained (defended) as a reluctance to interfere directly in Greece's internal political affairs. Most opponents of the regime have regarded our apparent "hands-off" attitude as constituting militant support for Papadopoulos and company, since they believe that only active hostility from the U.S. government could topple them. One could get into an endless argument on this score, but suffice it to say that a hands-off policy hardly squares with the hundreds of millions of dollars of military assistance we have given the junta since the coup, nor with the strong (but often behind-the-scenes) political support we have given by lobbying in their favor in such organs as NATO as well as in other bodies to which we do not even belong, such as the Council of Europe, where we discouraged friendly governments from taking any action that might annoy the Greek Colonels. If all this was "noninterference"—for example, take merely the massive military aid to a regime that stays in power only because it enjoys the support, or at least the sufferance, of the Greek armed forces—then I would like to know where the definition of "interference" begins.

As time passed, I was no longer advocating intervention to encourage the immediate departure of the junta from power—which appeared increasingly impracticable—so much as advocating a policy of putting the maximum distance between ourselves and the oppressive and inept Greek Colonels, while still maintaining relations with the Greek government as such. This is what is known in State Department parlance as assuming the posture of "a very low profile." I thought we could easily afford to cease the highly visible hobnobbing with the Colonels by our ambassador, our spooks, and our resident military, as well as the constant high-level visits by American generals and admirals, cabinet officers, and other VIPs from Washington that so outraged the opposition and convinced them that we had really learned to love the junta.

As an illustration of this syndrome, I cite the serenading of Prime Minister Papadopoulos by a group of American schoolchildren singing Christmas carols in his office in December 1969. The regime naturally played this up for all it was worth, and I received some early morning phone calls from irate opposition friends as soon as they saw the pictures in the progovernment Athens newspapers. They assured me that no such gesture had ever been extended to any of the democratically elected prime ministers of Greece. In my dual capacity as embassy representative on the board of the American Community Schools and as acting political counselor (Arch Blood was chargé), I called the superintendent of schools to find out who had authorized this activity. He told me it had been the idea of a Greek American (and, as I later learned, ardently pro-junta) teacher at the elementary school on the American air base at Ellenikon. The teacher had checked with the school principal, who had checked with the superintendent, who had thought it would be okay.

I told the superintendent that in the future no such activity involving a high-level Greek government official should be undertaken without first checking its propriety with the ambassador, the chargé, the DCM, the political counselor, or at least someone in the Embassy Political Section. He promised me he would. I was recently dismayed, and depressed, to learn from the report on Greece by Clifford P. Hackett to the Subcommittee on Europe of the House Foreign Affairs Committee (August–September 1971) that the serenading of the prime minister by American grade schoolers was repeated a second time on Christmas Eve of 1970! The first time it had happened I had assured my opposition friends that it had been a mistake, the inspiration of a pro-junta teacher, unauthorized by the Embassy, and obviously of no significance as a demonstration of our policy toward the junta. What explanation do you offer the second time it happens, other than that you were a fool?

Perhaps it was authorized a second time, but I presume not by Ambassador Tasca, who in mid-December 1970 saw his entire policy go up in smoke when Papadopoulos stated in a speech that there would be no progress toward a democratic, constitutional regime during the coming year—this despite promises Tasca thought he had extracted in return for our resumption of full military aid. I suppose the serenading will be repeated at Christmastime in 1971, for by this time it must have achieved the status of a tradition.

To conclude this discourse on the problem of foreign intervention, I should like to look at it from one more angle, a peculiar one. In the spring of 1970 Ambassador Tasca, having made up his mind that he was going to work with the Colonels rather than against them, hit upon what he thought was a good argument for refraining from putting pressure on the junta. He proposed that those who wanted us to act against Papadopoulos were advocating a sort of NATO "Brezhnev Doctrine" under which we would be trying to impose our concepts of "democracy" on one of our allies, just as the Soviets had overthrown Dubcek's government for failing to conform to the USSR's version of Communist orthodoxy. This argument had a superficial appeal to some, but a brief examination shows how wrongheaded it was. The Soviet intervention in Czechoslovakia was designed to remove from power a liberalizing regime that was clearly vastly popular with the Czech people and to put in its place a regime that would do the bidding of a foreign power, the Soviet Union. The advocates of American intervention in Greece against the Colonels, by contrast, wished to remove from power a regime that had imposed itself on the Greek people and to permit the establishment in its place of a government that would result from the democratic choice of the Greek people through free elections. To put it bluntly, the Soviets intervened in Czechoslovakia to thwart the will of the Czech people, whereas the United States was being asked to intervene in Greece to permit the Greek people to express their will. As I have tried to show elsewhere, analogies can be the most misleading devices of the political analyst.

So, if one must resign oneself to the fact of life that the great powers are going to interfere in the affairs of lesser powers, like it or not, one is forced to ask the question, intervention for what? At this point I feel I must pass from realism to idealism, for I believe that while a nation should in general refrain from interfering in the affairs of other nations, when involvement is inevitable or already in existence, it should carry out its intervention in support of the principles it professes, at the same time allowing its adversaries to show their true faces by the "Brezhnev Doctrines" they use to justify their brutal repressions. Intervention may be second best, but intervention on behalf of anything other than the extension of human freedom and dignity is distinctly third best. In the case of Greece, a small but loyal ally of the United States, an intervention to help restore the right of the Greek people to choose those by whom they wished to be governed would not have earned the resentment of that people, who once again must display their own capacity for bravery and sacrifice, pride and endurance.

Princeton/Kampala
1971–72

ALL'S WELL THAT ENDS WELL?

In 1988 I received the Christian A. Herter Award from my peers in AFSA (American Foreign Service Association). This was the award for a senior officer. It and two other annual honor awards, the Harriman for junior officers and the Rivkin for midlevel officers, were approved by a committee based on nominations from the field. Mine came to me as a complete surprise, and resulted from a nomination by a staff member serving under me when I was ambassador in Athens. But it was not for anything I was then doing in Athens, but rather for my policy dissents in the 1960s. All three awards had been instituted to recognize FSOs who had allegedly shown some bravery by dissenting from official policies. Originally the citations specifically mentioned "creative dissent" and the awards were known as "the dissent awards."

But by this time some genius at AFSA had turned more politically correct and had moderated the last part of the citation. Mine read: "for extraordinary contributions to the practice of diplomacy exemplifying intellectual courage and a zeal for creative accomplishment." In the revision the word "accomplishment" had replaced "dissent." But I had failed to change policies. I had accomplished very little. Despite the adulteration of the message, this is my proudest memento from my Foreign Service career.

As mentioned earlier, in 1971 Arch Blood, after being recalled from Dacca peremptorily, had received the very same Christian A. Herter Award in recognition of his dissents from East Pakistan.

APPENDIX A

SEFERIS AND THE CLINTON SPEECH

In April 2007 the Athens daily newspaper *Ta Nea* published a 161-page book on the fortieth anniversary of the April 21, 1967, coup and the junta that ruled Greece until 1974. The editors asked me to provide a statement of around 650 words on whatever subject related to that period I chose. For reasons that seemed compelling at the time, I did not mention that much of the credit for including the paragraph in President Clinton's speech in Athens was owing to the intervention of our then ambassador in Athens, R. Nicholas Burns. I thought his career in the Foreign Service, which in fact culminated with his service as under secretary of state for political affairs in the George W. Bush administration, would not have been helped by publicly giving him credit for this courageous but possibly unwelcome act. I had lent him the early draft of this book to read as part of his preparations for going to the Athens post, and he told me later that that was what had led him to convince the president to include this passage in his speech. My statement, as published in the *Ta Nea* book in Greek translation, follows.

I wish to use the space you have graciously allotted to me to ensure the inclusion in your 40th anniversary reporting of two texts that have special meaning for me. The first is the statement issued by George Seferis on March 28, 1969. The illustrious poet, diplomat, and intellectual conscience of democratic Greece had spent the previous fall in the United States as a

Visiting Fellow at the Institute for Advanced Study in Princeton, New Jersey. At his few public appearances, Greek students had questioned him as to why he hadn't spoken out publicly against the junta. His response was that people in Greece were muzzled, and he thought it not right to take advantage of the freedom he enjoyed in the United States to do what was not possible in Greece.

But on his return to Athens he decided he would speak out, no matter the consequences. After explaining his earlier silence, this is what he said:

> It is almost two years since a regime was imposed upon us utterly contrary to the ideals for which our world—and so magnificently our people—fought in the last World War. It is a state of enforced torpor in which all the intellectual values that we have succeeded, with toil and effort, in keeping alive are being submerged in a swamp, in stagnant waters. I can well imagine that for some people these losses do not matter. Unfortunately this is not the only danger that threatens.
>
> We have all learnt, we all know, that in dictatorial regimes the beginning may seem easy, yet tragedy waits at the end, inescapably. It is this tragic ending that consciously or unconsciously torments us, as in the ancient choruses of Aeschylus.
>
> The longer the abnormal situation lasts, the greater the evil.
>
> I am a man completely without political ties, and I speak without fear and without passion. I see before us the precipice towards which the oppression that covers the land is leading us. This abnormality must come to an end. It is the nation's command.
>
> Now I return to silence. I pray to God that never again may I find myself under such compulsion to speak.

At the time I was serving as a first secretary in the American embassy and I certainly shared these sentiments wholeheartedly. I also aided somewhat in disseminating the Seferis statement abroad, including to Washington. On April 23, 1969, eighteen notable Athenian writers issued a parallel statement defending intellectual freedom and hailing the earlier one by Seferis with this final comment: "Let us hope that the poet's voice will not prove to be the voice of another Cassandra."

In the decades that followed I waited in vain for an official statement by a senior American spokesman that would constitute an apology for the misguided policy we had adopted toward the junta of the Greek colonels and then maintained throughout the seven years of its rule. That eventually came to pass when on November 20, 1999, President Bill Clinton, in a public address during his official visit to Greece, spoke as follows, after praising Greek valor in World War II:

> Twice since World War II, battles between democracy and despotism have again been played out on Greek soil; each time, thank God, democracy emerged victorious. I have been thinking about that history today again in both its painful as well as its proud aspects. When the junta took over in 1967 here, the United States allowed its interests in prosecuting the Cold War to prevail over its interests—I should say, its obligation—to support democracy, which was, after all, the cause for which we fought the Cold War. It is important that we acknowledge that.

The White House transcript of President Clinton's speech notes that there was "applause" by the audience at this point. It was about time that we said something that merited applause.

APPENDIX B

INTERNAL EMBASSY MEMORANDA, MARCH–JUNE 1968

MEMORANDUM   March 10, 1968

TO: The Ambassador
THROUGH: POL—George L. Warren, Jr.
FROM: POL—Robert V. Keeley
SUBJECT: Some Thoughts on our Present Predicament

"The hero of one country is almost inevitably the villain of another."
—Ernle Bradford, *The Great Betrayal: Constantinople 1204*

These thoughts, stimulated by the twelve-page "Points on Greece" paper sent to Mr. Battle on March 2, are offered on the basis that if one has a dissenting opinion it is a duty to offer it and that the reprehensible thing would be to keep silent.

It is oftentimes futile to rake over old history in a disputatious manner, but because our present predicament is so difficult to resolve it is necessary to have an agreed-upon understanding of how we got where we find ourselves today. Yet it is not germane to bring into the argument the entire political history of Greece in the Twentieth Century. Of course there has been great political instability in Greece in this century, wars, coups, abdications and so forth, but what is significant is how much stability has been displayed in *recent* years. To say that there have been 26 governments since

1950 is to make entirely the wrong point. The fact is that since 1952 and the electoral victory of General Papagos there has been an admirable degree of stability in Greece. It appeared that Greece had finally achieved the stability for which it had been striving for so long. Greek democracy was working. The proof is that in the period of 16 years from 1952 to 1968 Greece had only three different Prime Ministers who came to power through popular elections: Papagos, Karamanlis, and Papandreou. From this point of view Greece has been much more stable during this period than that model democracy, Great Britain. Greece experienced a degree of stability unusual even in Europe. To get the figure of 26 governments one must count the pre-1952 situation, the repetitions of Karamanlis and Papandreou, all the service governments, as well as all the governments that resulted directly from royal interventions in the democratic process and the unconstitutional changes of the most recent period. This is hardly legitimate arithmetic as a critique of democracy. The point is that Greek democracy was healthy when the electorate was permitted to exercise its democratic function. The voters put in power only three different Prime Ministers. It was the undemocratic and anti-democratic forces operating in Greece that were hurting Greek democracy; it was certainly not that that democracy itself was sick. To use a medical analogy such as is favored by the present regime, what has happened in Greece is like an incident in which a burglar breaks into a house, is surprised by the householder, whereupon the burglar sticks a knife into the householder and kills him. Now does this prove that the householder was sick with an incurable disease? Is that the conclusion that we draw from the fact that he was unable to overpower the burglar and place him under arrest? Or do we say simply, the burglar had a knife and the householder was unarmed?

Any democracy contains within itself anti-democratic elements, just as every body harbors germs within itself. But just because on occasion the germs multiply suddenly and make the body sick, do we say that the body is incurably diseased? No; the mere existence of germs does not define the state of health of the body, nor does the fact that they can occasionally deal a knock-out blow to a normally healthy organism.

Leslie Finer once said to me that he believed the principal propaganda achievement of the present regime was to convince people in Greece and abroad that Greek democracy was very sick prior to April 21, 1967 and that it therefore required drastic surgery. Mr. Finer thought this was just what he called it: propaganda, or a myth. The fact is, he said, Greek democracy was quite healthy, and its overthrow did not prove it was sick but simply that it was unarmed and it had enemies who were armed. The present regime originally justified its coup on the basis that a Communist takeover was imminent. When this line didn't wash with anyone, since no proof could be offered, they switched to the line that the "old politics" was completely corrupt and had to be overthrown. It appears that we too have accepted this line, for we are heard frequently these days saying, "Of course there will be no return to the pre-April 21 situation, and no one would want such a return." This position is worth examining a bit further.

What was wrong with the pre-April 21 situation as far as Greek democracy is concerned? There are two essential elements without which no democracy can be considered healthy or can survive. One is that there be genuinely free elections at regular intervals to permit the electorate to choose its leaders. The second essential element is somewhat more sophisticated and is an outgrowth of the development of political parties. It is that the losing party and its adherents be willing to permit the winning party to govern, that is, that they be "good losers." Now both of these have been problems in recent Greek history. The first serious difficulty came in 1961, when the Center Union refused to accept the verdict resulting from the elections as valid; it charged that the elections had been rigged, and George Papandreou began his first "unrelenting struggle." Many people concede that there was some "monkey business" in the 1961 elections, in other words, that they were not genuinely free elections expressing the will of the electorate. Thus the first essential of a healthy democracy was somehow subverted (by Karamanlis and company) and the Center Union refused to accept the verdict, thus denying the second essential, that the loser accept loser status. Eventually the Center Union won a clear-cut electoral victory, in the 1964 elections, which were considered honest by all sides. The first essential was back in force, but this time the losing side refused to accept the verdict and thus led us into our present predicament. They accepted the verdict at first, but after the July 1965 crisis they did not. The only proper course for the King at that time was to call for new elections and allow the electorate to lead the country out of its political impasse. But he was unwilling to abide by the will of the electorate, which he believed would support Papandreou and not him, so he engaged in a series of highly questionable maneuvers in order to avoid elections. The forces of the right and the anti-Papandreou center supported the King in these maneuvers.

Eventually the ERE and the EK came to an agreement, in December 1966, to resolve the impasse through holding free elections under the Paraskevopoulos government. This "deal" had some hope of resolving the conflicts growing out of the July 1965 dispute. But the trouble was that important elements in Greece still refused to abide by the electoral results, that is, if they returned the Papandreous to power. The palace, the army, the political right, the conservative establishment together created the climate that made the April coup possible by becoming open advocates of an "extra-parliamentary solution" (a coup or dictatorship), in fact of any "solution" that would prevent the Papandreous from returning to power. The Center Union forces were willing to abide by the election result, being fully confident that it would favor them. They wanted free elections and they were willing to abide by the results; in other words, they were in complete support of the two essentials of any healthy democracy. Their opponents were not: first they wanted to avoid elections, and finally they were unwilling to abide by the result. The installation of Kanellopoulos as Prime Minister to conduct the elections, instead of a service Prime Minister, was the final proof that the Right would not accept the principles of free elections and the consent of the loser.

This is why it is such a misreading of recent Greek political history to say, as many people do today, that the Center Union, or the Papandreous, or specifically Andreas Papandreou was largely responsible for creating the situation that brought on the death of Greek democracy through the April 21 coup. Those responsible for bringing on the coup were those persons who were subverting Greek democracy by preventing the holding of free elections when they were clearly called for, and by declaring in advance that they would not abide by the result if it turned out to be not to their liking (that is, a Papandreou victory). It is a clear perversion of logic to blame the death of a democracy on those who had openly declared their willingness to run for office in a free election (even under a government controlled by their opposition) and to abide by the result. This point, it should be stressed, clearly refutes the easy statement that Andreas Papandreou brought on or was responsible for the April 21 coup. To say that is to say that because antidemocratic forces overturned a functioning democracy it is the fault of the democrats and proves their unworthiness; because the man was murdered, he must have been incurably sick. Thus there are at least two myths current today: one is that Greek democracy was incurably sick prior to April 21, and the second is that Andreas Papandreou was the cause of that illness. The facts are that Greek democracy was reasonably healthy and all that was needed was for someone with power and influence to order the antidemocratic forces of the right to shape up and start behaving as if they accepted democratic principles and stop plotting to subvert Greek democracy. That was all that was needed to make Greek democracy survive.

The two prime requisites, which Greece has needed since World War II to have a healthy, functioning democracy, are:

(1) The elimination of the constitutional question, or the termination of the royalist-republican struggle. This was generally conceded to have been achieved after 1946, when the monarchy as an institution no longer was a central political question in Greece, after the return of George II and especially after the accession of Paul.

(2) The establishment of two strong nationalist parties, one conservative on the right and one liberal in the center, the left being conceded to the Communists. Papagos and Karamanlis succeeded in creating a strong conservative party, and from 1961 onwards George Papandreou and Sophocles Venizelos succeeded in creating a strong center party. As long as these two strong parties vied for power, alternated in power and in opposition, and accepted the principle that the winner of free elections would hold power, Greek democracy could function well. There is no question in my mind as to where the fault lies for the dishonoring of this last principle.

To look at democracy from another angle one might say that it suffers from three besetting evils: factionalism (in party organization), inefficiency (in administration), and demagoguery (in electioneering). Factionalism has been the particular bane of Greek democracy, especially in the post-Venizelos center. This evil had apparently been eliminated with the emergence of a strong, united, center party. The strength and unity of the center were not, however, very appealing to this party's opponents on the right. From the U.S. point of view, if not from that of the right in Greece, a strong center party should have been a priority *desideratum* toward assuring a healthy democracy in Greece. Inefficiency is something that democrats accept as one of the necessary evils of the system they prefer. In other words, they would rather have democracy with inefficiency than dictatorship with efficiency.

Demagoguery is the worst evil of democracy and the one most difficult to combat. But one does not eliminate it by eliminating democracy, elections, and political competition between parties, by subverting the entire democratic system. One eliminates it by exposure and overexposure, and by the faith that in the end the democratic electorate will choose honesty over demagoguery. Now it is said that Andreas Papandreou created the situation that led to the April 21 coup by being a demagogue. It is true that he indulged in demagoguery and political opportunism in the pre-April period, but the antidote to his demagoguery was exposure, not the elimination of the electoral process. To say that he was responsible for the coup is to say that he could have prevented it by shooting himself, by eliminating himself as a potential victor in the elections. Now does it make any sense to say that it is incumbent on a popular politician to commit suicide in order to save democracy because his opponents will kill democracy if he doesn't kill himself? Demagoguery was the weapon used by those who felt they had been unjustly deprived of the fruits of an electoral victory.

To say that Andreas was too rich for Greece's blood, that he brought into Greece's political life matters so disputatious that he infected Greek democracy and made it unhealthy, is a red herring. It is true that he challenged Greece's "establishment" in such a way that powerful groups in the country would do almost anything to keep him from coming to power. But to accept this view, as we apparently have—that it was Andreas who was the discordant element in Greek politics—is to range ourselves, along with the "establishment," against a large mass of the Greek electorate, which we do at our peril. As far as I am aware Andreas was attempting to attain power through normal democratic electoral means (even the junta has had to abandon the allegations over the Aspida affair) so to say that someone who is a potentially successful vote getter is a discordant element is to make a complete mockery of anyone's democratic system.

George Seferis, the Greek for whom I have the greatest respect intellectually and morally (though an intellectual he spent his life in practical political affairs), said to me recently, apropos of America's relations with Greece, "You must stop treating small poor countries like children and they will begin to behave like adults." He was alluding to what he felt was an attitude of condescension on the part of the Government of the United States, the attitude that expresses itself in the views so prevalent today that Greece is not ready for democracy, that Greece has tendencies toward chaos and anarchy as strong as those toward order, public tranquility and democracy, that democracy was not working well in Greece and that it must therefore "sleep" for a while. Aside from the justice of these views, or lack of same, with respect to Greece, there is an uncalled-for arrogance displayed by one democracy which is beset by internal problems of such a character that many of its major cities explode in mammoth riots every summer telling another country that it is not yet fit for democracy. Did Athens in 1965 experience anything like Detroit in 1967? There is also a glaring inconsistency when a country which is losing an average of 500 of its young men each week in Vietnam in order, according to its stated purposes, to assure to the people of that country the right to decide their own fate without coercion, when such a country tells another of its allies (Greece) that it is all right if its citizens have their similar rights suspended for a while. We struggle to have a democratically chosen government installed in Saigon in order to show that the war there is being fought for legitimate Vietnamese purposes, yet we are willing to see democracy suspended in another country which has democratic traditions predating the very existence of a free Vietnam. If one doubts that we have displayed a condescending attitude toward Greek democracy one need only read the recent statements on the Greek situation of former Secretary Acheson and former Ambassador Briggs, or listen to the views of most Americans who have been involved with Greek affairs in recent years.

I believe the United States is becoming mired in a tragic situation in Greece. The Greek political world is becoming increasingly polarized between the junta which holds all power in the country and Andreas Papandreou, who is increasingly mobilizing all opposition under his banner. Papandreou is not being successful because he is a brilliant organizer or because his ideology has wide appeal, but because he is working, because he has energy and he is using it, because he is providing the leadership which has been lacking to date. He is the only major political figure working full-time against the regime. This is having an effect on foreign opinion and it is being reflected in Greece. Recently I have begun hearing good words said about Andreas by people who used to have no use for him. Why? Because he is active at least. People are beginning to collect money for Andreas in Greece, ordinary citizens of small means but whose numbers are significant. A situation in which one would have to choose between the junta and Andreas would be a most unhappy one for most Americans in Greece, but it is even worse than that already.

A Greek friend of mine who has the widest circle of acquaintanceship here of anyone I know, from far right to far left, told me the other day, "If you could take a genuine public opinion poll in Greece today you could not find more than 3% of the people who have anything good to say for the United States. Practically, everyone is against you today." He pointed out that the government and its supporters are unhappy with us because we have not embraced them and have refused to restore full military aid. The government's opponents are against us because they think we have embraced the junta, and they cite things such as the reception aboard the aircraft carrier. The ERE people are angry with us because they feel we have deserted them, they who were always our best friends in Greece. The King's people are mad because we failed to support Constantine when he made his move, and they blame us for having led him astray to commit his foolish act. The Center people hate us because they feel we drove them from power and prevented them from winning the elections that were never held. The "apostates" claim we used them for our own purposes and then discarded them. The Communists are of course against us. Who are the 3% who are still with us? People who, like my friend, are pro-American "by nature." No matter what we do they'll be with us. But after all our investment in Greece 3% is a small lot to be left with.

How do we get out of this terrible situation? Well, I don't agree entirely with my friend! I think a great many Greeks are still looking to the United States to rescue them. They may be angry with us, but they still respect our power and our good intentions and if things work out in the end they will excuse what they feel to be the mistakes we have made recently. Even Andreas Papandreou is at this moment in the United States trying to mobilize American support. The junta may be mad at us, but they still want our support and assistance more than anything else. The opponents of the regime are somehow unable to abandon the idea that the U.S. government must have had its own reasons for having "installed" this coup government and that when our purposes have been served we will throw it out. They are counting on our coming to our senses eventually. That is why there has been so little overt opposition to the regime; not because people are happy with the situation, with the calm and order prevailing, but because they are counting on someone else, mainly the U.S., to do for them what they do not wish to take the risks of doing themselves, that is, getting rid of the present regime.

Looking at the present alternatives a moment, I see no disposition on the part of any American in the Embassy, in the U.S. government, in the U.S. community in Greece, to vote for taking the side of Andreas Papandreou and his opposition movement. In other words, the consensus is that Andreas is not rescuable. More than that, he is considered America's Number One Enemy in Greece. Why is there so much passionate hatred of Andreas on the part of Americans involved with Greece? It is hatred that goes beyond anything felt for an out-and-out self-proclaimed Communist. This question has interested me ever since I became re-involved in Greek affairs in 1966 and I have spent a lot of time trying to sort this question out. It struck me from practically the first moment, for when I arrived in Washington to have a few days of consultation before coming to Athens, the then assistant desk officer, Dick Barham, began by giving me a violently anti-Andreas diatribe and I immediately wondered what this was all about. Nothing he told me adequately explained the passion of the anti-Andreas sentiment that I noticed everywhere among Americans in Greece. With this near-unanimity of anti-Andreas passion one would be tempted to conclude that there must be something to it, it must be legitimate, he must really be the Devil Incarnate after all. But I think we must face the question of Andreas Papandreou quite frankly, because I don't think he is going to disappear, but rather I think his role will loom larger and larger as time passes, and because people feel that he is such a danger to U.S. interests in Greece it is worth exploring the problem in some depth. I believe that one reason why Americans hate Andreas so much is that he was formerly an American and we tend to be intolerant of anti-Americanism displayed by a former American whom we adopted as a citizen. There is something of the feeling that he has been traitorous, that since we accepted him as a U.S. citizen he has no right to criticize our government or our policies or our role in Greece. In other words, Americans are reacting to the anti-Americanism of a sort of American "turn-coat," one of the most evil figures in our lexicon.

Now the question is, what makes Andreas so anti-American? I think there are several explanations at least, but I could not presume to determine what their relative weights are:

(1) One of his greatest handicaps as a Greek politician was that he was a former American, and in the beginning he was considered in some circles to be the Americans' fair-haired boy. There were even rumors spread about him that he was an American agent whom we were trying to infiltrate into the Greek political scene. Also, Andreas was a Johnny-come-lately who suddenly arrived on the scene threatening to take over the Center Union over the heads of many other politicians who had been working away here for years and felt they had priority in the succession to old George. Andreas doubtless felt it incumbent on himself to prove that he was no American stooge and what better way than to be more anti-American than the next guy? Did he have to go so far to make this point? Perhaps not, but there were other reasons.

(2) Once the Center Union was in power Andreas probably came to feel that the USG's involvement in internal Greek affairs was too great and derogated from Greek sovereignty. This was a genuine feeling, and was based on the observation, once the EK was in power, that the palace and the army acted as totally independent power elements which were closely allied to the Americans. Even more important, the KYP was quite an independent operation with close links to its American counterpart and probably under little control by the government. In trying to rectify this situation from the EK government's point of view a direct clash with American interests was created. This is not the place to go into further detail on this subject. But I think we could agree that the palace, the army and KYP were all basically hostile to the Center Union.

(3) A feeling that the U.S. did not give the support it should have to the GOG in the Cyprus crisis of 1963–64. The EK government was in power during this period and felt entitled to greater support from NATO and the U.S. in its dispute with Turkey. The reaction to the neutral attitude of the

U.S. in the form of anti-American feelings on the part of Andreas and other EK people should not surprise us, for the same anti-American feelings were generated in Turkey because of our failure to take the Turks' side in the dispute. This is one of the natural hazards of being a great power, of being caught in the middle in major disputes between countries such as India-Pakistan, Arabs-Israel, Nigeria-Biafra and so forth. The anti-Americanism bred by our neutrality is understandable and should be something we could live with, since we have to.

(4) Andreas reacted to what he felt was anti-Andreas sentiment in the U.S. Mission in Athens and the U.S. government generally by becoming more anti-American. This continues to this day and is connected with the feeling that the U.S. government has always favored the Center Union's opponents, the ERE with its conservative allies in the palace and the army, and has been decidedly biased against the liberal forces in Greece. Obviously this subject could be argued at great length, but the feeling among Center people other than Andreas is widespread, so it is not a phenomenon limited to Andreas. If evidence of anti-Center bias is required, one need only cite the recent published statements of former Secretary Acheson and former Ambassador Briggs. Admittedly the latter is somewhat eccentric, but it is unconscionable for a former American Ambassador to this country to declare in public print that we're much better off now than we were when the Papandreous ruled, quoting Mr. Acheson's crack about "the old fool and the young rascal" and in the same breath referring to the "good" Karamanlis. If that isn't taking sides in internal Greek politics then I have never seen it. By the same token Mr. Acheson may be aging and his memory may be failing so that he cannot remember the words he wrote (or approved) about Greece in the Truman Doctrine message to Congress, but it is the height of condescension to try to tell the Greek people today that they are not worthy of a democratic system. He might just as well tell the Africans that they do not deserve to be liberated from the colonial yoke. Perhaps he will. Think of an imaginary situation a year from now, following a takeover of the British Government by a group of military conspirators distressed with the Labor Government's disengagement from its world commitments and unhappy with its poor performance at home. What if the then former Secretary Rusk and former Ambassador Bruce wrote letters to the *Times* saying they regretted the necessity for the military coup in Great Britain but at least that was better than to have that great American ally ruled "by that old fool Harold Wilson and that young rascal George Brown."

Wouldn't we wonder whether Messrs. Rusk and Bruce had viewed British domestic politics in an unbiased and disinterested manner in the period prior to the British coup, while Wilson and Brown were in power? Former Ambassador Briggs's statement is a dead giveaway on the question of official American prejudice toward the Greek political parties and personalities; he was our Ambassador in Athens when the 1961 election was held here. (In the interest of brevity I will skip over the Laughlin Campbell and Vincent Joyce incidents, but these clearly played a large role in the bad relations between the American Mission and Andreas Papandreou.)

(5) Andreas engaged in demagoguery, opportunism, political pragmatism, or whatever one wants to call it, by taking anti-American and anti-NATO positions calculated to appeal to the left-of-center voters whom he hoped to convert into personal supporters in order to enhance his power in the Center Union. This was a calculated effort to wean away from the far left party (the EDA) and into the fold of the Center a group of people who had genuine anti-American feelings. I suppose Andreas calculated that the right-of-center spectrum included within the Center Union was closed to him because rival Center politicians had this area "locked up." So he decided to make his push on the left-of-center, and his anti-American positions went very nicely with this effort.

All in all, Andreas has been anti-USG and anti-US Embassy, but strange as it may sound I think he is pro-American.

Beyond the above I believe I detect in Andreas a certain strain of super sensitivity bordering on paranoia, which causes him to react violently to what he regards as prejudice against himself, rather than shrugging it off as a natural antipathy in view of the threat he posed to established interests, American and Greek. Andreas does not have the thick skin that most professional politicians grow. But I have also long felt that Andreas' power and prominence were created for him by his enemies, who have displayed the same sort of paranoia.

Does this account for the passion of the hatred of Andreas? If he were not so hated perhaps he would not have so many adherents. As the Arabs say, "The enemy of my enemy is my friend." And to revert to the quotation at the beginning of these remarks, one might propose to write Andreas off, label him Public Enemy Number One, and do our damnedest to eliminate him as a political force in Greece. The difficulty with this course is that we may simply succeed in making him a hero to the mass of the Greek people who will thereby become even more convinced in their anti-Americanism. The villain of one country is almost inevitably the hero of another.

Now to take the other alternative, should we give the junta our full support? My Greek acquaintances may be fantastically limited in variety, but I have yet to talk with a single Greek (who is not an official of the present government) who is an enthusiastic supporter of the present regime. Admittedly I've never exchanged more than greetings with Nick Farmakis. There are enthusiasts in the business community, but many of them are Greek-Americans who have the most passionate hatred of all for Andreas Papandreou, and fear him to such an extent that they like the junta all the better for it.

I believe we must take the long-range view and in the long range I think we will lose out with Greek opinion if we come down strongly on the side of the junta. As the situation increasingly polarizes into Junta vs. Andreas obviously more people will flock to the banner of the junta and its popular base will enlarge somewhat. But I do not believe it will command the popular support necessary for a long stay in power. More than that, I do not think the junta will succeed. This belief is based on the demonstrated incapacity of the junta leadership to cope with Greece's problems, economic and other. Perhaps they could get some good people to take over in their name, but I doubt that they will want to do this.

More important is that the Greek people are refusing to cooperate with the junta and without that cooperation the junta cannot succeed. The Greek people have been mild in their opposition to the regime thus far, but they are sitting on their hands, allowing the economy to slide downhill, and hoping someone will step in to rescue them. I believe most Greeks want the junta to fail, for they feel that if the junta succeeds it will merely be encouraged to stay in power longer and longer. When will the economy have grown enough, when will the bureaucracy have been cleansed enough, when will the threat of communism have been sufficiently reduced, for the junta to say that its job is finished? Whereas if the junta fails, someone (the U.S.) can be counted on to step in and give them the *coup de grace*. It is amazing that so many people continue to count on the U.S. to solve the situation in Greece. There exists a strange paradox between the great amount of dissatisfaction among Greeks with the recent performance of the United States and the still vast hopes entertained that in the end the U.S. will rescue them.

Rather than being stuck with the junta, why don't we work to get rid of it? This is presumably what we have been doing. The prognosis regarding our success is, however, highly doubtful. We have been working to have constitutional democracy restored. This would logically mean the departure of the junta from power. Yet they give no appearance of wanting to give up power at an early date. Nor do they engender confidence that they really believe in democracy or believe that it is a good system for Greece. They give every indication of thoroughly detesting parliamentary democracy, politicians and democratic politics in general. They much prefer efficiency to democracy.

They could give Andreas Papandreou some lessons in demagoguery, if we define that activity as appealing to people's passions and prejudices to gain their support and as making extraordinary promises of what they will accomplish, promises they cannot hope to fulfill. Perhaps we could call them "sincere demagogues" in the sense that they believe their own impossible promises. Most demagogues are insincere. Huey Long said every farmer was entitled to 40 acres and a mule. Joe McCarthy said that one Thursday he would release a list containing the names of 207 (or some such number) card-carrying Communists in the State Department. Both of these politicians were demagogues. One was eliminated by assassination; the other was stripped of his power by his parliamentary colleagues. No democracy is ever immune to demagogues; we have one today in the person of George Wallace. Let us hope we can take care of him by democratic means.

What does all this mean for our policy in Greece today? We should first of all avoid being driven into making a choice between the junta and Andreas Papandreou at the head of a unified and virulently anti-American resistance movement. If we do nothing, or not very much, we risk being driven into that position eventually, and perhaps sooner rather than later on. The best alternative would be to restore a healthy democracy to Greece just as soon as possible, by means of genuinely free elections, with all parties and factions committed to respect the electoral outcome. We should insist that the present regime publish a new democratic constitution at the earliest possible date, without further delay, hold a referendum on it, and declare in advance that genuinely free elections will be held three months after the referendum. They should then turn power over to a non-partisan service government immediately after the referendum to govern the country in the pre-electoral period. Perhaps the King could return right after the referendum with a pledge to guarantee the freedom of the elections and the restoration of a constitutional democracy.

The surest guarantee that domestic Greek Communism would continue to fade as a threat was the existence of an entrenched democratic political system coupled with steady and rapid economic growth. The junta has suspended both of these and has thereby opened the door to resurgent Greek Communism. In no historical case has Communism thrived in a democratic, developed country. We must somehow reestablish Greece as a democracy on the road toward the status of a small but strong, developed, secure Free World power. The junta stands in the way of the achievement of this goal and must therefore be removed from power.

Obviously, the formula set forth above would be most unpleasant medicine for the junta to swallow. This fact would only evidence their lack of interest in restoring genuine constitutional democracy to the country. They could very well refuse to carry out such a program. In that case I believe our best course would be to withdraw all support from them in an effort to force compliance with our program. There would be certain risks in such a policy, but I firmly believe that we have much greater leverage over this government than we apparently believe we have and certainly much greater leverage than we have yet used. I believe the present regime needs our support to survive in the long run and this gives us a great deal of influence over how things will develop in Greece. Our job is to get them to act in ways we believe are necessary to save Greece for the Free World; our job is not to get them to like us.

One might object that the policy I propose is unrealistic, in that it would not be accepted by the junta. Actually I think it is at least as realistic as the policy we are pursuing, which is to try to talk the present regime's leaders into eliminating themselves from power, in other words trying to encourage them to commit political suicide. For if they restore truly democratic constitutional government they will have signed their own discharge papers, and if they rig things so that they can perpetuate their rule under supposed constitutional and democratic norms we will only be kidding ourselves that we have solved our problems here; we will merely have postponed the day of reckoning.

Since I have posed the situation as one of choosing between the stark alternatives of the junta and Andreas Papandreou, it is proper to ask how my program, which would dispose of the junta, would take care of the problem of Andreas Papandreou. There are two answers to this. One is that Andreas Papandreou operating in a Greece ruled by a healthy democracy would be a much lesser danger for the United States than would be a Greece polarized between a fading junta and a violently anti-US resistance movement headed by Andreas. The second answer is that we could use our program for restoring democracy to Greece as the first step in an attempt to rehabilitate our relations with Andreas Papandreou and the dynamic that he represents in the Greek political world. The most dangerous course, I believe, would be to write him off as a non-entity or a has-been in Greek politics. Greece today is ripe for Andreas Papandreou or someone else very much like him. A resistance movement is a great way to rehabilitate a fallen hero. And the hero of one country is almost inevitably the villain of another.

    cc: MIN—R. D. McClelland
    POL:RVKeeley:js 3/13/68

March 19, 1968

    Ross:

One afterthought to our discussion of yesterday.

The emotionalism you found in my draft is not due to my concern over what has happened to Greece, that it has lost its democratic system and so forth. My serious concern is that as an American I feel we are losing Greece as an ally in the Free World, if we persevere on the present course. The present regime is pro-US and pro-NATO, and offers us a short-term guarantee, but someday the Greeks will once again freely choose their own government. When that time arrives I fear there are going to be more powerful anti-American elements in Greece than there were in the past, and the longer that the day is put off the more anti-American feeling there will be. This will be our loss as Americans, not as friends of Greece.

There are others (Kay Bracken, Dan Brewster) who have as long and as close associations with Greece as I do, and they come to conclusions very different from my own. I don't question their objectivity any more than I should like them to question mine. What I do detect in them is a defensiveness about the correctness of past US policies with which they were associated.

My Greek "relatives" and their friends, being members of the "*Kolonaki* crowd," are unanimously right-wing and pro-junta; they have hardly influenced my views about Greece.

On the question of objectivity, I am concerned that the views of the many Greek-Americans who serve here are all in accord on two things: one, that Greek democracy was incurably sick, that the junta is good for Greece and the Greeks, and that the Greeks deserve no better, and second, that their fellow Greek-American Andreas Papandreou is the Devil Incarnate. There are influential Greek-Americans in the Embassy, in CAS (especially), in JUSMAGG, in the local business community. There was a time in the Foreign Service when prior connection with a foreign country disqualified one for service there, because of fears over objectivity and because we didn't like to place people in positions where they could be "blackmailed." You couldn't serve in a post with which your *wife* had any previous connection. As far as Greece is concerned that practice has been abandoned by all agencies, it appears. To my regret. Today it appears, at least in some agencies, that being a Greek-American especially qualifies one to serve in Greece. I do not agree.

—RVK

TO: MINISTER—Mr. McClelland   April 26, 1968
FROM: POL—Robert V. Keeley
SUBJECT: One Year Assessment (A-558)

Here are a couple of thoughts stimulated by the long analytical study of the situation one year after the coup. Attention is directed specifically to the final section on "Recommendations for U.S. Policy."

I think there is something important missing from this section. That is, there is a portion dealing with "The Short Range," meaning the next few months, and then another portion dealing with the period after the September referendum. Actually both of these periods are in the short range; they don't look beyond the next year. There is no section dealing with the long-range implications of the policies we have been pursuing or are advocating now. I believe this has been missing from all of the policy papers we have submitted in the past year: we have failed to look at the long-range implications, by which I mean what will (or may, as best we can guess) happen in the next five to ten years.

For example, this consideration is entirely absent from the discussion of the MAP issue and the recommendation that we restore MAP deliveries in order to be able to influence the present regime in favorable directions in the short range. This is fine as far as it goes, but there is no mention of the other important aspect that a restoration of MAP by the USG will throw the regime's opponents into a mood of despair and will cause them to conclude that we have finally embraced the junta completely and irrevocably. The junta will not fail to play up this latter theme loud and long. The only thing we have done since April 21, 1967 which has helped to persuade the regime's opponents that we are not really delighted with the junta and with the coup is the MAP suspension. If we reverse that policy we should recognize (and take into account) that although our relations with the junta will decidedly improve, our image with the regime's opponents will change from gray to very black instantaneously. If this is a price we are willing to pay, then so be it, but I think a policy paper should put this factor into the equation when making such a serious and well-considered recommendation.

The second thought is stimulated by the paragraph at the bottom of page 42 where the point is made that severe pressure by the USG to force the Greek regime "to conform to the demands of democratic idealism" could merely have the effect of reducing the significance of the United States as a factor in the Greek situation. I take it that the argument here is that if we ever concluded that the present regime was not going to leave power peacefully but decided to remain in control for a very long time, then any effort by us to dislodge them might simply eliminate the U.S. as a factor in Greece. Therefore we ought to be willing to reach some sort of compromise with the regime.

I think this is a very short-sighted view. Again, I think we are failing to look at the long-range implications. If we tried to oust the regime, we might run the risk of eliminating ourselves as a factor in Greece *in the short run,* that is for as many years as the junta could remain in power despite the complete hostility of ourselves and our friends. So far so good. But what really needs saying is that if we failed to make such an effort to oust the regime once it had demonstrated that it intended to stay in power regardless of anything, then we would be running an even greater risk of eliminating ourselves permanently as a factor in Greece *in the long run.* If we chose instead to compromise with the junta then our influence here would be so intimately linked with the junta's survival that it would die whenever the junta eventually died. This is a choice we may be facing, and not too far in the future, so I think it's important to keep the long-range implications in view as well as the short-range considerations that tend to dominate the argument in A-558.

The same principle applies with respect to our military bases, staging rights, VOA facilities, Sixth Fleet visitation privileges and so forth. The best way to preserve these, *in the short run,* would be to embrace the junta. But in the long run the best way to preserve them might well be to avoid at all cost an over identification with the junta (for opponents of the regime normal MAP deliveries to Greece would constitute such an over identification). Do we want "Ellenikon" (in Kay Bracken's shorthand phrase) guaranteed for the next one, two or three years? Or do we want it for the next ten or twenty years? The time may not be far away when we will have to face the horns of this dilemma.

POL/RVKeeley:rr
4-26-68

cc: AMB
POL

OFFICE OF THE MINISTER

May 4, 1968

Bob:

I apologize for the length of this paper, and I do not thereby propose that we conduct this dialogue through an extended exchange of such memoranda. However, significant differences of appraisal are clearly involved which are going to have to be resolved if POL is to play an effective role in the important policy planning job which lies before us in Athens. I therefore felt the discipline of putting my thoughts in writing was warranted.

                                                                                  Ross

TO: POL—Mr. Keeley   DATE: May 3, 1968
FROM: MIN—R. McClelland
SUBJECT: Your April 26 Comments on A-558: Assessment of Greek Situation a Year After the Coup

The following are my preliminary reactions to your views.

    A long-range perspective is certainly desirable in conducting foreign relations. Under the present conditions of amorphousness and uncertainty in Greece, however, I find such a perspective difficult to achieve in any definitive terms. In particular we do not yet have a reliable enough "fix" (in the navigational sense) on the various factors which must be taken into account to be able to plot a future course as specifically as you would have us do.

    I gather from your earlier paper that you believe the risks of even a short-range, tactical accommodation with the junta are unacceptable because of the potential long-range alienation of the Greek people which could, in your opinion, result. You observe in your present memo that "a restoration of MAP . . . will throw the regime's opponents into a mood of despair and will cause them to conclude that we have <u>finally</u> embraced the junta *completely* and <u>irrevocably</u>" (underlining mine). I'm not sure that the evidence supports so categoric an assumption or that we could not manage to offset such a reaction by frankly explaining our real purposes in the proper Greek quarters. I should however be interested to know what leads you to this conclusion. Can we at this stage, for example, equate the "regime's opponents" with the Greek people as a whole?

Although I don't know Greek psychology as well as you do, the proposition seems valid to me that in order to deal effectively with anybody, especially a Greek, you have to mix some "carrots" with the "sticks," as we said in A-558. You appear, however, to feel that we could do better in our attempt to push the government toward more convincing constitutional progress if we maintained a critical and aloof attitude toward it and did not respond in any other way. Maybe so, but do you, at the same time, disagree with the premise underlying our present tactic that we would be in a stronger position to come down hard on this crowd for having given some prior evidence of taking them at their word? Continuing to treat a man, let alone a government, as though you questioned the sincerity of his motives, seems to me a very shaky basis on which to found any expectation of influencing him constructively.

On page 2, para 2 of your memo you say: "I take it the argument here is that if we ever concluded the present regime was not going to leave power peacefully but had decided to remain in control for a very long time, then any effort by us to dislodge them might simply eliminate the U.S. as a factor in Greece."

If my reading of our present thinking is correct, we certainly have not reached any such truncated conclusion. I would ask you, moreover, to consider the points made further along in this paragraph of A-558 (page 42), notably the statement: "The question would remain whether any actions *within the acceptable range of U.S. policy* would have the effect of dislodging the present regime in Greece and replacing it with a government more consonant with contemporary Atlantic community standards, or would merely salve the American conscience while *reducing* the significance of the U.S. as a factor in the Greek situation." (Note that we didn't say "eliminate.")

The present stage of developments in Greece does not *yet* permit the conclusion you seem already to have reached that all efforts to force this government back into tolerable constitutional channels are doomed to failure because of the essentially dictatorial and intrinsically malevolent nature of its purposes. We may, not too far down the road, have to reach such a conclusion and revise our policies accordingly. But even were this to be the case, it is nevertheless far from clear that the correct and inevitable policy alternative should be to attempt to get rid of it. Although I don't like clichés, diplomacy, like politics, remains very much "the art of the possible." So, before seriously advocating such a drastic course, I think we would have to weigh a number of factors very carefully and have a much more accurate reading of the situation than we now do.

We are already on the horns of the proverbial dilemma in our relations with Greece since we are confronted not with any convenient choice between a good course and a bad one, but rather with two unattractive and risky propositions: trying to make something more acceptable to Greece and to the democratic world out of the present government (a grubby and unheroic enterprise at best), or possibly undertaking a course of action (e.g. trying to dislodge them) which—quite apart from the fact it might not succeed unless we could count on resources which are unlikely to be forthcoming from Washington, or if it did, take several years—could lead to serious internal strife, economic harm, etc., in Greece whose extent and consequences are impossible to foresee at this stage (although one can safely predict that they would add up to a substantial rehabilitation task).

I am therefore not yet prepared to accept the assertion on page 2, 3rd para of your memo that "if we failed to make . . . an effort to oust the regime once it had demonstrated that it intended to stay in power regardless of anything, then we would be running the even greater risk of eliminating ourselves permanently as a factor in Greece *in the long run*."

I would be very interested to have your considered and detailed views on how we might practically go about "ousting" the present Greek Government if it turns out to be the sordid and authoritarian clique many intelligent people fear it is.

There is another factor, which caused us considerable travail in composing A-558, to which I invite your attention and on which your estimate would be most welcome: the question of the true attitude of the Greek people toward the present regime.

I take it from the tenor of your observations that you believe the present government is not only so universally detested by the Greek people as a whole, and so unalterably bad, as to render any effort on our part to work with it or *on* it as not only an unacceptable policy alternative but one which could seriously jeopardize our long-range relations with the country. While I can personally sympathize with you from a sentimental viewpoint, I'm not sure we can permit ourselves the luxury of surrendering to these dictates of the "American conscience," however morally edifying they may be. Moreover, I do not believe that we have enough evidence *at this juncture* to conclude that everybody in Greece shares the obvious feelings of hostility and indignation with respect to the present regime which the intellectual community has. There are large chunks of the population (as we tried to point out in the section on public attitudes in A-558) about whose real views we know very little; and it is dangerous (as well as easy), I fear, to extrapolate the opinions of an elite at the top as though they applied to the whole population. This is not to say, I hasten to add, that the views of the leadership stratum of Greek society are not, and particularly, could become extremely important, but merely that they are not the entire picture, and hence not sufficient evidence on which to base radical and far-reaching policy recommendations.

Another consideration on which I'd be interested in your thoughts: if we are to get into the risky business of ousting other people's governments, what assurances could we have regarding the form of the successor regime? Would we be able to exercise sufficient control over the course of events (which are not readily predictable) to make sure that what replaced the present government was unmistakably better for Greece and for U.S. interests in Greece than what might result from a concerted effort to change the present set-up? If a substantial breakdown in the internal fabric of Greece occurred, would we be able, short of the type of massive intervention we undertook in 1946–49, to prevent the emergence of a political situation which could conceivably be worse than what we now have or what might be made out of it?

I frankly question at this point what I take to be your underlying thesis, namely, that a continuation of the present regime spells irrevocable disaster for Greece while what its opponents want (and, what type of opponents, by the way, are you talking about?) will manifestly provide a better solution to Greece's longstanding problem of mis-government. I do not think we know at this stage. As the coming months unfold we may well have to consider what *feasible* policy alternatives there are to trying to push the present ruling group into adopting acceptable goals and modes of action. I however sincerely doubt (and I say this out of a sense of genuine pragmatism and not cynicism), that the available alternatives will ever permit us to mount the barricades of liberation.

MIN: RDMcClelland:efm

TO: MIN—Roswell D. McClelland   May 17, 1968
FROM: POL—Robert V. Keeley
SUBJECT: U.S. Policy Toward Greece

I welcome the opportunity to continue this dialogue on U.S. policy toward Greece, and am responding in writing to the questions posed in your memorandum of May 3, both because it is beneficial to try to set down one's views in language as precise as possible and because in this way one can share one's thoughts with other colleagues who are equally interested in these important matters. I apologize even more for the length, but there are far-ranging considerations which affect one's overall conclusions.

To recapitulate, you asked the following questions:

—What leads me to the conclusion that a restoration of MAP would throw the regime's opponents into a mood of despair and would cause them to conclude that we had finally embraced the junta completely and irrevocably? Can we at this stage equate the regime's opponents with the Greek people as a whole?

Brief answer: The partial suspension of MAP has been the only concrete and public evidence we have given since April 21, 1967 that we are not entirely happy to have this regime in power in Greece. Most Greeks believe we at least accept the regime today. Full restoration of MAP would be interpreted as an embrace of the junta, no matter what explanations we offered. I do not equate the regime's opponents with the Greek people as a whole. More on this below.

—Do I disagree with the premise underlying our present tactic that we would be in a stronger position to come down hard on this crowd for having given some prior evidence of taking them at their word (about a restoration of a constitutional, democratic regime)?

Brief Answer: You concluded from my earlier paper that I was advocating a policy of all stick and no carrot. If I believed that the present regime was sincerely interested in restoring constitutional and democratic rule at an early date I too would advocate a combination carrot and stick tactic as the best means of speeding up that process. Since I believe on the contrary that the regime is most strongly motivated by a desire to perpetuate its rule for the longest possible time unhampered by the restraints of democratic principles and processes, I am concerned that our present carrot and stick course is merely wasting for us valuable time that would be better used in support of a vastly different policy.

—Is it not too early to conclude that all efforts to force this government back into tolerable constitutional channels are doomed to failure?

Brief answer: It is too early to reach such a conclusion if one demands that we have "conclusive" evidence in hand. Yet there is a most serious risk in waiting for such evidence to appear (for example in the form of a flat declaration by Papadopoulos that he intends to remain in power for five years come what may). The risk is that when we have obtained such evidence we will discover that it is much too late to do anything about it, for the assets we possessed for affecting the situation will have disappeared during the time we were waiting to make up our minds about the true intentions of the regime.

—How might we go about ousting the present regime?

Brief answer: I do not advocate that we try ourselves to oust this regime. Briefly, I suggest that we help create a climate in Greece which would encourage the Greek people to act to replace the present regime with one more to their (and our) liking. The most important thing we could do to help create such a climate would be to concert with our allies to withdraw support of all kinds from the present regime to show the Greek people that we do not condone what has been done to their democratic institutions and that they do not have to fight the United States and its allies as well at the junta but the junta alone. Since the Greek people are unarmed I would expect that the initial favorable change would be brought about by die-hard pro-Western and pro-NATO elements which still exist in large numbers in the Greek armed forces, who would act to remove the present junta from power because it had alienated Greece's allies, had brought about a break between Greece and its natural friends in the West and the Free World, and which, if allowed to remain in power any longer, would lead the country to ruin and destruction. Once the present junta had been replaced by a truly pro-Western military group which was not interested in power for its own sake but rather in restoring Greece to its traditional place in the bosom of the Western world, then there would be opened up infinite possibilities for working out a smooth and orderly transition back to democratic, constitutional rule within a reasonable period of time.

—What is the true attitude of the Greek people toward the present regime? How much popular support does it enjoy? Is the opinion of the intellectual community representative of the whole?

Brief answer: I do not know the answers to these questions. But I do believe that the junta, despite the vulnerability to sycophancy from which it suffers in common with all undemocratic regimes whether they be monarchies, dictatorships or aristocracies, is much better informed than we are on the true extent and nature of its popular support. I am therefore willing to take the government's actions (not its statements) as evidence of the support it believes it enjoys, and the evidence in this regard is fairly conclusive. One year after the coup we still have martial law, a strictly controlled press, no permitted political activity, civil liberties in suspense, no public discussion of national issues, control of the population exercised by inducing fear of arbitrary arrest, and so forth. Surely a regime which enjoyed the support and/or tolerance of a substantial majority of the population would not need to maintain such strict controls in addition to the overriding weapon of coercion deriving from the fact that the government also commands the only armed forces in the country.

As for the intellectuals, history has demonstrated that they often have a way of being the first group to adopt a cause or an idea which only gradually gains popular acceptance. But if we wait to act until we have conclusive evidence in hand that the people as a whole are following the lead of the intellectuals, then again we will have sacrificed the tactical advantages of acting in time in favor of the desire to act with absolute certainty. When a third of the population has reached the stage of opposition to the junta of being willing to take up arms against it, we will be faced with a civil war. The way to avoid a civil war is to anticipate the trend that is leading toward a total alienation of that third of the population.

—If we were to get into the risky business of ousting other people's governments, what assurances could we have regarding the form of the successor regime? Would we be able to exercise sufficient control over the course of events (which are not readily predictable) to make sure that what replaced the present government was unmistakably better for Greece and for U.S. interests in Greece than what might result from a concerted effort to change the present set-up? If a substantial breakdown in the internal fabric of Greece occurred, would we be able, short of the type of massive intervention we undertook in 1946–49, to prevent the emergence of a political situation which could conceivably be worse than what we now have or what might be made out of it?

Brief answer: This is of course a key question. Briefly, we would certainly be able to exercise more influence over a successor regime if it were led by a military group dedicated to restoring a democratic government to the country rather than, as with the present group, people who see themselves as messiahs and revolutionary statesmen. And a subsequent democratic regime would certainly be more subject to favorable influences of all kinds, since it could not escape the normal checks and balances of a democratic political system acting in a free environment. The present ruling group holds all power in Greece in a very few hands and therefore is subject to the least possible external influence. No one could be sure about post-junta events and there are no guarantees in this type of situation. One must take certain gambles in order to avoid even larger risks.

This is what went very wrong in Greece in the winter and spring of 1967. Andreas Papandreou inspired fear in many quarters, but he was attempting to obtain power by democratic means within a democratic system. If his enemies had been wise they would have done their damnedest to preserve that democratic system, for even if they had lost the first (electoral) battle to Andreas, he would still have had to work within a democratic system and would have been subject to all of its very important restraints on radical courses of action. For example, if he had tried to take Greece out of NATO (which I strongly doubt he intended) the Greek monarchy and armed forces could have exerted their considerable counter-pressure against such a course and most probably would have prevailed. Now the checks and balances have been destroyed along with the system, so that if the present regime wants to pull the country out of NATO there is no one who could stop them (at least in the first instance). For this reason almost any other regime would be "unmistakably" better than the present one if it were even one degree less a dictatorship.

As for a breakdown in the internal fabric of Greece, that is occurring today and is likely to continue at an accelerated pace so long as the present regime of incompetence refuses to seek skilled help. Our massive intervention of 1947–49 arose from the fact that Greece was torn by a civil war (it is apparently forbidden in the State Department lexicon to call this episode a "civil" war, but the fact is that the fighters on both sides were indigenous

Greeks, and that is the traditional definition of a civil war). The longer the present regime stays in power the more likely it is that the final outcome will be a civil war. An attempt by us to encourage the Greek people to oust the junta would not be likely to precipitate a civil war, but would instead materially assist in resolving the situation before it degenerated into a civil war. "Massive interventions" result from a failure to take much less drastic action when such a limited intervention was still possible. Frankly, the worst conceivable situation in Greece for us would be one in which the population had become polarized between the present ruling junta and an armed resistance movement dominated by the Communists. Vietnam in Europe.

—Do we know at this stage that a continuation of the present regime spells irreversible disaster for Greece while what its opponents want (and, what type of opponents, by the way, are you talking about?) will manifestly provide a better solution to Greece's longstanding problem of misgovernment?

Brief answer: In the first place, Greece has never before been as misgoverned as it is today, according to the testimony of many people who know much more about the subject than I do. Yes, there is less bribe taking; yes, there are no strikes; yes, the buses run on time. But an objective analysis of the government's handling of the economy since April 1967 would not award any prizes to the junta. The present regime's propaganda notwithstanding, Greece had a tolerably able and efficient government by 1967, so that even a minority government (of Stephanopoulos), which benefited by practically no popular support and by only a precarious parliamentary majority based on fear and convenience and royal pressure, could keep the country on an even keel and even make some mild progress in the field of foreign relations. This was all partly the result of twenty years of massive American effort. If Greece did not have a tolerably efficient administration by 1967, as well as a reasonably healthy democracy (whose main failure was that the armed forces were dominated by anti-democratic elements), then those twenty years of American effort were a failure, a proposition to which I for one do not subscribe.

As for the regime's opponents, I believe what they want restored is what they had: a democratic system, freedom of choice, the freedom to make mistakes from time to time, but a system that the people will support in the long run because it gives them the individual freedom they cherish. If I am right about what the regime's opponents want then I don't see how we could raise any objection, even if it did not solve the problem of mis-government. Of course here I betray my own sentiments as an absolute democrat, that is, one who believes that what people want they ought to have and that efficiency is an entirely secondary and subordinate consideration.

Discussion

A good beginning would be to look for a moment at what the supporters and opponents of the regime think about it and why. For the adherents and apologists I suppose the compelling arguments are that the coup was inevitable and the arrival in power of the junta an unavoidable event in Greek political history, that the present government can accomplish reforms and restructurings that no political government dependent on a parliamentary majority could ever achieve, that somehow the coup stopped a drift toward Communism, that the colonels' revolution is a positive force for good in Greece, and essentially that any other of the available alternatives, either in April 1967 or today, would have been or would be much worse for Greece and for the Free World.

The regime's critics and opponents, for their part, use the exactly reverse sides of these same arguments: that a coup was not inevitable but rather avoidable, that there were and are other possible desirable alternatives, that the present regime cannot accomplish anything constructive because the Greek people will not cooperate with it, that the coup was a most unfortunate development in Greek political history which will have evil consequences, and that the aftermath and eventual outcome of the colonels' revolution will inevitably be a strengthening of the Communist forces in Greece.

We are dealing here with philosophical arguments and with the opinions of those who oppose the regime on grounds of principle, not for personal reasons having to do with loss of job or status or with individual hardships allegedly suffered. For persons who oppose the regime on grounds of principle, that is, for true democrats, there is a basic wrong in the present situation that can in no way be corrected or worked out or smoothed over, for these people believe that the ruling junta is composed of anti-democrats who do not want democracy for Greece, who do not believe that democracy is a good system for the country, and who will therefore not permit Greece to have democracy so long as they have the power to prevent it.

These are views held by intellectuals, by "thinking" Greeks, not by Mr. Gallup's "ordinary citizen." But the views of intellectuals are important because they can influence the thinking and behavior of other citizens who are not so reflective initially. For the intellectual who is also what I call the true democrat, democracy is the best system of political organization and he adheres to this faith regardless of the fact that sometimes democracy produces results that are distasteful to him intellectually. For him the preservation of the democratic system is more important than any of the myriad uses or misuses to which it can be put. His belief in democracy is unadulterated by any other dogma, for he believes that the system offering freedom of choice is the best one regardless of any possible outcome. He does not subscribe to the theory that it is all right for people to choose their own government so long as they don't choose system x. If the people want to choose fascism, as they did in Italy and Germany in the '20's and '30's, he makes no objection. He regrets it perhaps, because the people may thereby be abolishing their democratic rights to free choice for as long as the dictator they have elected can maintain himself in power. The true democrat says, well, at least they made their choice. If the Greek people want a military dictatorship, or if they want instead to be ruled by parliamentary demagogues, then so be it, but the democrat will accept this outcome only if the people have been given the right of free choice in the initial stage.

The person described above is not an imaginary individual. Most Greeks, the non-intellectual as well as the better-educated, are highly individualistic and deeply cherish their personal freedoms. They are by and large democrats. Democracy is the political philosophy most appealing to the individualistic person. For such a person the present Greek regime is an anathema (to use a good Greek word) because it is the antithesis of all he believes in. The present regime is repugnant to him partly because Papadopoulos' political philosophy (if we can use such a grand term to describe his speechifying) calls for the interests of the individual to be sacrificed to the exigencies of the state. For the democrat the individual and his personal freedoms are much more sacred than any state; he is opposed to totalitarianism (or statism) in all its forms. But for the opponent of the present Greek regime something even more repugnant than Papadopoulos' elevation of the state into the position of the supreme good is his belief that only he is capable of deciding what is good for that state, that is, he and a small group of close associates who share with the Prime Minister his narrowness of outlook caused by the disabilities they also suffer of a provincial origin, limited education, confinement within a rigid military organization during all of his mature years, and a professional preoccupation with conspiracy as a way of life.

One might argue that the tastes and distastes of the Greek people, or of an important segment of the Greek people, have nothing to do with the matter at hand and that by the same token the United States Government has no business finding this or that regime repugnant or laudable. There are several aspects of this matter worth considering.

One is that as the leader of the Free World the United States must not overlook the large role played in international affairs by the psychological factor; we must pay some attention to questions of ideological competition and what is sometimes called "the battle for men's minds." We cannot afford to be narrowly pragmatic in pursuing our own nationalistic interest while ignoring others' opinions on the stands we take internationally. The one thing we have to offer the rest of the world, the committed and the uncommitted, is that we stand for freedom of political choice; we believe in self-determination and in the right of peoples to dispose of their own destiny. And this is about all we have to offer that truly distinguishes us from our ideological opponents. We cannot prove that our system achieves economic development quicker, or that our system makes a nation militarily stronger, or that under our system people are healthier or live longer, or that we are better able to achieve any other possible human goal. Some things we do better at certain times and in certain places, and the Communist powers can make the same claim. But what they cannot claim is that they guarantee freedom of choice to people. We have made that claim and it has had a powerful impact internationally. Unfortunately we have so often compromised with the suppression of freedom of choice around the world—in Hungary and Haiti, in the Dominican Republic and Dahomey, in Palestine and Panama and dozens of other places—that the claim may be becoming hollow. If we appear to acquiesce in, even to welcome, the disappearance of that freedom of choice for a people closely allied to us and who have looked to us for leadership and support for two decades, then our international ideological stature as the upholders of freedom of choice, of self-determination and the consent of the governed, is dealt a very severe blow.

We must look at our bilateral relations with Greece in the context of the overall image and prestige of the United States in the world, hard as this may be to face. For many of our real and potential friends around the world Greece in 1967–68 has been one more example of the USG's willingness (eagerness, even) to embrace authoritarian regimes so long as they are also anti-Communist and pro-U.S. This is seen as another proof that we have a blind spot where Communism is concerned. We oppose Communist regimes because they are totalitarian and because they oppress the human individual in the name of some "higher" goal (a dogmatic Marxist view of history, economics, society, politics and so forth) whereas we are supposed to believe that there is no higher earthly goal than humanity itself. It should make very little difference to us which supposed "higher goal" is being served by an oppressive totalitarianism, whether it be Communist or anti-Communist. Some great crimes against humanity have been committed in the name of Communism, and some other great crimes have been committed with the justification that they were part of the fight against Communism.

Our job should not be to make the present Greek regime more palatable to Greek and international public opinion by urging them to stop doing certain things that outrage opinion, or by glossing over these things, or by "presenting them in a better light" (public relations); our duty is to show that we really believe what we say about a people's right to freedom of choice.

Now one might argue that we should be strictly pragmatic in our relations with foreign states, that we should do and say nothing about what kind of government any country or people has, but simply try to work with whatever we find in existence in a given country. This would be well and good if we were a small and minor power like Switzerland interested mostly in trade, in selling cuckoo clocks and in keeping its bankers' coffers full. But in the present case we are the United States, the leader of the Free World, and we were the closest ally of democratic Greece. We didn't just suddenly arrive on the scene one day and find an authoritarian military regime in power in Athens and decide to enter into relations with it, accept it for what it is, not interest ourselves too much in what the Greek people feel about it, but just do the best we can to get along with the regime and work with them as good allies.

The facts of the situation are quite different: we were already deeply involved in Greece and had been deeply involved for two decades. We had had a lot to do with creating the Greece that existed on April 21, 1967; we were not just passers-by. If Greek democracy failed or was overthrown, we could not help but be partly responsible. Even if we deny that we were in any way responsible, we are held to be partly responsible by a large and important segment of the Greek population. These facts are as important as any others in the present situation.

I do not equate the Greek people with the opponents of the regime (and did not mean to do so in my paper of April 26), but both the opponents and the adherents of the regime by and large believe that we have not been unhappy with how things turned out in Greece (this helps to explain the bewilderment of the regime's leaders with our stand-offish policy, for they are the only Greeks who have a good idea of what our real attitude has been). The regime's opponents hold us very much responsible for what happened to their country because they see us as having approved of the coup, of having welcomed the military dictatorship, of having given it our continued military, economic, political and psychological support and in fact of having been its main prop. We must deal with these feelings because they are genuine even if we know that they are based on false information or wrong impressions.

We can say to ourselves in the privacy of our Embassy that we had nothing to do with the coup and that it's certainly not our fault. This does not wash with the average Greek. He is prone to believe that most important events in his country's political life are controlled by devious string-pulling behind the scenes, he never accepts the obvious motive as the genuine one, and in terms of his own political affairs he has long been inclined to ascribe a very large role to the "American factor," in fact a much larger role than we have probably ever played here. Since he believes that the USG calls the shots in Greece the average Greek absolutely refuses to believe that we are not largely responsible for the junta's being in power today simply because he believes that if we had not wanted the junta we could easily have prevented it from coming to power. Since the apparent evidence is that we did not try to stop it from coming to power then we must have wanted to see this happen if we did not actively encourage it to come about.

That we did neither is beside the point. Along with the Buddha I believe that to refrain from an action is itself an action (it is not difficult to prove this proposition logically). Thus failure to do anything to stop a military dictatorship from coming to power in Greece is not a policy of passivity, of "wait and see," but it is a policy of materially assisting this development to come about, if one is deemed to have had the power to do something to prevent it. Even if one could not have been successful in preventing it, the failure to make a clear and open attempt to stop it is bound to be interpreted as having given positive assistance to the junta. The fact that we have taken a generally passive attitude toward developments in Greece (perhaps on the reasonable basis that our power to affect developments here has been grossly exaggerated) does not convince the average Greek that we lack the power to influence the course of events here but rather it convinces him that we must be happy with the way things have been going. In the psychological sphere the important thing is not the true facts of the limitations on our power to influence developments in Greece but what the average Greek believes the true situation to be. We can't go on the VOA and say, "We're very sorry but there's practically nothing we can do about the situation in your country." We'd be laughed off the air. The average Greek believes that we like the junta, else we would have done something, somewhere, sometime to show our displeasure.

Doing nothing is doing something. In today's world, with the reality of America's super-power status, non-intervention is an action. We do have very great power to affect developments in Greece, simply because the Greek people believe we have such power. In such a situation the appearance of power becomes the reality of power. Even the junta thinks we are more important to them than we really are. Non-acceptance by the U.S. government could be a very powerful weapon if it were ever to be exercised. By the same token close identification with the regime is a similar weapon used in the other direction. The more closely we become identified with the regime the more hostile to us will become the regime's opposition. As things progress we risk being driven into the most undesirable choice of siding with the regime or with its opposition, which by that time could very well be Communist-led or dominated. The choice we would make is obvious, but what it could lead to is a Vietnam in Europe.

The question of our MAP policy is critical to this issue of identification with the regime, for a restoration of normal MAP will signal to the regime's opponents that we have embraced the junta. Frankly, I fail to see what a restoration of MAP heavy materiel deliveries is designed to accomplish. Presumably it is a "carrot" intended to encourage the regime to continue taking steps toward its departure from power. But how will it help accomplish this goal? Will the junta be less inclined to stay in power out of gratitude for our having given them additional military assistance? I seriously doubt it. What a restoration of MAP will mean to Papadopoulos and company is that we are happy with them and that they should just keep on doing more of the same, continuing in the same direction, and we will be even happier with them. Well, if the direction in which they were moving were towards their own removal from power and the replacement of their own with a more democratic regime, then our policy would make logical sense, that is, our "carrots" would be encouraging them to proceed in the direction we want them to go. But what if the true direction in which they are heading is one of entrenching themselves in power for the long pull by one means or another? Does not the MAP policy we have been advocating then mean that we wish to encourage them to remain in power, to entrench themselves further, for an even longer period, and that we're quite happy with their program of long-term rule?

The problem here is to know which path they are pursuing, what their intentions are. I think we are just kidding ourselves if we think the present regime sees itself as short-term and transitional. Every good indication they have given us points to the conclusion that Papadopoulos thinks of himself as a statesman, the savior of Greece in its hour of need, that what we have on our hands is a full-fledged revolution designed to change the course of Greek political history in a drastic fashion, in the manner of the Metaxas dictatorship. If Papadopoulos and company are actually planning to stay for the long term is it any business of ours? It is, if we believe that by so doing they will stimulate the creation of an opposition movement, that the opposition movement will become dominated by extreme leftists, that Greece will become polarized between the junta and the Communists, and that we will eventually be forced to choose between the regime and its opposition (between Batista and Castro, for example). Then it is very much our business.

The trouble with waiting until the regime has fully clarified its intentions with respect to the longevity that it envisages for itself is that it will probably then be too late for us to do anything to affect the outcome. Perhaps it is already too late. The junta is already pretty well entrenched, although their nervous reactions to minor provocations like the Rallis statement make one wonder how secure they feel themselves. The fact that time is working against us rather than for us (in the sense that when we decide we must act it may already be too late) is the reason that I have been arguing, since April 22, 1967, that we must make up our own minds about the junta's intentions, and not wait for them to clarify them for us. If it is the junta's wish to stay in power indefinitely it has a very good reason for wanting to obscure or disguise its true intentions for as long as possible. The fact that the junta's key members have consistently been unwilling to discuss, privately or publicly, the subject of what longevity they envisage for themselves is a very good clue as to what their true intentions are. By the time they have fully clarified their intentions for us I fear that we will have become paralyzed into a policy of acceptance and there will be nowhere for us to go but downhill.

On the issue of the regime's intentions, I propose one simple question: the regime is now proceeding toward the adoption of a new constitution for Greece in a national referendum; do we believe that their aim in this respect is to give the Greek people a new charter on the basis of which they can have restored to them a normal democratic regime at the earliest possible date with the full exercise of their traditional democratic freedoms, or do we believe that this constitutional exercise is viewed by the regime as but one step in the legitimization of itself in power as a "normal" regime that may have come to power through a revolution but that has as much right as any freely elected government to rule the country?

I cannot stress too much the importance of the matter of timing. From April to December of 1967 we waited for the regime to clarify its intentions. We accepted the constitutional revision scheme as evidence that the junta was moving toward restoring a normal, constitutional, democratic regime to the country. The King, however, became frustrated and did not accept their declarations at face value. We had depended on using the King as a last resort in case we should ever decide that the junta had to go. The King acted on his own, failed, and in the process used up most of the assets he and we had (in the form of loyalist, non-junta senior military officers) to effect a drastic change in the junta's stay in power. The policy of waiting while true intentions are clarified is one of wasting assets until there are none left to carry out the policy that one finally arrives at. Before we will act we apparently want incontrovertible proof that Papadopoulos and company are totalitarian and not just democratic reformers. They are not likely to give us such proof until it is too late for us to do anything effective.

We appear to be hesitant to act because we have no very clear idea of how much popular support the regime enjoys. I would certainly not advocate doing anything against a regime that enjoyed the support of the Greek people, no matter how it came to power and no matter what its political ideology. If the Greek people wish to be ruled by a military dictatorship that is their privilege, and we should respect their decision. A critical question in any discussion of what U.S. policy toward Greece should be concerns the degree of popular support the present regime enjoys today and how much support it is likely to have as time passes. I have no definitive answer to this question, and I doubt that anyone does at this point. The regime undoubtedly has its adherents. How many they are I do not know. There is also a large group of people who tolerate their rule, do not wish them well or ill particularly, who are waiting to see how things will develop, and who appear to be content to remain inactive politically for the time being. Then there are the regime's opponents. How many they number and how important a factor they are I do not know.

The opponents are certainly not confined to the intellectual world alone, but even if they were their political significance would be much larger than their numbers would account for. To cite a contemporary example of the political importance of the intelligentsia, in the United States it was the intellectuals who were the first group to become disenchanted with the Vietnam War. At the beginning they were derided as misguided people who were so insignificant in terms of the total electorate that they could safely be ignored by the country's political leadership. But in the space of three years the opposition to the war among the intellectuals has had an enormous impact on the country, so that today the small number of three years ago has grown to a clear majority of the American electorate. (I don't mean a majority of Americans want us to "pull out" of Vietnam. I mean a majority have become highly critical of the war itself and how it has been managed.) The recent opinion polls, when compared with those of two and three years ago, demonstrate the dramatic impact of the intellectual elite on mass popular opinion (in the U.S. the impact was relatively rapid because of the extensiveness and freedom of our communications media).

The same phenomenon is observable in totalitarian societies, where the free flow of thought is severely circumscribed. For example, the recent dramatic changes in Czechoslovakia are in good measure the product of years of ferment within the country's intellectual circles. And by contrast, in Germany in the 1930's a few prominent non-Jewish intellectuals opposed the Nazis, but many lent them vigorous or tolerant intellectual support (some because of fear of the Communists), which materially aided the Nazis in consolidating themselves in power and in maintaining their hold over the minds of the German people. Had the non-Jewish German intelligentsia massively and forthrightly opposed the National Socialist movement, Twentieth Century history might have been quite different.

Today it is extremely difficult to gauge popular sentiment toward the regime in Greece because all normal means of free public expression have been abolished or brought under strict government control. Without freedom of speech, freedom of the press, freedom of assembly, freedom of association, freedom to organize in groups for political action, freedom to run for and hold political office, freedom to choose one's representatives in government at the local and national levels, without these freedoms being practiced how is one to judge what the people think? The regime is doubtless much better informed on this subject than we are, for example from being aware (but not telling) how many of the constitutional "ballots" it receives from anonymous citizens contain scurrilous denunciations and insults.

On the question of the regime's popular support I would be willing to go on the evidence it offers itself, although not on its statements. If it enjoys popular support why, one year after the coup, do we still have martial law, why is the press still rigidly controlled, why are former politicians constantly being placed under house arrest, why is everyone afraid to talk in public, why is there no free exchange of ideas, why have there been no elections? A popular regime does not require the props of a police state to maintain its control over the population. If the old regime politicians have been thoroughly discredited why does the government react with panic every time one of them issues a statement? Obviously the regime knows full well it does not enjoy mass popular support or it would be willing to relax some of the more rigid controls on the public activities of the Greek people and would restore to them some of their personal freedoms, at least the freedom from arbitrary arrest if not the freedom to disagree with Papadopoulos in public print.

Some people say that the regime will eventually hold elections, when it has decided that it has purchased enough popularity through its many outrageous measures of vote buying to win the elections legitimately, or that it can control the outcome with a minimum of electoral fraud. The curious thing is that a government with nearly unlimited powers has been unable to build any solid popular base after a year in power. Its vote buying has placed the demagoguery of the old regime politicians in the category of chicken feed. Would any pre-April 1967 party leader have dared to raid the national treasury to the tune of $300 million to buy the electoral support of the rural population, or any other segment? Perhaps the explanation of the government's failure to buy support successfully lies in what a Greek friend said to me about the cancellation of farm debts: "Of course they'll take anything this government will give them, whether they be farmers, workers or businessmen—they'd be fools if they didn't take anything they are given—but that doesn't mean they'll thank anybody for it. Give them a chance in an election and they'll vote for the restoration of their freedom."

The only fair test of the regime's popular support would result from presenting the issue to the people in a referendum or an election, but one held under conditions of freedom, with freedom of speech, press, assembly, political organization and so forth in full and guaranteed operation, with anyone free to run for office, and everyone free to vote for the candidates of their choice. In the absence of these conditions no regime can legitimately claim to benefit by *any* degree of popular support for there will have been no legitimate measuring of that popular support. All would be guesswork or mere unsubstantiated claim (which is the condition under which we are operating today).

To turn to a final question, how would we go about getting rid of this regime if we decided that that would be in our interest? I do not think direct intervention by the United States Government would be necessary. The first thing we should do would be to concert with our allies and get them to agree on a common policy. Most of our allies are inclined to follow our lead as regards Greece, and some are even more unhappy with the present regime than we are. Only Portugal would probably object to a program for ousting the junta. France, which is an enigma, might not go along with us, but in that they would simply be consistent with themselves. The policy on which we would concert with our allies would be one calling for the cessation of all kinds of support to and cooperation with the junta, to stop assistance of all kinds, political, military, economic, psychological, and to make it clear, inside and outside Greece, that Greece's allies are united in opposition to the junta's continuance in power.

Obviously this would not cause the junta "to fall of its own weight." I would not expect Papadopoulos to resign on hearing this news. But I think we could trust the Greeks to take care of their own affairs then. I would expect that pro-Western elements in the Greek armed forces would blame Papadopoulos and his group for having caused a definitive break in Greece's ties with the Western world, a break which could only do serious damage to the Greek nation, its people, its economy, and its military posture. I would expect an anti-Papadopoulos group to organize within the Greek armed forces and to remove him from power by one means or another in order to restore Greece's traditional ties of friendship with the West.

Papadopoulos might try to counter such an effort by moving into the neutralist camp or into close friendship with the Communist states. If he did so I believe he would only confirm his internal opponents in their determination to get rid of him, for then there would be no question about his opportunism, obsession with remaining in power and skin-deep anti-Communism. The mass of the Greek people want no part of Communism and they see the future of their country as one of continued close alliance with the West, with free Europe and the United States. I believe they could be counted on to "throw the rascal out" if he tried to maintain himself in power by bringing about a drastic re-orientation of the country. Pro-Western and pro-NATO elements still predominate in Greece's armed forces, I believe. Anyone who would seriously argue that Papadopoulos would turn to the Russians if we were to cut him off must also then agree that his anti-Communist stance of today is more opportunistic than genuine. Many people believe that he is much more pro-Papadopoulos than anti-Communist. One could argue that a program for ostracizing the Greek junta would only cause the Greek people to rally to the side of their government. I doubt this sincerely, for I believe that a regime which had caused the country to be isolated by all its traditional friends, by the entire Western alliance, could hardly be a cause to which the Greek people would rally.

The point is that Papadopoulos is using what appears to most Greeks to be our support or at least friendly tolerance of his regime to stall off any internal opposition. Most Greeks believe, as many have put it to me, "Your CIA and your military like this regime." Believing as they do that the U.S. supports the junta, they are not inclined to go into active opposition because they feel they would be taking on not only the junta but the United States as well, and they consider us a very formidable opponent indeed. If we withdraw our support from the junta we would be doing three things at least: we would be removing from Papadopoulos a strong psychological prop (for he has made the most of what *appears* to be USG support of his government), we would be encouraging the junta's opponents to act against the regime to oust it, and we would be giving a clear demonstration that the junta's opponents would not have to take on the United States as well as the junta if they tried to topple the regime. One should not underestimate the influence of the "American factor" in Greece today, both in its negative and positive aspects: by our apparent support of the present regime we discourage its opponents from trying anything really serious in the way of opposition (we turn the fearful into cowards); on the other hand, by showing ourselves to be definitely opposed to the junta we would give a spark of encouragement to the opposition, for we would be telling them that they have the USG on their side, not on the side of their enemies. The point is that since April 1967 we have not shown ourselves to be neutral as between the junta and its opponents. Regardless of what we ourselves understand about the policy we have been pursuing in Greece, the average Greek thinks that we like this regime and have given it our support. This fact alone has played a powerful role in propping up the junta and in discouraging its opponents.

I have never advocated nor do I now advocate "ousting other people's governments." Any government which is freely chosen by the people over whom it rules is their own legitimate government and we have no business trying to oust it. However, the present regime in Greece is not a case of some "other people's government." This regime was not chosen by the Greek people but was chosen by its own members, who imposed themselves on the Greek people by force of arms. This is not rhetoric; it is the plain fact. If the Greek people like and want this government then I would certainly advocate our following quite a different policy. But this is a case of another people's government which was imposed on them against their will, and the people involved are the people of an allied nation, which gives us a definite and legitimate interest in their fate.

The question is not whether our "intervention" to obtain the departure of this group from power might destroy the fabric of Greek society. They are already in process of destroying it. If we failed to intervene to help effect their ouster once it became clear that the end result would be civil war between the government faction and its opposition, than we would be guilty of having permitted the destruction of the fabric of a Greek society which we invested billions of dollars to rebuild during the past two decades. We are hearing today from so many quarters that our failure to act now will lead to a civil war eventually that I believe it is time we re-examined the assumptions underlying our present policy toward Greece.

I cannot guarantee (and no one can) what a successor regime would be like. Under a democratic system no one can offer guarantees of that sort. But what it is fairly safe to predict is that Communist and other far left strength will increase steadily the longer the present state of affairs continues, so that when there finally is a successor regime the extreme left in Greece is likely to be stronger than it is today, and certainly much stronger than it was on April 21, 1967, when it was destined to come in a very poor third out of three in free parliamentary elections. The only thing we can say with some confidence is that the sooner we have a successor regime in Greece the less likely it is that it will be an extreme leftist one.

POL:RVKeeley:js 5/22/68

[In an attempt to close on a jovial note, I appended to the above memo a copy of a *New Yorker* cartoon showing five generals in uniform, four seated around a table and the fifth standing, all five hoisting glasses of champagne. The caption had the standing general offering the following toast: "Our junta, gentlemen! May it ever be right! But our junta, right or wrong!"]

TO: POL—R. Keeley DATE: May 31, 1968
FROM: MIN—R. McClelland
SUBJECT: US Policy Toward Greece: Chapter III

Bob:

Your lengthy May 17 memo was as always, revealing, and contained a number of persuasive analyses and arguments bearing on the difficulties of our present situation in Greece. It also contained welcome evidence over earlier versions of greater concreteness in your thinking of how we might cope with the problem. I must confess, however, that your proposals still fall considerably short, in my view, of being a useable plan of action. I will try to limit my comment to what strike me as major shortcomings.

1. Your central recommendation, as I read it, is that the best way to resolve the present Greek dilemma in order to avoid eventual communist control and/or civil war is to withdraw all support from this government forthwith, persuade our NATO partners to do likewise, and unequivocally denounce it as an unacceptable dictatorship. This policy would be designed

to promote the overthrow and replacement of the junta *from within*, primarily by pro-Western, pro-NATO and presumably democratic elements in the Greek armed forces.

While this scenario has a clear-cut, incisive, "let's stand squarely on principle" quality about it which understandably appeals to the American mind, it immediately raises (at least in my more relativistic approach) a host of problems which I fear would have to be faced, however sordid they may be and indicative of the unpleasant necessity which usually faces us in the foreign relations business of working out compromises and of having to settle for something less than the ideal.

If we were to adopt such a radical stand with respect to the junta (which would indeed be tantamount to a declaration of war on them), we would obviously have to be willing to accept a serious curtailment, and possibly even the complete suspension, of a whole range of factors which weigh significantly in our relationship with Greece. You do not mention any of these. First and foremost among these would be our extensive military facilities, and in particular what we were told just this last weekend by the Wood-McClintock mission are crucial and irreplaceable communications links. These are critically tied in to 6th Fleet operations in the Mediterranean, for instance, which are increasingly important in view of the stepped-up Soviet presence in the area. Secondly, as you know, there are substantial American economic investments in Greece which remit earnings to the States, as well as a not negligible volume of commercial trade. What would happen in this sector if we cast the present government into outer darkness? Whatever value one may personally attach to a military alliance system as the most effective response to the Soviet challenge, NATO still occupies an important position in the strategic defense of the southern European flank which would be seriously breached if Greek cooperation were no longer available or were substantially weakened. Admittedly one could argue that the GOG, even if publicly proscribed, might not go to extremes as a matter of self-interest; but one cannot be at all sure what the dimensions of the reaction of injured national pride might be on the part of the narrow minds which characterize the Greek revolutionary group.

I have genuine doubts that it would prove possible to convince the Department of Defense (should we, for purposes of argument, espouse your thesis) that the risks you discern in our present policy of trying to push this regime back into acceptable constitutional channels are greater than those which could result from a boycott. Whereas we might succeed in persuading some of the Western European NATO members like Holland or Belgium, whose strategic interests and responsibilities in the eastern Mediterranean are far less than ours, to go along with such a policy, I doubt that the Germans, especially their business community which has substantial investments and trade interests in Greece, or the French would be very enthusiastic about doing so. Resounding party resolutions by the Western European Socialists are one thing, but severing concrete ties with a country at the government-to-government level are quite another one.

I would also anticipate definite political difficulties within our own U.S. backyard in obtaining acceptance of the course you advocate. Could it be sold, for instance, to the Greek-American community, large and conservative segments of which uncritically accept the version that the present Greek rulers saved the country from communist anarchy and hence support them? Analogous reactions could be expected from other right-wing circles in the U.S. And could we, under circumstances of official ostracism, expect to continue normal diplomatic operations in Athens; and if not, what would happen to such substantial elements of Greek-American relations as the immigration flow (for example, under the new 5th Preference quota)?

My recent Rhodesian experience leaves me very skeptical, I'm sorry to say, Bob, regarding the feasibility of organizing international boycotts of countries on grounds of political principle and of the successful outcome of such undertakings (and Lord knows the denial of democratic rights was even more flagrant in So. Rhodesia and the prejudice to U.S. relations with the rest of Black Africa far more serious and widespread than is the case with Greece).

I wish I could share what I suspect is your belief (although you did not carry your scenario this far), that were such a concerted stand taken against the present Greek regime the internal forces of opposition to it would rapidly coalesce and succeed in displacing it so that the period of risk to our military and economic interests here would be short-lived. This would partly depend, of course, on how rigorous the ostracism was and what assistance, if any, we were willing and able to give a domestic opposition movement. But since the likelihood of getting such a policy organized, and even if it were, of its being vigorously pursued, is discouragingly slight, embarking on it at all under such inauspicious circumstances would, I fear, simply court the obvious risks without much promise of achieving the desired results.

Moreover, even if the U.S. undertook unilaterally to withdraw support from the present GOG and condemn it, I do not find it easy to predict that an authoritarian regime of this kind, which is in substantial control of the security apparatus, could be readily overthrown. The Coup Group would unquestionably dig in their heels and become more oppressive and intransigent than before. The chauvinistic, hard-line faction could take over, and the well-known scenario set in motion which could also end in the type of "Batista-Castro" polarization you see down the road if we continue on our present course. In the process more damage could well be done to the fabric of Greek society than is likely under our present policy.

This line of reasoning (with which you may or may not agree, and if you don't I would be interested in knowing why) forces me to conclude that your recommendation, at least in its present "absolute" formulation, does not fall within the range of feasible U.S. policy alternatives. This leaves us with trying to figure out how we can adapt our present admittedly unsatisfactory policy or some variant of it, to cope as effectively as possible with the present Greek dilemma.

Here, I must say, Bob, I do not subscribe to as dire and apocalyptic a view of the situation as you do. Perhaps I am more optimistic by nature, or possibly just more thick-skinned. In the first place I do not consider the time factor as critical as you do. Given the resiliency of the Greek people and their long experience of political vicissitudes, I think that it would prove a much more difficult and lengthy process for the junta to bring the country to the "ruin and destruction" you predict. In point of time, the "Colonels" have really only been in undisputed control of the country since December 13, 1967, that is for about six months. In historical perspective this is still only a short period. This regime could conceivably go on in its present form for two or three years, I submit, without disastrous or irreversible consequences for Greece. The Metaxas dictatorship lasted somewhat longer than that; and the Greeks seem to have made a fairly satisfactory political recovery from that experience.

I say "fairly," since I find myself (based, admittedly, on a very superficial knowledge of the country) somewhat less confident regarding the Greeks' capacity for democratic self-government than you do. At the same time I fully agree with you that they certainly deserve a far better break than they have previously had in respect to freedom of choice of their own government. We probably bear some responsibility for not having at least tried to prevent the reactionary establishment from subverting Greek democracy after 1965; and again I share your belief that going ahead with the Papandreou elections of May 1967 would have been decidedly preferable to a military dictatorship, especially the present one (although I am told the alternative was weighed in Washington, and the conclusion was "six of one and half a dozen of the other" when a Generals' coup was anticipated). On the other hand, feeling guilt-ridden over our putative complicity in this train of events is, I fear, more conducive to moral indignation than it is to devising some practical way of making the best out of a lamentable situation.

I certainly do not advocate, nor do I think the Embassy's present policy does, that we wait around indefinitely for incontrovertible evidence, which will probably never be offered to us as such, of the presumably dictatorial intentions of the coup group while they continue to consolidate their power and eliminate all potential sources of opposition. I however believe we have little or no choice at this stage but to await the constitutional plebiscite of September, and more particularly the concomitant indications of the regime's future intentions with respect to enforcing the constitution and holding elections which I think the regime will not be able to avoid at that time. This does not mean that we should necessarily remain passive meanwhile, particularly if we receive reliable evidence that they are planning to seek (and also planning to engineer) popular endorsement of their remaining in power for an unreasonable period before applying the constitution (and I would personally define "unreasonable" as anything beyond the second anniversary of the coup). In this case I for one would certainly recommend that we ask for instructions to make forcefully clear to them in that event that the continuation of this sort of undemocratic rule in Greece would be totally unacceptable to the United States and could lead to a serious deterioration of our relations.

Your paper seems to imply, I am distressed to note, Bob, that the Embassy, or the CIA or Washington or somebody in a position to call the shots is somehow anxious to "embrace" this crowd, as you put it, and quite willing, indeed even "eager," to accept them as really not appreciably worse than the politicians who ran the country before, give them credit for being sincere in their intentions, etc. I don't really think anyone seriously feels this way; and the imputation is unfair and out of place. It does not, in any event, contribute to arriving at a dispassionate estimate of the problem and how it might be resolved. I don't know anybody around here in a position of influence who kids himself that Papadopoulos is not bent on holding onto control for as long as he can in order to carry out his revolution. Since we can't remove him, however, the best alternative in the circumstances would seem to be to deal with him and to try to compel him to be as sincere as he professes to be about returning his country to democracy. Maybe it won't work, but we are not in a position to say so flatly at this stage. Meanwhile, I do not regard this as a somehow despicable undertaking. It is simply part of our often difficult job as Foreign Service Officers; and whether we happen to find it consonant with some absolute and more desirable political ideal is unfortunately beside the point. If in the end we don't like the heat, we're always free, in the old dictum, to get out of the kitchen, or at least look for another more congenial one.

[Handwritten: P.S. I attach a short paper recently written by Harry Odell FYI.]
MIN: RDMcClelland: efm

TO: POL—R. Keeley   DATE: June 6, 1968
FROM: MIN—R. McClelland
SUBJECT: Postscript to my Previous Comment on your May 17 Memo

Bob:

You noted, I recall, that "efficiency is an entirely secondary and subordinate consideration" in relation to a functioning democracy (in Greece). I agree with you that the two concepts are on different levels of significance, and the former is certainly not a substitute for the latter. On the other hand, in a half-developed country like Greece is, still in the process of transition from an oligarchic society to a modern democratic one, efficiency (in the most extensive sense of the term, which, in my thinking, would include good administration, effective management, progress based on merit, the most equitable social distribution of resources, etc.) *should not be sold short.* Indeed, I would regard the two concepts of efficiency and democracy as closely interrelated. A functioning democracy should produce efficient national performance (or at least prevent gross mismanagement) because of its inherent checks and balances while a well-run administration is certainly a necessary adjunct of a viable democratic system. But unfortunately the "Colonels'" administration is not a particularly efficient one.

When some of my good Spanish friends would really take their hair down a few years ago (and the vicissitudes democracy has suffered in Spain are even greater than those Greece has experienced) they would assert that what their country really needed was to be administered quietly and efficiently for perhaps 10 or 15 years by somebody like the Norwegians or the Swiss. While the experience would be undoubtedly dreary, they felt that after it they would be better equipped to make a success of political democracy.

MIN: RDMcClelland :efm

TO: MIN—Mr. Roswell D. McClelland   June 7, 1968
FROM: POL—Robert V. Keeley
SUBJECT: U.S. Policy Toward Greece—Chapter IV

I do not wish to prolong this dialogue beyond a point of usefulness, nor do I wish to have the last word, but you have raised some new questions that have apparently been inadequately discussed heretofore. I promise that this will be my last contribution to this series.

Your memorandum of May 31 quite rightly raises questions about the risks the policy I have advocated would pose for the continued availability of our important facilities in Greece and our economic and other relations with this country. I have not been unaware of the importance of these considerations, but I felt that they had been adequately mentioned in earlier memos. The remaining points I wish to make are the following:

(1) I believe that NATO is at least as important to Greece and its security (of which the present government is perhaps even more aware than prior civilian governments) as Greece is to NATO and to U.S. interests in the Eastern Mediterranean. Therefore I do not believe any GOG would want to sever its military ties with NATO and the U.S., ties which underlie our facilities here. In any case it is a question of time: basing our policy for relations with Greece on the desire to preserve our military facilities at all costs can preserve them for one, two or three years and perhaps even longer, but does run the risk of losing them in the longer term. Since the Near East is likely to remain unstable for some years to come, with the Soviets playing a much enlarged military role in that area and thereby endangering our own interests, we should be concerned with maintaining our facilities over the longer term so that we will be able to play a role when the Near East again erupts into war. I believe we should avoid tying our facilities rights to the survival of the junta.

(2) I do not share your fears about what might happen to US-Greek economic relations. As with the military area our economic relations are at least as important to Greece as they are to us. Specifically, Greece needs a great deal of foreign capital, private and governmental, to assist in its economic development. The United States is one of the prime available sources of such capital in large amounts. I doubt that any GOG would want to take actions that would cut the country off from this source of investment capital.

(3) You doubt that we could convince the Defense Department that the risks associated with our present policy are greater than the risks which could result from the boycott I proposed. I believe this is beside the point. If the State Department determines a policy which it believes to be the correct one, its duty is to try to convince the President that this is the right course to follow, against the vigorous objections of the Defense Department if necessary. It is of course State's duty to take security and alliance (and facilities)

considerations into account in determining our national foreign policies, but I believe it is wrong for State to decline to advocate a policy line just because DOD wouldn't go along.

(4) You also mention political difficulties at home in obtaining acceptance of the course I advocate. The course we are following today has already created political difficulties at home, but this is also beside the point. As civil servants and professional diplomats I believe it is wrong for us to advocate (or fail to advocate) one policy or another because some segment of the American populace or electorate favors or opposes that policy. If the President is prevented from adopting the policy we as diplomats advocate because of domestic political considerations that's his business. But it should not influence the recommendations we make, which should be based on our national interests as we see them. It would be unfair to a President to anticipate how much weight he might assign to domestic political factors; we should decide what we think is best for our country, without worrying about the President's domestic political problems, and then it is up to the President to decide whether he likes our recommendations and to what extent he believes he can sell them or live with them domestically.

The Near East is a prime example. Should our Embassies in Beirut, Amman, Tripoli, Jeddah (plus the six or seven we lost last year) be advocating a U.S.-Israel military alliance because such a policy would be vociferously supported by the segment of the American electorate most influential on our policies toward the states of the Near East? It might be very good domestic politics (which is the President's job) but it would be abysmally bad diplomacy.

(5) As for Rhodesia, the policy we have pursued there has been unsuccessful in achieving some of our short-term objectives (I don't believe our sole objective has been to bring down the Smith regime but also to placate African opinion), but this does not mean that it has been a wrong policy in the world-wide and long-range scheme of things. It may be the right policy and it may be successful eventually.

(6) I agree that "this regime could conceivably go on in its present form for two or three years . . . without disastrous or irreversible consequences for Greece." But I do submit that the consequences for the U.S. position in Greece and our relations with post-junta Greece could be disastrous for us. Greece as a country and people will most definitely survive its post-April 1967 history, but will it end up as the close and friendly ally of the U.S. that it used to be? I very much doubt it if the present regime continues in power for a number of years.

(7) On a question of historical interpretation, I do not agree that the Greeks made a fairly satisfactory political recovery from the Metaxas dictatorship. Some of the most destructive and bloody years of modern Greek history (1944–1949) were a direct outgrowth of the political right-left polarization caused by the Metaxas dictatorship. This is very much in the mind of the average Greek today. If we want the same sort of "fairly satisfactory political recovery" then we are asking for a civil war.

(8) I do not feel guilt-ridden about our role in Greece since 1965 or any other year. It is not out of moral indignation that I keep referring to the past, but only to see if we can learn from past errors of judgment or action or inaction not to make the same mistakes again. Deciding there is no difference ("six of one and half a dozen of the other") between the planned Generals' coup and the probable outcome of the scheduled May 28, 1967 parliamentary elections is a perfect example of what I regard as the disastrous thinking we have done in the past about Greece.

(9) I am distressed to receive the impression that my efforts to put forward my views to those who carry the responsibility for our relations with Greece are considered to be out of place and unwelcome, or at best are misunderstood. I have consistently tried (perhaps unsuccessfully) to avoid injecting any issues of people but only issues of policy into this dialogue. I have reread my memo of May 17 and I cannot find a single place where I have imputed any views to any individual or organization. It is not I who says we are or are not embracing the junta; in all cases I am speaking of what some Greeks think we are or are not doing. I am concerned with the impression we create on people locally.

I have not said so before, but there *are* influential people in our mission who, as you phrase it, are "quite willing, indeed even 'eager' to accept them as really not appreciably worse than the politicians who ran the country before, give them credit for being sincere in their intentions, etc." Although I have not made any such allegation it would not be unfair for me to do so, for there are people who have expressed themselves to me in precisely those terms and I take their words at face value.

But the question is not what individual members of this mission think about the present Greek regime. What I was discussing in my May 17 memo was the impression our policies create among the Greek people (as well as internationally) and my feeling that most Greeks (both pro- and anti-junta and the indifferent) believe that we are quite content to see this regime in power here. I am aware that this does not square with our actual policy.

I for one have tried to carry out our policy, as determined in Washington and here, faithfully. My dissents have been internal, within the family so to speak. I do not find it distasteful to carry out a policy which I consider inadequate. I do not consider the program we are engaged in (to encourage a rapid return to a constitutional, democratic regime) a despicable undertaking. I do not criticize anyone in the slightest degree for doing his duty as an FSO. That is all I have been trying to do.

It is certainly not I who dislikes the heat in the kitchen. I do not comprehend how it comes about that if one expresses internally a position at variance with the official line one is thereby showing that one dislikes (or "can't stand," as President Truman put it) the heat in the kitchen. I can very much stand the heat, I find this kitchen congenial, and I plan to remain in this particular kitchen until ordered to leave it. I regret it if I seem to be adding heat to an already overheated kitchen, but my aim has been to try to make people aware of the true temperature, not to inflate it artificially or pretend that it's really quite cool.

Addendum

Mr. Odell's paper is an interesting apologia for a policy of doing nothing. Americans tend to believe that the absence of activity is nullity, but this is not a universally accepted notion. In the case of Greece and the U.S. if we do nothing we will have done something in the minds of most Greeks, for they would interpret a do-nothing policy as one of positive acceptance and support of the Papadopoulos regime, whether they like, despise or are indifferent to that regime.

Mr. Odell quite rightly invokes the adage about accepting the inevitable before it becomes inevitable. I go one step further and believe that the wisest and most skillful diplomacy is one in which a nation discovers the inevitable before it happens and then exploits it to its own advantage. But in the present situation in Greece the important inevitability is not the one Mr. Odell points to—that is, the probability of a lengthy period of military-supported dictatorship in Greece. Were this the important inevitability the policy Mr. Odell advocates might be the most sensible one in the short term, that is, for as long as that dictatorship endured.

Mr. Odell invokes the name of Franco. Were Papadopoulos a Franco and did it look as though Papadopoulos would be in power for another thirty years Mr. Odell's policy might make a great deal of sense, for those thirty years at least although in the long run it could turn out to have been a grave error. I don't think Papadopoulos is or can become a Franco, and even so I don't think that Franco has been as successful as Mr. Odell thinks he has been. Someone with my inexperience in Spanish affairs shouldn't even mention the subject to someone with your experience, but it does seem to me that Franco has not solved the problem of Spain; he has merely postponed the day of reckoning, admittedly for more than 30 years. Franco's success has not been that the issues and personalities which so divided Spain have passed from the scene. Franco has exploited the Spanish people's wish to avoid a renewal of the bloody civil war which so damaged their country. But today there is a whole new generation which has had no direct experience of the civil war and which may therefore not be overcome by fear of its renewal. This is all very apropos of Greece, for it is the memory of a bloody civil war that today inhibits many Greeks from taking direct action against this regime. But there is a younger generation which is not so impressed by the blood shed in the past, and it is this generation which may take things into its own hands.

The important inevitability in the contemporary Greek situation is that someday the military-supported dictatorship will pass from the scene, as inevitably happens with all dictatorships. My concern has been with when that will take place, how it will come about, what will succeed the dictatorship, and most of all where the United States will stand in Greece when that day comes. If we adopted Mr. Odell's policy I fear that the U.S. standing in Greece would be exactly zero or worse at the time when the dictatorship made its inevitable departure. The inevitability we should be discovering today and exploiting to our advantage is not the one we have (a military dictatorship in being) but the one that has not yet come about (the passing of that dictatorship).

Mr. Odell's proposal is based on one premise that I consider most questionable. He presents this indirectly when he asks if there is "any convincing evidence that the bulk of the Greek people—or the American people for that matter—are actively upset and unhappy about the Greek situation?" Mr. Odell's argument is based on the opposite conviction, that the bulk of the Greek people are reasonably satisfied with their present situation. Were I convinced of this I too would advocate the policy so cogently presented by Mr. Odell, that is, a sort of "hands off and keep our heads down and our eyes averted" program.

This week I had a long talk with Mr. and Mrs. Alan Berlind. Alan is an FSO who formerly served in this Embassy and who has most recently been in Accra. His wife is of Greek origin. He has just spent three weeks in Greece and his wife three months. They have talked with a great many Greeks from many different walks of life and they have the feeling that they are hearing honest private views, she because she is Greek and he because he is not attached to this Embassy although he is known to be an American official. I would trust their sampling of Greek public opinion more than my own. Unlike most Americans, whose commonest Greek contacts are among the Athenian establishment, the Berlinds talked with middle class and lesser types, tradesmen, professionals, skilled workers, civil servants, teachers, a cross-section of ordinary urban citizens, in Athens, and in Patras, where Mrs. Berlind's family originates. They found nearly unanimous and deep-seated opposition to the regime; only one person they talked with spoke favorably of the present government (this person, incidentally, has a brother in one of the island detention camps). The three dominant themes the Berlinds reported to me in the thinking of the Greeks they talked with were: opposition to the present regime, inability to comprehend U.S. policy toward Greece which they deem to be support of a regime that is opposed by the bulk of the people whom it governs, and a hopeful anticipation that the U.S. Presidential elections will result in a drastic reversal of U.S. policy which will bring about the downfall and departure of the Papadopoulos regime and thus avert a civil war (this was prior to the assassination of Robert Kennedy, of course). They say that in Patras resentment of the regime has increased recently as a result of police pressure applied to get people out to cheer Papadopoulos when he recently visited there, to display flags, and to write and hand in signed statements on the constitutional draft supporting the government (this mostly among civil servants and employees of state corporations).

Mr. Odell refers to the "reservoir of basic good will" we have in Greece that we risk weakening if we do things that in themselves can have no real effect on the situation. I am sorry to say so, but it is precisely that reservoir that I sense is running dry because of our failure to take a clear stand before the Greek people on the basic issue of: "Do the Greek people have a right to freedom of choice just as much as do the American people?"

POL: RVKeeley : js 6/7/68

Notes

PROLOGUE

1. MacVeagh to Roosevelt, Oct. 15, 1944, *Ambassador MacVeagh Reports: Greece, 1933–1947*, ed. John O. Iatrides (Princeton: Princeton University Press, 1980), 627.
2. *Ambassador MacVeagh Reports*, 583.
3. Ibid., 608.
4. Ibid., 659–62.
5. Lawrence S. Wittner, *American Intervention in Greece, 1943–1949* (New York: Columbia University Press, 1982), 67.
6. Ibid.
7. *Ambassador MacVeagh Reports*, 711.
8. Ibid., 713.
9. Department of State, *Foreign Relations of the United States* (hereafter *FRUS*), 1948, vol. 4, 12.
10. John O. Iatrides, "The United States and Greece in the Twentieth Century," in *Greece in the Twentieth Century*, ed. Theodore A. Couloumbis, Theodore Kariotis, and Fotini Bellou (London: Frank Cass, 2003), 80.
11. Wilson D. Miscambie, *George F. Kennan and the Making of American Foreign Policy, 1947–1950* (Princeton: Princeton University Press, 1992), 82.
12. *Ambassador MacVeagh Reports*, 727.
13. Ibid., 723.
14. Ibid., 713–14.
15. Iatrides, "United States and Greece," 83.
16. U.S. Association for Diplomatic Studies, "Dealing with Greece: Fifty Years (1940–1990): American Diplomats Recount Their Experiences" (manuscript, 1993), 99.
17. *FRUS*, 1955–1957, vol. 24, 598.
18. *FRUS*, 1961–1963, vol. 16, 614.
19. Ibid., 617.
20. Ibid., 662–63.
21. Ibid., 664–66.
22. Ibid., 667–68.

23. Ibid., 673.
24. Ibid., 676–79.
25. Ibid., 686–87.
26. Thomas J. Schoenbaum, *Waging Peace and War: Dean Rusk in the Truman, Kennedy, and Johnson Years* (New York: Simon and Schuster, 1988), 419.
27. *FRUS*, 1964–1968, vol. 16, 412–15.
28. Iatrides, "United States and Greece," 98.
29. *FRUS*, 1964–1968, vol. 16, 416–18.
30. Ibid., 418–19.
31. Ibid., 422–23.
32. Ibid., 425n4.
33. Ibid., 426–27.
34. Ibid., 427n3.
35. Ibid., 430.

CHAPTER 1

1. Hannah Arendt has written that in our century memoirs "have become the most deceitful genre of literature" (*New York Review of Books*, November 18, 1971, 31).
2. In bureaucratic slang this is called "bootlegging a copy."
3. Arthur M. Schlesinger Jr., *A Thousand Days* (New York: Houghton Mifflin, 1965), 402–3.
4. Relevant portions of Colonel Marshall's testimony before the subcommittee are: "I know from previous testimony that it is now pretty well established that there was no imminent danger of a Communist takeover at the time the coup took place. That is, none that would justify military seizure of power. . . .

"Now, in that perspective what did happen was not what romantics would call a revolution. It was an open mutiny by the armed forces, and rebellion by those mutineers against the King and the Constitution of Greece. All subsequent events bear witness to that view. . . .

"In my opinion this is the most important aspect of the Greek situation and the greatest danger for the future Greek-American and Greek-NATO relations: the belief on the part of the Greek people that the United States did support this mutiny and that it continues to do so. It is my opinion that it is very necessary we convince the Greek people that we did not and do not support this junta." House Committee on Foreign Affairs, *Greece, Spain, and the Southern NATO Strategy: Hearings Before the Subcommittee on Europe of the Committee on Foreign Affairs*, 92nd Congress, 1st sess., 1971, 115–16.

CHAPTER 2

1. The CIA is often accused of arranging the overthrow of "hostile" regimes. In reality it expends much more money, energy, and brainpower saving "friendly" regimes from being overthrown.
2. Compare Roger Hilsman, writing about Vietnam: "Thus the new leader would necessarily be anti-foreign, and he would talk and act as anti-American as he could without actually denying himself American support." *To Move a Nation* (New York: Doubleday, 1967), 366.
3. It is curious that Andreas, supposedly so hostile to NATO, was planning to attend a conference of economists of the NATO member countries scheduled to be held in Rome in the summer of 1967. By the time it was held he was languishing in Averoff Prison. A petition protesting his imprisonment was circulated at the conference and was reportedly signed by all the economists attending.

4. In his book *Democracy at Gunpoint: The Greek Front* (New York: Doubleday, 1970), 106–12. I have also heard this account from Andreas directly, when he admitted more candidly that he had suggested Campbell's recall to Carl Kaysen.

5. *FRUS* vol. 16 was prepared and completed by editor James E. Miller in 1999 and was published—that is, printed—by the Government Printing Office in 2000. However, all copies were locked up in a GPO warehouse under the label "Embargo: This publication cannot be released." This action was revealed by reporter George Lardner Jr. in an article in the *Washington Post* on July 28, 2001, that mainly concerned a similar suppression of a different *FRUS* volume covering Indonesia, Malaysia, and the Philippines in the same 1964 to 1968 period. In the latter case the concern was over revelations that we had aided the Indonesian government by identifying thousands of Indonesian communists who were then killed by the regime in the mid-1960s. The Indonesia volume had already been distributed to libraries throughout the world when the suppression order came, and had even become available on a Web site.

In the Greek case the CIA denied sole responsibility for the embargo and explained that it had worked closely with the State Department. A later report in the *Post* by Lardner published on August 17, 2001, focused on the Greek volume and quoted the editor, Miller, as saying the controversial documents concerned proposed U.S efforts to influence Greek politicians and elections with money, though these proposals had been turned down by the 303 Committee in Washington. Miller noted that the Johnson presidential library in Austin had already made some of the documents public. He also said that an arrangement had been made to release the volume in 1995 but that the CIA station chief in Athens "got the U.S. ambassador there to say the sky would fall in," and CIA officials in Athens convinced a visiting congressional delegation that publication "would destroy Greek-American relations." Miller scoffed at the idea that the disclosures would prompt Greek terrorists to launch attacks against Americans. The notion that Greek terrorists "sit around reading *Foreign Relations of the United States* volumes to get their ideological direction is absurd."

This whole flap dated back to 1990 with the publication of an *FRUS* volume on Iran that made no mention of the widely known CIA-backed coup in 1953 that overthrew the elected Iranian government and restored the Shah to his Peacock Throne. That suppression had so outraged prominent members of the academic community that many resigned from the State Department's advisory board for the *FRUS* series. Lardner noted that Congress responded the next year with a law explicitly requiring that each volume be "a thorough, accurate and reliable documentary record."

In 2001 I got into the act in two ways. Stimulated by the Lardner articles, I sent a letter to Senator Paul Sarbanes on August 25, 2001, enclosing the Lardner July 28 article and calling Sarbanes's attention to the embargo on the *FRUS* volume on Greece. I asked if he would "consider making a parliamentary inquiry, asking the State Department to provide an explanation as to why this publication has been suppressed, in the hope of shaking it loose." I have not found in my files a response from Sarbanes, but Lardner reported that Senator Joe Biden had taken the matter up with State, "on behalf of an inquiring letter writer," with no known results.

On September 10, 2001, I sent a letter to Marc Grossman, State's under secretary for political affairs, explaining why I had not asked him a question in the Q and A period after his talk to the Foreign Service retirees attending "Foreign Affairs Day" just completed. I referred to the press reports about the embargoes on both the Indonesia and Greek volumes of *FRUS* for 1964–68, and the earlier fiasco with the Iran volume about 1953, and asked for an explanation of the reasons for the embargo on Cyprus, Greece, and Turkey and some indication of when it might be lifted. I mentioned my personal interest in that volume based on my service in Athens at the time. I never received a reply, which is understandable, for the next day, September 11, 2001, there occurred the terrorist attacks on New York and Washington, which surely put my request on a very back burner at the State Department.

CHAPTER 3

1. I recall—with some surprise at my audacity—an occasion on which I felt required to contradict Tom Pappas when he said, trying to justify the coup to Mrs. Jacob Javits (at a luncheon at the McClellands'), "Andreas wanted to have the people swear in the government in

Constitution Square whether his people won the election or not. Something simply had to be done!"

CHAPTER 4

1. Compare, for example, the situation in East Pakistan in 1970–71. Would there not have been a great difference in the climate of world opinion had Yahya Khan moved to suppress the movement for autonomy in East Pakistan *before* rather than *after* the Awami League had won its overwhelming electoral victory and thus legitimized its demand for autonomy?

CHAPTER 5

1. Ambassador Talbot's personal secretary has assured me that my statement is not true of Ambassador Talbot, and she knows, since she kept his appointment calendar for years. My sweeping statement encompasses Talbot, nonetheless, for it is my recollection that at the time of the coup and its aftermath Talbot wanted nothing to do with any newsmen. It was about eight days after the coup before Talbot would agree to meet with the American correspondents, and this session, which I sat in on, was noteworthy for the reluctance of the ambassador to provide any interesting "inside" information and for his lack of candor as to the U.S. government's attitude toward the coup.

2. The king, unlike Papadopoulos (if my analysis is correct), had been trying to determine the U.S. government's attitude toward a "coup" (though of course he didn't call it that). Why was he less sure of the U.S. attitude than was Papadopoulos, who apparently didn't feel it necessary to secure an advance reading? It was not that Constantine was less sure; he was simply more cautious. He was not a desperado type like Papadopoulos. Also, as a head of state he didn't have to fear exposure of his plans; to whom would the United States have reported him? On the other hand, the king had less need of an advance reading as to how the United States and the other Western allies would react to a coup: in his case they would have had even less choice when faced with a fait accompli, for whom else was there to recognize?

CHAPTER 6

1. In fact, as a basis for social stratification in Greece, education is probably of equal importance with wealth.

2. The CIA likes to pretend that it does not take "policy" positions but merely provides intelligence data and analyses on the basis of which others—for example, the president or the State Department—determine policy. Thus, in a speech to the American Society of Newspaper Editors on April 14, 1971, Richard Helms, director of the Central Intelligence Agency, asserted (according to the *New York Times* account published the following day) "that the agency had no stake in policy debates. 'We cannot and must not take sides,' he said. When there is debate over alternative policy options in the National Security Council, to which he is an adviser, 'I do not and must not line up with either side.' If he recommended one solution to a problem, those recommending another would suspect 'that the intelligence presentation has been stacked to support my position, and the credibility of CIA goes out the window,' he said."

Mr. Helms may here be accurately describing how he believes he behaves in National Security Council meetings, but if he believes the above remarks to be an accurate description of his agency's performance, he is either naïve or disingenuous. In the first place, the preparation of any intelligence estimate—like a piece of journalism or any other form of reporting—involves selection, and the process of selection grows out of and inevitably displays a certain point of view on the question. The intelligence presentation inherently takes a position of advocacy willy-nilly.

But more important than this is the fact—which has been confirmed for me by observation of CIA personnel in four countries and in Washington—that the agency certainly does have a stake in policy debates and works assiduously to promote its own point of view. In the specific case of Greece, the CIA had a profound and perhaps understandable distaste for Andreas Papandreou and all he stood for—a feeling that was mutual. More significantly, the agency's personnel were incapable of taking an objective view of the Papadopoulos regime. From the moment it came to power, the CIA was its ardent advocate and defender, often to the point of a ludicrous and demeaning sensitivity to any criticism of it. The agency did itself no honor by embracing such an inept and oppressive regime.

3. Townsend Hoopes, *The Limits of Intervention* (New York: D. McKay, 1969), 16.

4. A felicitous phrase used by Paul C. Warnke in a seminar at Princeton's Woodrow Wilson School on April 8, 1971.

5. This means "Government of Greece," a State Department acronym system growing out of the desire to shorten telegrams.

6. Marion Mitchell's presentation of our policy options in Greece was a perfect illustration of the "Option B" concept described by Leslie H. Gelb and Morton H. Halperin in their article "The Ten Commandments of the Foreign-Affairs Bureaucracy," *Harper's Magazine*, June 1972: "Option B solves a lot of problems for the bureaucrat. Bureaucrats do not like to fight with each other. Option B makes everybody a winner (by letting everyone do the essence of what he wants), preserves the policy consensus, and provides ultimate comfort to the bureaucrat—deference to his expertise and direct responsibility. Very few will be so dissatisfied as to take their case to the public.

"Unfortunately, while this process allows the President to keep his house happy, it also robs him of choice. The alternatives he is given are often phony, two ridiculous extremes and a jumbled, inconsistent 'middle course.' Unless a President knows enough and has the time to peel off the real alternatives from within Option B, he ends up being trapped by the unanimity of advice."

Their illustration of this bureaucratic ploy is drawn from Vietnam. President Johnson was presented with Option A: use maximum force (rejected because the Soviets and Chinese might respond). Option C: immediate unilateral American withdrawal (rejected because it would lead to a Communist victory). And Option B: bomb a little more each time and seek negotiations. Of course Option B triumphed.

Miss Mitchell's two extreme options were A—break relations; C—embrace the junta. Of course there was another triumph for Option B: recognize the regime, work with it, attempt to influence it to restore a democratic government.

The Vietnam Option B was ridiculous, as pointed out by Gelb and Halperin. The bombing was preventing negotiations; the American buildup obviated the need for the South Vietnamese to shoulder more of the burden of fighting; and our program of giving the Thieu regime all the aid it wanted without conditions gave Saigon no incentive for reform.

As for Miss Mitchell's Option B, recognition of the Papadopoulos regime removed the incentive for it to make any commitments in order to obtain the recognition it needed so badly; the U.S. government's working with it merely strengthened its hold on power and prolonged its existence; and all attempts to influence it to restore a democratic government were bound to be futile, since it came to power on a program of total rejection of democracy for Greece.

Gelb and Halperin's fourth commandment is called "veto other options," which is the technique of disqualifying an option by declaring it to be "infeasible." This is precisely the means that were used by the policy makers of the Marion Mitchell school to dispose of my proposal that we encourage the replacement of the Papadopoulos regime with something more to the liking of the mass of the Greek and American peoples.

Gelb and Halperin's ninth commandment is "Don't tell likely opponents about a good thing." Their illustration is the thwarting of a McNamara effort to cut down on military assistance to Taiwan by Pentagon bureaucrats, who resorted to shipping to Taiwan masses of "excess or long supply" equipment outside the Military Assistance Program. This is precisely what the Pentagon did in the case of Greece during 1967–70 to circumvent the government's policy of withholding some military assistance promised to the Greek government in order to exert pressure on it. The Pentagon succeeded in completely thwarting this effort by arranging to give Papadopoulos and company even more military assistance than they would have received had there not been a partial embargo on MAP. The method was identical: provision of "excess and long supply" items.

CHAPTER 8

1. A. Papandreou, *Democracy at Gunpoint*, 275.
2. Margaret Papandreou, *Nightmare in Athens* (Englewood Cliffs, N.J.: Prentice-Hall, 1970).
3. The lack of any identifiable mention of Louise's and my meetings with Mrs. Papandreou in her account of her relations with the Embassy makes her description of her treatment somewhat more consistently shabby than it actually was. But I believe her story is in accord with the spirit if not the letter of the truth, for two reasons: (1) she *was* treated entirely shabbily by everyone else in the Embassy, including its highest-ranking officers, notably Talbot and her old friend Norbert Anschuetz; and (2) she understood that our contacts with her, although initiated by her, were not encouraged by the Embassy and were undertaken on our own responsibility.
4. Later John Tsouderos, an unemployed apostate ex-deputy, offered to help Bruce at the Farm School, and he took the occasion to fill Bruce with anti-Andreas invective and gossip. Prior to their entry into Greek politics Tsouderos and Andreas had been close friends, to the extent that Tsouderos was godfather of one of Andreas's children. They had had a falling out and had become political enemies, even before Tsouderos's "apostasy." When Andreas was in prison, John once crossed the street to avoid speaking to Margaret. About the same age, the two of them had unusually similar backgrounds. Both were sons of liberal prime ministers of Greece and thus carriers of famous Greek political names, American-educated economists, Center Union deputies, and ministers in the Papandreou government of 1964–65. Their relations with the CIA differed diametrically.

CHAPTER 9

1. On November 21, the same day we had a drink with her, Margaret smuggled out of Greece three letters from George Papandreou to the prime ministers of Sweden, Denmark, and Norway, which in effect gave his consent in advance to the king's countercoup. The letters read in part: "I would like to formally re-assert my dedication to the principles of democracy, my commitment to the NATO alliance, which I consider essential to our survival as a Western power, and to the form of the regime of crowned democracy in Greece.

"It is my belief that a solution lies in a two-stage return to parliamentary government. The initiative must be the King's, for he is the only force today which can move the country in the correct path. If he takes the initiative he will have my backing 100 percent, and I speak for the entire party, as well as the majority of the Greek people which we represent.

"He will need, however, the full backing of the United States and Western European powers."

Papandreou expressed the hope that this proposal could be transmitted by the prime ministers as soon as possible to President Johnson and the leaders of the Western European countries. M. Papandreou, *Nightmare in Athens*, 339–40.

2. *Two NATO Allies at the Threshold of War: Cyprus, a Firsthand Account of Crisis Management, 1965–1968* (Durham: Duke University Press, 1990).

3. Without identifying me as her interlocutor, Margaret Papandreou gives her recollection of this talk in her book *Nightmare in Athens* (357): "I talked to an Embassy man of lower rank two days after the royal coup, and he predicted that Papadopoulos would declare a republic,

saying he could make this legal by a plebiscite on a republican form of government, and call the plebiscite much earlier than the announced date of the constitutional referendum, which was scheduled for September 1968. 'He would be crazy not to do it,' he remarked dryly. I gathered that this official felt Papadopoulos had the cards on his side, that the Americans would not withdraw their support even under these new conditions because of the importance they gave to Greece strategically. After all, were they to dismantle the American air force base at Hellenikon, which does the servicing of all United States government aircraft between Athens and Pakistan? Were they to stop using Phaleron as a refueling port for the Sixth Fleet? What about the base on Crete, a center of communications for the entire Middle East? The United States needed the territory of Greece as a base and as an arsenal. Papadopoulos, on the other hand, needed United States support because nonrecognition, he feared, would encourage those forces which wanted to pull the rug out from under his personal rule. It was a question of judgment and his assessment of the situation was that he had to work out a compromise solution which satisfied the Americans and kept the conservative army elements happy. The young radicals he would deal with later. The solution was to be no return of the King, but no change in the form of the regime. The King's job remained open for the future."

CHAPTER 10

1. Ambassador Talbot did provide Washington with a very full account of his January 8 session with the Papandreous. The full text (four pages plus) was published in *FRUS* vol. 16 as Document No. 353, Athens cable 3099 of January 9, 1968, 721–25.
2. M. Papandreou, *Nightmare in Athens,* 369. According to Talbot's reporting telegram, the meeting took place on January 8, not January 12.
3. A. Papandreou, *Democracy at Gunpoint,* 293–94.
4. I take these quotes from Andreas's book *Democracy at Gunpoint,* 296–97. However, they merely corroborate what I learned in Athens at the time from reports from Pattakos and other sources.
5. Ibid., 295–96.

CHAPTER 11

1. One prominent and humane opposition leader in Athens once assured me, however, that he and his associates were willing to permit Papadopoulos and his entire gang to board a charter aircraft at Ellenikon Airport and fly to the destination of their choice so long as they never returned to Greece. They could also presumably have claimed their military pension rights.

I must stress that this was the attitude of an extremely sophisticated, cosmopolitan, I would almost say aristocratic, man to whom the concept of "honor" is not silly and old-fashioned, and has more to do with *noblesse oblige* than with revenge. A more typical Greek characteristic, I am afraid, is vengeance, the requirement that one exact retribution for wrongs done to one's family in order to restore its self-respect, even decades after the event. To illustrate, there occurred a few years ago a most gruesome instance of vengeance in a courtroom in Iraklion, the capital of Crete. While a criminal proceeding was under way, a middle-aged male spectator sitting on a bench just behind the defendant reached around with a knife and slit the defendant's throat from ear to ear, killing him on the spot. The murderer was grabbed by the court policemen and hustled off to jail. A lawyer assigned to assist him later told the press that the murder had been a vengeance killing. Some twenty-six years earlier the murderer's brother had been denounced to the Nazi occupiers as a member of the resistance and had been executed. The man who had denounced him to the Germans was the man whose throat had been slit in court.

It is not the sophisticated intellectuals of Athens that Papadopoulos and his gang fear, but men like the Cretan peasant whose memories lasted twenty-six years.

CHAPTER 12

1. I once asked this question of the American diplomat who knew Andreas best, and he answered with an anecdote that sounds apocryphal but probably is not. One Sunday morning the president (as George Papandreou was universally called, even in the family, as president of the Center Union party) came by Andreas's house in Old Psychiko. George was in the chauffeured limousine to which his post as prime minister entitled him. Andreas was washing his car, a typical Sunday morning activity for a middle-class American family man. George admonished his son, saying that it was highly improper for a member of the government, a minister, to be seen washing his car. That was the chauffeur's job. Andreas replied that his father should forget his old-fashioned ideas, and in fact it was a good thing for a minister to be seen working with his hands, to set an example for the Greeks, all of whom have a deep disdain for manual labor of any sort. True enough, said George, but if Andreas wanted a career in Greek politics, it behooved him to behave like a Greek, at least in public, and not like the typical American that his political enemies mocked him as being. Andreas gave up washing his car himself.

2. It was the writer Vassilis Vassilikos, author of Z, who to my mind best analyzed and explained the peculiar phenomenon observed by so many, that a great many Greek Americans of the first and second generations are supporters of the junta, even after observing the Colonels at close range on a visit to Greece. Vassilikos observed (I do not have the exact quote) that these Greek Americans have a love-hate relationship with the land of their origins, but the hate predominates, for they are mostly the children of very poor rural Greeks who had themselves to emigrate to America (or whose parents had to emigrate) in order to make even a modest step up on the ladder of life. They retain a subconscious hatred for the country that forced them to expatriate themselves, and they hate even more those Greeks who did not emigrate, either because they didn't need to or because they were able to "make it" at home. Clearly they have a disdain for the Greeks who did not emigrate and believe that the Colonels are exactly what these Greeks deserve. In fact the Colonels closely resemble these Greek American emigrants in their social origins. They stayed behind and made it by using their guns.

In this regard Andreas Papandreou was not an emigrant at all. Because of native abilities and the good fortune of being born the son of George Papandreou, he had it made either in Greece or in America. He was a critic of Greece, not a hater.

3. This was Mrs. Raphael Demos, whose husband, the Greek-born distinguished professor of philosophy at Harvard, had died earlier in 1968.

4. M. Papandreou, *Nightmare in Athens*, 20.

5. Should my superiors' views have been discounted because of their obvious and deep disdain for the Greeks as people? My instincts answer yes, their views should have been discounted for this reason; but my desire for consistency argues no.

6. I also once attended a lunch with the female members of the royal household, when Ambassador and Mrs. Talbot were entertaining them and needed some extra males to balance the unescorted ladies: the widowed Queen Mother Frederika, the spinster sister of the king, Princess Irini, and Queen Anne-Marie. My recollections of this lunch are three: the bland repast (Irini is an insistent vegetarian); the wholesome Scandinavian beauty of Anne-Marie; and the imperious, egocentric, name-dropping conversational style of the queen mother—"So I said to Krishna Menon, 'Krishna, you may be a socialist and I may be a royalist but it all amounts to the same thing!!'"

CHAPTER 13

1. I understand that Talleyrand wrote, "Nonintervention is a political and metaphysical term and means about the same as intervention."

Acheson, Dean, xvi, 29, 215
AFSA. *See* American Foreign Service Association
Alken, Ib, 144
ambassadors, U.S. *See also* embassy, U.S.; Talbot, Phillips
  Briggs, xx, xxi, 19–20, 29, 215, 216
  Grady, xviii–xix
  Keeley, xxviii, 201
  Labouisse, xx, xxi–xxii, xxiv, 25
  MacVeagh, xiii–xv, xvi, xvii–xviii
  Peurifoy, xix, 7
  power, xx
  relations with Greek politicians, xx
  Tasca, 2, 180, 199–200
American Community Schools, 198–99
American Farm School, 70, 143, 262n4
American Foreign Service Association (AFSA), Herter awards, 181, 200–201
American Women's Organization of Greece (AWOG), 171–72
Anne-Marie, Queen, 128, 264n6
"Annual U.S. Policy Assessment for Greece" (1967), 51–55, 56–58
Anschuetz, Norbert
  background and career, 6–7
  as chargé d'affaires, xxiv, xxv–xxvii, 7, 128
  Farmakis and, 86–87, 112
  friendship with Papandreous, 140, 141
  Lansdale and, 77
  memoranda received by, 116–17, 122, 123, 134
  Nixon's visit and, 128–29
  Owens and, 3
  Papandreou (Andreas) and, xxv, 7, 34, 39–40, 44, 67
  Papandreou (George) and, xxv–xxvi
  reaction to coup, 86, 106–7, 114–15
  reports to Washington, xxv, xxvi–xxvii, 84
  staff assignments, 3–4
  Talbot and, 7
  transfer to Washington, 141, 144
anti-Americanism
  in Greece, xvii, xx
  of Papandreou, xxv, 28, 45, 51, 52, 53, 169, 214–16
apostate government, xxvi–xxvii, 23–24, 26, 37–38, 107
Arab-Israeli crisis, 130, 131
ASPIDA plot
  allegations, xxiv–xxv
  investigation, xxv
  Papandreou and, xxv, 36, 45, 48, 56–57, 134, 135, 140, 163
  politicians accused of complicity, 36, 48
  trial, 36, 40, 45, 163, 167
asylum requests, 93–94
Athens
  Acropolis, 129, 189
  ancient, 190–93
  on coup day, 81–83
  funeral of George Papandreou, 186–90
Averoff Prison, 105, 141, 165
AWOG. *See* American Women's Organization of Greece

Bangladesh. *See* East Pakistan
Battle, Lucius, 80, 130
Bhutto, Zulfiqar Ali, 105, 181
Bitsios, Dimitrios, 37, 96
Blood, Archer K., 180–81, 199, 201
Bracken, Katherine (Kay)
  ambition to become DCM, 3, 8, 9–10, 174
  as author's boss, 18, 35, 51, 143–44, 177, 180
  background and career, 7–8

Bracken, Katherine (Kay) (*continued*)
   countercoup and, 156
   Lansdale and, 77
   memoranda written to, 85–86, 99–100, 102–3, 115–17, 121–22, 133–35, 136, 137–38
   Papandreou (Andreas) and, 167
   as Political Counselor, 3, 10–12, 45, 58, 86, 195
   reactions to coup, 97, 98, 105–7, 112–14, 117, 121–22
   reaction to countercoup, 154
   reports to Washington, 84
   retirement, 174, 180
   staff assignments, 3
   Talbot and, 8, 174
   view of military junta, 172
Brewster, Daniel, 15–17, 67, 68, 80, 83, 87, 92
Briggs, Ellis O., xx, xxi, 19–20, 29, 215, 216
Britain
   ambassador to Greece, 96
   relations with Greece, xiii, xvi, 31
Buchanan, Patrick, 128
Bundy, McGeorge, xxvii, 32
Burchinal, David, 104
bureaucracies
   dissenters, 195
   "Option B" concept, 261n6
   oral demarches, 2
   policymaking, 195–96
Burns, R. Nicholas, 203

Calligas, Stephen, 118
Campbell, Laughlin, 30–33, 164, 176
censorship, 97, 129
Center Union party. *See also* Papandreou, George
   American views of, 21
   antimonarchist position, 58
   apostate government and, xxvii
   campaign of 1961, xxi
   deputies, 45, 93–95
   election prospects (1967), 53, 57, 59, 60, 61, 71, 72–73, 125
   elections of 1961, 192
   elections of 1963, xxiii
   embassy relations with, 3, 26, 34, 55
   followers of Andreas Papandreou, 29, 38, 51, 72, 94, 185
   government (1963–65), xxiii–xxiv, 27, 28
   leaders, 146–48
   potential coalitions, 38, 57
Central Intelligence Agency (CIA)
   Campbell as station chief, 31–33, 176
   contacts with coup leaders, xxii, 59–60, 87, 112, 115
   cover of agents, 23
   Greek intelligence service and, 28, 50, 87
   information on coup leaders, 91–93
   lack of intelligence on coup, 87–89, 93
   Maury as station chief, xxi, 82, 87
   Papadopoulos and, xxii
   Papandreou (Andreas) and, 27, 30, 32–33, 48, 88
   Papandreou (Andreas) on role in U.S. foreign policy, 47
   polls, 59–60
   position in policy debates, 260–61n2
   on possible treason trial of Papandreou, 134–35
   potential interventions in Greek politics, 41, 59–60
   relations with Greece, 20–23, 195
   station in Greece, xvii, xix, 20–23, 31–33, 34, 50, 79, 88, 175–76, 259n15
   surveillance of Papandreou residence, 143, 170–71
   U.S. diplomats and, 21, 23
   view of coup, 103
   welfare activities of wives, 171
Christian A. Herter awards, 181, 200–201
CIA. *See* Central Intelligence Agency
Clinton, Bill, 203, 205
Cohen, Ed, 165
Cold War
   Berlin crisis, xxi
   superpower competition, 181–82, 197
   Truman doctrine, xvi–xvii, 7
   U.S. foreign policy, 205
Communists. *See also* EDA
   after coup, 117, 129–30
   stigma of, 29–30
   in wartime resistance movement, 29
Communist threat
   in Greece, xv–xvi, 74, 75, 89, 218–19
   as justification for coup, 95, 100, 125
   Truman doctrine, xvi–xvii, 7
Congress, 14–15, 140, 166, 199
Constantine II, King
   advisers, 124
   apostate government and, xxvi–xxvii
   countercoup, 14, 136–37, 146–50, 151–57
   coup responsibility of, 124
   as crown prince, 32
   elections of 1967 and, 61, 67
   exile, 156, 170
   Generals' coup plan and, 61, 124, 127
   historical role, 196
   Kanellopoulos government and, 57, 126
   Maury and, 12

military government sworn in by, 95, 118
Nixon and, 128
Papandreou (George) and, xxv, xxvi, 23, 24, 25, 36, 124
public views of, 102
reactions to coup, 95–96, 113–14, 118, 120, 127
relations with military junta, 96, 152–53
relations with United States, 260n2(ch5)
Sulzberger and, 37
Talbot and, 67, 69–70, 96, 127, 152, 153, 154
in United States, 140
U.S. military attachés and, 156
warnings from United States to prevent coup, 54–55, 68–69, 74
countercoup (December 1967)
advance knowledge of, 14, 146–50, 152, 157
aftermath, 157–60, 163
date chosen, 157–58
embassy reactions, 154, 155–56
failure, 154–57
launching, 153
planning, 136–37, 146–50, 151–52
politicians supporting, 149–50, 153, 262n1(ch9)
coup of 1967. *See also* military dictatorship
American military reactions, 14–15, 103–4
arrest of Kanellopoulos, 82–83, 95
arrests of potential enemies, 89
author's reactions, 99–103
CIA and, 59–60, 103
compared to Turkish coup, 105–6
embassy reactions, 84–85, 86, 93–95, 96–97, 98, 103–7, 112–14, 117
events of day, 81–83
Generals' coup preempted by, 77–78, 84
justifications, 62, 95, 100, 101
king's reactions, 95–96, 113–14, 118, 120, 127
leaders, 89–93, 100–101, 103, 123–24
military reactions, 107–8, 127
planning, 87–88, 123–24
presentiments, 61, 65
prevention efforts, 73–74
prospects, 71–72, 86
public reactions, 102–3, 107
responsible parties, 123–27, 209
timing, 72–74, 77–78, 108
U.S. involvement assumed by Greeks, 87
U.S. policies leading to, 106–7, 124, 127
U.S. press reaction, 133–34
vignettes, 93–98
Cyprus
author's visit, 55
Greek Cypriot leaders, xxiv–xxv, 56

Cyprus issue
author's work on, 18–19, 55–56, 138
crisis of 1963–64, xxiii–xxiv, 8, 29, 132, 214–15
crisis of 1967, 150–52
embassy staff, 3, 18
Greek position, xvii, xxi
Greek-Turkish dialogue, 19
Papandreou (Andreas) on, 28–29, 48, 50, 132
summit meeting, 150–51
Treaty of Guarantee, 18
U.S. position, xxi, xxiii–xxiv, 28–29, 132
Vance peacekeeping mission, 150, 151
Czechoslovakia, 200

Day, John
career, 11–12
expertise on Cyprus issue, 18
as internal political affairs officer, 3, 84, 86
meetings with Papadopoulos, 154
memoranda, 67
trip to Washington, 93, 115, 116
walkout of Papandreou speech, 44–45, 49
DCM (Deputy Chief of Mission). *See* Anschuetz, Norbert; McClelland, Roswell D.
democracy
constitutional monarchies, 35
in Greece, 190–93, 207–10, 211–12, 249
restoration (1974), xxiii
transition planning, 137–38, 144–45
in United States, 47, 211
Denmark
diplomats in Greece, 144
government formation, 62, 63–64
Deputy Chief of Mission (DCM). *See* Anschuetz, Norbert; McClelland, Roswell D.
Diakoyiannis, Kyriakos, 135, 140, 167
dictatorships. *See also* military dictatorship
consequences, 74–77
Metaxas, 35, 74–75, 252
U.S. relations with, 114
Duran, Bonte, 171

East Pakistan, 180–82, 201, 260n1(ch4). *See also* Pakistan
Eaton, Samuel Knox, 13, 93, 95, 96–97, 104, 112
Economic Cooperation Administration (ECA), xix, 16
economic mission, U.S., xvi, xviii, xix, 16, 194

EDA (Union of the Democratic Left)
  arrests of leaders, 89
  election prospects (1967), 53, 60–61, 71, 72–73
  elections of 1964, 26
  emergence, xxi
  murdered deputy, 36
  newspapers, 97
  Papandreou's appeal to, 29–30
  predicted reaction to coup, 73
  supporters, 172
  voters, 30, 60–61
EENA group, 91, 134, 135, 163
Egypt, comparison to Greece, 139
Eisenhower, Dwight D., xx, xxi
EK party. *See* Center Union party
elections
  of 1946, xv, 35
  of 1952, xix
  of 1961, xxi, xxiv, 29, 32–33, 191–92
  of 1963, xxiii
  of 1964, 24, 25–26, 60, 184–85
  constitutional referendum (1968), 138, 238
  fraud, xxiv, 29, 32–33, 191–92
  reform proposals, 147
elections of 1967
  anticipation, 38–39
  author's predictions, 52, 53–54, 57, 60, 71
  campaigns, 62, 64
  efforts to prevent Papandreou victory, 61, 67, 72
  preparations, 58–65, 125
  prospective results, 53–54, 59, 60, 61, 79–80, 125, 170
Ellenikon air base, 195, 199, 262–63n3
embassy, U.S. *See also* ambassadors
  buildings, xvii
  CIA officers, 176
  at close of World War II, xiv–xv
  Greek employees, 94, 97–98, 118
  interpreters, 118
  labor attaché, 84
  in late 1940s, xvi–xvii, xviii–xix
  military attachés, xix, 13–15, 19–20, 81–82, 90, 156
  Political Section, 3, 20, 22, 62, 97–98, 144
  reactions to coup, 84–85, 86, 93–95, 103–7, 112–14, 117
  relations with Greek politicians, 26
  reporting officers, 84
  senior staff, 6, 19, 84–85, 105–7, 193
  social occasions, 128, 145
  telegrams from Washington, 65–69, 79–80, 87

treatment of Margaret Papandreou, 95, 140, 141, 142, 164–65, 166–67, 168, 169, 262n3(ch8)
welfare activities of wives, 171–72
ERE party. *See also* Karamanlis, Constantine
  election prospects (1967), 53–54, 57, 59, 60, 71, 125
  elections of 1961, xxi
  elections of 1964, 26
  Kanellopoulos government, 56, 57, 58, 126
  members of apostate government, 23
  negotiations in 1966, 37
  potential coalitions, 38, 57
  support of monarchy, 58
  United States and, 29, 32, 52, 53–54, 55
Ethnos, 45, 64
Ethridge, Mark, xv

Farmakis, Nick, 86–87, 95, 112
fascism, 172–73
Fermor, Paddy Leigh, 17
Fielding, Xan, 17
foreign policy. *See* Greek foreign policy; U.S. foreign policy
Foreign Press Association, 44
Foreign Relations of the United States (FRUS), volume 16, 40–41, 65, 120, 259n5
Foreign Service Regulations, 194
France, NATO withdrawal, 77
Franklin D. Roosevelt, 161–62
Frederika, Queen, xxi, 36, 96, 264n6
FRUS. *See Foreign Relations of the United States*

Galbraith, John Kenneth, 140
Garoufalias, Petros, xxv
Generals' coup
  intelligence on, 61–62, 91
  leaders, 90
  Marshall's support of, 14
  planning, 61–62, 87, 88, 108, 127
  preemption by Colonels' coup, 77–78, 84, 124
George, Father, 171–72
George II, King, 35
Goutos, Argini, 146
Goutos, Michael, 146
governments, Greek. *See also* military dictatorship
  of apostates, xxvi–xxvii, 23–24, 26, 37–38, 107
  caretaker, 37, 38
  of Kanellopoulos, 38, 56, 57, 58, 126
  of Karamanlis, xix–xx, xxi, xxii–xxiii, 50
  in late 1940s, xviii
  Metaxas dictatorship, 35, 74–75, 252

of national unity (1974), xxiii
negotiations in 1966, 37–38
of Papandreou (1963–65), xxiii–xxvi, 27, 28, 50, 126
Grady, Henry, xviii–xix
Greece
  civil war, xv–xvi, 29–30, 229–30
  democratic tradition, 190–93
  foreign domination, 192–93
  German occupation, xiii, 29
  situation at close of World War II, xiii–xvi
  vengeance, 263–64n1
Greek Americans
  businessmen, 50
  CIA officers, 42, 88
  involvement in Greek politics, 42, 88
  in State Department, x, 91–92, 220–21
  teachers, 199
  views of Greek politics, 220–21, 246, 264n2
Greek foreign policy. See also Cyprus issue; U.S.-Greek relations
  NATO membership, xvi, 50, 250
  relations with Britain, xiii, xvi, 31
Griswold, Dwight, xviii
Grivas, George, xxiv–xxv, 56, 151
Guatemala, U.S. intervention, 7, 102

Hackett, Clifford P., 199
Hamilton, Bill, 155
Handley, William J., 41–43, 66
Hart, Parker T. "Pete," 150
Helgerson, Robert, 44–45
Heller, Walter, 167
Helms, Richard, 88–89, 93, 260–61n2
Herter, Christian, xx
Herter awards, 181, 200–201
Hodja, Nasreddin, 148–49
Hoopes, Townsend, 104
Houghton, Robert, 2
House Foreign Affairs Subcommittee on Europe, 14–15, 199, 258n4
Humphrey, Hubert, 5

IDEA fraternity, 48, 91, 124, 135
India, 181–82
Intelligence and Research (INR), State Department, 42, 91–92, 170
intelligence services. See Central Intelligence Agency; KYP
Iran, 48, 167
Israel, 130, 131

Johnson, Lyndon B.
  Cyprus issue and, xxiii–xxiv, 132, 151

  Papandreou (Andreas) and, 132
  Vietnam War decisions, 261n6
Joint United States Military Assistance Group Greece (JUSMAGG), 13, 19, 90, 104, 143
journalists. See also newspapers
  imprisonment, 139
  press freedom, 129
  relations with, 84–85
Jouvenel, Bertrand de, 142
Joyce, James Vincent, 30–31, 58, 164
JUSMAGG. See Joint United States Military Assistance Group Greece

Kanellopoulos, Panayotis
  countercoup support, 153
  elections called, 60
  at funeral of George Papandreou, 186, 188
  negotiations in 1966, 37, 38
  overthrown by coup, 82–83, 95
  as prime minister, 56, 57, 58, 126
Karamanlis, Constantine. See also ERE
  elections of 1961, xxiv
  elections of 1963, xxiii
  national unity government, xxiii
  opposition to military junta, 152
  Papandreou (Andreas) and, 27
  in Paris, xxiii, 16, 125, 152
  as prime minister, xix–xx, xxi, xxii–xxiii, 50
  relations with United States, xix–xx, xxi, xxii, 16
  responsibility for coup, 125–26
  royal family and, xxii–xxiii, 36
  visit to United States, xx
Kardamakis, Vassilis, xxii
Katzenbach, Nicholas, 80
Kaysen, Carl, 32
Keeley, Edmund (Mike), 17, 127, 141, 142
Keeley, James Hugh, xv, xxvii, 17
Keeley, Louise
  funeral of George Papandreou, 186–90
  journalist friends, 45
  Kay Bracken and, 45
  Margaret Papandreou and, 140–41, 142–43, 149, 163–64, 165
  welfare activities, 171
Keeley, Mary, 17, 107, 141, 142
Keeley, Robert V. See also memoranda
  as acting political counselor, 179
  as ambassador, xxviii, 201
  arrival in Athens, xxvii–xxviii, 18
  assignment to Athens, 2–4, 17
  childhood years in Greece, 17, 70
  diplomatic career, 9
  as external political affairs officer, 3–4

Keeley, Robert V. (*continued*)
  Herter award, 200–201
  as internal political affairs officer, 180
  McClelland and, 9, 10
  performance evaluations, 177, 179
  second tour in Athens, 177–78, 179, 180, 198–99
Kennedy, John F., xx, xxiii, 4–5, 48
Kennedy administration, xxii, 25. *See also* Rusk, Dean
Khan, Yahya, 180–81, 182, 260n1(ch4)
Kohl, Walter, 187–88, 190
Kohler, Foy, 42–43
Kokkas, Panos, 97–98
Kollias, Constantine, 95, 96, 112, 118–20, 145, 153
KYP (Greek intelligence service)
  CIA and, 28, 50, 87
  coup officers' ties with, 87, 103
  Papandreous and, xxv, 28, 135, 176
Kyris, Vassillis, 107

Labouisse, Henry, xx, xxi–xxii, xxiv, 25
Lagakos, Leonidas, 93–95, 188, 189
Lagoudakis, Charilaos, 91–92, 170
Lambrakis, Christos, 37
Lambrakis, Grigorios, 36
Lansdale, Bruce
  American Farm School, 70, 143, 262n4
  friendship with Keeleys, 17, 38, 70, 163
  Hodja stories, 148–49, 157
  Margaret Papandreou and, 142–43
  Tsouderos and, 262n4
  views of political situation, 70, 77, 122
Lansdale, Tad, 142–43
leftists. *See also* ASPIDA plot; Communists; EDA
  American embassy staff and, 22, 23
  CIA views of, 20–21, 23, 34
  election prospects (1967), 53, 54
  imprisonment, 129–30
  in 1960s, xx–xxi, xxii
  Papandreou's appeal to, 29–30, 51, 60–61
  reactions to coup, 102
  views of political situation, 78–79
Lehman, Dick, 88–89
Linkletter, Art, 129
Livanos, Dionysos, 82–83

MacVeagh, Lincoln, xiii–xv, xvi, xvii–xviii
Makarezos, Nikolaos, 87, 90, 162
Makarios, Archbishop, xxiv, 56
MAP. *See* Military Assistance Program
Markezinis, Spyros, 128–29
Marshall, George, xvi

Marshall, Oliver K. (OK), 13–15, 137, 152, 156, 258n4
Maury, Jack
  career, 12–13, 19, 33
  as CIA station chief, xxi, 41–42, 82, 87
  on coup day, 82, 87
  lack of intelligence on coup, 93
  reaction to coup, 106–7
  royal family and, xxi
Mavros, George, 146–48, 152, 153, 157
McClelland, Roswell D. (Ross)
  as author's boss, 179
  author's memos and, 175, 176, 177–79, 223–55
  background and career, 8–9
  Bracken and, 9–10
  as deputy chief of mission, 8–10, 144, 171, 172, 178
  Papandreous and, 166
  retirement, 10
  view of military junta, 172
memoranda by author
  "Annual U.S. Policy Assessment for Greece," 51–55, 56–58
  arguments for toppling military government, 99–100, 115–17, 122–23, 197
  on Mavros conversation, 146–48
  McClelland's responses, 177–79, 223–26, 244–49
  "One Year Assessment," 176, 221–22
  "Our Present Dilemma," 99–100
  on Papandreou (Andreas), 28–30, 33, 133–35
  "Possible Formula for Evolution Toward Resumption of Political Activity in Greece," 137–38
  "*Post-Mortem* on Responsibility for the Military Dictatorship in Greece," 123–25
  reasons for writing, 1–2
  "Some Thoughts on Our Present Predicament," 175–76, 206–20
  "Some Thoughts on Prospects for and Means of Restoring a Democratic Regime in Greece," 144–45
  "Status and Prospects of Greek Democracy," 136
  "The Meaning of Fascism," 172–73
  "The Present Political Crisis," 70–78, 85–86, 122
  "U.S. Policy Toward Greece," 227–44, 249–55
  "U.S. Posture Toward Coup," 121–22
  on U.S. press reaction to coup, 133–34
Metaxas dictatorship, 35, 74–75, 252

military, Greek. *See also* ASPIDA plot;
    military coups
  American military contacts with, 14, 90
  EENA group, 91, 134, 135, 163
  IDEA fraternity, 48, 91, 124, 135
  information on members, 90
  navy, 107–8
  officers trained in United States, 90–91
  purges, 136–37, 170
  reactions to coup, 127
  royalist officers, 14, 40, 152, 153
military aid
  Kennedy administration policies, xxii
  to Pakistan, 182
  to Turkey and Iran, 48
  U.S. public's view of, 113
Military Assistance Program (MAP)
  embargo after coup, 13, 96–97, 100, 104,
    109, 112
  embassy and, xix
  equipment, 14
  Greek views of, 48, 194
  to military regime, 131, 182, 194, 198, 199,
    221, 261–62n6
  original goals, 182
  Papandreou government and, xxv–xxvi
military attachés, xix, 13–15, 19–20, 81–82,
  90, 156
military coups. *See also* coup of 1967;
    Generals' coup
  threats and rumors, xxi–xxii, 48
  in Turkey, 105–6
  U.S. warnings against, xxii
military dictatorship (1967–74). *See also*
    coup of 1967; U.S.–Greek relations,
    with military junta
  amnesty for political prisoners, 163
  censorship, 97, 129
  collapse, xxiii
  comparison to Egypt, 139
  constitutional referendum, 138, 175, 238
  countercoup and, 136–37, 153–54
  Cyprus crisis (1967), 150–51
  foreign ministers, 151, 160
  insecurity, 115, 119, 120, 121, 151, 152, 159,
    162
  Kollias as prime minister, 95, 96, 112,
    118–20
  opponents, 129–30, 203–4, 231–32, 239,
    255, 263n1(ch11)
  popular support, 229, 239, 240–41
  speculations on future of, 144–45
  threat of treason trial for Papandreou,
    133–36, 141, 158–59, 163
military mission. *See* Joint United States
    Military Assistance Group Greece

Mitchell, Marion, 16–17, 111, 261n6
Mitsotakis, Constantine, xxvii, 24
monarchy. *See also* Constantine II
  anti-monarchists, 35–36, 57, 58, 126, 145
  female family members, xxi, 36, 96, 128,
    264n6
  future of, 76
  history, 35–36
  Karamanlis and, xxi, xxii–xxiii, 36
  Papandreou (Andreas) on, 64, 126
  as political issue, 35–36, 57, 58, 59, 126–27
  relations with United States, xix
  supporters, 58, 59

Nasser, Gamel Abdel, 139
National Security Council, U.S., xx, 97,
  260n2(ch6)
national unity government (1974), xxiii
NATO (North Atlantic Treaty Organization)
  ambassadors of members, 159
  coordination of members, xx
  French withdrawal, 77
  Greek membership, xvi, 50, 250
  Greek public's view of, 50
  military aid, 48
  Papandreou (Andreas) on, 30, 50, 77
  Prometheus plan, 89
  Turkish membership, xvi
navy, Greek, 107–8
Navy, U.S., Sixth Fleet, 119, 120, 121,
  161–62, 171, 262–63n3
newspapers. *See also* journalists
  American, 37, 133–34, 162
  censorship, 97, 129
  Greek, 59, 97, 162, 199
New York Times, 37, 133, 162
Nixon, Richard M., 6, 127–30
North Atlantic Treaty Organization. *See*
  NATO

Owens, John, 3, 11, 41, 42, 67, 80

Pakistan, 105, 117, 181. *See also* East Pakistan
Papadopoulos, Georgios. *See also* coup of
    1967; military dictatorship
  American schoolchildren singing to,
    198–99
  American views of, 103, 137, 139
  career, 101
  compared to Nasser, 139
  countercoup and, 136–37
  coup planning, 87–88
  Cyprus crisis and, 150–51
  education, 101
  Farmakis and, 86

Papadopoulos, Georgios (*continued*)
  intelligence service ties, xxii, 59–60, 87, 103
  as prime minister, 154, 158, 159, 163
  relations with United States, 161–62
Papagos, Alexandros, xix
Papahelas, Alexis, 65
Papandreou, Andreas
  academic career, 27, 165–66, 167, 168
  American embassy views of, xxv, 3, 26–28, 30–34, 39–40, 49–50, 51, 53, 58, 67, 176
  American views of, 37, 50, 88, 105, 213–14
  Anschuetz and, xxv, 7, 34, 39–40, 44, 67
  anti-Americanism, xxv, 28, 45, 51, 52, 53, 169, 214–16
  appeal to leftists, 29–30, 51, 60–61
  arrest, 89, 95
  ASPIDA plot and, xxv, 36, 45, 48, 56–57, 134, 135, 140, 163
  author on, 28–30, 33, 76, 133–35, 183–85, 210–11
  comparison to Bhutto, 105
  Constitution Square declaration of government rumor, 62–64, 259–60n1
  contacts with U.S. embassy staff, 55
  Cyprus issue and, 28–29, 48, 50, 132
  Democracy at Gunpoint, 135, 164, 169
  departure from Greece, 165–66, 167–68
  effects of countercoup, 158–59
  execution feared, 132–33
  exile, 33–34, 168–69
  foreign supporters, 133, 140, 163
  historical role, 196
  imprisonment, 105, 132, 141, 142, 165, 258n3
  Joyce and Campbell episodes, 30–33, 164, 176
  meeting with author, 163–64, 168
  on monarchy, 64, 126
  on NATO, 30, 50, 77
  negotiations in 1966, 38
  opposition to U.S. involvement in Greek affairs, 28
  on Papadopoulos, 103
  parliamentary immunity, 45, 56–57
  personality, 76, 216
  political career, xxv, 27, 184–85, 214
  political faction in Center Union, 29, 38, 51, 72, 94, 185
  relations with Americans, 28, 32–33, 34
  relations with father, 183–84, 264n1(ch12)
  release from prison, 162–66
  resistance to military government, 34, 166, 168–69, 212
  responsibility for coup, 126–27
  seen as demagogue, 24, 29, 125, 210–11
  speeches, 44–51, 63
  threat of treason trial, 133–36, 141, 158–59, 163
  Tsouderos and, 262n4
  U.S. citizenship, 27, 28, 140, 214
Papandreou, George. *See also* Center Union party
  Andreas and, 183–84, 264n1(ch12)
  arrest, 95
  countercoup support, 149–50, 153, 262n1(ch9)
  Cyprus issue and, xxiv, 132
  death, 186–87
  elections of 1961, 192
  elections of 1963, xxiii
  elections of 1964, 26
  elections of 1967, 39–40, 64, 79–80
  funeral, 185–90
  house arrest, 185
  on kindred party system, 32
  negotiations in 1966, 37
  oratorical skill, 64
  political strategy, 126
  as prime minister, xxiii–xxvi, 27, 28, 50, 126
  resignation (1965), xxvi, 4, 23, 24, 25, 36
  seen as demagogue, 24, 37, 125
  Talbot and, 34
Papandreou, Margaret
  children, 140, 143, 162–63, 189
  CIA surveillance of residence, 143, 170–71
  death of George Papandreou and, 186–87, 188, 189
  departure from Greece, 168
  effects of countercoup, 158–59, 262–63n3
  on Greek democracy, 192
  Nightmare in Athens, 140–41, 166, 167, 192
  relations with Keeleys, 140–44, 149–50, 158–59, 163–64, 165, 168
  Talbot and, 95
  U.S. embassy treatment, 95, 140, 141, 142, 164–65, 166–67, 168, 169, 262n3(ch8)
Pappas, Tom, 50, 259–60n1
Paraskevopoulos, John, 37, 38, 45, 48–49, 56–57
Pattakos, Stylianos
  on constitutional referendum, 138
  English-language knowledge, 90–91
  as interior minister, 129–30, 136–37
  Nixon's visit and, 129–30
  Papandreou passport issued, 166, 167–68, 169
  relations with United States, 162
  reputation, 129

Paul, King, xix, 35, 36, 188
Perama, 171–72
Peurifoy, John, xix, 7
Pipinelis, Panayiotis, 151, 160
police, 64, 65, 143
political parties, 31–32. *See also* Center Union; EDA; ERE
political situation. *See also* elections
 in fall 1966, 23–26
 negotiations in 1966, 37–38
 in spring 1967, 16, 39–40, 56–58, 70–78, 125–26
Porter, Paul, xv–xvi
prime ministers. *See* governments, Greek
Progressive Party, 128–29

Rankin, Karl, 168
Rockwell, Stuart, 15, 42, 65–69, 80, 176–77, 195
Rolling Stones, 65
Roosevelt, Franklin D., xiii–xiv, xviii
royal family. *See* monarchy
Royal Navy, Greek, 107–8
Rusk, Dean, xxi–xxii, xxiii, 4, 5–6, 104, 151

Salonika
 countercoup, 153, 155–56
 U.S. consulate general, 155
Schacter, Margie, 141, 149, 170–71
Schlesinger, Arthur M., Jr., 5–6
Sedgwick, Shan, 168
Seferis, George, 186, 203–4, 211
Silva, Walter, 155, 196
Sisco, Joseph, 130
Six-Day War, 130
Sixth Fleet, 119, 120, 121, 161–62, 171, 262–63n3
Sofoulis, Themistocles, xviii
Soviet Union, 181, 200. *See also* Cold War
Spandidakis, Grigorios. *See also* Generals' coup
 coup planning, 61, 90, 91, 108
 king and, 96
 in military government, 84, 95, 112, 115
Stamatelopoulos, D., 92
State Department
 dissenting views in, 193–96
 Greek, Turkish, and Iranian Affairs Office, 8, 15, 105
 Greek Americans in, x, 91–92, 220–21
 Greek Desk, xxv, 6–7, 15, 27, 41, 111
 Intelligence and Research, 42, 91–92, 170
 NEA Bureau, x, 15, 80, 130
 Near East and South Asia assistant secretaries, 4–5, 33, 105, 130
 reactions to Greek coup, 111, 115, 261n6

 relations with CIA, 21
 telegrams to Athens embassy, 65–69, 79–80, 87
Stephanopoulos, Stephanos, xxvii, 4, 23–24, 38
Stoddard, Philip, 91
Sulzberger, Cyrus, 37

Talbot, Phillips
 analogies used, 104–5, 139, 167, 174–75
 background and career, 4–6
 Bracken and, 8, 174
 contacts with coup leaders, 112, 118–20, 132–33, 145, 154, 159–60, 161–62
 on coup day, 82–83
 Cyprus issue and, 151
 dissenting views and, 179–80
 at funeral of George Papandreou, 186, 188
 Greek politics and, xx, 25, 39, 41–43, 152
 Lansdale and, 77, 149
 meetings with author, 122–23, 157
 meetings with George Papandreou, 34
 meetings with journalists, 85, 260n1(ch5)
 meetings with king, 67, 69–70, 96, 127, 152, 153, 154
 meetings with Margaret Papandreou, 95, 166
 mistakes, 127
 Papandreou (Andreas) and, 164–66, 167, 168, 169, 184
 personality, 5
 reactions to coup, 93, 95, 96–97, 104–7, 112–14, 122–23, 127, 198
 reports to Washington, 83, 84, 87
 resignation as ambassador, 6
 secretary, 179–80, 260n1(ch5)
 senior staff, 8–10, 123
 at State Department, 33, 104–5
 telegrams to Washington, 83, 95
 visit to United States, 128, 139
 wife, 8, 142, 171–72, 174
 working style, 2, 5, 6
Tasca, Henry J., 2, 180, 199–200
Thessaloniki
 American Farm School, 70, 143, 262n4
 election campaigning in, 64
 trial of Lambrakis assassins, 36
Thompson, Malcolm (Mac), 10–11, 93, 108–11, 114–15, 144
Toumbas, John, 24, 107–8
Truman, Harry S., xvi, xvii
Truman doctrine, xvi–xvii, 7
Tsaldaris, Constantine, xviii
Tsirimokos, Elias, xxvii
Tsouderos, John, xxvii, 24, 262n4

Turkey. *See also* Cyprus issue
  military coup (1960), 105–6
  NATO membership, xvi
  occupation of Greece, 192–93
  U.S. military aid, 48
Tzinieris, Aleko, 62–63, 97–98

Union of the Democratic Left. *See* EDA
U.S. foreign policy. *See also* Cold War
  Cyprus issue, xxi, xxiii–xxiv, 28–29, 132, 150, 151
  East Pakistan crisis (1971), 181–82
  Guatemalan intervention, 7, 102
  interventionism, 197
  Papandreou (Andreas) on, 46–48
U.S.-Greek relations. *See also* embassy; Military Assistance Program; State Department
  ambassadors' roles, xx
  American presence in Greece, xvi–xvii
  annual policy assessment, 51–55, 56–58
  asymmetry, xvii, 211
  author's dissenting views, 201
  author's recommendations for intervention, 73–74, 200
  at close of World War II, xii–xix
  cultural mission, xvi
  democratic transition planning, 137–38
  economic mission, xvi, xviii, xix, 16, 194
  failure to prevent coup, 106–7, 124, 127
  foreign investment, 50
  Greek views of U.S. role, xvii, 24–25, 46, 54, 197–98, 211, 212–13, 236–37
  military bases in Greece, 195, 199, 262–63n3
  military mission, xvi–xvii, xix, 19, 46, 49–50, 81–82, 103–4, 137
  in 1950s, xix–xx
  in 1960s, xx–xxvii
  in Nixon administration, 130–31
  Papandreou (Andreas) on, 46, 50
  with Papandreou government, xxv–xxvi, 28
  in period before 1967 elections, 40–43, 51–55, 67–70, 79–80, 259n5
  Truman doctrine, xvi–xvii, 7
U.S.-Greek relations, with military junta
  acceptance, 118
  Clinton's apology, 205
  countercoup and, 153–54

  demilitarization scenarios, 174–75, 199, 217–19
  discussions in embassy, 102, 108–11, 112–14, 121–23, 154, 172–73, 182
  dissenting views of author, 175–80, 193–96, 219–20, 221–22
  FDR luncheon, 161–62
  insecurity of coup leaders, 115, 119, 120, 121, 162
  low profile posture, 198
  military aid, 131, 182, 194, 198, 199, 221, 261–62n6
  official recognition, 130–31, 159–60, 261n6, 262–63n3
  publicity, 161–62, 198–200
  recommendations for U.S. intervention, 99–100, 110, 111, 113–14, 115–17, 121, 197, 241–44
  six-month assessment, 145
  State Department paper, 111, 261n6
  Talbot's meetings with leaders, 118–20, 145, 154, 161–62
  toast to leaders, 145
U.S. Information Service (USIS), 30–31, 59, 85, 139, 169, 171

Vachliotis, Andreas, 135, 140, 167
Vance, Cyrus, 150, 151
Vardinoyannis, Paul, 134
Vassilikos, Vassilis, 264n2
Venizelists, 35, 107
Venizelos, Eleftherios, 35
Venizelos, Nikitas, 3
Venizelos, Sophocles, xxiii
Vietnam War, 116, 195, 211–12, 239–40, 261n6
Vlachou, Eleni, 37, 59, 97
Vladimiros's restaurant, 78–79
Voice of America, 31, 138, 186, 187, 190

Warren, George, 144, 175, 176
Washington Star, 133
Weiner, Tim, 88–89, 93
women's organizations, 171–72
World War II
  German occupation, xiii, 29
  government in exile, xiii, xiv
  situation at close of, xiii–xvi

Zographides, Kiveli, 149, 158, 187, 188
Zographides, Tito, 149, 158, 171, 187, 188

www.ingramcontent.com/pod-product-compliance
Lightning Source LLC
Chambersburg PA
CBHW021356290426
44108CB00010B/260